Origins of the
Magdalene Laundries

Origins of the Magdalene Laundries

An Analytical History

REBECCA LEA MCCARTHY

McFarland & Company, Inc., Publishers
Jefferson, North Carolina, and London

LIBRARY OF CONGRESS CATALOGUING-IN-PUBLICATION DATA

McCarthy, Rebecca Lea, 1966–
 Origins of the Magdalene laundries : an analytica history / Rebecca Lea McCarthy.
    p.   cm.
 Includes bibliographical references and index.

 ISBN 978-0-7864-4446-5
 softcover : 50# alkaline paper ∞

 1. Mary Magdalene, Saint. 2. Mary Magdalene, Saint — Cult. 3. Women in Christianity. I. Title.
 BS2485.M28   2010
 226.092 — dc22   2009050029

British Library cataloguing data are available

©2010 Rebecca Lea McCarthy. All rights reserved

No part of this book may be reproduced or transmitted in any form or by any means, electronic or mechanical, including photocopying or recording, or by any information storage and retrieval system, without permission in writing from the publisher.

Front cover: Magdalene in her uniform, ca. 1776

Manufactured in the United States of America

McFarland & Company, Inc., Publishers
  Box 611, Jefferson, North Carolina 28640
    www.mcfarlandpub.com

This work is dedicated to my parents, Kathleen Margaret Grossman and Lee Scott Grossman, both of whom passed away during its writing. Kathleen and Lee were fundamental in encouraging me to pursue, research, and seek out the truth behind the mysteries of the Magdalene convents and asylums. Further, both were readers at different points in the long process of writing and preparing this work. I miss them both.

Table of Contents

Preface   1
Introduction   7

PART ONE: MARY MAGDALENE AND THE RISE OF MAGDALENISM

One — Mary Magdalene and the Mother Mary   17
Two — The Rhetorical Framing of the Magdalene and Women in the Early Middle Ages   40
Three — Medieval Prostitution, Regulation, and Repentance   64

PART TWO: THE STATE, COLONIZATION, AND THE FEMALE AS CITIZEN

Four — Ancient Irish Law and Women's Status in Precolonial Ireland   93
Five — The Colonization of Ireland and Her Women   113
Six — The Rise of the Irish Magdalene Laundries   135
Seven — The Rise of the English Magdalenes and the Magdalen-House   168
Eight — The Twentieth Century Magdalene Laundries   196

Chapter Notes   219
Bibliography   247
Index   255

Preface

The image, perceived personality, presentation and packaging of Mary Magdalene has had a great and significant impact on women; particularly on marginalized women in society. Transformed from an affluent financial and emotional supporter of Jesus' mission to a simple repentant prostitute, the Magdalene becomes the symbolic representation of women's forced and premeditated fall from "moral" grace. This work follows that symbolic and pragmatic fall by examining not only the evolving image of the Magdalene in relation to women's status in society, but also the Magdalene convents for repentant prostitutes in Europe (approximately A.D. 1200–1699), and how these institutions, influenced by the rise of the capitalist world system, were transformed (A.D. 1700–1996) into forced-labor asylums, "houses," and laundries under the guise of spiritual deliverance.

I became interested in this subject in 1996 when two independent lines of research collided — research for a play on Margaret Sanger and the rise of birth control in the United States, and a personal investigation into my Irish roots — and I did an Internet search for birth control and Ireland. This accident was to change my life, sending me back to school to eventually earn a Ph.D. and devote the next several years studying the so-called Magdalenes. The hits returned by this nescient Internet search were several articles regarding a Dublin convent in High Park, run by the Sisters of Our Lady of Charity, and their 1993 real estate deal. Apparently, under the land being sold off by the church were the unmarked graves of 133 "Magdalene Repenties," women forcibly removed from society and compelled to work for the Catholic Church and the state of Ireland as laundresses (the last Magdalene laundry closed in 1996). Far from being an isolated case in Ireland, the Magdalene institutions can trace their roots to the early medieval Catholic Church, Pope Gregory the Great's (A.D. 540–604) branding of Mary Magdalene as a reformed prostitute, the rise of Church-sanctioned marriage,[1] and Pope Gregory IX's papal bull (1227) which endorsed convents for repenties, or the "white ladies."[2] These repentant convents (which functioned as halfway houses to marriage) spread widely throughout the Holy Roman Empire, an outgrowth that coincided with the centralization of economic and political papal authority in the twelfth and thirteenth centuries. This centralization created a social and political monopoly on social norms, "ritual, solace, appeasement, status and ultimately, salvation."[3]

The Magdalene convents thrived throughout Europe in the early Middle Ages, even through the economic and political crises experienced during the fourteenth century, and were slowly transformed with the advent of the modern capitalist world system, pinpointed by Wallerstein (1974) as the sixteenth century.[4] With the expansion of territorial land, the development of strong state machineries, and new forms of labor methods and control, the Magdalene convents slowly became institutionalized into forced work-houses, hospitals, and halfway houses, through state law and private philanthropy. This transformation occurred alongside colonization, land enclosure, and the redefinition of women's rights to property. Furthermore, economic, political and social transformation, as well as re-agrarianation by the end of the sixteenth century, helped to reinforce a strict feminine moral code, which marginalized many women. This re-moralizing created a new culture for the Magdalenes, and by the seventeenth century repenties started calling themselves Magdalenes.[5] However, the nature of the Magdalene institutions differed between the core and colonized (peripheral) nations and market centers. For example, Magdalene institutions in England, a core market power, can be characterized as halfway houses financed mostly through private philanthropy where men and women worked to take care of their "fallen" sister, and where the "Magdalene culture" was romanticized through the writings of Horace Walpole and Wilkie Collins. In England's colonies, such as Ireland, Magdalene laundries were maintained into modern times as forced-labor "homes," where any woman deemed a moral threat to society could be taken, imprisoned in these "convents," and forced to perform manual labor. Finally it is important to note that these modern laundries (1700s–1900s) existed throughout the world including core market centers of England and the United States, as well as peripheral and semi-peripheral market centers such as Australia, Scotland, Canada and other parts of the world.

Why did the Magdalene institutions transform from halfway houses into modern forced-labor camps in some areas, while becoming philanthropic ventures in other parts of the world? The answer, I believe, lies in a convergence of events wherein economic and territorial reorganization, as well as new divisions of labor, worked to redefine social norms differently in the core and peripheral market centers of the emerging capitalist world system. This shift can be best viewed in the cases of England and Ireland, where colonization, and the forced transition from a pastoral to an agricultural society, undermined traditional Irish Brehon Law, laws that looked more favorably on women's rights (social and property) than English law did. English colonization also reformed and reinforced a Romanized Catholic culture in Irish society, which further limited woman's rights. In turn, this intensification helped create a new division of "female" labor that was later exploited by the church and the state of Ireland. Although similar convergences occurred in the other core and peripheral nations, the dichotomy between England and Ireland offers an exemplar case study in which to examine the finer effects resulting from the rise of a world capitalist-economic system in relation to concepts of nationhood, citizenship and labor arrangements.

Research Plan

Considering the wide historical and social ramifications of the Magdalene convents, laundries, and asylums, this study is interdisciplinary in nature and will take an in-depth look at the sociological, rhetorical, and historical origins behind the institutions and the reasons why they were allowed to exist unchecked in Ireland. The research for this project will consist primarily of historical analysis, rhetorical analysis of period literature, and secondary analysis of existing historical data from Magdalene homes found in the Middle Ages and later in Ireland and England. Further, I examine existing news articles, sermons and other accounts concerning prostitution, reform, and the status of women. It is important to note, however, that the convents (nineteenth and twentieth centuries) in England and Ireland were not legally bound to keep records of those entering the Magdalene convents, or of their financial transactions. Further, after a great deal of negative publicity in the last ten years, many religious orders that supported and perpetuated the laundries are no longer sharing what records they do have with researchers, and have actively sought to legally impede investigations. As a result, any analysis of historical records that were once kept by these asylums and convents must be approached apprehensively, and conclusions made with extreme caution. Similarly, surviving Magdalenes are also reluctant to share their stories, because of the emotional and physical abuse suffered and their still-open wounds. Those wounds were again opened in May (2009) when *Ryan's Report*, an investigation regarding the abuse of children in the Irish state- and church-run industrial schools and laundries, was released by the *Commission to Inquire into Child Abuse*. The findings: "Physical and emotional abuse and neglect were features of the institutions. Sexual abuse occurred in many of them, particularly boys' institutions. Schools were run in a severe, regimented manner that imposed unreasonable and oppressive discipline on children and even on staff."[6] Since approximately 25 percent of the children in the industrial school system were children of Magdalenes, and many of these female children were made into Magdalenes themselves, this report is not only relevant, but also central to the modern fallout of what I term *magdalenism*, defined here as the process of identity inversion for the sake of controlling a class of women in the name of moral righteousness and power.

Theoretically, I am approaching this project through an economic, state developmental, and rhetorical analytical framework rather than simply a social/cultural and spiritual lens. Such an analysis allows me to trace and understand the underlining conditions that made the laundries possible and different in different nations. To date, there have been several publications exploring the Magdalene laundries in Ireland (Finnegan's 2004 *Do Penance or Perish: Magdalen Asylums in Ireland*, and Smith's 2007 *Ireland's Magdalen Laundries and the Nation's Architecture of Containment*), the Lock Hospitals (Luddy's 1995 *Women and Philanthropy in Nineteenth-Century Ireland*, and *Women in Ireland, 1800–1918: A Documenentary History*), and discussion regarding the convents and laundries in relation to Mary Magdalene (Haskins' 1993 *Mary Magdalen: Myth and Metaphor*, and Jansen's 2000 *The Making of the Magdalen: Preaching and Popular Devotion in the Later Middle Ages*). However, these publications tend to examine the Magdalene phenomenon from a social/cultural viewpoint, which is often divorced from the larger global and economic convergences at play. I propose to tackle the problem from a comprehensive historical point of view that is theoretically guided by the social and cultural, as well as the global and the economical. Such an analysis is vital because it not only sheds new historical light on the connection between religious, economic, social, and political convergences in relation to the rights of the "other," but also offers a blueprint for understanding how such convergences might occur in our modern world where religious morals merge and clash with modern efforts at globalization, and where the rights of the marginalized are defined within these convergences. As such, this work incorporates and takes inspiration from such social theorists as Immanuel Wallerstein (*The Modern World-System* Volumes 1–3), David Held ("The Development of the Modern State"), Edward Said (*Culture and Imperialism*), and Erving Goffman (*Frame Analysis: An Essay on the Organization of Experience*); as well as rhetorical scholars such as Kenneth Burke, Gerald Hauser (*Vernacular Voices: The Rhetoric of Publics and Public Spheres*), Thomas Goodnight ("The Personal, Technical, and Public Spheres of Argument: A Speculative Inquiry into the Art of Public Deliberation"); and the linguistics scholar George Lakoff. In the end, it is my hope that such a comprehensive approach will uncover the cause and motivations behind such institutions, and why we, as a society, were so willing to tolerate such offences to our very own, by our own hand.

Images

Many images included in this book are reproduced from period publications no longer under copyright protection, such as "The Magdalene in her Uniform," the Australian Sister of Mercy's advertisement for a Magdalene Laundry — listed in the 1897 Queensland *Handbook of Information for the Colonies and India*." The modern images of the Good Shepherd Convent at Cork Sunday's Well were taken by photographer and social historian Mark Davis. The Good Shepherd Convent, orphanage, and laundry was constructed in the 1800s, closed finally in the 1970s, and was severely damaged in a 2003 fire. Further, this Cork laundry is featured in chapter six of this work, along with a related discussion regarding the *Contagious Diseases Act* and a mass protest by the Magdalene inmates after being forced into the laundry at Sunday's Well. These images taken by Mr. Davis document the convent and graveyard as it stands today in 2009. Mr. Davis resides in the UK and has dedicated thousands of hours of research, sourcing firsthand accounts, creating oral and pictorial histories, while sourcing information through archives in an effort to redress and address social injustices suffered by thousands of patients who were locked away in "public" institutions, such as the laundries. The hope is to sustain memory regarding the institutional realities of the nineteenth and twentieth century, even as society marches on. Mr. Davis' extensive work can be view online at www.silverstealth.co.uk and www.highroydshospital.co.uk.

Acknowledgments

This book was originally conceived as a master's thesis for Rollins College, under the direction of Dr. Arnold Wettstein, in 2001. Since writing the thesis, I returned to school and earned my Ph.D. in comparative studies (sociology, rhetoric, and philosophy) from Florida Atlantic University. My additional education has provided me with new and rich insights, all of which I wanted to bring to this project. For this I must thank not only Florida Atlantic University in general, but also several mentors who gently guided me to new directions: Dr. Jan Hokenson, who encouraged a rigorous understanding of interdisciplinary research and how to better understand multiple threads of inquiry; Dr. David C. Williams, who introduced me to the wondrous world of Kenneth Burke, as well as the rhetoric used to define "nations" and "citizenship"; Dr. Mark Frezzo, who offered me hours of wonderful conversation and instruction regarding social organization, the effect of "power," the rise of a capitalist economy, and the different social devices and modes used to exclude members of society from citizenship and full participation. Also, I must thank Dr. Farshad Araghi, who encouraged me to see beyond the "religious" influences, and to look also at the economic pressures that changed the landscape for not only the Magdalene laundries, but Ireland, England, and women's rights. I would also like to thank the *Justice for the Magdalene Group* for the insights, struggles and resources that they openly offered. Other important mentors, readers and supporters include Beth Kuwahara, Dr. Peggy Schaller, Trudy Mercadal, Dr. Noemi Marin, Kelly Whorton, and all those who listened to me theorize, ponder, and obsess over this history. If any of the information contained within is questionable, these are my mistakes and not those of my mentors or supporters. Finally, I must thank my family, who has supported me on this very long journey: my mother, k. Margaret Grossman, who was equally horrified and fascinated by the long history of the laundries, my father, Lee Scott Grossman, and my husband, George Wabey, who has supported me without question throughout this journey and read and reread each chapter more times than he would like to remember. Additional emotional support has come from my sister, Deborah McCarthy, Emily Hadley, Jonathan Hadley-McCarthy, Fred McCarthy, the First Saturday of the Month Group, as well as my dear friend, Amy Snyder.

Finally, this book would not exist in its present form without the vast amount of primary resources that became available because of Google Books and their efforts to digitalize libraries of content: firsthand accounts of the laundries, convents and religious orders, handbooks and histories of the religious orders, period news and magazine articles, laundry advertisements, sermons, debates regarding the laundries on the parliament floor (1895–1907), period directories of religious institutions and other noncopyright material from the late 1700s to the 1920s. Google Books has provided scholars the ability to engage in primary research, in a way that did not exist till now. When limited by a lack of funding, many scholars find their ability to travel and conduct research at various locations difficult. Google Books has taken some of those limitations away by scanning historical documents that would have been difficult to obtain through traditional modes. Thus, this research would not have been possible without the wherewithal provided by Google Books or without the services provided by my local library in Rainier Beach, Seattle, Washington.

Introduction

> *I consider the word madgalenism as, equally with fornication and whoredom, applicable to the woman who, whether for hire or not, voluntarily surrenders her virtue.*[1]
> —*Lectures on Magdalensim*, 1843, by Ralph Wardlaw, p. 32–33.

The Magdalene Asylums

In 1996, while researching Ireland, that beautiful, mystical place my ancestors came from, I came across something that not only shattered many of my romantic notions about Ireland, but also contradicted my belief in women's rights — the Magdalene* Laundries. Granted, my grandiose imaginings of Ireland had an unrealistic tint: somehow Ireland's past had joined her present. Images of the great capitals of Connaught and Ulster, with Queen Medb and Cuchulain[2] still living, breathing, and having children who were half-God, half-human — indeed the Children of Dannan, protected by their otherworldly mist, must not have left Ireland even today![3] I was wrong. The great hero spirits of Ireland's past either never existed or left the island, residing in their ethereal plane until that time when the world will again be ready for them. Where were those strong women who shaped Ireland's story and her history? Where were Queen Medb and the very real Gráinne Uí Mháille (Grace O'Malley),[4] who was said to have taken on Queen Elizabeth and won? Of course there was Mary Robinson,[5] president of Ireland from 1990 to 1997, but she seemed an exception to the rule. So what happened to many of Ireland's women? Apparently, they were dressed in white, and sent away to Magdalene laundries, homes and asylums, hidden away behind fortified towers from a society that considered them immoral and sinful.

---

*There are two primary spellings of Magdalene: Magdalen and Magdalene. I will use the more traditional spelling of Magdalene throughout this work; however, the more common spelling of Magdalen is maintained by many and will be used in reference when appropriate.

In Ireland, September 1993, a city convent in Dublin's High Park (the sisters of Our Lady of Charity) sold off a good portion of their land to a real estate developer for a million pounds. Although such a transaction is not unusual, this business deal came with a much higher price than might be imagined: the price of human lives. Beneath part of the land being sold off by the city convent lay 133 bodies of women. These women were called Magdalene laundresses, or "Magdalene repenties," women taken forcibly from society and compelled to work for the Catholic Church and the state of Ireland as laundresses. Considered a threat to the social and spiritual "moral" code, these women (prostitutes, unwed mothers, troublemakers, and other "undesirables") disappeared from society behind cloistered walls, creating an invisible slave-labor market: "For more than 150 years, until the early 1970's, thousands of Irishwomen, were relegated to lives of unpaid servitude in Catholic convents, working as laundresses. They were hidden away — unwed mothers, daughters of unwed mothers, prostitutes, orphans, and nonconformists."[6] Just as these women were hidden away from society in life, the High Park Magdalene Convent continued to hide their presence in death when the Magdalenes' graves were destroyed to make way for real estate development. Before the graves were destroyed, there was no attempt to contact family members who might still be living. In fact, these women were unearthed, their bodies cremated (contrary to their faith and the Catholic tradition) and their ashes shipped to a nearby cemetery where they were re-buried in a mass grave without any headstone or remembrance allotted to them. Later, after public outcry, a gray headstone was erected in their memory: "A double grange on the edge of Glasnevin cemetery, the 133 bodies had been joined by 42 more. Under the heading 'St. Mary's High Park, In Loving Memory of,' 175 names and dates of death are listed on gray stone, the first in April 1858, the last in December of 1994. There are no religious trimmings on the grave."[7] What, I had to ask, was going on in our very modern world? One girl I read about had been born with the *curse* of being too beautiful; so to save her from a life of sin, she was placed in one of these laundries. She was assumed guilty before being old enough to understand what she might be guilty of. Why? And was this happening *only* in Ireland? Apparently not.

I soon learned that the Magdalene institutions (also known as laundries, asylums, houses and convents) started in the Middle Ages as a way to help reform prostitutes, an idea that spread and transformed from the Middle Ages to the twentieth century. Far from being an isolated case in Ireland, the Magdalene institutions can trace their roots to the early Medieval Catholic Church, Pope Gregory the Great's (A.D. 540–604) branding of Mary Magdalene as a reformed prostitute, and the rise of church-sanctioned marriage, as well as the widening definition of what constituted a prostitute and prostitution. I term this widening definition of how we view the prostitute and prostitution as *magdalenism*, defined here as the process of identity inversion for the sake of controlling a class of women in the name of moral righteous and economic gain. Just as the image of Mary Magdalene was transformed from financier and key supporter of Jesus' mission to that of a prostitute, the Magdalene repentant convents were also inverted when they ceased being halfway institutions designed to help prostitutes transfer into new employment, and instead became virtual labor prisons for poor and marginalized women. This transformation can be traced not only to the Roman Catholic Church's centralization of economic and political papal authority, which started in the twelfth and thirteenth centuries, but also to the rise of a capitalist world system. As capitalism slowly worked to change how division of labor, and ownership of production functioned in relation to territorial expansionism, the rise of the state, and the definition of citizenship, Magdalene institutions and women's roles also changed. This magdalenization transformation occurred alongside colonization, land enclosure, and the redefinition of women's rights to property and corresponding rights of citizenship.

Into modernity, however, magdalenism differed between the core and peripheral/colonized market centers of the world. For example, just at the time when England, considered a core market center at the turn of the twentieth century, instituted labor laws (*Factory Acts*) that regulated reform institutions, such as the Magdalene laundries, and legislated other protective measures for labor, Ireland (a peripheral/colonized center), even after obtaining her freedom, insisted that social-reform workhouses and factories should not be held to the same standards of industry. Concepts of economics, citizenship and moral worth are at the center of this debate. Whereas England eventually viewed women, female labor, and citizenship in relation to how her economic worth could serve herself and her country (in the home and in the marketplace), Ireland maintained that a women's worth could only be measured as unpaid labor in the home as wife and mother first, and as daughter and sister second. If a woman rejected these roles, she forfeited her rights as a citizen. Because citizenship and moral worth for women were so narrowly defined in Ireland, the process of magdalenism was more drastic than what was seen in England and other core market centers that promoted a wider definition of women's worth and rights in citizenship. Thus the central research question of this work is how and why did the Magdalene institutions transform from halfway houses into forced-labor workhouses in some areas of the growing capitalist world system, while becoming philanthropic ventures in other parts of the world? To answer this question, this work will look at the network of converging events, including economic and territorial reorganization, divisions of labor, as well as the diverse understanding of social norms in relation to magdalenism as found in England and Ireland. As stated in the preface of this work, this shift can be best viewed between England and Ireland. Undeniably, magdalenism and its consequences is truly amplified in the case of Ireland, where colonization, and the forced transition from a pastoral to an agricultural society, undermined traditional Irish Brehon Law, as well as women's rights to property and citizenship.

From the 1750s on, Magdalene institutions popped up all over Europe, Australia, the United States and Canada to alleviate prostitution and the social, political and pragmatic problems associated with prostitution. However as magdalenism took hold with the rise of Victorian values and the so-called Cult of True Womanhood, the definition of prostitution widened to include not only those who sold their body in exchange for profit, but the poor woman, the nonconformists, the single mothers, the young and poor truants, the abandoned wife, and any woman who was seen as a challenge to society's moral code. Standards set not only by society for women, but also by the Church (this is particularly true for Ireland, who defines nationhood and citizenship in relation to Roman Catholic morals) and other religious institutions that claimed that Eve was the cause for man's fall from grace; therefore, women must be kept submissive and under control, before they cause any more harm. Ironically enough, "she" was also expected to uphold the spirituality for the family, and for her own sex.

Who were and are these women affected by magdalenism? Why are they so easily disposed of, like dust swept under the carpet in a fortified tower? Why would enlightened societies become so callous toward these women in the name of God and moral righteousness? And what conditions existed that would allow for the laundries and asylums to rise? Furthermore, why is the name of Mary Magdalene given to these women? To answer these questions, we must rediscover who Mary Magdalene was, and why her image was inverted, and finally why her true reputation was swept under the carpet. Next, we must examine where myth and Biblical history leave off, and where the roots of modern history with the transformation into a capitalist world system, as well as the economic divisions between budding states, directly affected not only Magdalene institutions, but also social norms and laws that regulated women's role in society. Finally, we need to examine the Magdalene institutions themselves, the motives behind them and the history surrounding them. Keeping these ideas in mind, I would like to briefly outline the chapters involved in this work.

Chapter Layout

In general, this book will follow the ever-changing but persistent thread of Mary Magdalene, our relationship with her and our use of the Magdalene as the catalyst for symbolic and functioning rationale for action or magdalenism. The first part of this work, "Mary Magdalene and the Rise of Magdalenism" (chapters one through three), will lay out the foundation for the development and rise of the Magdalene convents, laundries and asylums, while the second part (chapters four through eight) will look at how and why the modern Magdalene laundries and asylums developed and functioned differently between the ones in the core market center of England and the colonized/peripheral market center of Ireland.

Chapter one will briefly examine Mary Magdalene as she is portrayed in the New Testament along with how her image was confused with the images of Mary of Bethany and the unnamed sinner from the Gospel of Luke, the prostitute who cleans Jesus' feet at the Pharisees' house. I will also examine Paul's views regarding the status of women in the early church. Next I will look at the other iconic role models offered to women, the Virgin or Mother Mary and how she has been portrayed in the Bible, as well as her transformation from "mother" to "eternal virgin" and the ramification of this new, unreachable focus.

Chapter two will explore the hagiographic texts depicting Mary Magdalene's story from where the Bible leaves off. I will also discuss how these symbolic tales help substantiate a strong and developing hierarchy that will place woman subservient to her male counterpart while separating the good from the fallen woman. These Magdalene narratives will also be explored in relation to marriage and the Catholic Church's monopoly on "salvation" and how this affected secular property rights. Finally, I will briefly explore the Medieval economy from A.D. 1000 to 1299 and how the economics of the time interacted with marriage and prostitution.

Chapter three continues this thread of inquiry but also looks at the evolving view of prostitution in relation to social life, reform, and the Magdalene. An investigation into the Magdalene cults and how they achieved popularity throughout Europe during the late twelfth century will be conducted. Since the start of the magdalenism process, these cults and prostitution reform efforts spurned a lucrative market that not only gained the attention of the Catholic Church, but also made the Cathedral of Sainte-Marie-Madeleine at Vézelay, France (said to be the last resting place of the Magdalene), a market and trade center. I will then investigate how Mary Magdalene's new image as a reformed prostitute worked to reinforce and encourage the newly developed Gregorian Christian marriage of the twelfth century. This developing line of argument will be followed to the introduction of the first Magdalene convents for prostitutes, and Pope Gregory IX's papal bull (1227), which endorsed convents for repenties, or "white ladies." These repentant convents functioned as halfway homes toward marriage and spread widely throughout Europe. I will explain how the popularity of these Magdalene convents coincided with the centralization of economic and political papal authority in the twelfth and thirteenth centuries. Further, the Church's monopoly on salvation also determined economic modes of wealth acclamation, which controlled prostitution, and orchestrated the rhetoric of salvation for prostitutes in Magdalene convents.

The second part of this work, "The State, Colonization, and the Female as Citizen," will focus on the rise, development, and functioning of the laundries and asylums in Ireland and England, ending with chapter eight, which looks at twentieth-century Magdalene laundries. Not only is Ireland a popular topic of discussion with concern to the Magdalene laundries, but as I mentioned above, Ireland also offers us the ideal case study for examining how laws and social morals concerning women were drastically altered because of the rising world-capitalist system, new divisions of labor, and territorial reorganization. Chapter four will focus on the status of women in pre-colonial Ireland, as well as the Irish culture, structure, and mythology. Next, I will present the important traditional Irish/Brehon laws that legislated marriage and family life (including inheritance and dowry), and how these laws were destroyed through English colonization — limiting women's rights and helping to create a legal opening for the later Magdalene laundries.

After visiting pre-colonized Ireland, chapter five will follow England's rise in the European world-economy (mid-sixteenth century) and the aggressive colonization tactics used by England to transform Ireland into an economic peripheral/colony. During the 1500s and 1600s, traditional Irish society was destroyed as English colonization dismantled Irish culture/society. Fundamental to this process was the destruction of Irish Law, the rise of the March Laws (a hybrid system of Irish and English law), to the exclusive use of English law. Using conquering techniques such as Henry VII's forced colonization, to Henry VIII's surrender and regrant policy, as well as Queen Elizabeth I's policy of divide and conquer — Irish land, traditional ruling/power structures, and social/cultural traditions (including the rights of women) were erased.

Chapter six focuses on the English poverty laws, workhouse laws and labor laws in relation to the Magdalene laundries and asylums in Ireland. Following the rise of the first Magdalene laundries in Ireland, from the first convent founded by Lady Arbella Denny (1767), this chapter will present the history of Irish magdalenism and the Magdalene laundries in colonized to free Ireland. It is interesting to note that although there were more recorded prostitutes in England, by the late 1700s there were more Magdalene asylums in Ireland. This is because concepts such as prostitution and "morally fallen" were more widely defined in Ireland than in England, including all women who became single/unwed mothers. Further, when private support for these homes weakened, the women were made to do needle work and laundry to earn their keep. These new, reformed workhouses produced the term "Magdalene laundresses"—a term adopted by the women in these institutions. Eventually all the privately owned Magdalene asylums were absorbed into mostly Irish Catholic Convents. Unlike many of the homes in England, Ireland's laundries and asylums became not only a place for reforming prostitutes and unwed mothers, but also places to hide away any woman considered a moral threat to society. Tracing the history of the laundries, I will end this chapter by demonstrating how labor factory laws, the modern Irish Constitution, along with the Catholic Canon Laws, came together in a silent marriage that allowed few rights for the Irish female, and no rights within the Irish reform institutions.

Chapter seven will focus on the Magdalene laundries, asylums and halfway homes in England. Mostly philanthropic ventures, these homes were financed through charitable organizations and functioned as halfway homes for women trying to leave prostitution. The first Magdalene home in England was founded in 1758, and was established by Jonas Hanway, Sir John Fielding, Joshua Reynolds, and William Dodd. These men and others led a group to help reform prostitutes, approximately 8,983 women, within an institution that lasted 150 years. I will also examine at length how English and Irish members of the British Parliament had great differences of opinion regarding labor laws in relation to the religious laundries. Although briefly covered in chapter six, chapter seven will trace how the *Factory and Workshop Act* debates between 1895 and 1907 demonstrate the practical and ideological difference regarding concepts of nation building and citizenship between English and Irish members of parliament. These views would directly influence magdalenism and the religious reform institutions, as well as the rights of women in these two different nations. In the end, the English members argued for inspection, labor protection and regulation of the religious laundries, while the Irish members of Parliament rejected such laws on the basis of religious exemption. Finally, chapter seven will also look at the rhetoric behind the English's romantic image of the reformed "Magdalene," which was celebrated in art, portraits of mistresses painted as Mary Magdalene, and popular literature, including the writing of Daniel Defoe (1660–1731) and Wilkie Collins (1824–1889).

The final chapter of this work will examine the modern fallout regarding the Magdalene laundries and other reform institutions in Ireland. From 1996 on with the real estate news and the subsequent cremation of the Magdalenes from the High Park laundry, there have been political, social, and economic ramifications faced by Irish society, the Catholic Church, and the Irish State. Investigations into the laundries and the widespread abuse of women and children (male and female) within the religious and state-run institutions has left many in Irish society feeling vindicated, ignored, and humiliated. The 2009 *Ryan's Report* is especially damaging, as it documents the extensive abuse of children within the complex arrangement of Irish orphanages, laundries and reformatories. What this report forgets to mention is that many of these children were the children of Magdalenes, single mothers who had their children forcibly taken away from them by the Irish Church and state. Because illegitimacy was seen as a crime, both mother and child suffered while the father, often unnamed, felt few or no official repercussions. Although many of the children of the Magdalenes were adopted out to Catholic families outside of Ireland, many were kept in the network of reformatory institutions, receiving little to no education and used as free labor resources themselves. This final chapter will then examine the modern fallout and how the many players are reacting to the reality of the Magdalene institutions and the process of magdalenism.

PART ONE

*Mary Magdalene and the
Rise of Magdalenism*

One

Mary Magdalene and the Mother Mary

> *In Defense of Eve*
> *A Man recently told me that the success of the trees in the Garden of Eden was due to the fact Adam and Eve were astronauts and had attained curious knowledge in horticulture, agriculture and jungle planning from other planets. I found this information plausible inasmuch as I had no reason to doubt the man. He then explained that the trees' fruit were actually precious gems and the apple was a pearl and every leaf on every tree was the color of water. Water and insects rule our planet. I found this information imminently possible because of the swamp I live in. He further illustrated Eve's eyes — little bottles of perfume and Adam's penis — a cowboy boot with a broken heel. Also, the Garden itself was lined in vacuum cleaners and sleeping bears. I told this man, who claimed to be God, Eve should have trusted Adam but she was tired of the smell of paradise and who wouldn't talk to a talking snake?*
> — Michael G. Hickey

When considering the Magdalene convents, asylums, and laundries throughout Europe and the United States, two polar "iconic" designations come to mind. The Sinner and The Saint. The Fallen Woman and The Nun. Mary Magdalene and The Virgin Mary. Although much of Western society now knows better, women throughout the ages have been portrayed as either one or the other, and more often than not, it is the sinner that is expounded in myths, stories, and legends. It is difficult to understand why women are limited to such either/or roles that simply discourages true empathy. Throughout his life and writings, the communication theorist Kenneth Burke reminded us that the key to communication was not an Aristotelian emphasis on persuasion, but the encouragement of identification, the "function of sociality."[1] But as Burke also points out in his *Rhetoric of Motives*, "identification is compensatory to division,"[2] that is, people tend to build, define, and reinforce their identity through what it is not: the fallen woman is not the virgin. The

Virgin Mary is not Mary Magdalene. This function of division works to create identification with a "public," but it also functions as the great divider — discouraging understanding between seemingly disparate social groups as well. To be the pure "virgin," it must also learn to despise "the whore," even as a helping hand is tentatively offered. Yet this either/or approach toward identification is rarely or entirely effective.

Considering the either/or designation assigned to the Virgin Mary and Mary Magdalene, many women cannot really identify with either image completely, since most women have their feet planted in both rings. As the voice of wisdom reminds us in a poem found in the Gnostic Gospels, "The Thunder, Perfect Mind": "I am the whore, and the holy one. I am the wife and the virgin."[3] Regardless, because all that is left is an either/or formula when examining the *Magdalenes*, as well as the iconic images used to represent available roles for women; this formula and from where it derived must also be understood. This chapter will briefly examine the Biblical accounts of Mary Magdalene and the Virgin Mary, and how these characters were later reframed in order to create a neat either/or identification for women. Further, it will end with a brief, yet important analysis and acknowledgement of the vital role that the "whore" played in framing both the Old Testament, and the life of Jesus Christ.

The Veiled Mary Magdalene

Just as little is known about the Magdalenes working away in laundries and asylums, little is also known about the true Mary Magdalene. Because of this historical uncertainty, the Magdalene's image has been distorted, deemphasized, and deconstructed throughout history. Mary Magdalene is mentioned sporadically and inconsistently in the four Gospels of the New Testament: Mark, Luke, Matthew and John. Three of these Gospels — Mark, Luke, and Matthew — tend to mirror each other, offering little difference in the portrayal of Mary Magdalene.[4] As Haskins points out, these three Gospels are "synoptic." Indeed, the stories tend to corroborate the events surrounding Jesus' rising from the grave and the role that Mary Magdalene played in this event:

> With minor variations, the same women are present, and the body is taken by Joseph of Arimathaea, who appears in no other episode in the New Testament. In Mark and Luke, the women go to the tomb with the purpose of anointing the body, and in Matthew they come to visit the tomb only as it has been sealed and guarded under Pilate's orders. In Mark, initially Mary Magdalen alone sees the risen Christ (and no-one believes her); in Matthew,[5] Mary Magdalen and the "other Mary" return to the disciples

and meet Christ on the road; and in Luke, the women tell the disciples and are not believed.⁶

The Gospel of John, however, offers us quite a different picture of the Magdalene. During the resurrection, Mary Magdalene is portrayed as standing with Jesus' mother at the cross: "Meanwhile, standing near the cross of Jesus were his mother, and his mother's sister, Mary the Wife of Clopas, and Mary Magdalene."⁷ In John's account, there are no mourners who watch from a distance, but only the women who ministered to Christ. Later, John tells us how Mary Magdalene did not see Jesus rise from the dead, but in fear ran to Simon Peter for help:

> Early on the first day of the week, while it was still dark, Mary Magdalene came to the tomb and saw that the stone had been removed from the tomb. So she ran and went to Simon Peter and the other disciple, the one whom Jesus loved, and said to them, "They have taken the Lord out of the tomb, and we do not know where they have laid him." Then Peter and the other disciple set out and went toward the tomb. The two were running together, but the other disciple outran Peter and reached the tomb first. He bent down to look in and saw the linen wrappings lying there, but he did not go in. Then Simon Peter came, following him, and went into the tomb. He saw the linen wrappings lying here, and the cloth that had been on Jesus' head not lying with the linen wrappings but rolled up in a place by itself.⁸

John's account differs greatly from those of Mark, Matthew and Luke; however, it is most akin to Luke's account of the resurrection. Indeed, Luke's account, which the orthodox Christian Church tends to agree with, does not recognize Mary Magdalene, or the *weak* women, as the true witness of the resurrection, but a man, Simon Peter: "Saying the Lord is risen indeed, and hath appeared to Simon."⁹ By endorsing Simon Peter as the first witness to the resurrection, and not Mary Magdalene, the Church could guarantee and continue the tradition of male dominance of Church leadership. This rhetorical reframing of the Magdalene's image, as well as that of the Virgin Mary, was to have great repercussions for the later Magdalenes and for women in Western tradition. Indeed it is the beginning of magdalenism — the inversion of Mary Magdalene's true identity. Since the final "branding" act of these images took place during the Middle Ages, these framing techniques used by the early Church Fathers will be discussed further in chapter two. Regardless, even if Luke denies Mary Magdalene her place at the resurrection, he does credit her as a woman of means, who helped finance, or as Cahill suggests, "bankrolled" Jesus' spiritual mission:

> She seems to have been a woman of substance and unconventional, for Luke tells us that she was one of "many women" who traveled with Jesus and his male disciples in an age and place where the mixing of the sexes

was unheard of and that these unusual women "provided for [everyone] out of their own means"—that is, bankrolled the operation.[10]

If Mary Magdalene was a woman of means, and able to travel with Jesus in order to administer to him and his followers, earning her the name *Apostola Apostolorum* (the Apostles' Apostle) along the way, how could she be denied her importance in the events of Jesus' time, and then have her identity transformed, inverted, and distorted into that of a so-called repentant prostitute? There is something very contrived and convenient in this transformation. At any rate, it must be remembered that Mary Magdalene lived in a very patriarchal society where women were not allowed to play powerful, leadership roles. For this reason alone, one could understand why the Magdalene's importance might be denied in the scriptures. Yet this denial of the importance of women and the role they played in the story of Jesus Christ helps us to understand why women, especially Mary Magdalene, are often hidden away or dismissed. *She* becomes a gender to be embarrassed by. An embarrassment that penetrates the Catholic Church, and some of the most enlightened saints of the Church have made it clear that outside of birthing, womankind equates a useless gender. St. Augustine, a converted womanizer, was known for his aversion to women after his conversion, which he demonstrates in his *De genesi ad Litteram* (9, 5–9) where he states, "If woman was not given to man for help in bearing children, for what help could she be? To till the earth together? If help were needed for that, man would have been a better help for man."[11] Not to be outdone, St. Thomas Aquinas is found to hold the same basic distaste for the female sex. In his *Summa Theologia*, under the chapter titled "Should Woman Have Been Made in the Original Creation," Aquinas, like Augustine, believes that women are only good as vessels for procreation (37).[12] Further, by quoting Aristotle, Aquinas reminds us that this misogyny has long roots indeed: "A woman is a misbegotten man."[13] Hence by denying women the respect of equality and Mary Magdalene the recognition of Biblical and spiritual significance, the church allowed no room for women teachers or for the *Apostle to the Apostles*—that is, Mary Magdalene. As St. Augustine and Aquinas both observed, a woman could be considered a partner in the realm of procreation, but in other goodly works a man is a better helpmate for a man. As such, in order for Mary Magdalene to be seen as a pivotal member of Jesus' entourage and the first witness to the resurrection, she had to undergo a metaphoric sex change operation.

Masculinizing the Magdalene

Mary Magdalene was denied and dismissed by her peers, but elevated by Jesus. However this elevation came with a price, and Mary had to deny her gender in order to be worthy of *the word*. As Susan Haskins reminds us, the Gospel of Thomas tells us that Simon Peter objected to the presence of Mary because "'women are not worthy of life,' [to which] Jesus replies, 'I myself shall lead her in order to make her male, so that she too may become a living spirit resembling you males.' He then adds, 'for every woman who will make herself male will enter the Kingdom of Heaven.'"[14] This attitude that one must be male in order to become a living spirit worthy of the Kingdom of Heaven, is the mind-set that kept women teachers out of the Church, establishing the idea that only the male apostle could hold significance and true spirituality. The Church, holding onto this fact, officially selected Peter, not the Magdalene, as the first apostle. This selection helped justify the logic of succession from Peter as the so-called first pope, to those who followed after.[15] So it was, according to Matthew, that Peter Simon was first to receive the keys to the "Kingdom of Heaven," not Mary Magdalene.[16]

However, the notion of women working for the Kingdom of Heaven was not immediately discarded, but had a consistent, smooth transition. It is obvious that Jesus accepted any man or woman willing to learn into his circle. Certainly, the Bible demonstrates that he did not deny women, nor did he insist that they *stay in the kitchen*. Proof of this is seen when Jesus visits Mary and Martha's (of Bethany) house.[17] Here, Martha is running around, gathering food and drink for her guests, as well as attending to housework. Mary, on the other hand, had decided to sit by Jesus and listen to his teachings. When Martha complains to Jesus about Mary and asks him to make Mary help with the household chores, Jesus surprises Martha by taking Mary's side, saying: "Mary has chosen that good part, which will not be taken away from her."[18] This small example demonstrates Jesus' respect for anyone, including women and their ability to learn. Yet this message about women becomes confused when reading further into the New Testament with the works of Paul.

Paul is credited with the authorship of several books in the New Testament, including: Romans, 1 Corinthians, 2 Corinthians, Galatians, Philippians, Colossians, 1 Thessalonians, 2 Thessalonians. It has also been suggested, and traditionally upheld by many that Paul was the author of Ephesians, 1 Timothy, 2 Timothy, Titus, Philemon, and Hebrews.[19] However, most scholars now agree that Paul did not actually write these last several books, and that authorship of these *apocryphal* texts might have resulted from Paul's followers.[20] Yet while examining the traditional attitudes regarding women's roles in society and the church, and how many of these views were justified, it is helpful to remember that apart from reality, Paul has been traditionally associated with all of these texts, even though as the French philosopher Alain Badiou reminds us in *Saint Paul: The Foundation of Universalism*, "Paul has no obvious historical legitimacy."[21] Nevertheless, justification regarding women's roles in the church and society has relied on these writings and on the authority of Paul.

It can be confusing to decipher just how Paul or his followers viewed women in the apocryphal text, because of the many contradictions that exist in these texts. For example, 1 Timothy (2:11–12) states: "Let a woman learn in silence with full submission. I permit no woman to teach or to have authority over a man; she is to keep silent." This statement is fairly clear and to the point: A woman has no authority over a man, and so she may not teach or preach in the church. Yet Paul knew of and praised many women who worked for the church as deaconesses. One such woman, Phebe of Cenchrea (a town near Corinth) was credited with carrying Paul's letter to Rome. In Romans, 16:1–2, Paul writes: "I commend to you our sister Phoebe, who is a servant of the church which is at Cenchrea; that you receive her in the Lord in a manner worthy of the saints, and that you help her in whatever matter she may have need of you; for she herself has also been a helper of many, and myself as well." Furthermore, when it came to men and women's sexuality, Paul suggested equality, although he did hold that those who could live without marriage (so by default, sex) should, so that they may fully commit themselves to God:

> It is well for a man not to touch a woman. But because of cases of sexual immorality, each man should have his own wife and each woman her own husband. The husband should give to his wife her conjugal rights, and likewise the wife to her husband. For the wife does not have authority over her own body, but the husband does; likewise the husband does not have authority over his own body, but the wife does.[22]

Strange these attitudes, when keeping in mind the statement from 1 Timothy; but then again, it would not be strange if Paul truly was not the author of this text as is now thought to be the case. Paul's statement as quoted above seems to suggest equal possession, a very *feminist* statement for the times. Besides sexual equality, there is still, nevertheless, Paul's statement to deal with that states how women were to be *silent* and were not allowed to teach. Paul might have felt this way for the majority of women, if he was the writer of 1 Timothy, but he certainly made exceptions.

Paul, while promoting his mission of Christianity, employed several women that helped promote his crusade. In 1 Corinthians (11:5), Paul reports that women actively preached during the liturgy, and he also tells of women prophesying, or more accurately preaching. As mentioned above, in Romans 16:1–2, Paul praises Phoebe, a deacon in her community. Further, in Paul's letter to the Romans, he commends Prisca, a "fellow worker in Christ Jesus."[23] In Philippians, Paul discusses two women, Euodia and Syntyche, who struggled beside him: "I urge Euodia and I urge Syntyche to be of the same mind in the Lord. Yes, and I ask you also, my loyal companion, help these women, for they have struggled beside me in the work of the gospel, together with Clement and the rest of my co-workers, whose names are in the book of life."[24] However, the most admired woman that Paul speaks of is Junia who, like Mary Magdalene, had to become male in order to gain spiritually respectability:

> Paul characterizes a woman named Junia as "outstanding among the apostles" (Rom. 16:7). In the time since he wrote Junia has undergone a sex change, and been renamed "Junias." But the old Church knew better: Jerome and Chrysostom, for example, take it for granted that Junia was a woman. Chrysostom writes: "what brilliance and ability this woman must have had to be thought worthy of the title of apostle, indeed to be outstanding among the apostles" (in *epist. Ad. Romanos homilia* 31, 12). Up until the late Middle Ages not a single commentator had seen a man's name in Romans 16:7 (ce. B. Brooten in *Frauenbefreiung: Biblische und theologische Argumente*, edited by E. Moltmann-Wendel, 1978, pp. 148–51). But in the Church's continual repression of women this woman's name was taken over by men.[25]

No matter how much women were an integral part of the Christ movement in the beginning, ultimately they had to either be recreated as male or remain a virgin to truly reach spirituality: "Then the kingdom of heaven shall be likened to ten virgins who took their lamps and went out to meet the bridegroom."[26]

Like Junia, Mary Magdalene underwent a type of sex change, but because she was so involved with the original movement, and because the church wanted to limit and eradicate women's participation within the hierarchical structure, Mary Magdalene's true identity became hidden. The denial of Mary Magdalene's significance to Christ and the role she played does not end here: as further insult, she no longer became known or remembered for being the divine witness to the Resurrection, or a *woman of means* who helped *bankroll* the operation — rather, Mary Magdalene became a repented prostitute where her identity was mistakenly, or more likely intentionally, confused with the other women in Jesus' life.

Which Mary Is She?

Many of us have grown up with the image of Mary Magdalene as the reformed prostitute, an image that has no Biblical support. In the New Testament, three different women are mentioned, and their identities often become intertwined. These are the women who, in addition to his mother Mary, ministered to Jesus. The first of these women, and an extremely important character for this project, is the sinner talked about in Luke:

> One of the Pharisees asked Jesus to eat with him, and he went into the Pharisee's house and took his place at the table. And a woman in the city, who was a sinner, having learned that he was eating in the Pharisee's house, brought an alabaster jar of ointment. She stood behind him at his feet, weeping, and began to bathe his feet with her tears and to dry them with her hair. Then she continued kissing his feet and anointing them with the ointment. Now when the Pharisee who had invited him saw it, he said to himself, "If this man were a prophet, he would have known who and what kind of woman this is who is touching him — that she is a sinner." Jesus spoke up and said to him, "Simon, I have something to say to you." "Teacher," he replied, "speak." ... "Do you see this woman? I entered your house; you gave me no water for my feet, but she has bathed my feet with her tears and dried them with her hair. You gave me no kiss, but from the time I came in she has not stopped kissing my feet. You did not anoint my head with oil, but she has anointed my feet with ointment. Therefore, I tell you, her sins, which were many, have been forgiven; hence she has shown great love."[27]

The next woman is Mary of Bethany, the sister of Martha and Lazarus, who is also mentioned in the Gospel of Luke:

> Now as they went on their way, he entered a certain village, where a woman named Martha welcomed him into her home. She had a sister named Mary, who sat at the Lord's feet and listened to what he was saying. But Martha was distracted by her many tasks; so she came to him and asked, "Lord, do you not care that my sister has left me to do all the work by myself? Tell her then to help me." But the Lord answered her, "Martha, you are worried and distracted by many things; there is need of only one thing. Mary has chosen the better part, which will not be taken away from her."[28]

The third woman mentioned is Mary Magdalene, who had seven devils cast out of her by Jesus Christ: "Now when Jesus was risen early the first day of the week, he appeared first to Mary Magdalene, out of whom he had cast seven devils."[29] Throughout much of western history, these women have been confused for one another, combined into one entity, and basically misunderstood: a misunderstanding that happens often when dealing with the image of women within the confines of the Church.

There are several reasons why Mary Magdalene might have been mistaken for the prostitute in the New Testament. The first reason is offered to us in the 1913 edition of the *Catholic Encyclopedia*: "Mary Magdalen was so called either from Magdala near Tiberias, on the west shore of Galilee, or possibly from a Talmudic expression meaning 'curling women's hair,' which the Talmud explains as an adulteresses."[30] It is not far-reaching to argue that this idea of Magdalene meaning *curling women's hair* (an adulteress) was later translated to imply a prostitute, since medieval laws required prostitutes to distinguish themselves from good women by not covering their heads. Thus Cahill argues: "Though the weeping prostitute with the uncovered curls is often assumed to be Mary Magdalene, (whence the words *magdalene* for 'prostitute' and *maudlin* for 'excessively weepy')."[31] Further, this hypothesis, the uncovered curly head of the weeping prostitute as Mary Magdalene, came about from the sixth century on, when Mary was also confused with the woman of Samaria.[32] However, this link, as Haskins also observes, is "even more tenuous than those between the Magdalen and Luke's sinner and Mary of Bethany."[33] There is also the theory that the description of Mary Magdalene being a woman that "seven devils had gone out,"[34] was interpreted to mean that she was a prostitute. However, the Biblical casting out of evil spirits tended to correlate with the curing of illness and not with immoral sexual behavior; as such, this argument falls flat especially when considering the lack of Biblical support: "When the evening was come, they brought unto him many that were possessed with devils: and he cast out the spirits with his word, *and healed all that were sick*."[35] The Gospel of Luke also suggests that Mary Magdalene was taken ill because of the seven devils, not because illicit sexual behavior invited the devils to reside within: "And certain women, which had been healed of evil spirits and *infirmities*. Mary called Magdalene, out of whom went seven devils."[36] As Chilton points out, unclean spirits or demons were "considered contagious, moving from person to person and place to place, transmitted by people like Mary who were known to be possessed."[37] It appears that the better argument here is that demons were understood in the same light as viruses are thought of today, in how they commute from person to person through air and or body contact. Since healing of evil spirits directly related to illness and not prostitution or loose sexual behavior, it is unlikely that Mary Magdalene could be mistaken for a prostitute because she had seven devils cast out of her. However, there is a third reason why Mary Magdalene might have been seen as the repented prostitute: a rumor that originated from Pope Gregory the Great.

Pope Gregory (pope 590–604), the last of the four original Doctors of the church, was known as Gregory the Great, and is the official instigator of the magdalenism syndrome. It has been suggested that the confused representation of Mary Magdalene as a prostitute came from the sixth century, when "Pope Gregory the Great mistakenly identified Mary with the sinner who anointed Jesus with oil. Thus she became a repentant whore."[38] Indeed, Pope Gregory stated that all three women (Mary Magdalene, Mary of Bethany, and the unnamed prostitute sinner in the Pharisees house in Luke 7:36–50) were actually one in the same during a speech he gave in 591.[39] The confusion could have stemmed from the fact that each of these women were said to have anointed Jesus. In Luke 7:38, the unnamed prostitute weeps on Jesus' feet, cleans his feet with her hair, and then anoints the feet with perfumed oil. In Mark 14:3, while Jesus is in Bethany at the home of Simon the Leper, a "woman," Mary of Bethany, anoints Jesus' head with "costly perfume of pure nard." In John 12:3, Jesus is again in Bethany at the home where Lazarus was raised from the dead, and Mary of Bethany is said to use a "pound of very costly, genuine spikenard ointment, and anointed the feet of Jesus, and wiped his feet with her hair." Finally, although Mary Magdalene does not anoint Jesus during life, she prepares to anoint his body after death, as was the custom (Lk 24:1–10; Mk 16:1). If the events of who was anointing Jesus and when are what led to Pope Gregory's confusion regarding Mary's identity, it is not terribly surprising that Pope Gregory mistook Mary as the prostitute sinner who anointed Jesus' feet with oil (Lk 7:38), since there were many traditions that linked sacred prostitution with the ceremony of anointing. In fact many of these traditions were still being practiced in the time of Jesus Christ.

The practice of anointing with perfume is part of an ancient tradition, a ritual performed by a sacred priestess in the Roman Empire, as well as in the Canaanites' religion. The priestess has been often referred to as the sacred prostitute, in honor of the Goddess image, the feminine image of God: "As priestess of the goddess, their importance dates back through the centuries to the Neolithic period (7000–3500 B.C.), back to the time when God was honored and cherished as feminine throughout the lands that are now known as the Middle East and Europe."[40] Sjöö and Mor explain this sacred practice of the priestess as the union with the "moon goddess":

> The moon Goddess was worshipped in orgiastic rites, being the divinity of matriarchal women free to take as many lovers as they chose. Women could "surrender" themselves to the Goddess by making love to a stranger in her temple. This has been called, by male historians, "sacred prostitution," but the word is totally misleading. This was not any kind of service to men, nor did any woman have to do this to live, it was a way for women to participate, for a ritual moment, in the transindividual being of the Goddess. The Goddess comes into being "in the moment of union"—a moment of psychic as well as sexual union. This was one way that men could partake in her essence also, through the body of a woman. The rite was meant to recharge the living Goddess, and to enlarge the woman's ego-consciousness into an experience of cosmic sexual power and flow. It was a way for each woman to experience herself as "the moon."[41]

In some periods of Jewish history, this custom was even part of ritual worship, including in the Temple of Jerusalem. Furthermore, Chilton links anointing with the process of exorcism and healing, stating that "when Jesus sent out the twelve apostles to heal, there is reference to anointing, as if it were self evident that this was part of their standard practices (Mark 6:13)."[42] Regardless of Chilton's suggestion that anointing was linked to standard Jewish spiritual practices, Starbird argues that it was looked down upon because, rather, the prostitute was also associated with pagan spirituality: "Some of the prophets of Yahweh deplored the influence of the Great Goddess locally called 'Ashera,'" a Neolithic Goddess who represented the tree of life.[43] Starbird, Sjöö and Mor all link anointing to the *sacred union*, the coming together in ritual worship, which was often accompanied by the anointing with oil, since anointing was a tradition followed before a wedding ceremony, and the joining with the Goddess, in ceremony, was seen as an reenactment of the marriage between the Holy God and Goddess: "The anointing of the sacred King was the unique privilege of a royal bride. For millennia this same action had been part of an actual marriage rite performed by a daughter of the royal house, and the marriage rite itself conferred kingship on her consort."[44] Consequently, the act of anointing Jesus' feet by a *prostitute* could be linked back to this controversial, yet still persistent ritual worship, because these cult rituals did not completely end until around the fifth century.[45]

Nonetheless, this is not the only confusion over the image of Mary Magdalene. There also seems to be puzzlement as to whether Mary Magdalene and Mary of Bethany was one in the same person: "Medieval interpretation further conflated the weeping prostitute, Mary Magdalene, and Martha's sister Mary into one person, whereas it appears to modern scholars that they were in actuality three different women."[46] Evidence and debate over Mary Magdalene and Mary of Bethany being one and the same person, has been going on for hundreds of years to the present day. Modern sensibility tends to either prove or disprove the theory by examining the meaning behind a person's name as a designation. For example, Picknell conflates the two biblical characters. Inspired by Starbird's work, Picknett believes that "Magdalene" is a title best understood as "Magdala" or "tower" rather than her place of origin.[47] Chilton offers a similar argument, pointing to Jesus' quirky tendency of offering somewhat sarcastic nicknames to his apostles — Simon was dubbed the "Rock" for his apparent "mental density."[48] However, Picknett argues that Mary Magdalene and Mary of Bethany is actually the same person, based partly on the argument that Magdalene is not a location, and because of the practice of anointing. As there is no evidence that Magdalene is a title or a nickname rather than a name that designates a place of origin (much like *of Bethany* does), it is more likely that these two women are indeed separate entities. In fact, traditionally the Greek fathers of the Catholic Church agree that there are three different Marys mentioned in the New Testament: Luke's sinner, Mary the sister of Martha and Lazarus, and Mary Magdalene. The Latin fathers of the Church disagree. From the Latin point of view, these three women were one in the same: "We believe that the one that Luke calls 'sinner,' that John names 'Mary' is the same out of whom, according to Mark, 'seven devils were expelled.'"[49] Much of this confusion is due to the Gospels themselves, and again the act of anointing. Mary anointing Jesus, and wiping his feet with her hair (Jn 1:3) is reminiscent of the prostitute in the Pharisees' house, wiping Jesus' feet clean with her tears and hair (Lk 7:38). Haskins suggests that John might have known about Luke's account, and so then associated Luke's sinner with Mary of Bethany:

> John may have known Luke's story of the unknown sinner, and have applied it to Mary of Bethany for, at the beginning of the Lazarus episode, he tells us very clearly, apparently anticipating his account of the event in his next chapter, that "it was that Mary which anointed the Lord with ointment, and wiped his feet with her hair, whose brother Lazarus was sick" (11:2). It has also been suggested that the relevant chapters in John have been transposed, and the John is referring to Mary of his own story.[50]

We have already discussed how Mary Magdalene had been confused with the *sinner* of Luke's story. Keeping this in mind, it is only a small step (with the help of the Gospel of John) to link Mary Magdalene with Mary of Bethany. Authenticity was added to this conclusion when Saint Bernard, the Cistercian Abbot of Clairvaux (1090–1153), agreed that Mary of Bethany and Mary Magdalene were the same person.[51]

This process of magdalenism, mystification, and the act of erasing identity not only robbed the Magdalene, Mary of Magdol (the tower) of her identity, but it takes away from the important role women played in Jesus' mission—something St. Jerome at least recognized in a letter to the virgin Principia in 412:

> Those unbelievers who read me may perhaps smile to find me lingering over the praises of weak women. But if they will recall how holy women attended to our Lord and Saviour and ministered to him of their substance, and how the three Mary's stood before the cross ... they will convict *themselves of pride rather than me of folly, who judge of virtue not by the sex of the mind.*[52]

Later, in that same letter, he offered an epithet for Mary Magdalene containing the words *fortified with towers*[53]: "and especially, how Mary of Magdala received the epithet 'fortified with towers' because her earnestness and strength of faith, and was privileged to see the rising Christ first before the apostles."[54] Regardless of the facts, the tradition of Mary Magdalene as *the repented prostitute* seems to stick with us even to the present day, and it remains an image used consistently by our society when dealing with the so-called fallen woman.[55] Indeed, even today, as religious scholar Bruce Chilton points out, Mary Magdalene cannot be discussed without also discussing her sexual habits, whatever those might have been: "She is often depicted as nude in the craggy rocks of La Sainte-Baume. Her long and lustrous hair covering the parts of her body that modesty conventionally requires to be covered, is a staple of iconography in the West to this day, making Mary Magdalene the Lady Godiva of Christian spirituality."[56] This image has penetrated our psyche, our traditions, and history, just as it stuck with the Magdalene laundries in Ireland and elsewhere, where Mary Magdalene was only understood as a role model for prostitutes and other marginalized women. Additionally, when considering how the Magdalene has been portrayed in relation to the Mother Mary — women are often faced with this simple either/or understanding of womanhood: the virgin or the whore.

Why does society continue to hold onto the myth of Mary Magdalene as the repented prostitute, even if it is not so? In part, this stems from the tradition of associating women with either the virgin or the whore in our myths and legends. True to form, the Christian religion offers women two different basic role models: Jesus' mother, the Virgin Mary, and Mary Magdalene, the reformed prostitute. There are women in the Bible that represent the *wife*, such as Sarah, who was married to Abraham; however, these women are not as dominant as the images of The Magdalene and The Virgin. Thus the Mother Mary and Mary Magdalene have become so prevailing in our culture's mind eye that Western culture looks to them rather than to Deborah or Rebekah in the Old Testament. The problem of this representation is that there is a polarization of ideals and the reinforcement of division: first, the absolutely unattainable pure status of the Virgin Mother, compared to the Magdalene, who represents a dive into sin. The classic reinforcing of good versus evil, an *us* versus *them* identification move built upon difference. Still between the two images, Mary Magdalene as the repented prostitute is more accessible to women because she seems more "human," whereas the Virgin Mary as traditionally promoted by the Catholic Church is rather unattainable to the mere mortal female.

The Virgin Mother Mary

The story of the Mother Mary and the virgin birth is only found in the Gospels of Matthew and Luke. Not only is the virgin birth discussed, but the lineage of Jesus is also described, demonstrating how Jesus is a direct descendent of King David, just as the prophets foretold.[57] The mythical story of Mary's virgin birth is a quick and simple one, if that is even possible. At around thirteen or fourteen years of age (the proper age for engagement, since she was engaged but not yet married to Joseph), the Arch-Angel Gabriel visits Mary at her home in Galilee, called Nazareth. This visit would change and challenge Mary's life, since Gabriel not only brings greetings from God, but also announces that she is going to have a son, Jesus. It is further explained to her that this son is no ordinary man, but the Son of God who shall reign over the House of Jacob forever, and that his Kingdom will have no end.[58] Mary, in Luke (Lk 1:35), is rightfully startled by this pronouncement and wonders how it is she will have a virgin birth. The angel Gabriel explains that the Holy Spirit will come "upon" her and "the power of the Most High will overshadow" her, and in this way the child will be born of the Holy Spirit and will be called the Son of God. Mary is also given the extra news that her cousin Elizabeth, who was old and thought sterile, was also going to have a son (John the Baptist)—another gift from God. Of course it is understood that Elizabeth will have a natural, not a virgin birth.

An interesting insight into Mary's character can be found in Luke's passage (the passage in Matthew is lacking in details regarding the specifics of this event). First of all, unlike the myths, stories, and movies made depicting this scene, Mary does not seem submissive or meek. In fact she is not scared when Gabriel shows up, because she never trembles. This is an odd fact, since it can assume that an angel showing up at a person's home was as rare then as it is now. Furthermore, such an occurrence, coupled with the pronouncement that "I have a special message for you directly from God," would be enough to send most humans running out of the house. As such, this young girl is no weakling; she is strong and sure of herself. When Mary finds out about the child she will bear, the Son of God, she is again not scared, but, oddly enough, slightly unnerved and curious as to the *mechanics* of a virgin birth: "How can this be, since I am a virgin."[59] This response is truly phenomenal even for a person of great faith. Considering the time period that Mary lived in, where a woman could be ruined, and stoned to death for looking in the direction of another man, Mary's reaction is not only brave but quite pragmatic as well. When Gabriel answers that the Holy Ghost will "come upon" her, she is not scared, but simply honored (another amazing reaction). This story, as read in Luke's account, offers us the most insight regarding Mary of Nazareth. Little is known regarding what kind of mother she made, because only a few mentions of the Mother Mary are discussed outside of the divine announcement. However, it can assume that she excelled in her role of mother, considering Jesus' character. It is later learned that Mary and Joseph go on to have more children, giving Jesus several brothers and a few sisters.[60]

Jesus leaves the family fold, after the death of Joseph, and embarks on his Holy destiny, grappling with his demons in the desert, preaching and, more often than not, stirring up trouble and controversy. Mary becomes worried about her son Jesus when she hears how his preaching is being received by the authorities, and so she gathers up her children, Jesus' brothers and sisters, for what is termed today as a family intervention. The Gospel of Mark

(3:33–35) tells how Mary and her gathered family tried to reach Jesus in order to help him in his time of controversy. However, when they arrived and are announced, Jesus denies their presence, saying: "Who is My mother, or My brothers?... Here are My mother and My brothers! For whomever does the will of God is My brother and My sister and mother." Is Mary daunted by this response from her son? This is not discussed. However, it can be supposed that as a mother she was likely scared for her son, since the political dust he was stirring up would bring about his death. In fact this is the last time that Mary is seen, at her son's crucifixion, watching along with Mary Magdalene, while Jesus is stripped naked and nailed to a cross. As a reader it is difficult not to wonder where all the other supporters of Jesus are. Where are Simon Peter (the apostle who will deny Jesus three times on this night), Matthew, and the other apostles? Sadly, they are nowhere to be seen, as the women stand alone watching the last moments of Jesus' life run from him. This is a very human, very real Mary presented in the accounts of Luke and Matthew. Except for her uncanny reaction to angel Gabriel's news regarding the virgin birth, she appears to be a rather traditional yet committed and strong mother and wife, simply doing the best she can under extraordinary circumstances. Indeed, this is a woman that can be looked up to and, rationally, one that other women can aspire to! However, the Mary that stood watching her son die, and the Mary who attempted the family intervention, is not the Mary that has come down to us through the ages. Instead, there is presented an impossible image, untouchable, and difficult to relate to.

What separates the very real woman described above from the iconic, untouchable Mary that most of us are used to? Her status as an eternal virgin. As mentioned above, it is written in both Mark (6:3) and Matthew (13:55) that Jesus has brothers and sisters, but it is traditionally held by the Catholic Church that the virgin Mary remained a virgin even after the birth of Jesus — this adjustment alone makes her an untouchable character. At face value, the fact that Mary might have had children the *normal* way after the virgin birth of Jesus would not, for the most of us, diminish this miracle event. Regardless, for a church that associates sex with sin it is vital for the myth that the Virgin Mary remains a virgin. Without a doubt, when the church emphasized celibacy, the idea of sex became increasingly taboo and sinful. This had to affect the Virgin Mary more than any other circumstance or character in the New Testament. After all, if God demanded purity and abstinence from sex, then the mother of Jesus must be pure during the birth, after the birth, throughout life, and in death. As St. Augustine insisted in the *Enchiridion*, sex is related to pleasure, and the combination of the two determines original sin: "Thus, according to Augustine, sexual intercourse or, more precisely, sexual pleasure is what carries original sin on and on, from generation to generation. 'Christ was begotten and conceived without any fleshly pleasure and so he also remained free from every kind of defilement by original sin.'"[61]

In an effort to explain away the passages that mention Jesus' brothers and sisters, the church devised several plausible explanations, one being that Joseph was married before he married Mary, and that these were his children, therefore Jesus' stepbrothers and stepsisters. Later, it would be unsuitable for Joseph to have been married before he wed Mary, and so these stepbrothers and stepsisters were then turned into Jesus' cousins. As Ranke-Heinemann reminds us:

> After New Testament times, from the second century on, Jesus' brothers and sisters were first turned into stepbrothers and stepsisters from the first marriage of Joseph, now a widower (Proto-Gospel of James 9, ca. 150); and finally in about 400 Jerome made the stepbrothers and stepsisters over into male and female cousins; and maintained that it was "godless, apocryphal daydreaming" to believe that Joseph had children from a first marriage. According to Jerome, only a virginal Joseph would be appropriate for a virginal Mary (*ad Matth*. 12). Thus Mary was a virgin after, as well as, before the birth of Jesus.[62]

There were two sides to the issue: some felt that God did not value virginity any more than he valued marriage; others contended that because the act of sex begat original sin, then Jesus, being the Son of God, must never have a connection to original sin. In the fourth century, Pope Siricius, pondering the question of sin and sex, determined that Jesus set down the rules for his own birth, and his rules demanded that the woman who was to bear him needed to be without sin, which is why Mary died a virgin: "Jesus would have taken no pleasure at all in the whole process of redemption.... Jesus would not have chosen birth from a virgin, had he been forced to look upon her as so unrestrained as to let that womb, which the body of the Lord was fashioned, the hall of the eternal king, be stained by the presence of male seed."[63]

Yet not every holy father of the church maintained Siricius' or Augustine's view on virginity and sex. For example, Saint Jovinian (ca. 347–419 or 420) took an alternative view regarding virginity, when he stated that virginity was not necessarily more pleasing to God than marriage, and he highly doubted that Mary remained a virgin throughout her life.[64] But Jovinian's views were rare, and other leaders such as Ambrose, the bishop of Milan (d. 397), led a fight against Jovinian and his opinions regarding God's views on virginity. Later Pope Siricius, who demanded that Jesus insisted on the virginity of Mary, excommunicated Jovinian and his followers in Rome. However, excommunication is not enough to stop *troublemakers* from rocking the boat; something more was needed, some hard evidence to prove, beyond a doubt, that Mary was a virgin and remained that way until her death. To end the question of whether Mary died a virgin or not, the proto-Gospel of James (the apocryphal Gospel said to be written by Jesus' "brother" James) was employed.[65] Bluntly put, the importance of this Gospel was that it offered *evidence* that Mary's hymen was not damaged during the birthing process that produced Jesus, allowing Mary to remain a virgin even after giving birth:

> And they stood in the place of the cave: and behold a bright cloud overshadowing the cave. And the midwife said: My soul is magnified this day, because mine eyes have seen marvelous things: for salvation is born unto Israel. And immediately the cloud withdrew itself out of the cave, and a great light appeared in the cave so that our eyes could not endure it. And by little and little that light withdrew itself until the young child appeared: and it went and took the breast of its mother Mary.[66]

Next, the midwife speaks to Salome about the miracle birth, but Salome does not believe her, or in the possibility of a virgin birth. Requiring evidence, Salome goes into the cave where Mary and Jesus are just getting to know each other. Here she performs an exam, checking to make sure the hymen is truly intact, but she becomes infected, burned because of her lack of faith. She is only healed by holding Jesus, leading her to believe that the savior had been born to a virgin.

> And Salome said: As the Lord my God liveth, if I make not trial and prove her nature I will not believe that a virgin hath brought forth. And the midwife went in and said unto Mary: Order thyself, for there is no small contention arisen concerning thee. Arid Salome made trial and cried out and said: Woe unto mine iniquity and mine unbelief, because I have tempted the living God, and lo, my hand falleth away from me in fire. And she bowed her knees unto the Lord, saying: O God of my fathers, remember that I am the seed of Abraham and Isaac and Jacob: make me not a public example unto the children of Israel, but restore me unto the poor, for thou knowest, Lord, that in thy name did I perform my cures, and did receive my hire of thee. And lo, an angel of the Lord appeared, saying unto her: Salome, Salome, the Lord hath hearkened to thee: bring thine hand near unto the young child and take him up, and there shall be unto thee salvation and joy. And Salome came near and took him up, saying: I will do him worship, for a great king is born unto Israel. And behold immediately Salome was healed: and she went forth of the cave justified. And lo, a voice saying: Salome, Salome, tell none of the marvels which thou hast seen, until the child enter into Jerusalem.[67]

Even though the Gospel of James is apocrypha, it provided the *evidence* that the fathers wanted ... proof that Mary was a Virgin and remained one until her death. The other children could not have been hers, since there could be only one miracle birth, and so she died far from sin and carnal knowledge.

The major problem with this line of thinking is that it denies the true Mary of Nazareth, since it inverts her identity in the same way as magdalenism nullifies the true identity of Mary Magdalene. It denies her strength, being a human mother capable of incredible love and faith. Instead, focus is only placed upon the *virginity* and the importance of *virginity*. Not unlike Mary Magdalene, Mary of Nazareth was robbed of her rightful existence — an irony when considering that out of all of Jesus' followers, these two women were among the few truly strong enough to watch his death in its entirety. Further by deeming the Virgin Mary always a virgin, absolutely free from all sin, she becomes an impossible role model for the ordinary woman. After all, women are required by the church to bring children into the world, to be fruitful and multiply, but whenever a woman abides by this commandment, she is accused of passing on sin — essentially making female *sin machines*. How can women live up to or live with such expectations? Of course there is confession and baptism; nevertheless, the woman, because she gives birth, enables the never-ending cycle of sin. As such, women can never obtain the purity of the Mother Mary, and in this women will always be failures. Thank God then for Mary Magdalene. Mary Magdalene, even as the repentant whore, is a woman most of us can relate to and look up to, because although she sinned, she was forgiven. Indeed, the image of the whore, a feminine presence that is flawed yet hopeful, is a prominent theme throughout both the Old and New Testaments of the Bible.

Whoredom in Our Midst

Both concepts, the virgin and the whore, are loaded ideologies that bring with them centuries of connotations linked to social, political, spiritual and economic influences. As such, and in light of the deconstruction of the historic Magdalene, it is important to also deconstruct the Biblical whore. Society often mistakes the iconic whore image for the real person(s) wearing the image. As Chilton kindly reminds us, *good* society tends to forget that women (and men) who turn to prostitution do so out of necessity, not simply out of a lustful need. Nevertheless, it is on lust, what in the Middle Ages was referred to as the sin of *Luxuria*, that society is focused: "Women didn't prostitute themselves from necessity; rather, they enjoyed sexual indulgence, which was considered to be sinful even within marriage."[68] Yet even the Bible, that which was claimed as defining the sin *luxuria*, view the whores, harlots and harlotry in a variety of ways.

How many images of the harlot or the whore are in the Bible? Frankly there are quite a few, including the entire Jewish Nation, if you take your Bible literally. The words harlot, whore and prostitute are used freely throughout the Old Testament in a few different contexts. For example, the term harlot, as it refers to a person who *prostitutes* his or herself, can be found in Proverbs (2:16; 5:3–20; 7:10–27; 9:13–18), Isaiah (23:15–16), Hosea (2:13), Deuteronomy (23:17–18), Leviticus (19:29, 21:9), and discussing Rahab, the prostitute from the city of Jericho, in Joshua (2:3–6, 6:17, 23, 25) and Hebrews (11:31), and Samson's Delilah (who is said to exemplify the harlot) in Judges (16:4–5), just to name a few. But the idea of harlotry is better understood through its metaphoric application, specifically as applied to the Children of Israel and their relationship with God.

Ezekiel[69] was especially fond of comparing Jerusalem with that of the harlot or whore in reference to *her* apparent faithless relationship with God. Not unlike "The Great Harlot," which stands for "the great city that rules over the kings of the earth" presented in the New Testament's book of Revelation,[70] Ezekiel tells the allegorical history of God's bride, the unfaithful Israel and how Israel's people had "trusted in [their] beauty, and played the whore,"[71] *sleeping* with the "Egyptians, [their] lustful neighbors, multiplying [their] whoring" to make God angry.[72] Chapter 23 offers the symbolic tale of two adulterous sisters (Ohalah and Oholibah, understood as Samaria and Jerusalem):

> Mortal, there were two women, the daughters of one mother; they played the whore in Egypt; they played the whore in their youth; their breasts were caressed there, and their virgin bosoms were fondled. Oholah was the name of the elder and Oholibah the name of her sister. They became mine, and they bore sons and daughters. As for their names, Oholah is Samaria, and Oholibah is Jerusalem."[73]

Ezekiel goes on to explain how the two cities had continued play the whore with the Babylonians, the Egyptians, and the Assyrians, and because of their actions God declared: "Therefore, O Oholibah, thus says the Lord God: I will rouse against you your lovers from whom you turned in disgust, and I will bring them against you from every side."[74] This metaphor is extended in the book of Hosea where Israel is compared to that of a faithless wife because God's chosen people were turning to other gods:

> Say to your brother, Ammi, and your sister, Ruhamar. Plead with your mother, plead — for she is not my wife, and I am not her husband — that she put away her whoring from her face, and her adultery from between her breasts, or I will strip her naked and expose her as in the day she was born, and make her like a wilderness, and turn her into parched land, and kill her with thirst. Upon her children also I will have no pity, because they are children of whoredom.[75] For their mother has played the whore; she who conceived them has acted shamefully.[76]

God's chosen people are also labeled as harlots in Isaiah, who begs them to amend their ways: "How the faithful city has become a whore! She that was full of justice, righteousness lodged in her — but now murders."[77] This theme continues throughout the Old Testament, pushing the limits of what quickly becomes a tiring metaphor, as Jeremiah looks for a righteous man among the harlot houses of God.[78] However, this theme of a nation of harlots is not reserved only for the people of Israel, but also for the nations of the world. In the book of Joel, for example, God judges all of the nations (harlots, the lot of them) and blesses his chosen people:

> For them, in those days and at that time, when I restore the fortunes of Judah and Jerusalem, I will gather all the nations and bring them down to the valley of Jehoshaphat, and I will enter into judgment with them there, on account of my people and my heritage Israel, because they have scattered them among the nations. They have divided my land, and cast lots for my people, and traded boys for prostitutes, and sold girls for wine, and drunk it down.[79]

A review of Old Testament harlotry would be incomplete without discussing the famed city of Jericho, which was filled with whores and harlots, enacting every sexual deviance and the central sin of worshiping gods other than Yahweh. However, this story offers the reader an interesting view of the harlot as hero: Rahab (later given as part of Jesus' lineage), who saved the lives of two Israelites when they came into the city to spy before an invasion. The book of Joshua tells how Rahab bargained for her life, but more importantly, how she truly believes that God meant the land for the Israelites: "I know that the LORD has given you the land, and that dread of you has fallen on us, and that all the inhabitants of the land melt in fear before you."[80] Later, because of her wisdom and kindness, this harlot is saved from the destruction of Jericho: "The city and all that is in it shall be devoted to the LORD for destruction. Only Rahab the prostitute and all who are with her in her house shall live because she hid the messengers we sent."[81] Story after story in the Old Testament dwells on the plight of the whore or the potential for harlotry. In Genesis 34, Jacob's daughter Dinah is raped and her brothers take revenge, making sure she would not be made into a common whore. There is also the story of Judah and Tamar, Genesis 38, showing Tamar taking on the role of a harlot in order to trick her father-in-law, Judah, into having sex with her so that she may rightfully bear a son, carrying on the family line. It is understood that this act of harlotry is done out of desperation to fulfill the law of procreation. In essence, Judah had gone back on a former promise that he would give one of his younger sons in marriage to Tamar after her husband, who was Judah's eldest son, had died, as was law and tradition: "And Judah acknowledged them, and said, 'She hath been more righteous than I; since I did not give her to my son Shelah.' And he did not lie with her again."[82] Finally, in addition to the harlot as a prostitute and as a metaphor, there are laws concerning prostitution as seen in Leviticus. Here, rules and laws concerning the holiness of priests are presented, and how that holiness should not be contaminated by marrying a prostitute, defined as any woman who has been defiled or married before.[83] Indeed, the only suitable woman for a holy man is a virgin: "A widow, or a divorced woman, or profane, or a harlot, these he shall not take: but he shall take a virgin of his own people to wife."[84] Not surprisingly, a rabbi's daughter is expected to be pure, lest she ruin her father. In fact, if the rabbi's daughter in question should profane herself, be raped, or in any way fall from virginal grace, by law she is to be killed by way of fire.[85]

The New Testament picks up the harlot theme where the Old Testament leaves it. As mentioned above, one of the most prominent allegorical uses of the whore figure comes in the book of Revelations and *The Great Whore*. Focusing on the symbolism behind the number seven, chapters 17 and 18 of Revelations depict the Great Whore: "Then one of the seven angels who had the seven bowls came and said to me, 'come, I will show you the judgment of the great whore who is seated on many waters, with whom the kings of the earth have committed fornication, and with the wine of whose fornication the inhabitants of the earth have become drunk."[86] This Great Whore is really the "great city that rules over the kings of the earth,"[87] who has seduced all the other nations by allowing them to drink of her "wine and the wrath of her fornication" and by committing fornication with her in order to gain riches and power.[88] From this text, the image of the harlot and the act of sex, in connection to economics and power, are presented as being the two largest corruptors and the downfall of humanity itself. The Great Whore becomes the hotbed for all that is wrong and evil — for all that cannot be forgiven. Regardless of this image, the New Testament actually offers the harlot forgiveness in the presence of Jesus Christ.

What makes many of the whores in the New Testament unique is the fact that Jesus never shuns them, something the Jewish community at the time found outrageous. Jesus seemed to take to women easily, never turning his back on them just because they were mere women: wife, virgin, or whore. One account (Mt. 9:20–22; Mk. 5:25–34 and Lk. 8:41–19) recalled when Jesus was walking with a great crowd of people on his way to help a young girl who was dying. On his way to her house, a woman who suffered from a constant menstrual flow touched the back of Jesus' robe in hopes of being healed. Jesus, noticing the departing healing power, asked who had touched him, and after she made her presence known, he told her to go in peace. Granted, in today's world the image of the whore is not associated with that of a woman who has a dire medical condition. But in Jesus' time, prostitutes, whores, and an unending menstrual flow all constituted a form of impurity stemming from either demonic activity or sin. As such, this story is an important one, because it demonstrates how Jesus was not afraid of the so-called unclean or impure. Consequently, Jesus' reaction toward this woman was a challenge against the ritual laws of purification, and stigma of impurity in all its forms: "You shall separate the children of Israel from their uncleanness."[89] Another example of how Jesus concerned himself not only with impurity, but true interpersonal relations can be found in John 4:6–42, where he speaks to a Samarian woman and requests a drink of water. The Samarian woman knows who Jesus is and asks him: "How is it that you, being a Jew, ask a drink from me, a Samarian woman."[90] The Samarian woman's bewilderment stems from the fact that Jews were not known to speak with Samarians, and because he was a Rabbi and she a woman of questionable honor (having had more than one husband). Not only was it unusual for a Jewish Rabbi to speak to a Jewish woman not his wife or family member, or even look at her, but to speak directly to and look at a woman who was not Jewish at all, and who had played the role of a harlot, was surprising behavior.

Finally, as discussed earlier, there is the touching account of the harlot from Luke (7:36–50) who enters the home of the Pharisee. Crying, this unnamed woman washes Jesus' feet with her tears and then wipes them clean with her hair, and she is forgiven her sins, which, it is stated, were many. Jesus does seem to be a very unique Rabbi for his time, especially in his interaction with women from all walks of life. Whatever lessons Christianity has taken from Jesus, it is apparent that one lesson not learned was true forgiveness for the so-called whore. Indeed, the word *whore* is now such a loaded term that it is almost impossible to see past the centuries of implications and connotations heaped upon the word. Furthermore, the allegorical implications of harlots and whores added another dimension toward women's reputation as naturally sinful beings. The themes are not hard to miss, since whoredom and fornication are often associated with Israel's sins and always depicted in the feminine (men, accordingly, cannot be Biblical whores). However, it is also apparent that God and Jesus forgave harlots, allegorical or real, as long as they would turn over a new leaf. The epitome of this tradition can be seen with the so-called repentant prostitute, Mary Magdalene. Mary Magdalene, a woman who had seven devils tossed out of her by Jesus, is seen as the repented whore, an image fabrication created and perpetuated by our society to keep marginalized women hidden, just as society hides the true image of Mary Magdalene. Yet unlike the constructed frame of the Virgin Mary, this Mary can be easily related to. For women, hope can be understood through this personality, whereas women can never reach the heights of the mythical Virgin Mother Mary. Thus it is no surprise that after the sainting of the Magdalene many women and men looked up to and adopted her as their personal saint.[91] In the Middle Ages, both mystics and repented whores sought out the Magdalene, and it is at this time that the first Magdalene convents for repented prostitutes appeared. Furthermore, it is also at this time that the either/or framing of the two Marys was accomplished, pitting the virgin against the fallen, women against women, and society against the whore.

Chapter Two

The Rhetorical Framing of the Magdalene and Women in the Early Middle Ages

Upon my bed at night I sought him whom my soul loves;
I sought him, but found him not; I called him, but he gave no answer.
"I will rise now and go about the city, in the streets and in the squares;
I will seek him whom my soul loves." I sought him, but found him not.
The sentinels found me, as they went about in the city.
"Have you seen him whom my soul loves?"

—*Song of Songs, 3:1–3*

The renowned French historian Georges Duby demonstrates in his work *The Knight, the Lady, and the Priest* that fundamental to the Medieval reforming of marriage and the relation between the sexes (between A.D. 1000 and 1200), was the notion of power and hierarchy.[1] As Davis writes in the introduction of this important work, what is at heart is the "notion of hierarchy. The husband has authority over the sexuality and property of his obedient wife; the church has authority over the laity in regard to marriage and other spiritual questions."[2] Add to the mix the rise of kings in feudal Europe, as well as the Catholic Church's nourishment of a cultural and economic monopoly,[3] power and hierarchy "justifies the obedience of the men who work, the superiority of the men who pray, and the overall — and new — power of the king above the men who fight."[4] Kenneth Burke in his definition of *man* defines humans as "the symbol-using (symbol-making, symbol-misusing) animal; inventor of the negative (or moralized by the negative); separated from his natural condition by instruments of his own making; *goaded by the spirit of hierarchy* (or moved by the sense of order); and rotten with perfection."[5] Like Duby, Burke realizes that action, in his case symbolic action, for good or bad, is motivated by our sense of order. Humanity's affinity for hierarchy is not deemed by Burke as necessarily a value-positive reality, any more than being "rotten with perfection" or the "inventor of the negative" (explained below) is a positive value call ... it just is. Humans lean toward systems of arranged order, and most prefer a predictable schedule of expectations and actualities, even when the actualities are less than ideal. People enjoy being able to know what is around the corner or under our bed, lest they are surprised by an unwelcome monster. But how hierarchal actualities can be created in relation to women's roles and place in society is what this chapter will be concerned with.

This chapter argues that the creation of hierarchal modes of social and economic action, in conjunction with the Catholic Church's nourishment of a monopoly over these hierarchal modes, formed the lived attitudes and expectations concerning women's place in the world, while rooting magdalenism. This formation can be understood through how the Catholic Church controlled and shaped the discourse regarding women's worth and roles through story, such as the stories of the saints and specifically Mary Magdalene, as well as through law concerning marriage and sexuality. In an attempt to control the discourse of salvation,[6] medieval woman, much like the Magdalene, became defined through her sex, and the understanding of *her* as a possession, rather than as an autonomous being. As such, this chapter will first present the concept of the Catholic Church as a cultural and economic monopoly that worked to control social and economic aspects of everyday life from the early to middle medieval period (approximately 1000 to 1300). As Otis observes while discussing prostitution, by the thirteenth century the basic cultural values of Western medieval society were dictated by the Catholic Church, and greatly motivated by "a particularly coherent system of sexual morality based on the restrictions of all sexual activity within the bonds of marriage and the decision that the only acceptable form of Christian marriage was perpetual monogamy."[7] Since much of this monopoly relied and depended upon the control of discourse regarding sexuality and social relationships, this chapter will also outline the concept of framing and how, through the use of identification and division, and what Burke terms the "negative," the Magdalene icon went through an inversion process where her image worked to reinforce the hierarchal reality as laid out by Duby, as well as the economic historians Davis, Davidson and Ekelund above. Next, this chapter will examine how the framing of the Magdalene mirrored the framing of women's roles during the Early to high Middle Ages. This structuring occurred through the newly formed spiritual and secular laws on marriage, the regulations of prostitution and red light districts, as well as promoting the salvation of the prostitute in Magdalene convents throughout Europe.

The Catholic Church as a Rising Monopoly

Traditionally, many considered history and the writers of history as non-interested recorders of political and social historical events. This theory is in itself a tradition that has come to us from the enlightenment on, as the empirical notion that history, science, and other modes of *logos* inquiry can be approached and understood from a *disinterested* point of view — that is, reported without bias. However, it is now realized that this *disinterest* is fiction, and so it must be remembered that history is recorded by people with social and political agendas. As Edward Said argues in his key work *Culture and Imperialism*, the past should not be nor should the political motivations of those who document the past be forgotten.[8] It is within this context that Duby tells his reader that it is impossible to understand the history of the Middle Ages or the Catholic Church without also noting that the church has a monopoly on this history because "it was the priests and monks who could read and write and therefore 'document' history."[9] This "cultural monopoly" was accompanied by a corresponding economic monopoly as well. As Davidson and Ekelund argue in "The Medieval Church and Rents from Marriage and Market Regulations," the early Catholic Church maintained a monopoly over "eternal salvation" through the control of texts, interpretation of texts (such as the Bible and other spiritual titles), as well as "temporal" products such as "social services" and "health care" through "downstream" and "upstream" levels of control.[10] This model worked through what the authors term the "monopoly of the good": "To make the good temporal in nature, characteristics and conditions for purchase downstream (sold locally by parish priests, bishops and church orders) had to be defined by the Papacy (the upstream or input part of the monopoly)."[11] As such, in order for "consumers" to obtain salvation, they had agree to and maintain certain spiritual and temporal modes of living that were first formed and supplied by the central apex of the "upstream" papacy and disseminated "downstream" by the papacy's administrative body (the Curia), and finally "sold" locally through the bishops, priests, abbots and nuns.[12] By controlling many of the temporal aspects of everyday life including marriage, sexuality and, by default, land ownership, the church was a pivotal spiritual and economic element of feudal Europe. Regardless, this monopoly would not have been possible if the church had not controlled the message and promise of salvation by linking the discourse of salvation to worldly functions of everyday life. This was accomplished in part by disseminating idealistic narratives of the saints, and so demonstrating how ultimate salvation could be achieved. For women, Mary Magdalene was central in this effort because, like the *everywoman*, the Magdalene was an imperfect character who sought spiritual acceptance through physical sacrifice.

Framing the Magdalene

In his definition of man, Burke states that he is not entirely happy with the term *inventor*, because it would be more accurate "to say that language and the negative 'invented' man."[13] In our case it is the negative that invented the Magdalene. As discussed in chapter one, part of what defines the Magdalene or the *whore* among us, is what she is not — her negative, or, in this instance, the Virgin Mary. If identification is ever on the cusp of division, then either/or frames of actuality rely on the negative for definition: "We can settle for the indubitable fact that all moral terms are of this polar sort ... that such positives and negatives imply each other."[14] Yet framing this *negative* and its corresponding *positive* image is not a given. That is, a process of negotiation to create symbolic meaning must first be had before the so-called either/or frames are taken as an everyday assumption. As Burke also points out, either/or frames limit each other and also limit meaning. A frame, then, is a word, phrase or concept that evokes a "conceptual structure used in thinking."[15] Lakoff, in his essay "Simple Framing" states that frames consist of "four morals":

1. "Every word evokes a frame";
2. "Words defined within a frame evoke the frame";
3. "Negating a frame evokes the frame"; and
4. "Evoking a frame reinforces that frame."[16]

As such, if you were told not to "think of an elephant," you would find the task impossible since the word "elephant" reinforces the conceptual image of an elephant. You cannot, for example, immediately envision a monkey, because "every time a neural circuit is activated [in the brain], it is strengthened."[17]

Lakoff's suggestion of *neural circuit activation* implies that "deep frames," defined by Lakoff and Halpin as conceptual frames rooted in our values and principles,[18] work on an unconscious *reaction* level in the same way that ideology is said to sway individuals. This becomes an important aspect of either/or polar ideologies and our relationship to them. Considering the either/or of the Magdalene versus the Virgin Mary, certain assumptions are brought to this pairing regarding their place in society and society's relationship to them. Unspoken assumptions about their meaning are practiced, while communication reinforces polar meaning on an unconscious level. To this end, the social theorist Goffman states that most of us are unaware of our organizational frames and would be "unable to describe the framework with any completeness if asked."[19] And so the Magdalene frame must be understood and deconstructed in order to understand how this frame was created, and how this construction promoted magdalenism.

The Gnostic Magdalene and the War of the Sexes

As discussed in chapter one, the early years of Christianity had a precarious relationship with the role of women. As is seen in the New Testament, women were both teachers for the church and told to be silent — to be seen but not heard in 1 Timothy. Although Pagels points out that from the year c. 200 there was "no evidence for women taking prophetic, priestly, and Episcopal roles among orthodox churches,"[20] the uncertainty about a woman's place in the hierarchal ladder would continue through the beginnings of Christianity, into the early Middle Ages where the role of women church leaders were still being discussed and negotiated. Much of the early debate can be viewed in the Gnostic Gospels, said to date anywhere around c. A.D. 120/150 to 400. However, the religious scholar and historian Elaine Pagels concurs with Professor Koester from Harvard that the pivotal Gnostic Gospel of Thomas might have been composed as early as, or even earlier than, the New Testament documents, which date to c. 60 to 110.[21]

The early Gnostic documents, especially the relationship between Mary Magdalene and Simon Peter, symbolically demonstrate the tensions involved in the negotiation process of women's roles in the church. The *Pistis Sophia* (or Faith Wisdom) and The Gospel of Mary, Pagels recounts, both present a tumultuous and hostile relationship between Mary and Simon Peter. In the *Pistis Sophia*, Peter claims the superiority of the male when he protests Mary's domination of the conversations with Jesus. Reminiscent of Timothy 1, Peter asks Jesus to silence Mary: "My Lord, we will not endure this woman, for she taketh the opportunity from us and hath let none of us speak, but she discourseth many times."[22] Jesus follows Peter's objection by telling him to listen to wisdom, *Pistis Sophia*, who is presented by Jesus in the feminine. Later in the text, Mary is frightened for herself when she is around Peter Simon. Janson,[23] Haskins,[24] Pagels,[25] and Picknett[26] all recount how Mary expresses her fear of Simon Peter to Jesus in the *Pistis Sophia*, saying Peter threatens her and hates her sex. The Gnostic Gospel of Thomas also demonstrates Peter's distain for Mary, since he demands that she should be sent away because women are not worthy of life. Jesus replies by making her a male, so that she may be worthy.[27] However, it can be posited that this creation of Mary as a male was for Peter Simon's sake, not for Jesus, whom, it has been shown, did not hold hostility toward women because of their sex throughout the New Testament, especially for those who wished to learn such as Mary of Bethany did, while sitting at Jesus' feet.[28]

These stories regarding Mary Magdalene and Simon Peter, as well as the contradictory notions regarding women's place in the New Testament, leaves us with an interesting problem: what active or passive role should women take in the new church and in the wider "Christian" society? This question becomes more important when it is recalled that although inspired by Judaism, Christianity rose partly in reaction to, and as a backlash against, traditional Judaism. Considering this relationship, it is not surprising that there is tension between Simon Peter and Mary Magdalene. If Jesus welcomed women learners into his fold as equals to male students, this would have been contrary to the Jewish understanding of a *woman's place*. Pagels reminds us that the "women of the Jewish communities ... were excluded from actively participating in public worship, in education, and in social and political life outside the family."[29] Simon Peter and the other of Jesus' apostles were from traditional Jewish families with traditional Jewish notions about women's place in society.[30] Thus, Simon Peter's attitude toward Mary Magdalene should not be a surprise, but Jesus' attitude toward women in general is a revelation. Further, there is another important element about this social reality in connection to building the Catholic Church: what repercussions would there be if Mary Magdalene, and not Simon Peter, were named the official observer of the risen Christ? As Picknett rightfully observers:

> If Jesus chose to show himself to Mary, *not Peter*, then this threatens a somewhat fundamental change. Although there is much theological pontificating on this subject, the essence is very simple: if there is a shred of doubt about the first person to see the risen Christ then the whole of the authority of the Catholic Church is dangerously in question.[31]

In the Gnostic Gospel of Mary, more of the Coptic texts found at Nag Hammadi in Upper Egypt, 1945–1946, Mary Magdalene is portrayed prominently as the first official observer of the risen Christ. Janson suggests that this Gospel is a direct affront to the assumption that it was Simon Peter, and not the Magdalene, who was first in the presence of the risen Christ: "As much as this was a commendation of the Magdalen's unwavering faith, it was also an implicit rebuke to Peter, who had not only denied Christ three times in the course of one evening, but had gone so far as to dismiss the Magdalen's announcement of the resurrection as 'idle tales.'"[32] Why is the relationship between Mary Magdalene and Simon Peter relevant, and does it matter, in the end, who was the first to see Christ rise from the dead? To answer the second question first, yes it matters. When the newly formed Christian Church proclaimed that it was Simon Peter and not the Magdalene who first saw Christ rise from the dead, they were framing and creating the hierarchal rules for how the Christian Church was to function in regard to gendering roles: men would lead and women would be silent followers. In a sense, the early church fathers were rhetorically creating the conditions of spiritual, sexual, and gender engagement within the church — the spiritual exigence of gender.

To answer the first question, Simon Peter then historically stands and speaks for the Catholic Church.

In "The Rhetorical Situation," Lloyd F. Bitzer postulated that "rhetoric is situational"[33] and that "the presence of rhetorical discourse obviously indicates the presence of a rhetorical situation."[34] A situational exigency, such as the event of Jesus rising from the dead, will demand and form rhetoric/discourse to address the particular need. The way a certain exigency is addressed and described, in this formulation, is determined by the event itself. However, in response to Bitzer's understanding of the rhetorical situation, rhetorical scholar Richard Vatz rightfully points out that "no situation can have a nature independent of the perception of its interpreter or independent of the rhetoric with which he chooses to characterize it."[35] Indeed, an exigency might call us to address it, but who "we" are, our values, goals, and aims all determine how a certain situation will be addressed. People actively work to frame the exigency in such a way as to fit that situation into their lives and worldview — people create a *deliberative rhetoric* of social values. As Vatz points out, people "translate" events by filtering them through a personal, value-laden, point of view.[36] Thus how a situation is presented is a deliberate choice, what information to include and what to leave out, who will be featured and who will not. The moments of an event are edited to match people's needs, which is exactly why it was vital to the early Christian Church fathers to assign Simon Peter and not Mary Magdalene as the first witness to the resurrection. Simply put, the creation and assignment of gender roles in society and in the Catholic Church rhetorically created a spiritual exigence of gender. Rhetoric, after all, is a form of creation. As Thomas Goodnight argued in his defining essay "The Personal, Technical, and Public spheres of Argument," not only does rhetoric create, but it is also an art of social definition: "My guiding assumptions are that Rhetoric is an art, a human enterprise engaging individual choice and common activity, and that deliberative rhetoric is a form of argumentation through which citizens test and create social knowledge in order to uncover, assess, and resolve shared problems."[37] In the end it was deliberative rhetoric, along with the development of social norms and patterns that effectively formed what the early church fathers considered the correct spiritual and social exigence of gender hierarchy.

Hegemonic Gender Creation

Like many other notions, gender is a social construction that should not be confused with sex. The rhetorical and social construction of gender is not understood through assigned sex, but through the relations between the sexes.[38] Factors used to regulate gender include accepted social roles, law, and economics, marriage, and gender lore, division between the public and the private spheres of life and living and, as Connell points out, the "connections between institutions": "Gender is institutionalized to the extent that the network of links to the reproduction system is formed by cyclical practices. It is stabilized to the extent that the groups constituted in the network have interests in the conditions for cyclical rather than divergent practice."[39] Simply, people form and determine gender relations not only out of their ideas and need for power, but also out of a need for a normative baseline of social interaction and expectation. Again, humans enjoy order and habit. Divergent practices can result in chaos and confusion — for this reason culture and society often rely on a hegemic agreement to maintain certain normative realities in our *networks* of human relations. Hegemony is defined here through an Antonio Gramsci lens of how the dominant power of a specific group is maintained through both force and consent — Gramsci writes in *The Prison Notebooks*, if it is perceived that there is something to be gaining from the current power arrangement/agreement, people consent to the so-called normative network — if people do not feel like they are getting something out of the arrangement, then the network will create consent *through* force. Because the concept of hegemony is an essential theme throughout this work, it is helpful to quote Gramsci's understanding of the concept:

  1. The "spontaneous" consent given by the great masses of the population to the general direction imposed on social life by the dominant fundamental group; this consent is "historically" caused by the prestige (and consequent confidence) which the dominant group enjoys because of its position and function in the world of production.

  2. The apparatus of state coercive power which "legally" enforces discipline on those groups who do not "consent" either actively or passively.[40]

It is important to note that Gramsci, writing in a Mussolini prison in the late 1920s, saw the abovementioned control/forced apparatus (which could be anything from discourse/rhetoric, assigned division of labor, to social and legal rights, and so on), as "constructed for the whole of society in anticipation of moments of crisis of command and direction when spontaneous consent has failed."[41] Hegemony, then, is "primarily a *strategy* for the gaining of the active consent of the masses through their self-organization."[42] Hegemony works to create a collective social and political will, by forming a historic bloc (many civil societies united together — such as social, religious and legal, as well as ruling, institutions) that unites a population under what becomes embedded ideology — it works partly through what Kenneth Burke termed "identification." Hegemony, however, is a delicate balance between state and civil society; a machine dependant upon the smallest parts to keep the whole working. If one nut, one bolt cracks, the machine becomes threatened, and counterhistoric blocs, or what Connell calls the "divergent," have an opportunity to rise and challenge the *normative* structure. This challenge, as Gramsci suggests, has a short window to function in because the "dominate" social class has more recourses available for quick mobilization of counter or damage control action. However, although it is comforting to understand the *dominate social class* as a set, central and predetermined group of puppeteers, power and hegemony are better understood as a machine that must be constantly maintained by the majority of consenters against breakage. This maintenance is often formed through discourse and narratives regarding society and our roles in society. The French historian and philosopher Michel Foucault will later argue, an important apparatus of power creation and control is knowledge, and knowledge is created through discourse.[43] Knowledge of Christian women, and how she as a gender should act her role in society, was partially created through the deliberative construction of the Magdalene narrative, refined in hagiographic texts. Although, as historian Ruth Mazo Karras points out, hagiographical texts cannot be taken as "reflections on actual events in the world,"[44] hagiographical texts did create social meaning for everyday people. As such, if the early Magdalene narrative portrayed a strong woman who helped finance Jesus' work and as the person who was the first witness to the resurrection, the new narrative had to reconstruct the Magdalene image—focusing on her early life as a sinner, and her later life (after the departure of Jesus) as one of repentance, sorrow, and silence.

Magdalene as the Beata Peccatrix—Blessed Sinner

Throughout the Middle Ages, the lives of saints served as guideposts to the "good" life. While examining the role of the *Vita apostolica* (stories regarding the apostolic life), Ernest McDonnell writes: "Socially, intense devotion to the apostolic life coincided with the communes and the louder articulation of townsmen on matters of faith and politics."[45] Even for the lay man or woman, the *Vita apostolica* and other such publications that told the life stories of apostles and saints provided a guide-map to social life, proper roles, and organization.[46] Undeniably, like the popular stars of today, the lives of the apostles and saints were of central importance and interest at this time. Medieval times breathed new life into the saints. Taking the place of the polytheistic house gods of the past, you could select from a multitude of saints for your specific needs: St. Jude if you found yourself in desperate circumstances, and St. Christopher, like the Greek Hermes, could protect you in your travels and against storms, or the plague.[47] There are literally hundreds of saints to choose from, each one of them offering protection and help in many areas. Their help could be obtained by prayer, whereas they would then convey your worries directly to God or Jesus for you. To be better assured that your concerns were being heard, you could take a pilgrimage to a saint's shrine. Pilgrimages were not only a popular pastime for the medieval man and woman; they were a form of required penance. Once in your lifetime, it was expected that the good Christian would take a pilgrimage, abandoning all wealth (at least for a short period of time), comforts of home, and walk the road that Jesus' disciples walked all those many years ago. These required pilgrimages created quite a booming business for those who represented and spoke for the saints. In fact, there was a black market for saintly relics. You could buy St. Jude's pinky finger, for example, and wear it around your neck for protection: "To the faithful, the dried and somewhat gruesome remains or dust so repugnant to pagans and skeptics were the saints themselves, to be revered, touched, passionately kissed."[48] The bones of saints (the cult of relics) were the most popular and, as you might imagine, many graves of paupers were raided for these so-called holy relics.[49] The church, of course, was also concerned about the remains of saints. As Haskin's recounts, the possession of a deemed "authentic" saint's bones brought wealth, power and stature to the local church that housed the saint and the local town in which the church resided: "Status because of the veneration of the relics themselves, and power because of their ability to attract the faithful in large numbers, and thus quite literally to transform the economy of the church or monastery and of the surrounding area."[50] The underlining hope was not to sell away pinky bones and ribs (although that certainly occurred) but to locate, sanctify, and honor the final resting places of important saints and by doing so, obtain the blessing of God's chosen ones. Indeed, Bynum and Gerson point out the vital importance of relics and how they took on an institutional importance, since by the "Second Council of Nicaea in 787, relics were required for the consecration of altars; and before the development, in the late twelfth and early thirteenth centuries, of procedures for canonization controlled by the papacy, it was the translation of the holy person's remains into the altar, or into a reliquary that rested on the altar, that often constituted the making of a saint."[51] In any case, to prove that a saint's remains were *authentic* took a great deal of footwork, miracles, and supportive *documentation*. Somehow a saint's life must be documented from beginning to end — and the narrative must match with the discovery of the relics, as well as offering a deliberative rhetoric framing events. With saints such as Mary Magdalene, where the Bible leaves off in the middle of her life story, it was important to find evidence that demonstrated what happened to the rest of her life, where she went and where she died. Such evidence was found in myths and legends, and was written down by holy men in *Vitae* (documentation detailing someone's life events and accomplishments).

In the eleventh century, Mary Magdalene's remains were said to be in Burgundy, lying in a church at Vézelay where the first cult of the Magdalene was established en masse. Originally dedicated to the Virgin Mary, a papal decree of April 27, 1050, reassigned this abbey's patron saint, making Mary Magdalene the Saint for the Season. The Vézelay abbey was located on a main pilgrimage route "that brought the faithful from Germany and the East down to the shrine of Santiago de Compostela."[52] Possibly wishing to capitalize on the pilgrim route, in 1058 the church at Vézelay started to claim that they had the relics of Mary Magdalene. As Jansen writes, this *inventio* was pivotal for Vézelay because it helped raise the status of the church: "The presence of the Magdalen's relics helped the sanctuary at Vézelay become so important that Bernard of Clairvaux preached the second crusade there in 1146, and pious Louis IX made four visits, even attending the *elevation* of her relics in 1267, at which time he received some of them for his personal collection."[53] At this point the subject seemed closed as to the location of the Magdalene's final resting spot. Nevertheless, on the ninth of December 1279, Mary Magdalene's remains were also determined to lie in the crypt of the Church of Saint-Maximin near Aix-en-Provence. To make matters more difficult, "discoveries" of the Magdalene's relics, in Latin *inventio*, had gone into overdrive, since "by the end of the thirteenth century Mary Magdalen had, it seemed, left behind at least five corpses, in addition to many whole arms and smaller pieces which could not be accounted for."[54] At any rate on December 9, 1279, Charles, "the crown prince of the house of Anjou, whose petty kingdom covered parts of France and Italy, ordered an excavation of the church crypt at Saint-Maximin in Provence. One chronicler said that the prince dug with his own hands, working so fiercely that sweat streamed off him."[55] The crypt had been opened, and the remains were authenticated by several wondrous miracles including a sweet smell wafting from the tomb.[56] Next, there was a place on the Magdalene's forehead where the flesh had not rotted off. As Chilton recounts, this spot of skin was where the "risen Christ" was said to have touched Mary to prevent her from embracing him.[57] Of much importance was the appearance of a "tender shoot" growing from where the Magdalene's tongue once was. Interpreted by Philippe Cabassole, chancellor of the Kingdom of Naples, in 1355, this shoot "signified that as apostolorum apostola, apostle of the apostles, Mary Magdalen had announced to the other apostles that Christ had risen from the dead and that subsequently she had preached to the pagans."[58] Of course there was no real way to truly judge the Magdalene's remains authentic. There was no DNA testing, no blood test or even science to prove such a thing. Chilton theorizes that these Magdalene "discoveries" were truly "inventions" used to help strengthen spiritual and, importantly, political standing: "Charles would have done no better if he had dug in Vézelay, or in Magdala, for that matter.... Her true relics are not physical, and never have been. Her bones are mixed in with those of thousands of other victims who were hacked to death in Magdala by the Romans in 67C.E."[59] However, what royalty wants royalty gets, and the remains were eventually pronounced authentic by church authorities. Besides, everyone knew from popular legend that Mary Magdalene had come to Gaul to preach to the pagans after Jesus had risen from the dead. Yet as mentioned above, what was essential not only for the relic's authentication, but for the creation of *traditional* hierarchal and social orders, was the narrative of the saints that offered a blueprint for living *well*—in this case, Mary Magdalene's life and death story. In order to sort out the confused mess as to where the Magdalene's relics laid,[60] and her life after Christ's ascent to heaven, church officials looked to three *Vitae*[61] to provide answers: *Vita eremitica* (also known as the *Vita eremitica beatae Mariae Magdalen*), *Vita apostolica* and the *Vita apostolico-eremitica* (a narrative that combines the two earlier *Vitae*). As historians Haskins and Joëlle Rollo-Koster also mention, many of the *Vita* documents originated from the Abbey of Vézelay toward the middle of the eleventh century in order to substantiate the order's claims of holding the true Magdalene relics.[62] These *Vitae* not only offered the church answers, but also supplied the believer with information on what happened to the Magdalene after the New Testament story ends. Like any good novel or story where the reader is captivated by one of the characters, the questions that arise are: What is next? What happened to the Magdalene after Christ ascended to heaven? Where does her story end? Does it end? And finally, how can someone emulate the Magdalene? What makes for a blessed and God sanctified life? Being the grand storytellers that humans are, they find a way to answer such questions.

The first *Vita* on Mary Magdalene, *Vita eremitica beatae Mariae Magdalen* was a hagiographic or what is known as an idealized biography of a saint. Thought initially in the Middle Ages to be written by the Jewish historian Flavius Josephus (c. 37–c. 100),[63] Jansen and Haskins both suggest that the text was fashioned from sometime in the early ninth century, possibly from a Cassianite monk living in a Southern Italian provenance.[64] Most likely this *Vita* was brought west by Greek monks fleeing Byzantium,[65] and eventually found popularity throughout Europe, and was known in England somewhere around the middle of the ninth century.[66] In this life account of the Magdalene it is explained that after Jesus rose from the dead and ascended to heaven, Mary Magdalene sought solitude in a desert near Marseilles for 30 years. She lived as a hermit in a dirty cave, without clothing, and survived on prayer—being brought up to heaven by the angels every night and given spiritual substance to live on. Far from the bold learner and teacher that is portrayed in the New Testament and the Gnostic Gospels, this Magdalene is a sorrowful woman whose later life was spent silently repenting her past sins of prostitution away from the eyes of the world. The Magdalene was no longer the *Apostle to the Apostles*, but the *Beata Peccatrix*, with a focus on the image of sinner who knows only the sorrow of past sins. The *Vita* tells us that when it was time for her to leave this world, she went to "a priest" (unnamed in this early version, and later designated as St. Maximinus), asks for clothing to cover her shame (her naked, one assumes, suntanned body), confesses her sins and then dies. This story tells only of her continued shame and efforts at repentance—a theme that will be later shared by the Magdalene women and nuns who will run the so-called *reformatories* for wayward women. Further, it is important to note the similarities between this *Vita* and the *Vita patrum*, which was a collection of legends that told the stories of the saints residing in the Eastern desert. One main Eastern saint is Saint Mary of Egypt,[67] another popular repented prostitute, who was assimilated with Mary Magdalene in the *Vita eremitica beatae Mariae Magdalen*.[68]

Legends surrounding saints who sought enlightenment in the desert are plentiful. Jesus even fought his own demons for 40 days in the desert. Traditionally, the desert is the perfect symbolic place for the inner contemplation of sin, because the stillness and solitude almost forces you to look inward. Further, when one considers miracles, the desert is a perfect example of one, thinking on all the life abundant in these often portrayed death traps. If Mary Magdalene survived in the desert for 40 years (mirroring Jesus' own struggles with sin), this in itself is a miracle. Regardless, it is enough for our current purposes to account for the similarities between Mary Magdalene and Mary of Egypt: both stories told of the repentance of a reformed prostitute who sought and found God, both were said to have lived in the desert without food or clothing, and both grow long golden hair to hide their nakedness.[69] Haskins links this particular part of the story to a fifth-century legend of St. Agnes, the Roman virgin bride of Christ who, "on refusing a suitor, was denounced to the local perfect as Christian. Nothing could induce the young girl to desist from her intention to preserve her chastity as a bride of Christ. When she was thrown into a brothel, her hair grew miraculously to cover her shame."[70] Regarding the Magdalene story, Haskins explains how these narratives were synthesized, and so the *Vita eremitica* was left ambiguous regarding where this desert cave was that the Magdalene retired to, who the "priest" was that she confessed to toward the end of her life, and just how her bones ended up so far from Palestine, where she lived in the first place. As such, a revision was presented and a late twelfth-century manuscript located her large desert cave "east of Marseille, not far from Montrieux."[71] Indeed, Misrahi reminds us that by the middle of the thirteenth century, the cave became a pilgrimage tourist stop and "received visits from Fra Salimbene in 1248 and from Saint Louis in 1254."[72] As Jansen explains, this revised "pious fiction" explains how the Magdalene's relics were in Burgundy. In this revision, a monk was sent to Provence to enact the "holy theft" (*Furtum Sacrum*) of the Magdalene's bones to save them from war and destruction.[73] The Magdalene's relics had somehow been delivered from Palestine and reburied in the Provence around 882 and 884, where they were again at risk of being destroyed.[74] Several different *Vita* revisions recount the final holy theft of the relics. The first account tells how the monk Aléaume has enacted the theft, but this account was also vague, lacking in detail. Filling in some important story points, the second revision explained that the Bishop of Autun, Adalgar, during King Carloman's reign,[75] had visited Vézelay accompanied by his knight Adalelme. The bishop tells Vézelay's abbot Odo where the tomb of the Magdalene was: "Adelelme was then sent off with an escort to Arles-the entire areas having been overtaken by the Saracens-to find the church in which the saint was buried, and then took the bodies (that of St. Maximinus was also included for good measure), and returned to Vézelay."[76] This revision is important because it tells both the name of the priest that the Magdalene confesses to before her death, St. Maximinus, and how and why the relics were brought to Vézelay. The final revision of the *Vita eremitica* offers us a change in players. Instead of the knight Adalelme, the Monk Balilon (also spelled Badilus) was sent to Provence in 749 to "rescue Mary Magdalen's imperiled relics from Saracen invades."[77] Sent by Vézelay's founder, Count Girart de Roussillon, Balilon is shown to the designated "rumored" last resting place of the Magdalen by an old man.[78] The church, and the surrounding area, is found in ruins, but by a divine miracle Balilon finds the saint's body unharmed and intact: "He was also granted a vision of the saint who informed him not to fear since his mission had been ordained by God. The next day, in classic *Furtum Sacrum*, as this sort of holy theft has been described, Badilus spirited Mary Magdalen's bones off to Burgundy."[79]

Unlike the *Vita eremitica beatae Mariae Magdalen*, the *Vita apostolic* offers the reader an entirely different Mary Magdalene, one more like the vibrant teacher described in the Gnostic Gospels, and it explains how the Magdalene came to rest outside of Palestine. This narrative takes up right after Jesus rises from the grave. After Christ's ascension, many his followers continue to be prosecuted by the Romans and other hostiles. In an effort to escape this early Christian persecution, 14 years after the death of Christ,[80] Mary Magdalene, along with several of Christ's disciples, takes to the sea and, after an arduous journey, lands in Marseilles. Depending on the version being read, the Magdalene is said to have taken this journey with Lazarus and Martha, her brother and sister (this *Vita* assumes that Mary Magdalene is the same person as Mary of Bethany, sister to Lazarus and Martha). Rollo-Koster also mentions a score of other people including St. Maximin, the apostle mothers, Mary Jacobe and Mary Salome, Martha's handmaid, Marcelle, and Mary's handmaid, Sarah.[81] Once the refugees land in Marseilles, they get to the business of evangelizing the pagan Gauls. Mary Magdalene is said to have personally converted the pagan prince of Marseilles,[82] which is why Aix-en-Provence easily converted to Christianity.[83] The *Vita apostolic* explains how the priest Maximinus became the first Bishop of Aix. In the revised editions of the *Vita eremitica*, when the Magdalene knew it was her time to die, she approached the Priest Maximinus, told him of her life and confessed her sins before dying. Maximinus buried her soon after. The *Vita apostolic* adds to this ending by stating that before her death, as her last apostolic act the Magdalene ordains Maximinus the first Bishop of Aix. When Maximinus dies, he is buried next to Mary Magdalene: "A special altar at the Church of St. Sauveur at Aix was dedicated to Maximinus and Mary Magdalen as the first founders of the city, which also claimed the honor of having been evangelized in the first century."[84] There are several important elements in this *Vita*. Although this *Vita* promotes the Mendicant order's emphasis on the good life being a balance between one's engagement with the world and the inner spiritual/contemplative life,[85] this narrative does not promote the hegemonic hierarchal order of early Christian society, because a woman, Mary Magdalene, is deemed the leader and preacher. Further, this woman leader had been involved with a sexual past, a fact that also makes her suspect. Yet both *Vitae* were popular, and by the twelfth century, the *Vita apostolic* was not only considered the "official" bibliography on the Magdalene's life, but it also became a standard for preaching material (*material praedicibilis*).[86] Nonetheless, a question remains: how can a society that frowns upon women teachers or women holding powerful positions in spiritual and life matters accept a female, evangelizing apostle as a role model? This question is not a coincidental one in relation to the Magdalene and her status.[87] Indeed, it can be theorized that the final *Vita*, the *Vita apostolico-eremitica*, which combines and splices together the *eremitica* with that of the *apostolic*, was written in order to downplay the Magdalene's role as a teacher, while focusing on her efforts and silent repentance. This new hybrid *Vita* puts forth the social image inversion needed to promote magdalenism in society.

Vita apostolico-eremitica tells the reader that after landing in Marseilles and helping to evangelize the pagan Gauls, Mary Magdalene then, while in Aix-en-Provence, converted the city to Christianity. With her final spiritual and humanitarian task completed, she retires to her cave in the desert for 30 years of repentance before she dies: "One of the commonest features of these late versions is the story of the penitential life. It is related that the Magdalen was so overwhelmed by the enormity of her past sinful life that she resolved never more to look upon the face of a man and withdrew to a cavern at La Sainte-Baume, which is still venerated as the site of her long penance."[88] By focusing on the Magdalene's 30 years of solitude, this spliced *Vita*, along with the later more popular "The Golden Legend," attributed to Jacobus de Voragine, framed the Magdalene's life as the repentant prostitute who gloried in God but repented in silent despair: "Saints who had been sinners embodied the message that confession, contrition, and penance could wipe away the worst of sins, and saints who had been prostitutes embodied it most dramatically."[89]

Besides explaining where Mary Magdalene's remains were and how they got there, these three *Vitae,* along with Burgundy's claim to her relics, helped to elevate the Magdalene from a notable character in the New Testament, to the rock-n-roll star of the Middle Ages. Yes she was a prostitute in her former life. Yes she was a sinner. But she was also the *Blessed Sinner* and the *Apostle to the Apostles*— more popular in some places than the Blessed Virgin Mary. She was *the example* for all sinners, an example of true forgiveness and repentance ... someone to emulate. And emulate her the Middle Ages did, since Mary Magdalene becomes not only the patron saint for repented prostitutes, but for lepers and mystics alike.[90]

But what is interesting to note is that like the evolving stories concerning the Magdalene, which first focused on her sins, then on her strength as a preacher and organizer, and finally back to an even stronger emphasis of her sin and repentance, medieval society also viewed the prostitute within this type of swing: first shunning her, then organizing her profession and finally once again shunning, but also outlawing her. The end of this chapter will focus on how medieval society, economics, and politics all worked to define the prostitute in light of the Magdalene. Although prostitution is often characterized as a social and public stigma, it must be remembered that it is also a business, and therefore affected by the economic, political, and social conditions of everyday life.

As discussed earlier in this chapter, part of how the Magdalene was viewed, how women in general were viewed, as well as other segments in society depended upon an active attempt at framing values and a hegemonic agreement as to which gender and social classes receive power in society. So far, at framing and hegemony in direct relation to the Magdalene's story has been explored. This chapter will end this examination by noting how converging factors of medieval economics, along with an evolving understanding of marriage, and the role that prostitution played, worked to define the prostitute and magdalenism in the early to middle period of the medieval times (approximately A.D. 1000 to 1299).

Setting the Scene: Medieval Economics from 1000 to the 1300s

By the tenth century, Europe was entrenched within what is termed *Feudalism*. Characterized by the historical social scientist Immanuel Wallerstein, although Europe during this time can be understood as a Christian civilization, it was neither a world-empire nor a world-economy: "Most of Europe was feudal, that is, consisted of relatively small, relatively self-sufficient economic modules based on a form of exploration which involved the relatively direct appropriation of small agricultural surplus produced within a manorial economy by a small class of nobility."[91] Consequently, although there did not exist a comprehensive economic system that linked Europe to the rest of the world, it is important to note that an overall social identity of "Christianity" provided a key element of social, political, and economic identity among many in Europe. This identity was hegemonically cultivated through force, such as was see with the crusades from the eleventh through thirteenth centuries, as well as being social and political reproduced through custom, law, rhetoric (discourse), and other socialization practices such as marriage (discussed below). Also during this time, Europe experienced expansion geographically, commercially, and economically.[92] As Otis states, what is now called the twelfth century renaissance was "characterized by a great demographic surge, the expansion and technological improvement of agriculture, the growth of industry and commerce, the religious and intellectual ferment associated with a renewed papacy, and the spread of schools and universities."[93] This expansion and growth also encouraged the further development of local trade (everyday goods and services) and a limited amount of long-distance trade (exotic or precious goods). Wallerstein further explains, this type of economic feudalism mostly benefited the feudal landlords, who had noble status and control of the "juridical machinery":

> A series of tiny economic nodules whose population and productivity were slowly increasing, and in which the legal mechanisms ensured that the bulk of the surplus went to the landlords who had noble status and control of the juridical machinery. Since much of this surplus was in kind, it was of little benefit unless it could be sold. Towns grew up supporting artisans who brought the surplus and exchanged it for their products.[94]

Ultimately, economic and social/political growth continued until the "crisis" of the fourteenth century, when the Hundred Year War turned feudal Europe into a war economy, which redefined everything from trade to social relations — and where reoccurrences of the plague worked to diminish the population, further changing social relations and, as will be demonstrated, creating a more conservative societal view toward sexual relations. At present however, it is important to note how economic expansion and church consolidation of power went hand-in-hand with the definition of marriage and how this definition helped give rise to prostitution. Thus, although the Catholic Church in the medieval period did not hold an economic monopoly, Davidson and Ekelund make a compelling argument that the church, through their efforts at defining and controlling marriage, was able to limit the growth of economic dynasties but, as a byproduct, increased both prostitution and the resulting business of saving the souls of former prostitutes. Although it is this byproduct that is of interest here, it is helpful to develop a cursory understanding of how marriage became defined as a spiritual and economical state.

Defining Marriage

Duby reminds us that the Catholic Church during the Middle Ages held a cultural monopoly not only because the monks and priests of this time period were responsible for keeping and documenting history,[95] but also because they helped shape public law under the guise of "public interest." Davidson and Ekelund suggest that the idea of "public interest" goes hand-in-hand with a cultural "monopoly," because public interest was understood through salvation — a product that *only* the Catholic Church could offer.[96] Although there are many factors that go into the determination of salvation, both marriage and, by default, sex were key elements because of the relationship between original sin and sexual relations. However, marriage had not always been closely monitored by the Catholic Church. As Duby points out, the early Middle Ages were about defining the church's role in society and the power struggle that ensued with the spiritual power of the church working to "dominate the temporal."[97] Fundamental to this struggle was the understanding of marriage and the rules for marriage, which were not set in stone. For example, marriage and sexual partnership in the early Middle Ages took on many forms. Besides the traditional marriage pack, there were pre-arranged abductions, concubines, unions between not-so-distant relatives, and divorce was common. Davidson and Ekelund identify three different types of marriages that generally existed from the early middle to late medieval period[98]: First there were secular marriages or marriage contracts between individuals who were not followers of the church (such as Jews, Muslims or other "pagans"). These marriages were not officially recorded by the church and could be dissolved without the need for official court rulings. Next, there were clandestine marriages, or unions between church followers, but arranged through private means, circumventing aid or help from the church.[99] Unlike secular marriages, the church did not view these marriages as dissolvable and at least until the Fourth Lateran Council of 1215, recognized such unions as legitimate. Regardless, the church in its efforts to control the conditions of marriage discouraged these unions and later made clandestine unions illegal. The final union was that of church-approved marriages. These marriages were blessed by a priest, and the unions adhered to many rules and regulations: "Parental, community, and Church consent represented by the priest's blessing were required as well, making it more difficult to hide a consanguineous marriage or the existence of a pre-existing clandestine marriage."[100]

Regardless of the eventual understanding of marriage as a church-sanctioned institution, marriage as a spiritual and social institution evolved slowly over time "by a meandering process feeling its way along for centuries during which layer upon layer of contradictory texts were piled up. But the theory did rest on one foundation, on God's message, on just a few words [in the book of Genesis] which none of the eleventh-century bishops ever forgot."[101] These few words could be found in the first few pages of the Bible: (1) Man should not be alone; (2) the sexes were created unequally because woman was taken from man's rib; (3) two bodies will merge into one as the man will "cleave upon his wife"; and (4) marriage did not do away with the unequal status between the sexes because it is woman's fault that humans fell from grace.[102] However, it was the Book of Genesis and the story of Adam and Eve that originally created great problems for the early fathers of the church and their views on marriage. Because marriage legally regulated sex, and because sex was related to original sin, the early fathers saw marriage as an organized institution for promoting sin. As such, the church first started to promote the best marriage as one of sexless partnership.[103] Saint Jerome even posited that Adam and Eve had remained virgins in paradise and only united sexually after the fall — making marriage and sex a sinful state. To be sure, as Duby argues, for the early fathers, sex even within the confines of legal matrimony, necessarily made the husband into a "fornicator" and "adulterer" (if he loved his wife too much), and the wife into a prostitute[104]— making marriage a sin.[105] The fear of sex and its relation to original sin was so extreme that the church laid down a set of rules regulating sex within marriage. Accordingly, married couples were not allowed to have sex:

- During the day.
- Nights before Sunday and holy days.
- Nights before Wednesday and Friday (penance).
- The three 40-day periods of fasting before Easter, before Holy Cross Day in September, and before Christmas.
- When a woman was menstruating.
- During the three months preceding or 40 days following childbirth.
- For 3 days after marriage (for young couples).

"The ideal couple, of course, was a pair who remained totally chaste by common consent."[106] Davidson and Ekelund also point out that the "liturgical cycle mandated abstinence throughout the year as well as during penance, with fines ranging as high as 40d."[107] It might be well imagined, the church's early stance on marriage and sex within marriage was not necessarily fashionable with the wider population and saw little support. As such, the church in its efforts to better control everyday life redefined its views on marriage and by the eleventh century had reframed marriage as a means to salvation: "The bishops realized they could not lead the laity to virtue by inculcating loathing of the married state. The way to achieve their object was rather to extol marriage and put it forward as a possible framework for a good life. And so to strengthen the foundations of secular society they set about improving the moral standing of marriage."[108] In this way, the church was able to redefine marriage as a religious rather than secular affair.[109] Further, the church's argument for marriage as a spiritual rather than a secular institution was strengthened in 829 when the leaders of the Frankish Church linked marriage to salvation by insisting that marriage must agree to certain rules set by the Catholic Church, including rules regulating exogamy, and so limiting marriage between family members to the seventh degree of kinship.[110] The Medievalist Ault tells us, by the high Middle Ages, marriage was deemed a sacrament. Not only was a religious ceremony mandatory, but also divorce was no longer allowed except when the church court deemed a marriage invalid.[111] If people did not agree to the church's terms in marriage as in other modes of living, they lost out on the opportunity for salvation (an ultimate goal in these times), and so the church could continue to garnish and maintain a cultural and political monopoly: "The Church's primary good, eternal salvation, became elusive for members of society who did not adhere to the evolving requirements. As a result, the Church was able to maintain demand for its services and to generate quasi-monopoly profits through its own innovations and by enhancing its market position."[112] One way in which the church sought monopoly over marriage was in how they levied punishments, conditions of salvation, if their rules were not followed. Davidson and Ekelund describe a variety of taxes, as well as the refusal to offer communion and or formal excommunication.[113] In this way an eventual hegemonic relationship between society, the church, and the institution of marriage was promoted by the initial use of force in order to encourage new *habits* among the *Christian* population. Regardless, within this formula, so-called *legitimate* marriage became based on monogamy, exogamy and "the repression of pleasure."[114]

The evolution and role of marriage is important to this project for several reasons. First, marriage determines social and political structures, creates and helps define social norms (marriage) in contrast to deviant practices (prostitution), officiates the act of procreation, and thereby "it distinguishes lawful unions from others and gives their progeny the status of heirs — i.e., it gives the offspring ancestors, a name, and rights."[115] As such, marriage determines property rights and inheritance rights, and so regulates wealth.[116] Most of this regulation of wealth was conducted through the church's restrictions against marriage between blood relations, since marriage between certain degrees of relations was forbidden.[117] This church law not only discouraged the growth of family dynasties, but it also worked to decrease the number of legitimate heirs available; and thereby, "increasing the likelihood of inheritance for [the church] itself"[118] in the form of bequests offered to the church in hopes of obtaining salvation in the afterlife. Although not a direct aim of the Catholic Church in relation to marriage laws, the church's legal ability to confiscate lands from illegitimate heirs also aided in the church's interest of breaking up dynastic power that challenged its cultural and social monopoly.[119] For example, Pope Gregory the Great was able to challenge dynastic power through the questioning of clandestine marriages and the legitimacy of the offspring from these marriages:

> A final example of Pope Gregory's enforcement involves the case of a woman in Florence who had married within the regulated degree of kin. Her husband had died and she stood to gain financially through retrieval of her dowry and the marriage gifts (Smith, 1972, p.83). The Bishop of Florence was ordered by the pope to determine the degree of kinship and if it existed, to "quash all legal instruments relating to the dower and gifts so that the errant woman might not derive material profit from her sin."[120]

But there was an additional byproduct of the church's rules regarding endogamy, and that was a rise in prostitution. First, by limiting the eligible marriage pool, outlawing divorce, and making concubinage illegal[121] (an official act of the Fifth Lateran Council in 1514), the church created and indeed encouraged a wider market for prostitution because a low-cost escape from a bad marriage was not available: "A dissoluble marriage would have had a relatively low opportunity cost for the partners to the marriage since an escape mechanism would have been in place. Concubinage and prostitution would not have been important medieval institutions if a low-cost escape was possible."[122] So it is in the end that the church, through its efforts to manage the sin of sex, ended up creating a market for unsanctioned sex, and the prostitute.

Defining the Prostitute

As in almost every other time in our history, prostitution ran rampant during the Middle Ages. In many ways prostitution is difficult to define because an understanding of what the term means has evolved over time. Regarding prostitution and the medieval canon texts, historian and legal expert James A. Brundage points out that although the term can be understood through both a moralist and jurist[123] point of view, the canon law of the Middle Ages was an offshoot of moral theology and so "never wholly escaped its moralistic heritage."[124] So it is that even the terms used to understand prostitution has this highbred influence. The word "prostitute" is taken from the Latin *prostitutus*, meaning "up front" or "to expose," referring to the fact that prostitutes were expected to appear in public with their faces uncovered, distinguishing them from honorable women who covered their faces. Otis, in her defining work on prostitution as a medieval urban institution in Languedoc, observes that the terms and rhetoric associated with prostitution changed throughout the Middle Ages, reflecting the social and organizational attitudes of the different time periods.[125] The early Middle Ages referred to the prostitute as *meretrix publica*. Although considered redundant (*meretix* refers to public earning power and *publica* refers to public rather than private), the phrase was taken from the Roman tradition meaning "a public person who earns money (*meretix*) from her activities." But as Otis points out, the term *meretrix* did not originally mean an immoral private woman, simply a woman who earned money by working in a public field. Over time, however, the term transformed and the idea of a sexual public working woman became associated with the business of prostitution: "The word *meretrix* continued to be used in the West after the decline of Roman cities, but it had lost ... its precise and specific meaning and had come to be used as a general insult implying illicit sexual conduct. The addition of the adjective *publica* was therefore necessary, in a period of rising prostitution, to distinguish the professional public woman from the private amateur."[126] This relation of the public woman as prostitute was also put forth in Marseille's thirteenth-century statutes, which included a chapter entitled *De meretricibus* [regarding prostitutes], where prostitutes were simply "'public girls' who day and night receive two or more men in their homes."[127]

Although modern society defines prostitution as the act of earning money through the sexual commerce of the body, what Rollo-Koster terms "promiscuity and trade,"[128] early texts including canon law made little distinction between the prostitute and the promiscuous woman.[129] In fact, the medieval civic authorities[130] rarely attempted to define the prostitute when they were creating laws regulating her work.[131] Prostitution and promiscuity were specifically associated with the female element, and she was held responsible for turning the male to sin, like Eve was said to do to Adam in the Garden before The Fall. This theme, starting with many of the hagiographic texts on female sinner/saints and then socialized through tradition, became so prevalent that by the end of the Middle Ages, sexual sin was "attributed specifically to women."[132] Thus a double standard existed where women were associated negatively with sex, and where men were the innocent bystanders simply being tricked by sinful women, and where this promiscuous nature was also naturally associated with women's inclination toward pride, greed, and a love for worldly things.[133]

Karras further points out, when the early hagiographic texts of Mary Magdalene are examined, a distinction between the prostitute and the promiscuous woman is made,[134] and yet in the end the "sin" was the same: "Though a need to earn a living might provide an explanation for prostitution, it was not an excuse; nor was noble birth an excuse."[135] Indeed, many of the *Vitae* described the Magdalene as originally being a promiscuous woman, and this was quickly tied into the profession of prostitution. Reflecting back to the Magdalene's beauty and her reported long hair that later served to cover her nakedness, it is suggested that the perfection of her flesh is what leads her to a life of sin: "Now Mary, from the time she became a woman, shone in loveliness and bodily beauty ... but because outward beauty is rarely allied to chastity, and affluence of possession may often be an enemy to continence ... she, as is usual at that age, followed after the pleasure of the flesh."[136] Through the story of the Magdalene it is seen how prostitution became framed by linking physical beauty with promiscuousness and then to prostitution, since "beauty was identified with temptation, seduction, and all the danger that women represented."[137] Later this slippery slope argument will be used by some in Ireland to justify removing young girls considered too pretty for their own good from society and into the laundries. Presently, it's enough to recognize that although the early Middle Ages acknowledged the fact that professional prostitutes traded the commerce of her body for money or goods, that the underlining sin was sex. Not sex for money, but the act of sex itself. Further, the sin of sex is made worse when it is practiced outside the confines of marriage and, instead, offered as a public commons. As such, defining the prostitute in the role of a public community, or as *meretrix publica*, was an important distinction because it allowed authorities to regulate *her* life through the terms of the *public good*. Prostitutes could be told where to live, how to dress and when to work because they were the "property of all men in a sense because they were the property of none ... [a concept that] was reflected in the regulations of brothels across medieval Europe that forbade prostitutes to refuse any customer or even to have particular lovers."[138] As a public tool, prostitutes could be ruled over and, in a sense, their lives directed. Here is an early form of magdalenism where image and truth is inverted in order to control and maintain the marginalized woman. Further, being magdalenized meant that you were public property to do with as pleased. To lose one's privacy in this way was an insult, and in fact to falsely slander someone by calling them a witch or a prostitute could cost you much — pointing to sixth century laws of the Salian Franks, Amt notes that if "anyone calls a freewoman a witch or prostitute, and it cannot be proven, let him be held liable for 2500 denarii, which make sixty-two and one-half solidi."[139] However, although there was an attempt to discourage and shame the prostitute, there was also a corresponding understanding that prostitution, and so the prostitute, was a *necessary evil*. Nevertheless, it would be an overstatement to suggest that the church recognized that their views and rules regarding sex and marriage actually caused a rise in prostitution; the church did see prostitution as a permanent reality and as a necessary evil.[140] To protect society from such immoral influences, both the church and the wider society in Western Europe believed that prostitution and the prostitute should be segregated and reformed,[141] as well as repressed, which was the tendency in the early and late Middle Ages, or tolerated only through organized institutionalization, which occurred in the High Middle Ages.[142]

Chapter Three

Medieval Prostitution, Regulation, and Repentance

> *Remove prostitutes from human affairs
> and you will destroy everything with lust.*
> —St. Augustine, *De Ordine* 2.4

In the Middle Ages, prostitution and its association with sexual promiscuity was seen as a legitimate and needed profession, as well as something to aggressively repress. However, as the historian Leah Otis demonstrates in her work on prostitution in medieval Languedoc, the medieval view of prostitution throughout Western Europe went through several phases including repression (early Middle Ages), general acceptance (twelfth through the sixteenth centuries), institutionalization (fourteenth through fifteenth centuries), and back to a space of repression from the sixteenth century on.[1] Like many other social attitudes, views regarding prostitution and women's roles in society were shaped not only by geography but, importantly, by economic forces that influenced cultural and social norms.

This chapter will examine prostitution, repentance, and the first Magdalene convents for repenties from the twelfth to early sixteenth century. As documentation and general scholarship regarding this time period's relationship to prostitution and reform convents/homes is limited, this chapter will necessarily make some generalizations regarding prostitution and how it was generally viewed throughout much of Western Europe. This chapter also makes use of Wallerstein's (1974) understanding of the rise of a capitalist world system and how it worked to affect markets, social attitudes and, as this work argues, the reform of the fallen woman through privatizing public works, and thereby reforming forms of labor relations.

Means of Separation, Osterization, and the Legal Status of the Medieval Prostitute

As discussed briefly in chapters one and two, prostitution was seen as a necessary evil by much of medieval society.[2] Although a sinful state, prostitution was understood to help protect public order, save the *good* or *honorable* woman from molestation, while preparing men for marriage.[3] Although everyday life helped justify the existence of prostitution, the church and other spiritually inclined authorities looked to St. Augustine and his publication *De Ordine* (2.4). In this work, St. Augustine defended prostitution's existence in the light of the lustful nature of sinful men who "would corrupt respectable women — even their own wives — or turn to sodomy if they did not have the prostitute as a sexual outlet: 'Remove prostitutes from human affairs and you will destroy everything with lust' [Augustine, *De Ordine 2.4, Patrologiae Cursus Completus Series Latina*]."[4] Accordingly, even though prostitution was undesirable, it was deemed necessary.[5] So it was that like other necessary but unpleasant realities in life, prostitution would be allowed, but under controlled conditions, so to avoid harming a good social order.[6]

At first, control was not in the form of the creation of red-light districts or official brothels, but by separating the honorable and the not so honorable people in society.[7] As towns were often contained by walls, one of the main separation techniques came by insisting that public prostitutes were to conduct their business outside the walls of the said town. This legal ordinance tended to be the normal mode of operation throughout Western Europe[8] and can be observed through several official articles of law. For example, Otis points to the 105th article of the customs of Carcassonne (beginning of the thirteenth century), as well as a municipal law from the city of Toulouse (dated August 31, 1201), both stating that prostitutes must conduct their business outside the walls of the town, and away from *good* and *honest* citizens.[9] Although required to complain to the vicar first, these laws further empowered *good* and *honest* citizens to punish and expel prostitutes who broke these ordinances. By placing the prostitute outside the walls in order to conduct her business, it was felt that the reputation of honest women (and men) was protected. This can also be seen in Arles' 1240 law (number 49), which states: "We statute that no public prostitute [*meretrix publica*] or procurer dare stay in Arles in a street of 'good men,' and if by chance they be found in such places, that anyone of that area or neighborhood have the power to expel them from the neighborhood, on his own authority, without punishment or contradiction of the court."[10] By segregating the prostitutes from the so-called good elements of society, authorities were able to both acknowledge and control prostitution.[11] Additionally, these laws furthered the either/or rhetoric that is needed to promote magdalenism, discussed in chapter two, behind the good/honest versus the bad/dishonest woman — the virgin versus the whore. In this case, authorities were able to enforce and maintain hegemonic hierarchal relations by creating both a verbal and physical difference between these two artificial categories.

Segregation and control took several forms from the early Middle Ages to the late 1500s. Although asked to conduct business mostly outside of the walls of town, prostitution flourished inside those walls as well. When in the town proper, prostitution created the need for regulations that would distinguish *the harlot* from the *good woman*, while keeping the prostitute out of certain public areas where her presence might encourage illicit behavior among the population. For example, prostitutes and Jews were not allowed to touch food in the market without purchasing what was handled.[12] Further, while in town the *meretrix publica* had to stay away from gaming houses, bathhouses, and taverns.[13] Part of necessity of keeping prostitutes away from these entertainment houses came from what St. Augustine had identified as the weak tolerance of male sexuality within the confines of casual social scenes: "As for male sexuality, it was no secret to the canonists that men have a natural appetite for carnal relations with women. These lawyers were also aware that casual conversations with members of the opposite sex might easily lead to greater intimacy, an outcome which became even more likely when conversation was enlivened by intemperate drinking."[14] This law is reflected in the Parisian guild regulation of the thirteenth century: "No man or woman of the foresaid trade may maintain in their houses or baths either prostitutes of the day or night, or lepers, or vagabonds, or other infamous people of the night."[15] Besides bathhouses and taverns, prostitutes were to stay away from churches and schools alike, which can be seen from the statutes and sumptuary laws of Marseille (1253–1257): "Prostitutes must not stay among good men (*inter probos homines et honestos*), as well as rule in Arles and Avigon, and that these women must not stay near churches (*prope alias ecclesias*)."[16]

Additional steps were taken to create an either/or dichotomy between the so-called "good" woman from her fallen counterpart by separating the two social classes though clothing and sumptuary laws.[17] Witnessed mostly during the thirteenth and fourteenth centuries, the sumptuary laws created a separation between the classes by making sure that people dressed appropriately, according to their social station in life. Remembering Duby's insightful argument that the Middle Ages were based upon strict hierarchy,[18] it is not surprising that those in the highest social class, in order to maintain their place of power and the general hegemony of society, wanted to ensure that, for example, the newly rich merchants did not dress the same or better than the nobles, considered their social *betters*.[19] Further, these sumptuary laws punished prostitutes for dressing in such a way as to impress a clientele, and as a result women in the cities were "charged with excessive opulence of dress."[20] For example, the French cities of Toulon, Aix-en-Provence, Marseille as well as others in the Southern part of France imposed sumptuary laws. Rollo-Koster points out that "Marseille and Toulon ordered prostitutes to wear single-color garments, and Aix-en-Provence ordered them to be veiled."[21] London prostitutes also were subjected to these laws. Amt and Shahar[22] both discuss laws from fourteenth century London that made prostitutes wear distinctive clothing, while forbidding them to wear the fashion of the so-called better class — maintaining hierarchy, hegemony, and the discourse of *difference*: "On the 13th day of February, ... it was ordered by the Mayor, and Aldermen, and Common council, that all common harlots, and all women commonly reputed as such, should have and use hoods of ray [a striped cloth] only; and should not wear any manner of budge, or *perreie*, or *revers* [types of fur], to the contrary of this Ordinance found upon her."[23]

Punishments for disobeying these laws included mostly fines and the confiscation of clothing and other possessions.[24] However, as Brundage points out, the general authorities, although condemning prostitution, spend little time worrying about the punishments because the prostitute, by her very nature, was thought to be behaving in a way that was normal for her sexual character.[25] In this way, social and political hegemony was also maintained between the sexually *good* and sexually *bad* woman within the rhetoric of *necessity* and *nature*. Prostitutes, it was promoted, simply could not help their sexual natures. It was, as it might be said today, in the DNA. Because of this, prostitutes were given a scapegoat clause in that although their profession was shunned and sex for pleasure was a sin, because of their natures such women could take *the fall* for the rest of society. Prostitution, as a necessary evil, must endure — but it must not affect those who are born with pure or more adult natures. By arguing that nature (and possibly, by default, God) promoted and provided individuals who were not pure — authorities could once again justify prostitution within a Christian environment, while treating lightly the sin of sexual pleasure committed by the prostitutes themselves. So although fines and the confiscation of clothing and other possessions did provide a small income for town coffers,[26] in general the punishments for prostitutes were light compared to those levied on other related elements of the profession. If the prostitute was simply acting as was in her nature to act, then it was those who took advantage of the prostitute's nature that were the true criminals — brothel keepers, adulterers, and especially family members who forced a girl into prostitution against her will: "When it came to punishments, they gave most of their attention to the penalties to be inflicted upon those who used the prostitute's services and upon the pimps, procurers, and brothel keepers who made those services regularly available."[27] For example, adultery was severely punished and, unlike the prostitute who simply was doing as nature spoke to her, if a wife was found to be an adulterer, the husband (in many towns) had the right to kill her and whomever his wife was with "but without any further delay."[28] In Sicily, as in other areas of Europe, there were several unforgiving laws that dealt with madams who tried to recruit women into the business of prostitution, with penalties such as slitting the wrong doer's nose: "[They] should be punished by the slitting of their noses as are adulteresses according to the statutes of our grandfather, King Roger."[29] What is interesting about the Sicily laws, and title LXXXIV of these laws, is the language that suggests that women would not wish to take part in prostitution; rather, there are other sinister elements, those who "solicit the shame of wives, daughters, sisters, and finally virgins and honest women that some good man has within the walls of his house":

> But we order that those who attract the minds of women, who, since they have lived freely and were under no one's protection, have given themselves to the wills and pleasures of men at any time (*though it is not really believable that they would desire to give themselves for the first time*), should be beaten after they have been convicted by legitimate proof of committing such acts, and they should be marked on the forehead in recognition of the crime they have attempted. Such madams should know for sure that if they attempt to repeat what they have done again, they will certainly and without doubt be subjected to the slitting of their noses.[30]

Particularly harsh were the laws that regulated the occurrence of mothers or other family members who forced a child into prostitution against her will in order to provide an income for the family.[31] Like madams, the mothers who commit such crimes were ordered to have her nose slit because, the Sicily canonist wrote in title LXXXV of *The Liber Augustalis* laws, "We believe that it is not only unjust but cruel for other mothers, who give their consent, and for their daughters, who may not be able to marry a husband because of their poverty, but who also cannot even sustain life, to be subject to this penalty when they expose themselves to the pleasure of some man who gives them sustenance for life and other favors."[32]

Although the medieval mind tended to forgive the prostitute (to a limit) her nature, and although the laws judge harder those who would take advantage of her nature, the twelfth- to thirteenth-century prostitute was still seen as one of the lowest elements in society. Brundage argues that the prostitute's status was so low that she was actually understood as being *below* the law, and so not required to obey the law. In general, then the prostitute was "beneath the law's contempt."[33] Accordingly, the prostitute could not inherit property, or act as her own defense should a charge be brought against her.[34] In this case, the prostitute's word was not taken seriously in some instances, and she actually had to hire a representative to speak for her. Further, just as she could not speak for herself in court, she also could not denounce others in court as well.[35] These last limits on her legal rights stemmed from the vestiges of Roman law that equated the prostitute with the infamous person.[36] However, Otis points out that around the mid-fourteenth century, to the sixteenth century, these limits on the prostitute's legal status dissipate[37] and she starts to enjoy the same legal rights as other women in her time.[38] Regardless, it must be noted that although the prostitute's legal status was questioned throughout the twelfth and thirteenth centuries, her right to be paid for her services were basically protected.[39] Amt points to early thirteenth-century Norman laws that reflect this right: "If anyone takes a prostitute by force and does not vie her her price, he shall be in the Duke's mercy for all his chattels, and the prostitute shall have her price, and her damages shall be paid, if her clothes were torn; and if the abductor has no money, he shall do penance in the Duke's custody for eight days."[40] Once the service was provided, the prostitute's client had no right to take the money back, and she did nothing wrong in accepting payment. This attitude was reflected in the canon law and was expressed by the twelfth-century canonist Thomas Cobham, who stated: "Prostitutes should be counted among the wage-earners. They hire out their bodies and supply labour. It is wrong for a woman to be a prostitute but if she is such, it is not wrong for her to receive a wage. But if she prostitutes herself for pleasure and hires out her body for this purpose, then the wage is as evil as the act itself."[41] However, if payment was not received at the time of the transaction, then the prostitute's right to payment was less clear since the client could easily suggest that this woman, below contempt of the law, was lying about services provided.[42]

The Institutionalization of Prostitution and Early Attempts at Reform

As mentioned at the top of this chapter, the late Middle Ages saw the institutionalization of prostitution and, as such, a corresponding effort at reforming the no-longer-working prostitute either by marrying her off, or having her adopt the religious life.[43] Whether city officials felt that sexual promiscuity was a threat to the honest community,[44] or there were larger security issues with having prostitutes congregate outside the walls of a town,[45] the solution of institutional regulation of prostitution become popular during this time. First there were several efforts at creating official "red-light" districts in many towns. Otis lists documentation for the founding of red-light districts in the suburbs of Montpellier in 1285.[46] Here, "hot street" was established by the authorities as a section of town where prostitutes were legally required to gather, work, and live. This change of attitude from simply placing the prostitute outside the walls of the city worked to enhance her rights to live and work without being threatened by the so-called good members of society.[47] Other red-light districts followed and often looked to Montpellier as its model, including the French districts in Nîmes, and smaller towns such as Lacauue (Tarn), established around 1337.[48] As suggested above, some of these districts were established on the grounds that sexual promiscuity was damaging the community.[49] One such example can be found in the French town of Narbonne, who in 1335 established the district in order to stop scandal and limit harm done to the good portion of the population:

> We, the said Aymeric ... give ... and liberally concede to you, the said consuls, ... in order that the several scandals and evils which are said to touch the town of Narbonne should be avoided, that there be and can be henceforth a *postribulum*, *lupanar* or "Hot Street" in some suitable place in Narbonne ... with the same modalities, forms, privileges, uses and customs with which the *postribulum* of Montpellier exists and has been the custom to exist, that is, that in the said *postribulum* ... no one can be arrested by the subvicar or sergeants of our court or by others of our men, by day or by night, for adultery.[50]

Yet, as Otis demonstrates, a larger reason for the creation of red light districts, and later official municipal brothels, was to maintain security for the town. The concern came from the *elements* that were often attracted by the presence of prostitutes — that is, criminals, thieves, and the like. To be sure, there was unofficial business being conducted outside the walls of towns, and some of these businesses attracted dangerous individuals. Further, during the crisis of the fourteenth century, which saw the Hundred Year War, as well as several plagues, and the general decline of agricultural activity, crime and prostitution climbed,[51] requiring many towns to consider strengthening their security. Addressing this security concern, town prostitutes were moved back inside the walls of their respective towns. So it is that the town of Albi in France eventually relocated the red-light district from where the Bishop of Albi had placed it, to a securer location in town. Recounted by Otis, this particular instance also demonstrated how it was that secular authorities rather than religious ones asserted their rights and power over the question of prostitution. No longer a spiritual issue, because prostitution attracted a discouraging element in society, it was a security issue, and so a secular problem. In Albi, the Bishop had deemed it his right and domain to move the prostitutes to where he saw fit in the town. However, the secular authority of the consuls objected to this proclamation and in 1366 complained to the lieutenant governor of the King of France. The result was simple: placement of prostitutes was an issue of security more than a concern for spirituality: "The lieutenant governor ordered the prostitutes to be expelled from the place where the bishop had put them and placed in an area more suitable to the security of the town and the honor of Saint Anthony."[52] This struggle of power regarding spiritual versus lay authority over market conditions in connection with legislating morality will become an important issue between the future core market, England, and the peripheral state of Ireland. Indeed, fair labor regulations as applied to Magdalene laundresses and prostitutes will be determined by these questions: should religious law also direct secular law? In which modes of society and how deeply should religious morals sway lay law?

Nevertheless, in the high Middle Ages, along with the creation of red-light districts came the construction of official municipal brothels and homes. Both Otis and Shahar note that these official/municipal brothels were a partial reaction against the unofficial institutions: "Existence of official public houses implied the illegality of other brothels, protection of the *filia communa* was paralleled by the condemnation of the illicit prostitute."[53] Whereas the officially deemed prostitute was protected by law and allowed to practice her profession, illicit prostitutes were not and made up some of the poorest part of the community.[54] However, it was the officially recognized brothels that would later lead to the repentant homes for prostitutes. Further, as will be discussed below, by rhetorically defining the legal prostitute against the "good women," while the municipal earned profit from her services, the local government was actively promoting and perpetuating magdalenism. Because of this fact, it is important to briefly note the rise and function of municipal brothels. In Albi, the building of an official brothel occurred in 1419, and in 1425 King Charles VII placed the municipal brothel of Toulouse, also in France, under his "personal safeguard."[55] The practice of royal control of prostitution became the norm, according to Otis, in at least the Languedocian towns, where it was "the king's prerogative to authorize the establishment of a municipal brothel, and the task of his royal officers to supervise the realization of such a project."[56] There were some privately held brothels that were also legal; however, most of the legal homes of prostitution were public institutions. Moreover, although major repairs and additions in the legal brothels fell to the town to provide, municipal brothels were farmed out to individuals to run for an agreed upon period of time between the "renter-manager" and the town.[57] In the end, official brothels brought in a good amount of income for the town and the seigneurs of the towns, which means they were actively promoting magdalenism.[58] In addition, these municipal brothels were numerous until after the crisis of the fourteenth century, where funds and population declined,[59] forcing prostitutes to move into a single home in some instances. What is interesting is that laws governing the activity of these homes basically put prostitutes in the position of living a "cloistered" life, not unlike nuns, where their ability to roam freely was greatly hindered,[60] while the town authorities and others profited off their labor.

Reforming the Prostitute—Timeout for Church, Penance, and Conversions

It could be argued that as long as there has been prostitution, there has been a corresponding effort to rally for and/or against the institution; therefore, it can also be argued that as long as prostitution has existed, so has there been a campaign to reform members of the profession. It is not surprising then to recognize that just as the Catholic Church might have felt that prostitution was a necessary evil, they also felt a need to reform those who entered into the profession for the sake of the public good: "the prostitute symbolized human frailty and provoked the benevolence of God's grace. Reform entailed two possibilities, marriage or the convent. Both institutions were to bring these females back to the realm of sexual austerity. In both cases, remedies implied male ideological control of female sexuality."[61] One such famous reformer was Humbert de Romans (1194 to 1277), a retired Dominican master general, who in his *Ed Eruditione Praedicatorum* listed sermons devoted to nuns, noble ladies, the wealthy bourgeoisies, poor females, as well as the prostitute.[62] As chapter two discussed, medieval society was "goaded by the spirit of hierarchy,"[63] and there should be little surprise that Humbert divided his sermons up socioeconomically (like the medieval society the sermons were addressing). Nor should it be a surprise that unlike other preachers in this time, Humbert dedicated approximately one-fifth of his sermons to women,[64] partly in response to the fact that women outnumber men in the high Middle Ages.[65] Regardless, Humbert felt that women spent too much time appreciating the world of material wonders[66] (an argument that will extend well into the 1800s), and needed to embrace God more. When it came to prostitution, Humbert believed that fornication was the greatest sin "for which a whore was to be compared to dung as she was the greatest filth."[67] Associating women and not men with this particular sin, Humbert saw women as being imperfect creatures in general. However conversely, he also celebrated women as a gender. The female worth was that a woman was man's helpmate (not his servant), because she was taken from the center of man, Adam, not from his "foot as might have been the case."[68] Further, Humbert argued that the honor of delivering the son of man was given to a woman (the Virgin Mary), and it also was a woman (the Magdalene) who was the first witness to the rising Christ.[69] In his *De modo prompte cudendi sermones* Humbert states:

Notice that the Lord gave many privileges to women, not only over animals, but over men.... He created man in his world but women in Paradise. He formed the male from the slime of the earth. Which is of little worth, but the female from the rib of man. He did not form her from the lower part of man, that is from the foot, lest man have her for a slave, but from the middle part of the male, that is from the side rib, so that he might have her for a companion.... At the time of the resurrection Christ first appeared to a woman, namely Magdalen.... In the state of glory no mere man will be king ... but a mere woman will be queen. Also no pure man will be above the angels ... as will a pure woman ... and this will be in the person of the Blessed Virgin.[70]

Regarding the prostitute, Humbert wrote that the *meretrix* was everywhere.[71] In his sermon *Ad mulieres malas corpore* (To women evil in body), Humbert explains that it is not only the corruption of the prostitute's body and soul that must be of concern, but also how her bodily corruption will corrupt others.[72] Therefore, it was very important for him to encourage all priests to preach to women, including prostitutes, because even Mary Magdalene herself, once a prostitute according to Humbert as well, rose to amazing heights by embracing the church and Jesus Christ. Yet the spiritual ascension of women could only be found by removing the need for worldly goods so that only God and spirituality was left. In his sermon to *conversi* assigned to the *cura mulierum* (those who were employed with the guardianship of women in spiritual institutions), Humbert states:

> It is certainly advisable to help religious women ... because they are in much need due to their defect, which they have both in sense and strength; and because this help provides a safeguard against danger which they might incur if they worked personally for their own business. Moreover, through such aid they are able to acquire greater liberty to be free for God and religion. Therefore, the converse should ... help religious women in worldly things, working diligently for them ... and faithfully caring for their goods, alms and friends.... [They should work] so that they will have sufficient food, clothing, housing and other such necessities, so that anything which might cause peculiarities, complaints and despondency might be removed and so that they might show more good will in service to the Creator.[73]

All women could choose to become religious women. Although sinners, including Jews, lepers, and prostitutes, were seen and understood to be exiles, they could be saved.[74] The only way a prostitute could save herself, proclaimed Humbert, was to reject her profession and repent. In order to help her out, the church suggested that prostitutes who wished to reform compare themselves to Pelagia, Mary the Harlot, Afra, Thaïs, and of course, Mary Magdalene — all prostitutes who reformed and later became saints.[75]

In France, around 1100, the first-known preaching campaign to redeem prostitutes began, and the first Magdalene houses appeared. Robert of Arbrissel (ca. 1045–ca. 1117), became a wandering or itinerant preacher after being encouraged and inspired by Pope Urban II in Anjou, 1095.[76] A charismatic preacher, Robert was said to have gathered several infamous women and convinced them to repent their former ways.[77] The story has it that several prostitutes, goodly virginal women, and religious wives were greatly moved by his sermons, and followed Robert around everywhere he went.[78] In time, the crowds of hopeful women grew so large that Robert built a double monastery at Fontevrault (by the regions of Anjou, Poitou and Touraine) to house these women (and some male followers as well): "Having attracted a huge, heterogeneous and enthusiastic following of women, he was faced with problems similar to those encountered by a good number of other late eleventh-century hermits, and responded to the need to provide them with an institution."[79] Virgins and widows lived in a house under the patronage of the Virgin Mary, while the repented whores lived in a house dedicated to Mary Magdalene.[80] However, the monastery in general limited the contact between the men and women — assigning men to a life of labor, "spiritual for the clerics and physical for the laymen," and women to a "silent life in the cloister."[81]

Although converting the prostitute to the holy life was more common in the high Middle Ages,[82] the other solution was to find a suitable man to marry the prostitute, a practice that was officially promoted by Pope Innocent III on April 29, 1198, in the decretal *Inter opera caritatis*:

> Among the works of charity ... not least is that of recalling a person erring from his mistaken path, particularly to invite women living voluptuously and selling themselves indifferently to whomever into society of legitimate marriage, so that they may live chastely. We decree that for everyone who will extract public women from the whorehouses and marry them, because they do so, their sins shall be remitted.[83]

However, even before Innocent's decree, Henry of Le Mans (ca. 1115) worked to marry off those women "living voluptuously." Like Robert of Arbrissel, Henry of Le Mans was also a traveling preacher that attracted the fallen woman who "listened to his sermons and repented."[84] Although later condemned by the church as a heretic, Henry had a great idea: Force the prostitutes to give up their wicked ways in a public arena, and then marry them off to the bachelors of the town who, after all, should have been married by this time anyway. Setting his plan into motion, Henry gathered up the fallen women in Le Mans and had them "strip [their selves] naked, and 'burn their dresses and hairlocks in front of everyone.' Thereafter, 'all the street-girls were given a piece of material costing four solidi, hardly enough to cover their nakedness, then, on Henry's demand, the young men of the town married them all.'"[85] To make this last demand financially possible, Henry abolished the requirement of a dowry.[86] Heretic or not, Henry was onto something and, as the church was experiencing a revival in penitence, Pope Innocent III, as mentioned above, added to the incentive for men to marry fallen women by the remission of their sins. Several priests made Pope Innocent III's decree their mission, notably among them was Fulk of Neuilly, a student of Peter the Chanter, who preached to usurers and prostitutes about repentance in Paris.[87] In 1206, with the help of Peter of Roissac, he founded a community for repentant prostitutes, Saint-Antoine des Champs,[88] and then established a second home in 1226.[89] As Brundage explains, rather than abolishing the custom of the dowry as Robert of Arbrissel had, Fulk "induced the bourgeoisie of Paris to subscribe more than a thousand *livres* to create a dowry fund for reformed prostitutes, and the university students of the city scraped up a further 250 *livres* to augment the fund."[90] And so efforts to reform prostitutes spread like weeds, with many of the women being honorably married off and the rest of them being housed in Magdalene institutions throughout Europe, including Germany, Italy, Spain and France.

The church, however, was not the only interested party in saving these lost souls, as the community had a claim in such work as well. Municipal authorities did not want pillow talk and old, now considered useless prostitutes causing havoc in society by whispering secrets better left in bed. Further there were economic concerns as well, because just as the community had provided municipal brothels, they felt the need to provided "homes" for retirement and preparation for marriage:

> A former prostitute of the municipal brothel was not only a deserving recipient of municipal charity but also a potential object of suspicion. It was feared that, if not aided by the community, the former prostitute might well resort to activities inimical to the commonwealth: procuring for illicit prostitutes, arranging adulterous trysts and the deflowering of virgins, and concocting love potions and abortive mixtures.[91]

Thus, communities often supported all efforts of the church to reform prostitutes and added to those efforts organizationally and financially as well. First the municipal brothels encouraged the spiritual betterment of working *official* prostitutes by requiring them to listen to spiritual sermons.[92] Further, although the prostitute was discouraged from leaving the official brothel, she was not barred from attending church on Sundays or feast-days.[93] Prostitutes were also barred from working on Christmas or on the Feast of the Virgin Mary, as well as Holy Week. During Holy Week, all business in the official brothels stopped, and the working prostitutes were encouraged to join the religious celebrations. Otis points to the early-fourteenth-century police regulations of Nîmes forbidding prostitutes to work during holy week (ca. 1353), and similar regulations found during this period in Uzès where the prostitutes were made to leave town for the whole month.[94] Although there were exceptions to the rule,[95] during Holy Week the many brothels actually relocated the prostitutes to a different location, and the women were financially provided for by the Municipal. Otis examines Albi's account book of 1506, which "records that 7s. 6d. were paid 'to the poor sinners of the Good House of Albi ... so that they stop sinning for Holy Week.'"[96] By providing for the prostitute's room and board, the municipal felt that these poor sinners had a better opportunity to repent and that the community who supported prostitution through the maintenance of official brothels was not also guilty of not providing proficient means for reform and repentance. Indeed, some of the costs included not only food and lodgings during Holy Week, but even the purchase of rosaries.[97] Although repentance and reform was rare during Holy Week events, Otis reports that there were exceptions. For example, reported "in March 1526 all the women of the brothel of Albi decided to withdraw from their former worldly life to dedicate themselves to God."[98] Reform, however, was not easy, because even as preachers offered the hope of salvation if prostitutes were to leave their profession, this salvation came at a high price. When the retired prostitute entered a refuge, like a Magdalene convent, she exchanged her already limited civil freedoms for moral regulation, because a fallen Magdalene had to be protected from herself and her wayward nature.[99] Regardless, the early campaigns to save a woman from herself and through the development of Magdalene convents started in earnest between the twelfth and thirteenth centuries.[100]

Repentant Homes and Convents

Although the establishment of repentant homes for prostitutes can be traced to before the thirteenth century, Rollo-Koster states that the largest "phase" of repentant institutions for reformed prostitutes occurred between the thirteenth and fourteenth centuries,[101] right before and in conjunction with institutional efforts at creating official spaces for the existence of prostitution. Generally these convents and homes came in two forms: (1) reformatory spaces that functioned as halfway houses preparing the former prostitute for marriage, and (2) real religious convents functioning strictly under religious rule. It has been argued that the failure of many of the halfway homes is directly related to the character of the women — women who just could not or did not wish to reform: "Quite often, such contemporary reports on the institution were biased by a circular logic.... To many chroniclers, the attempt to reform the 'uncontrollable' nature of wayward women might seem doomed to failure, while the demonstration of the institution's failure only provided proof of these women's incorrigible character."[102] There is much merit in Rollo-Koster's primary argument that the problem did not simply rest on the character of the inmates, but rather on the fact that the halfway homes were missing the "institutional and protective apparatus of a genuine religious order."[103] Regardless, the success and/or failure of the homes did not deter their growth throughout Europe.

During the late thirteenth and early fourteenth centuries, several towns in France had communities for repentant women. There were, of course, Fulk of Neuill's convents mentioned above, and, in Paris, William of Auvergne founded an Augustine rule called the Fille-dieu (1226), which was supported by Saint Louis.[104] Otis also mentions a community founded in southern France in 1294 that is known through the mention of a donation in a Toulouse will.[105] Further, in Marseille (ca. 1272), a *bourgeois* by the name of Bertrand was reported to have established a home for reformed prostitutes as well.[106] This home was later acknowledged by Pope Nicolas II.[107] Like William of Auvergne's home, many of these religious reformatories were under Augustinian rule in France, including the Avignon convent (ca. 1257), which will be discussed in detail below. Other locations included "Toulouse (ca. 1300), Carcassone (ca. 1310), Narbonne (ca. 1312), Montpellier (ca. 1328), while Limoux made a foundation in the fourteenth century."[108] Otis uncovers the most information from the Montpellier home, which received its start in 1204. The oldest known institution for repenties in this region, Otis states that it was established "near the Gate Saint Gilles" and received papal favor in 1294. There was also a second community for reformed prostitutes established by the municipality, and these two communities "existed side by side in Montepellier from 1319 to 1387, when they merged, probably as a result of the depopulation of urban monastic communities in the wake of the Black Death."[109] Jansen's dates most likely reflects the municipal home before the merging of the two communities. Further, Otis points out that this community functioned more as a halfway house than a religious institution, taking in not only the old and retired prostitute, but also helping the younger prostitute reenter society though marriage.[110] Finally there is mention of a 1516 community in the town of Toulouse founded by the preacher Mathiew Menou after the conversion of local municipal prostitutes.[111]

Germany also found itself populated with prostitutes, and the problem of what to do with them when their deemed usefulness waned. They had tried regulation, and preachers had tried sermons, but the most fashionable solution was again the Magdalene convent.[112] The best known order of penitent prostitutes in Germany is described to us in the *Chronicle of Colmar*. An anonymously written late-thirteenth-century history, *The Colmar* tells the story of how a Magdalene convent, *Sorores Poenitentes Beatae Mariae Magdalenae*, came into being during the middle of the thirteenth century. In 1225, a preacher and chaplain by the name of Rudolph of Worms, the canon of Saint Maurice of Hildesheim,[113] was on a preaching mission to convert prostitutes, when he met a group of prostitutes at a crossroad. This story is very familiar as it parallels that of Robert of Arbrissel: "As he approached them they cried out to him: 'Oh sir, we are without resources and cannot find any other way of subsisting. Give us just a little bread and water and we will do whatever you wish.'"[114] Surprising these poor hungry prostitutes, Rudolph did not wish for sex, but only to reform and help the poor women. Like many before him, Rudolph set out to find husbands for as many of the fallen sisters as he could, and for the rest, a place in the convent of the Penitent Sisters of Blessed Mary Magdalene (*Sorores Poenitentes Beatae Mariae Magdalenae*). This Magdalene convent was so popular that it was officially recognized and approved by Pope Gregory IX in 1227: "The pope issued a bull giving a veritable juridical status to these communities, to whom the Augustinian rule and the institutions of Prouille were recommended."[115] Like France and Germany, Italy also promoted homes for the repentie Magdalenes as well.

In general, the work done to reform prostitutes in late-Middle-Ages Italy represented a private spiritual calling rather than a municipal or community endeavor, a phenomenon that will be seen later in the eighteenth and nineteenth centuries. The self-punishing (or flagellant — somebody who whips themselves as a form of penance) penitent members of *Santa Maria Magdalena* felt that one of their important charitable activities was to reform prostitutes. In 1240, because of a Dominican preaching campaign in the city of Pisa, *the Sorores Repentite Hospitalis S. Marie Magdalene de Spina* was instituted for former prostitutes.[116] There was also Saint Aldobrandesca of Siena (ca. 1249–ca. 1309),[117] widowed and without children after seven years of marriage, who devoted herself to care for the sick as well as the fallen.[118] However, one of the more dramatic episodes regarding the rescue of the *covertite* lies with Agnes of Montepulciano (a religious virgin, ca. 1268–ca. 1317), who worked to reform her fallen sisters. Agnes was created, it seems, to enter spiritual life. Born and raised in the small Tuscan village of Gracchiano-Vecchio, at nine years of age, Agnes asked her parents to place her in the convent at Montepulcian. While still quite young, Agnes moved to the convent at Procena to become the assistant to Sister Margaret. While at Procena, Agnes was soon elected as the convent's abbess, and at the age of 15 she received special permission from Pope Nicholas IV to assume the position. Her spiritual zeal won her great fame, and eventually the town of Montepulciano built a new Dominican rule convent for her: "The building was erected on the site previously occupied by several houses of ill fame which had been a disgrace to the town."[119] Inspired by the placement of the convent, Agnes worked to save the former prostitutes from the sight, directing their repentance.

Regardless of the saints and their interests in reform, several other homes for the *convertite* were established throughout Italy in 1243, 1255, 1257, 1338 and finally in 1353:

> In 1243 a convent for *convertite* was founded in Viterbo, by mid-century Bologna and Messina could each claim their own, and in 1257 Santa Maria Maddalena la Penitente in Florence's Borgo Pinti district had been established. In 1255, Alexander IV charged Juan of Toledo, titular cardinal of San Lorenzo in Lucina, to establish a house for *convertitte* in Rome in the church of Santa Maria sopra Minerva. By the early fourteenth century, Genoa had established a convent and Pisa yet another one, of which Domenico Cavalca was appointed confessor in 1329. Meanwhile in Florence, the sermons of Simone Fidati da Cascia had so inspired the members of the *Compagnia di Santa Maria delle Lauge de Santo Spirito*, a confraternity associated with that Augustinian church, that by 1338 they had founded yet another refuge for ex-prostitutes: Sant'Elisabetta delle Convertite. Venice followed suit in 1353.[120]

One of the most interesting stories, however, comes from Queen Sancia, of the Kingdom of Naples. As Jansen presents the tale, in 1304 Charles the II decreed that all prostitutes, and other people of notorious reputation, had to leave the principle piazza of the port district of Naples.[121] Adding to his father's work, Charles' son and heir, Robert the Wise, physically expelled the questionable *element* from the piazza of San Gennaro, which was near the monastery of San Severino. But it seems as if the fallen and the seedy still resided in Naples, since Robert's secretary, Niccolò d'Alife, also complained that there were many prostitutes living in his neighborhood as well. Because there apparently was an overwhelming problem with the sheer number of fallen women in Naples, and since laws and force did not seem to be the solution, another answer was sought. Thus in 1342, the pious Queen Sancia (Robert's wife) took things under her own wing and founded the convent of *Santa Maria Maddalena* in Naples.[122] In fact, Queen Sancia established several religious homes including "the Clarissan convent of Santa Croce, to which she retired, and two convents for penitent prostitutes, Santa Maria Magdala and Santa Maria Egiziaca."[123] These efforts were so valued that Pope Clement VI, in a Papal Bull dated November 21, 1342, put her institutions under papal protection and "noted that there were already 340 sisters, the abbess included. The pontiff remarks, furthermore, that of that number, some have expressly professed the rule and also vowed chastity, poverty, obedience, and perpetual enclosure."[124] Truly devoted to the cause of spiritual reform, Queen Sancia never forgot her repentant converts, and she dedicated much of her life to these communities, as well as endowing them generously in her will.

The Order of the Penitents of St. Mary Magdalene spread throughout Italy and the rest of Europe during the high to late Middle Ages, which helped popularize the cult of Mary Magdalene. These organizations became so popular that out of 51 new foundations, 32 were of the order of the Penitents of St. Mary Magdalene.[125] However, other convents that housed repentant prostitutes, and not named for Mary Magdalene, also used the Magdalene as their patron saint. It must also be mentioned that even though most of the surviving material on Magdalene convents illustrates how these repentant women lived in the homes for the rest of their life, most of the houses for penitent prostitutes were meant to be temporary situations — since it was hoped that many of the women would marry. Regardless, not all the former prostitutes were married off, and so many ended their life in these convents. Further, it should not be underestimated how much fallen women identified with Mary Magdalene. Although technically the nickname of *Magdalenes* would not be adopted by such women until the seventeenth century, Mary Magdalene's association with the prostitute really began during the Middle Ages. However, unlike Mary Magdalene who was said to adjust quickly and easily to the reformed life, most women did not. For example, in the case of Queen Sancia's communities, often the repentant prostitute had a difficult time in the Magdalene convent because their entire way of life was turned upside down.[126] In order to provide a stable environment (protecting the women from themselves), strict rules were enacted to control the women from a physiological point of view, as well as a moral one, a tradition that will be seen through 1996 with the closing of the last Irish Magdalene laundry. Although most documents laying out rules and regulations for these repentant sinners are lost, there is one very interesting document that still exists: The Latin statutes of the Repentant Sisters of Saint Mary Magdalene of the Miracles of Avignon, granted by Pope Gregory XI in 1375.[127]

Avignonese Repenties

The Historian Rollo-Koster states that the first mention of Avignonese Repenties dates to 1293, when the construction for the house was ordered by Guasbert du Val, the bishop of Narbonne, followed by the construction of the adjoining chapter built by John XXII in 1320.[128] The construction site selected was originally where public executions had once been performed, and it is here that the convent started as a small, "jail-like" home. In the 1370s, a larger home was built by an order from Pope Gregory XI, which included "a larger house with new sleeping quarters, a cloister, and a choir. From their own private oratory, the *Repenties* could participate in masses and communicate and confess through two large barred windows adjoining the chapel without being seen by the outside world."[129] Following the Augustinian rule, the house was officially established on the fourth of July, 1376: "A rule is established for the sisters to lead a dignified, honest, and regular life and to harvest the fruits of penance through which they will reach the glory of paradise. If some of the sisters fear this rule let them remember and meditate upon the words of the apostle: worldly discipline is not a cause for joy but for pain; the rewards will only come later."[130] Not unlike the care for many of the municipal brothels, the Avignon community worked closely with the Sister Repenties. Financial support was provided, and the "rectors of the Monastery make regular visits to make sure the women were living as they should."[131] In 1370, the home went from being owned by the community to being maintained and held by the church. However, this arrangement did not last long, and in 1376, Rollo-Koster reports that control was given back to the Avignon community: "This financial support demonstrates that popes and the Avignonese inhabitants looked upon the institution with approbation."[132]

The repenties lived under strict Augustinian rule, and because one of the main purposes of this community was to change former prostitutes and other women into nuns, the repentant Sisters lived under several strict rules. First, only women under the age of 25 years could enter the convent (*mulieres peccatrices juvenes que sint infra etatem vigniti quinque annorum*)[133]: "We decree and ordain that from this moment on, there will be received in the said monastery only young women of the age of twenty-five years who in their youth were lustful, and who by their beauty and formliness could still be prompted by worldly fragility and inclined to worldly voluptuous pleasure and to attract men to the same totally."[134] If a fallen woman qualified through age and beauty, she was given a trial period within the convent (about eight to ten days), and had to swear an oath of obedience and chastity for the time spent in the convent.[135] It is very interesting and sad to note that many women allowed into this community had to be not only of a certain age, but also of a certain degree of beauty. As will also be discussed and observed in relation the Irish Magdalene laundries, the beauty of a woman was enough to condemn her to a life of confinement, since it was believed not only that her beauty would cause her to be weak and vain in the flesh, but also that such beauty would condemn men, who, it was claimed, would not be able to resist such wiles. Francesco Sansovino (1521–1586), a sixteenth-century historian and literary critic, expresses this belief when speaking about how only very beautiful reformed prostitutes were accepted into convents.[136] Apparently, these women were the most at risk, because their extreme beauty alone would cause them to sin and, in turn, cause others to sin as well, something Humbert had also warned against. Regardless, the concern was to save the woman who still could be seduced into the profession, which is why the convent did not admit women considered *ugly* or *homely*, or even *old*. Regardless, once accepted into the community, the young woman was asked to give up all her possessions and clothing.[137] After the trial period was over, the other sisters would then decide whether to admit the "novice into their ranks."[138] Because this Avignonese community was more in the line with a convent than a halfway house, the sisters were protected by fortified walls from the outside world, and expected to live the life of a nun: praying, confessing, scrubbing floors, and doing laundry, of course. They worked for the good of the convent community and to save their souls. Further, after entering as a novice, everything these women did, said, and wore was controlled by church authorities. These women were expected to live as a nun would live, and the authorities believed that they were protecting the fallen woman from herself and society from the fallen. A few of the more interesting regulations were those that regulated dress, speech, and food.

The clothing provided for the women in the convent was a stark difference to what they may have worn during life outside. This is not a surprise, since the aim of the convent was to promote humbleness rather than vanity. First, hair was to be cut off, since long hair represented pride, and fashionable clothing was set aside for habits.[139] Traditional wear for repenties included a white robe, cap, and veil[140] made of "white wool cloth neither delicate nor precious."[141] The clothing had to be loose, "not too tight and difficult to put on," as well as decent: "From their exterior honesty must their interior purity shine."[142] This standard wardrobe is what eventually gave the repentant prostitutes the nickname of the *Ladies in White*; regardless, these uniforms were a far cry from the beautiful clothing worn by women of this period. The habits were tent-like structures, and no comfort was allowed, because comfort would remind these women of the luxuries of life they had left behind — remembrances, it was argued, that would tempt her back into her old ways.[143] Furthermore, the women had to sleep fully clothed, no matter the weather, and could not sleep with each other for warmth. Finally, they had to keep their faces veiled; a sign of modesty, and interestingly enough, it was a custom that was outlawed to them in their former lives as prostitutes. Besides clothing, speech was also closely regulated. As discussed earlier, when society works to control knowledge through language, there is a corresponding effort to control social relations, which is partly why speech in this community was closely monitored. Excessive speech was looked down upon and silence found to be golden: "When they were allowed to talk, their conversation had to be humble, decent, and charitable. The divine office had to be recited with devotion, pausing when necessary, with no laughter, making of faces, or other disruption. The Repentant sisters had to abstain from illicit words, blasphemy, lies, oaths, and gossip."[144] Not only did the convent forbid slang and other foul expressions, but the intent behind speech was also regulated.¹⁴⁵ Like dress and speech, food, because it could remind the repenties of carnal and bodily joys, was limited, with the sisters also being prohibited "from stealing food and from eating or drinking in their cells or with their confessors."¹⁴⁶ Finally, if a woman was caught speaking, eating or behaving out of turn, punishment would be exacted and would range from receiving only bread and water, to being placed into isolation.¹⁴⁷ For a particularly bad violation of the rules, such as if a member of the order was caught fornicating, there was the potential punishment of "excommunication and temporary or perpetual incarceration with or without irons."¹⁴⁸ Simply put, life in these convents could be difficult, but it was not without its own benefits including offering these women the ability to obtain and maintain financial security as a maintained community.

Pope Gregory XI had such a fondness for this community that he exempted them from paying tax, a rarity in these times. Further, the Avignonese repenties' community ended up garnishing and acquiring great wealth during its existence. Rollo-Koster documents several charitable "testamentary" donations and endowments made by the larger lay population in the form of real estate that made the repenties "respectable landlords." Between 1351 and 1416, the repenties community was offered 24 different bequests from men and women alike:

> With the exception of one burgess who left to the *Repenties* sixty silver gros, a Florentine merchant who left them a house, and an innkeeper who left them his inn, all the others bequeathed vineyards capable of producing an income. In addition to those properties, the *Repenties* controlled several houses in the seven parishes forming medieval Avignon. During the fourteenth century, they owned seven houses in the parish of St. Marie Madeleine, seven in the parish of Notre Dame la Principale, five in the parish of St. Symphorien, four in the parish of St. Didier, four houses and a garden in the parish of St. Geniès, three houses in the parish of St. Pierre, and four houses and two gardens in the parish of St. Agricol. Those thirty or so properties had been donated by men, which is not surprising, since, because of the patriarchal/Roman character of Provençal law, women rarely divested their properties.¹⁴⁹

Further, all income that the sisters' labor earned returned back to the convent and not the lay community or the church,¹⁵⁰ also adding to the financial soundness of the repenties community:

> Between revenues from their properties in Avignon, L'Isle, and Montelher, the *Repenties* grossed yearly revenues of 109 florins, 1,104 sous, 195 deniers, 43 livres, 11 francs, 2 sous tournois, 3 patats, 12 pogs, and 16 silver gros. In addition, they received yearly 108.5 emines of wheat, 35 of barley, and 1/4 and 1/5 saumées of fruits. Payments were scaled throughout the year, due at the Nativity, February, March, Easter, Pentecost, St. John the Baptist (June

24), the Assumption (Aug. 15), St. Michael (Sept. 29), and All Saints' Day (Nov. 1). The bulk was received on August 15. During the fourteenth century, the *Repenties* were clearly wealthy.[151]

All told, until their land and holdings were confiscated by the municipality in the late sixteenth century, the repenties could be said to have held great power, because of their holdings and because of the success their order had in ultimately offering a real alternative for the fallen woman. Rollo-Koster argues that the success of the Avignonese Repenties can be found in the fact that the community, unlike other "halfway" homes of the time, adopted and lived the conventual life within the inspiration of Mary Magdalene.[152] Sadly, in 1575 the Cardinal George of Armagnac "expelled the Repentant Sisters of St. Mary Magdalene" when he was looking for a suitable convent for the order of the Minims, and sent the repenties sisters to the hospital of St. Michel.[153]

The aforementioned examples of life and behavior lived by the Avignonese Repenties should not be considered the model for every community in Europe. As Otis points out, there is little documentation left regarding these reformatories,[154] but what documentation that does exist points to two different types of institutions: First, a strict convent-like environment such as the Avignonese Repenties lived; or second, homes designed to be halfway houses, which prepared the former prostitute to reenter society through marriage or other means.[155] To demonstrate the difference, Otis examines the Occitanian statutes of the Repentant Sisters of Saint Catherine, in Montpellier (ca. 1339). Unlike the Avignonese community, Saint Catherine did not have an age or beauty limit; any kind of female sinner could apply (not only former prostitutes), and the waiting/trial period was a year — giving a woman enough time to choose marriage or another occupation before committing to the order itself. Further, unlike the Avignonese community, Saint Catherine was not cloistered, and the women could come and go as they pleased, as long as they "did not eat or drink in town (*en la vila non auzon beure ni manjar*)."[156] Considering the looser regulations, the non-cloistered environment, the lengthy trial periods, and the fact that support was totally offered by the municipality rather than a joint effort between the community and the church, Saint Catherine does appear to be more of a social rather than a religious solution.[157] The problem with this type of set up, as Rollo-Koster argues, can be found in their lack of a "coherent vision," as well as the "institution and protective apparatus of a genuine religious order."[158] Because these other homes functioned more as temporary shelters rather than a permanent solution for change, the women were only offered brief help and direction. If after a year stay, the woman looking for reform still did not have a husband or a new career, she was forced to leave (unless she wished to become a nun) — left to fend for herself in a world that looked down upon *her* as hopeless and *dis-*

honest. Regardless, both types of the early repentant communities offer a glimpse into the running and origins of the later institutions for fallen women. Thanks to the popularity of Mary Magdalene, tolerating prostitution as a necessary evil, the need for saving souls along with the growing interest in the fallen woman, the Middle Ages started a trend that would be followed into the twenty-first century. It is hard to tell, however, how well these Magdalene institutions succeeded in reforming the fallen woman. Certainly, a great percentage of these women were successfully married off (in such a religious environment, and with the added incentive of having all your sins remitted). There is evidence to show that many other women became nuns, or, if not, at least embraced the life of a nun within the fortified towers of the Magdalene convents.

Nevertheless, both reform and prostitution experienced a shift during the sixteenth century, when the institutionalization of prostitution was dismantled as a public endeavor, leaving the profession to be privatized. In France, as the rest of Europe, there was a ruthless backlash on women, since her legal status declined from the Middle Ages throughout the sixteenth century, something that will be observed in Ireland as well, partly as a reaction against new feminist literature.[159] Brundage states that this transition started to occur during the late fourteenth and fifteenth centuries, where active efforts to reform prostitutes gave way to simple and often harsh penalties for those who worked in the profession.[160] Further, Otis and Rollo-Koster document a shift from repenties' shelters and convents to both *nunnery penitentiaries* as well as traditional prisons: "Medieval penitential solitude was thus abandoned after the mid-sixteenth century and was replaced by penitentiary enclosure. During the seventeenth century, when women entered various oppressive refuges, galleys, hospitals, and prisons of Provence, they stepped into these shelters 'as the Magdalene had entered the Sainte-Baume'— this time not so much for penance as for punishment."[161] Finally, Brundage and Otis connect this transition to the demise of acceptance for prostitution,[162] and a corresponding effort to reform prostitutes, to the rise of Protestant and specifically the Calvinistic sensibility, which took a much harder view of prostitution than did the Catholic Church of even the early Middle Ages. The difference being in the concept of the *necessity* for social evils — for fundamental Protestantism, prostitution was simply evil, and not to be tolerated for the sake of *necessity*:

> Some of Calvin's Puritan followers took a considerably less benign view. They saw adultery and prostitution as both physical and spiritual offences that merited stern retribution, physical and spiritual, in this life as well as hereafter. Fornication or adultery, they believed, resulted from serious mental and spiritual shortcomings. Christians must keep their hearts and minds

pure and avoid situations that might lure them to pursue fleshly desired outside of marriage.[163]

Although there is strong merit in this link between society's waning tolerance for prostitution and Protestantism, a stronger argument can be located in how a convergence of events affected the world of Western Europe at this time. The most important of these changes is found in the evolving economy of the Middle Ages, where the crisis of the fourteenth century and the war economy it had fostered evolved slowly into a capitalist world system. As a result, labor practices changed, and prostitution became a privatized enterprise where repenties were forced into the labor market as cheap labor, eventually forced to work in laundries, as well as other industries such as hospitals as a form of repentance.

Rise of the World Capital System and the Turn to Privatization

As discussed previously, from the fourteenth to mid-fifteenth century, European civilization experienced a crisis as a result of the Hundred Year War, plague, famine and a shrinking economy. Because commerce, geography, and demography shrunk, and as war became a focus, trade and early capitalist expansion was halted for a war economy:

> The slow deterioration of the situation was then rendered acute by the beginnings of the Hundred Years War in 1335–1345, which turned western European state systems toward a war economy, with the particular result that there was an increased need for taxes. The taxes, coming on top of already heavy feudal dues, were too much for the producers, creating a liquidity crisis which in turn led to a return to indirect taxes and taxes in kind.[164]

Wallerstein points to several occurrences that converged to create what is now called the crisis of the Middle Ages, or the dark ages: First, war and plague decreased the population. Next, climate changes and the drop in population created a corresponding problem with agricultural production, which added an extra burden to the peasant population.[165] Agricultural problems also added to a "fiscal burden" experienced by the upper classes that then restricted their overall consumption. This lack of consumption affected the whole of the economy from production and money circulation, "which increased further the liquidity difficulties which led to royal borrowing and eventually the insolvency of the limited royal treasuries, which in turn created a credit crisis, leading to hoarding of bullion, which in turn upset the pattern of international trade."[166] The result of these and other factors caused peasant discontent and revolts, and so municipalities as well as private individuals were forced to sell larger estates to survive.[167] This of course can be related to the decline of municipal financing of public works for prostitutes that occurred from mostly the late fourteenth to fifteenth centuries.[168] Regardless, what is important is that this move also helped transform the overall medieval economy, since large estates were often sold or rented out to what Wallerstein terms "the better off peasants." This is actually seen in how the Municipal farmed out the official brothels to individuals for a specified amount of time. As Otis describes, in the fifteenth century an "indirect" system was worked out in which the municipality would farm out a brothel (*arrentement*) to an individual who, as the "middleman" or woman, would gain the profits from the house after paying off an agreed-upon and fixed sum to the municipality who owned the brothel.[169] Otis dates the earliest records of this kind of arrangement to the Toulousan's account books of the fifteenth century. Also of interest is that these official "brothel farms" were often found in "medium-sized towns on important trade routes."[170] When located on a trade route, these brothel farms were more competitive in terms of a fixed price, and they demonstrate the arrangement that Wallerstein points to — renting or selling out estates to well-off peasants. As Otis observes, the farmers (the renters of the brothels) were most likely property holders themselves, because they had to "satisfy the requirements concerning security and guarantee of payment of the farm."[171] But these renters do seem to be well-off peasants, because documents of the time documenting brothels being farmed out to craftsmen, and not those of the upper classes: "Among the sixteenth-century farmers there were a weaver, a barber, a carder, a stonecutter, and a hat maker."[172] It is important to note that renting out estates to well-off peasants helped change the basic dynamic of traditional Middle Age feudalism based on tribute and feudal rent to what became a world capitalist economy:

> It was precisely the immense pressures of this conjuncture that made possible the enormity of the social change. For what Europe was to develop and sustain now was a new form of surplus appropriation, a capitalist world-economy. It was to be based not on direct appropriation of agricultural surplus in the form of either of tribute (as had been the case for world-empires) or of feudal rents (as had been the system of European feudalism). Instead what would develop now is the appropriation of a surplus which was based on more efficient and expanded productivity (first in agriculture and later in industry) by means of a world market mechanism with the "artificial" (that is, nonmarket) assist of state machineries, none of which controlled the world market in its entirety.[173]

The European world-economy came into existence in the late fifteenth and early sixteenth century.[174] Linked by economic rather than political arrangements, this system was and is based on capitalism. Capitalism here is defined within a rather Marxist tradition: an economic system where wealth and the production of wealth are based in and around privatization, rather than being publically/commonly controlled, and where the laborer becomes a commodity; thereby, controlling "the social relations of production and the associated sociopolitical order."[175] In a capitalist world system, the state and politics enable capitalism by "assuring certain terms of trade in other economic transactions. In this way, the operation of the market (not the free operation but nonetheless its operation) creates incentives to increased productivity and all the consequent accompaniment of modern economic development."[176] In helping the market system along, the state will tend to support and promote laws that regulate labor relations in such a way that labor stays a relatively low cost commodity that serves the wider market system. In regards to prostitution and the reforming of prostitutes, as convents and halfway homes gave away to penitentiaries, there was a change in labor relations where former prostitutes were forced to work not only for repentance, but as free labor serving the state and, as shall be seen in Ireland, the church. By the sixteenth century, repenties had taken to work instead of being maintained in a home. Otis points to the repentant sisters of Toulouse, who worked in the town hospitals, for example.[177] But it is important to note that the trend during this time was away from reform homes and convents and toward prisons, where, again hated, prostitutes found themselves sent to: "the convent [which] also served as a prison for certain female criminals; an arrêt of the Parliament of Toulouse dated 3 September 1518 records that Condorine de Menville, whose crime is not mentioned, was sentenced to be 'put in the convent of the repentant sisters of Toulouse to serve God and the said convent perpetually ... with a prohibition never to leave ... on pain of hanging and strangulation.'"[178] Because prostitutes in the late Middle Ages were again considered as being *beneath the law*, the prostitute was often described as being of questionable worth because she was somehow defective and indeed simple, like a child. This will be seen in how the Sisters of Mercy and the Order of the Good Shepherd Nuns will describe the repentant prostitutes in the seventeenth to eighteenth centuries as being their "children." Because, it was argued, the fallen woman was *simple of mind*, reflecting back to the genetic, or nature argument found in the early Middle Ages, it was thought a waste to provide such a person with an education because she would not comprehend or appreciate it anyway. Armed with such rationale, the repenties became slave labor though the justification of their *simple* nature (reminiscent of the justification often used to maintain slavery).

Finally, it is important to discuss that the development into a world capitalist-system did not occur evenly throughout Europe. Proving once again that humans are "goaded by the spirit of hierarchy,"[179] a developmental and economic hierarchy developed where new growing states (rather than feudal political and social systems) divided into "core and peripheral" market areas. In such an arrangement, the peripheral/colonized economic centers worked to support the core market centers of the world: "The solidarity of the system was based ultimately on this phenomenon of unequal development."[180] This relationship became possible because of the geographical expansion of the world in relation to long-distance trade. As Howell observes in *Women, Production, and Patriarchy in Late Medieval Cities*, "It was in the context of this competitive market situation that early forms of capitalism arose, usually when long-distance merchants, using the leverage over artisans and local tradesmen which access to imported raw materials or markets gave them, took over production processes themselves."[181] Within this new geographic relationship, core states (such as England) benefited from the labor and resources of semi-peripheral and colonized/peripheral states (this work will examine Ireland, but Wallerstein focuses on Eastern Europe and Latin America). Population within the peripheral states experienced a "second serfdom" becoming a coerced workforce through colonialization by core states. As will be examined in the next few chapters, England's colonial efforts in Ireland forced coercive labor practices when England replaced Irish landowners with English subjects. These new powerful English landowners then worked to enslave much of the Irish population through force. One offshoot of this new world economic system was the rise of not only coerced labor, but also slavery: "If slavery is to pay when applied to large-scale enterprises, there must be plenty of cheap human flesh on the market. You can only get it by war or slave-raiding. So a society can hardly base much of its economy on domesticated human being unless it has at hand feebler societies to defeat or to raid."[182] With the case of prostitution and the corresponding effort of repentance, there was often a great difference in how these women were dealt with depending upon their geographic location in this new world capitalist system. Although not looked to as being equal members of the community, repenties in core states (this work examines those in England) tended to fare much better and were treated better than those Magdalene repenties in peripheral states (this work will specifically examine those repenties in Ireland). The difference being one of true reform. Whereas many women in Magdalene homes in England received training (including literacy education) to help her return to the marketplace in a respectable position, and her labor was somewhat regulated and institutions inspected, Ireland's Magdalene convents and laundries eventually imprison their inmates (often for life), and did not offer education and training outside of the training needed to provide free and coerced labor for the convent and often for the state itself.

PART TWO

The State, Colonization, and the Female as Citizen

Chapter Four

Ancient Irish Law and Women's Status in Precolonial Ireland

> A Medb co méd búafaid
> Nít cerb caíme núachair
> Dearb leam is tú is búachail
> Ar Crúachain na clad.
> Art glor is art gairgnert.
>
> O Medb great in boastfulness!
> The beauty of a bridegroom does not touch you.
> I am certain that you are master in Crúachu of the mounds.
> Loud your voice, great your fierce strength.
> —O'Rahilly, Táin Bó Cúalinge

Ireland has the most interesting and *closed door* history on the Magdalene convents, asylums, and laundries. These later institutions were not maintained exclusively for reforming prostitutes, although this how they got their start. Eventually, any undesirable, marginalized, odd, headstrong, or unwed woman was placed into Magdalene laundries. The second half of this work, *The Colonization of the State and Women*, will examine the relationship between the core market state of England, and England's peripheral/colony, Ireland. The discussion regarding the process of colonizing Ireland (chapter four and five), will demonstrate how Ireland's understanding and formulation of citizenship and nation building, in relation to women and the laundries, led to the encouragement of widespread magdalenism, as well as a convent asylum system that profited off unchecked and unregulated coercive labor. Originally private charitable institutions, the Irish Magdalene laundries became institutionalized, administered and controlled by the Church of Ireland, while being financially and legally supported by the Irish State. Anyone who has any knowledge of Ireland's strict Catholic and moralistic society will not be amazed by the fact that women who did not fit into the mold were hidden away—

fortified behind towers. It is simply another example of magdalenism and of keeping women under control, with the idea that they, along with their sexual drives, cannot be trusted. Regardless, it is essential to acknowledge that Ireland today is an extraordinary contrast to the Ireland of yesteryear. Concerning women, law, and structural society, these two Irelands reflect two different civilizations. Indeed, what makes the Irish example extremely interesting is that before the colonization of Ireland by England, Irish women under the early Irish law, or what is often referred to as the Brehon Laws, were treated more fairly in life and marriage than their modern, Romanized counterpart. However, between the late 1500s to the 1600s, a convergence occurred where a combination of colonization, land enclosure, labor dislocation from means of production, reforming questions of citizenship and reinforced traditional Roman Catholic ideology, as well as Protestant patriarchy worked to demote women's status in modern Ireland to, essentially, that of conditional and, for the Magdalene, non-citizen status. Conditionally, the modern Irish woman (1800s–1990s) could enjoy citizenship rights in the home as mother, wife, daughter, and sister. Here, her rights were recognized, while her labor remained unpaid. If she was to break unspoken moral codes of conduct and fall outside of the narrow bonds of contingent citizenship, she could become a Magdalene. As a Magdalene, the modern Irish woman lived and existed in the role of non-citizen and, like her medieval prostitute counterpart, was understood as being *beneath* or *outside* the law. When comparing the rights given by law to woman in early versus later Ireland (including free Ireland), what is revealed is that the ancient Irish female enjoyed more complete citizenship rights. Although under the Brehon laws women were seen as being legally incompetent,[1] women were granted citizenship rights that allowed them the ability to make a contract, own land and other property, as well as rights protecting any offspring in case of rape or abduction.[2] Subsequently, once demoted to little more than a possession and often to a non-citizen by later Irish law, it became easy for society, state and the Catholic Church to hide away unwanted women into Magdalene laundries, while forcing them to work as slave labor — legalizing magdalenism on a vast scale. In this chapter, the general societal structure of early Ireland before colonization will be examined, as well as the ancient Brehon Laws dealing with marriage and sexual relations. Such a presentation sets the scene for how the convergence of economic, social, and spiritual practices occurring in Ireland between the late 1500s to the early 1600s ended up creating ripe conditions for the later rise of the laundries. In chapter five, these convergences in relation to the rise of the capital world system will be discussed, as well as the process of England's colonization of Ireland. As viewed partly through Marx's primitive accumulation, the concept of landownership, enclosures, and the English insistence on agricultural practices had a devastating effect for the Irish population and the traditional Brehon Laws, which ruled over gender relations. Through this transition of land ownership, enclosure, privatization, and dislocation of the Irish people, there was a corresponding push and pull between traditional Roman Catholic and Protestant teachings that insisted on a strict patriarchy that fundamentally changed relations between the sexes in Ireland. Chapters six and seven will compare and contrast the Magdalene laundries in Ireland and England from the late 1700s to the last laundry that closed its doors in 1996. Central to this tale is the story of how core versus peripheral states work to grow, develop, and nurture nationhood in relation to economics and inclusion or exclusion of national citizenship. By looking at the numerous attempts to regulative, stipulate, and legislate poverty, gender relations, and labor organization within a growing capitalist system, what will be revealed is a stark contrast in how nations work to hegemonically control and maintain citizens, while defining nationhood. Thus by focusing on the *Factory and Workshop Act* debates, 1895 to 1906, in the British Parliament (chapter seven), this work will be able to clearly demonstrate the structural, ideological, rhetorical and organizational difference between Ireland and England's approach to citizenship and nationhood. Finally this book will end by examining the modern fallout regarding the Magdalene laundries and the process of magdalenism in Ireland. With the release of the *Ryan Report* on institutional child abuse in Ireland, released May 2009, there is a deeper realization that magdalenism, conceptually widened as a concept to including all unwanted and deemed disposable members of a society, has victimized and divided Ireland. Yet Ireland is not entirely unique, for a similar victimization occurred in Australia and is presently happening to women and other marginalized members of various countries in Africa and the Middle East. Magdalenism, it seems, is not new or old but an evolving and persistent way to marginalize, control, and profit off of our fellow human. However, understanding the motivation behind magdalenism must first take us to the pre-modern state of Ireland. That is, Ireland before English colonization.

Understanding Precolonalized Ireland

Before being able to grasp the monumental structural and cultural convergences that Ireland and her people experienced as a result of England's colonization process in the late 1500s to 1600s, it is helpful to view Ireland before colonization, and how Ireland viewed women's rights and status within its social structures and laws. In *The Rise of the Network Society,* the sociologist Manuel Castells rightly points out that "cultures manifest themselves fundamentally through their embeddedness in institutions and organizations...."

This organizational logic manifests itself under different forms in various cultural and institutional contexts."[3] In order to understand how Ireland's culture and society, its institutions and organizations, were fundamentally changed, her people displaced from their own culture, and her women placed into Magdalene laundries, it is helpful to be familiar with her institutions and organizations before the process of transformation. Precolonized Ireland was unlike most of feudal Europe in several fundamental ways. First, Ireland was never colonized by Rome and so was not saturated with Roman law and culture or institutional organization. Historian Anne Chambers in her work *Granualile*, where she examines the life of the Irish female pirate Grace O'Malley, states: "The Romans overcame Celtic nations from Asia Minor right across to Britain. Only Ireland had remained outside Roman influence."[4] Regarding early Irish law, the Irish scholar Fergus Kelly also notes that surviving Celtic law texts reflect the monastic influences of spelling, script, punctuation and abbreviations, as well as grammar,[5] demonstrating canon but not Roman influence.[6] Accordingly, although it is suggested that St. Patrick brought with him not only Christianity but Roman law, it is nevertheless apparent that what little Roman law and culture was brought to Ireland, it was not enough to transform Irish law, cultural, or organizational systems since the overall structure of Irish society from the time of Patrick to the 1500s was comparatively unchanged.[7]

Further, the feudal system with its division between lord and serf did not exist in Ireland until the colonization of Ireland by England; and, as Irish historian MacManus points out in his longstanding work, *The Story of the Irish Race*: "The system in Ireland was something more like the patriarchal system of the east. The tribe resolved itself into family groups called *derbfine*[8] centering around one leading family from whom the chief was always chosen."[9] This leads us to the third distinctive aspect of Irish hierarchy[10]— the law of rulership inheritance was not necessarily or absolutely determined by the bloodline of the eldest son born until, again, English colonization. Reminiscent of Duby's observation of medieval European society's emphasis on hierarchy, Kelly also describes the law of rank in early Ireland as both hierarchal and inegalitarian.[11] Although based in family, inheritance was divided up among the family, not simply going to the eldest son.[12] Regarding leadership, whenever a king or chief was selected by a clan, there were general elections in which only the strongest and the considered wisest ruler was chosen.[13] Steven G. Ellis, in *Ireland in the Age of The Tudors 1447–1603*, states that this type of rule was referred to by the English as "custom of gavelkind" and that "theoretically, he who was 'eldest and worthiest' was chosen by the territory's gentry in their assembly, at which both related and unrelated clans of different surname was present."[14] Unlike Romanized law, being the eldest son did not guarantee the right, or absolute assumption, to election or property, and there were even laws that stipulated for the loss of social and political rank, as well as the gaining of such rank regardless of when you were born.[15] Rather more often than not, as Ellis explains, leadership and hierarchy were determined by "a bloody succession struggle ... a source of serious instability within the lordship and an incentive to outsiders to intervene."[16] Such unromanized organizational structures can also be viewed with the "class" system in early Ireland.

Class Distinction in Medieval Ireland

The class system in Ireland was not a caste system because only a very few members of the population could be considered "serfs," or, as it is called in Gaelic, *fuidir* (semi-freemen or a tenant at will — slaves, in Gaelic were called *mug*). The concept of a *fuidir* class is a difficult one to grasp because the early social/political class system was not like that of England or other Romanized states that sported a centralized government or kinship. Irish class and structural/organizational system rather contained a series of clans organized around territorial kingdom space, or *túaths*, which each had its own hierarchical system. So although a sense of shared culture united the Irish Celts, there was not a corresponding sense of political/governmental culture. Within this territorial set-up, the highest rank in privileged (*nemed*) society was that of the supreme king or the *rí ruirech*, followed by the overking (or great king) of a few petty kingdoms (*rí túath*), and then petty kingship or a king in charge of a single petty kingdom.[17] As Foster explains the system in *The Oxford Illustrated History of Ireland*: "The *tí túaithe*, King of a local petty kingdom [*túath*[18] or territory]; the *ruiri* [*rí túath*] 'great king,' who was overlord of a number of petty kings; and the *rí ruirech* 'king of the overkings,' who was the king of a province and a ruler of considerable power and significance."[19] Donnchadh Ó Corráin, a scholar of early Irish history, states that there were 80 to 100 different petty kingdoms in Ireland, but it is impossible to know how many existed at any given time.[20] By the eighth century, the *rí* and the *ruiri's power* were disappearing, which meant that the *tí túaithe* (local kings) was most prevalent. Like Ó Corráin, MacManus suggests that geographically, there were approximately two hundred *túaths* in Ireland at any given time and that each *túath* was ruled over by the petty king or the *tí túaithe*.[21] Furthermore, each *túath* land area was subdivided into *ballyetaighs* (around 30) and the *ballyetaighs* were further divided into twelve *seasreachs* (about one hundred and twenty acres). The *ballyetaighs* were basically designated as land for the "grazing for four herds of seventy-five cows each," guaranteeing that enough space was available so that cows would not have to touch each other.[22] Fundamental to this system, compared to the future English system of privatization through land enclosures, was the important concept of *kin-land*.[23] As Kelly points out, the early Irish did value private rights to property, ownership and even extended some private rights over mines and fishing rights.[24] Nevertheless, those that did have exclusive rights to land rented out large portions to tenants or *céiles*, who "formed the *féine*, or the general body of the people."[25] With regard to land "ownership," however, as Steven Ellis points out, land was held by members for a limited amount of time, thereby presenting a different understanding of "private" ownership than is normally associated with privatization:

> Land was usually held by individual members for a limited term, frequently one year only but sometimes longer, and then redistributed among coheirs, a practice which militated against intensive exploitation of the land, improvements or substantial buildings: even the nobles lived in cabins made of boughs of trees and covered with turf. Since land was plentiful, however, and peace precarious, there was in any case little incentive to development; but if the co-heirs agreed, a permanent partition of the lands could be made.[26]

Besides land, nobles also rented out cattle to client citizens (*céile*),[27] free and unfree: "The céile who owned his own stock, or who had to borrow but little, was of much higher standing than the céile who had to borrow or rent his stock. The former was called a free céile, and the latter an unfree because he was bound to those above him by so many obligations."[28] This setup also brings out another unique feature to ancient and medieval Irish civilization — that of wealth. Unlike other feudal and caste systems, wealth was determined not by land but by cattle. Social anthropologist Audrey Smedley, in *Race in North America*, points out that like other nomadic people "in the Old World," the Irish, as a herding people, gained their wealth in cattle.[29] Importantly and distinctly from English agricultural practice, land could be commonly shared, whereas cattle had to be owned outright or rented. Furthermore, agriculture and farming emphasis was not fundamental to Irish culture as evidence suggests that precolonized Ireland relied little on formal farming techniques.[30] These aspects, Irish wealth versus agricultural concerns, would become a fundamental point of contention between the Irish and the English. This ideology and structural difference, as well as the demotion of women's rights in relation to such contentions, will be examined in the following chapter.

Situated below the *céile* were the *féine*, which consisted of two classes: those free (Cottier or *bothach* and the hereditary serf or *sencléithe*)[31] and those unfree (*fuidir*). The *bothach* and *sencléithe* were the general laborers, horse tenders, herdsmen and so forth who were supported by their family, but who had no land rights or a voice in the tribal council.[32] However, they were considered "citizens" or members of the tribe. According to MacManus, the *fuidir*, on the other hand, were not considered "citizens," were beneath the law, and consisted of "strangers, fugitives, war captives, condemned criminals or people who had to give up their freedom in order to work out a debt or fine that they could not pay."[33] Regarding the *fuidir*[34] Kelly states that unlike base clients and freemen of legal "independent" capacity, the *fuidir* could not make a "legal contract without the permission of his lord."[35] Citizenship then was only denied to those people of the *túath* who were basically considered outlaws or who gave up citizenship status as a result of mounting debt and therefore were not able to provide for their sustenance. However, their status as non-citizens was not an absolute designation and could be changed:

> They had the right of renting a little land and gradually acquiring property — till, in the course of a certain number of years, having accumulated some substance, and having proved to the tribe that they were people of character, they could, by the general voice of the tribe, be received into the fold, and become of the *féine*.[36]

Finally, it is important to note that all these class relations, property rights, as well as wealth and servitude were conducted through the Brehon civil laws. Early Irish law can be pieced together through surviving Wisdom[37] and Law[38] texts that date from the fourteenth to the sixteenth century; however, as Kelly points out, linguistic evidence "shows that many of these texts were originally written in the seventh–eighth centuries."[39] Further, when the Christian missionaries arrived in Ireland (fifth century), early Irish law was already well established without "outside influence."[40] The Christian influence brought with it not only the Christian Canon but also the introduction of Latin letters, which "revolutionized the transmission of legal material" (established between the seventh and eighth centuries).[41] The most extensive collection left of Ireland's ancient law-books is what is commonly referred to today as the *Senchus Mor* (Literal translation being the "Great Tradition"): "The most important collection of Old Irish Law-texts.... It seems likely to have been put together at a law-school (or law-schools) in the territory of the Northern Féni, i.e. roughly the Northern midlands."[42] Fundamental to the *Senchus Mor*, and indeed all of Irish law, was the concept of public opinion over legislative law. Likewise, the foundation of law was based around oral contracts "'for,' says the old law-giver, 'the world would be in confusion if verbal contracts were not binding.'"[43] Since this system of civic law was based within the concept of contract, it reflected a mindset different from Roman Catholic civic law embedded in the philosophy of patriarchy.

De-evolution of Women's Rights in Ireland

A disturbing dichotomy exists between the status women once held in ancient Ireland, compared to the status of "modern" Irish women up to the end of the twentieth century. In fact, the difference in rights held by women in ancient times are so extreme that one wonders if they are examining the same country altogether. Unlike most Anglicized countries, women had more rights by law in ancient Ireland through the sixteenth century than they enjoyed throughout much of so-called modernity. It would seem, at least when dealing with the subject of women's status, that Ireland has de-evolved, while much of Western society has evolved toward a more just, equal balance in governing the rights of gender. The most common argument offered as to why an Irish woman lost her status in society is that of the Catholic Church and its relationship to Irish government and society in reacting against English *Protestant* influence. This line of rationale is similar to both Otis'[44] and Brundage's[45] argument that prostitutes lost their status in Medieval Europe because of Protestant and specifically Calvinistic creed. Although this argument has some merit, it is deterministic and does not really consider the wider picture, involving multiple factors apparent in this transition, including the change in hegemonic power relations between Irish and English organization, as well as economic factors. Up until the end of the 1500s, women still enjoyed considerable, although not absolute, rights under Brehon Law one thousand years after the coming of St. Patrick and the Catholic Church. Although the Catholic Church is partially responsible for diminishing women's status in Ireland, it is the destruction of the Brehon Laws because of institutionalized, centralized, English law, and later the modern state, that ultimately robbed women of their rights and citizenship status. In effect, the Irish Catholic Church was only reacting against these new conditions. In order to understand the relationship between women's status in ancient and "modern" Ireland, the influence that Brehon Laws had on women until the end of the sixteenth century must be explored; and, second, what happened to women once the Brehon Laws were outlawed through the process of colonization must be considered as well. This overview will form the basis of why Irish women were condemned to Magdalene laundries, because losing their rights under ancient law meant a loss of freedom, respect, and ultimately citizenship for modern women in Ireland.

The documented history for Ireland began around the seventh century during the early Irish Christian era. Until this point in time, the Celts had an oral history rather than a written one. As Kelly observes, until Giraldus Cambrensis's *Topography of Ireland*[46] in the late twelfth century, there is really no outside documentation of Irish history or culture besides the native and

Latin "law-texts, wisdom-texts, sagas, histories, praise-poetry, annals, genealogies, saint's lives, religious poetry, penitentials and monastic rules."[47] To comprehend any of Ireland's early history before the seventh century, and how it regarded the feminine element in society, it is helpful to consider the sagas, myths and legends of Celtic Ireland. Many scholars contend that oral history in the form of sagas represents the "poetic imagination" of the creator, and therefore cannot offer an accurate picture of the society. The philosopher Hegel, in judging civilizations in his 1813 work, *The Philosophy of History*, theorized that an absence of written history hinders the important role of memory, the collective, cultural memory of a society. It creates, for Hegel, an absence of memory.[48] However, this work argues that these myths/sagas help reflect the political and social atmosphere of the time they were created, and provide us with a mirror into the past, a reflection of what was and what might have been. Furthermore, these tales are uniquely Celtic and, therefore, fairly void of "imperial" assumptions found in later stories about the Irish. Again, as Edward Said argues, a great deal of literature based in the eighteenth through twentieth century is embedded with imperialistic ideology, which assumes the rightful place of the dominating few over the dominated many.[49] Further, as early Irish law also demonstrates, stories, poetry and the poets were central to early Irish society. Indeed, Kelly reminds his reader that the only "lay professional who [had] full *nemed* [privileged] status" was the poet (*fili* or *éces*).[50] Further, it was the poet who could damage or increase a person's status through verses of either satire or praise. In this capacity the poet and his or her[51] story were seen as embodying supernatural power that could be used for both good and evil.[52] Because the poet and the poet's stories were so central to early Irish culture, in looking at Ireland's pre-dominated literature, a better picture arises depicting law and life before English colonization.

Celtic Ireland as Understood Through its Stories

Ironically, it is said that Ireland's pagan sagas were saved from extinction because of St. Patrick's crusade to convert Ireland to Christianity. Catholic monks carefully documented the Celtic sagas, leaving us a glimmer of the pagan Celtic civilization, and the early roles and status of women in Ireland:

> Christianity came over from Britain, propagated in particular by St. Patrick (who died in 461). It overwhelmed Ireland, putting an end to the Druidic worship. But, in contrast with the case in Gaul, Christianity did not destroy the Gaelic language or the Celtic traditions. It could even be argued that the Irish Church saved all there was to be saved of Celticism: it was the monks who transcribed the precious literary manuscripts with their typically Celtic and pagan inspiration into the Gaelic language.[53]

It is difficult to think about Ireland without reflecting on her feminine elements, as her history is riddled with and dominated by women: Warrior Queens, Fairy Women, Druidresses and Goddesses. Peter Ellis, a popular scholar in Celtic mythology, states, "We not only have a pantheon of goddesses but numerous mortal women who display a range of characters and positions in society. There are powerful women, weak women, serious women, capricious women, vengeful women and ambitious women."[54] Ireland itself was named repeatedly after goddesses: first as Banba, then as Fotla, and finally as Eriu (Erinn), all which were powerful women and deemed descendants from the Danann goddess Brigit, who went from being a pagan goddess to a Christian saint — Saint Bridget. In this light, women seem to be at the forefront of defining Ireland. However, Kelly strongly argues against such a reading, stating that although women are prominently portrayed in Old and Middle Irish literature, he believes that this portrayal is an exaggeration of reality, because "the annals provide no instance of a female political or military leader,"[55] except for one noted exception:

> In non-literary sources I know of only one dubious reference to a female ruler or military leader. This is in a difficult passage in the law-text *Bretha Crólige* which lists some categories of women who are particularly important in the *túath*, including "the woman who turns back the streams of war" (*ben sues srutha coctha for cula*) and "the hostage ruler (?)" (*rechtaid géill*). The former could refer to a female military leader, through the glossator may be right in identifying her as an abbess for female hermit "who turns back the many sins of wars through her prayers." The term *rechtaid géill* is equally obscure: the glossator takes it to refer to a woman ruler who takes hostages, citing Queen Medb as an example.[56]

Although Kelly might be right in his instance that powerful women were the exception and not the rule, it is equally important to point out not only the bias language used in the above passage ("dubious reference," "difficult passage," "obscure") but also the consideration of who, gender wise, wrote the laws of Ireland down in the law and wisdom texts? First, Kelly's use of "dubious" is troublesome because this is a loaded rhetorical term when used in relation to women, their access to power, and their relation to law. Why is the text or reference dubious only when it is in relation to women? Is the authorship in dispute or possibly the text itself? Because Kelly does not address the intent behind this key term, the reader is left to wonder if he simply wants to dismiss any reference that allots the female a higher role in the community than he is comfortable with. Indeed, every passage that discusses a female in relation to power positions in Kelly's *A Guide to Early Irish Law* is accompanied by words of doubt and suspect. Regardless, what should also be noted by Kelly, and is not, is what Duby[57] referred to as the "cultural monopoly" of those who had to the power to read and write and subliquently, to place in print the early Irish law. Yes, there is little mention of women in power positions in the surviving law texts (most of which are little more than "fragmentary quotations imbedded in a mass of later commentary"),[58] but these texts were written by men, Christian monks and possibly clerks, who were likely all from the same class of learned men.[59] And so these authors were influenced by not only Irish culture but also Catholic Canon religious law, which, as was demonstrated in Part One of this work, held a "dubious" (borrowing Kelly's term) view of women in general. Regardless, although Kelly is likely correct in his assessment that women did not regularly hold powerful positions in ancient Ireland, it would be absurd to ignore those moments when women leaders are mentioned and indeed celebrated in early law and literature simply because it was not mentioned often enough.

Whether the women in Irish myths and lore are renowned goddesses or common everyday women, one of the most endearing and fantastic aspects about their characterization are the fact that they are all well-rounded, well-developed, and dynamic characters. This aspect, for myths and folklore in general, is unique. Most forms of myths tend to offer the reader one-dimensional characters. There are good characters that are innocent and/or clever, and bad characters that are wicked (witches, demons and crooks). In general, the typical myth offers us little growth and development of character. Good almost always triumphs over evil, and justice becomes predictable as the bad characters usually get exactly what they deserve — nothing more and nothing less. However, Irish myths sharply depart from this typical form of storytelling, and even more delightful, offer female characters that are dynamic and fully developed. As Peter Berresford Ellis succinctly explains, "The dumb blonde would not stand much of a chance in ancient Celtic society. Indeed, neither would the women who denigrated her femaleness. Mind and body were not separate issues in the myths but complementary sides of the whole person."[60]

Since "mind and body" were not separate forbidden issues, it is not surprising to find that sexuality was also something freely explored by both male and female characters in Irish lore. Sexual freedom is seen not only in the male characters, but in the female characters as well. Indeed, unlike many other Romanized cultures, such sexual expressions in women were not seen as something evil or dirty, but rather a natural way of being — a stark difference to modern Ireland, where a woman's sexuality is greatly feared. This difference can be viewed with Rosemary Mahoney's, *Whoredom in Kimmage: The World of Irish Women*, observation regarding the plight of modern Irish women:

> I had seen the article. An *Irish Times* reporter had discovered in the French magazine *Marie-Claire* a negative report on the status of Irish women and had written up a précis of the report. The French journalist had written,

"just two steps away from here, women are still living in the middle ages." The *Marie-Claire* article was a bleak portrait of a society where Catholic priests objecting to the use of condoms were allowed to announce on the radio that the AIDS virus was "smaller than the pores in a condom," where husbands beat their wives, and families of nine lived on a mere £160 per week, and where sex education was seen as "an incitement to debauchery." In short, Ireland was a society which, "by the voices of the Constitution and the Church, exerts an enormous pressure on women in order that they conform to an obsolete ideal of femininity and motherhood." I had seen the report and had to acknowledge that much of it was true.[61]

Conversely, the female character in ancient Irish literature was almost required to be a wise, complex and, often, openly sexual character like her male counterparts. Cahill demonstrates this idea while looking at the powerful Queen Mebd in his work, *How the Irish Saved Civilization*:

> The sexual frankness of these characters is unlike anything in classical literature, even in the folk epics of Homer ... Medb's offer of "her two friendly thighs" to seal the bargain with Daire is obviously thrown in casually. And it is just as obvious that Medb is not the remotest sense a needy woman — the very phrase would curdle before her! Rather, in early Irish literature both men and women openly admire one another's physical endowments and invite one another to bed without formality.[62]

Queen Medb is not the only strong female character found in Irish mythology, since there is a plethora to choose from, but for purposes of this example, Queen Medb's story is important because it will later serve to demonstrate women's rights in early Irish law.

In the famous Irish epic, the *Táin Bó Cuailnge*, which is often referred to as the Irish *Iliad*,[63] one of the main characters is the warrior queen Medb. She is described as a "very determined, forceful, strong, devious and oftentimes bloodthirsty queen" of Connacht.[64] The *Táin Bó Cuailnge* recounts Queen Medb's desire for the famous Bull of Cuailnge that lived and belonged in the Kingdom of Ulster. She makes several different attempts to obtain the bull, but when all fails, in true Irish fashion, she raises an army from the many kingdoms of Ireland, and prepares to invade Ulster and take the bull for herself. The story of Queen Medb shows her as a dynamic and strong woman, since she rules like a king, wars like a man, and takes lovers as she sees fit. Yet she is always feminine. One interesting comment made by Queen Medb, to her best-known husband, Ailill, was regarding her view of how she sees a life mate:

> My husband must be free from cowardice, and free from avarice, and free from jealousy; for I am brave in battles and combats, and it would be a discredit to my husband if I were braver than he. I am generous and a great giver of gifts, and it would be a disgrace to my husband if he were less gen-

erous than I am. And it would not suit me at all if he were jealous, for I have never denied myself the man I took a fancy to ... and I never shall whatever husband I have now or may have hereafter.[65]

By portraying highly developed and dynamic female characters in Irish mythology, it is demonstrated how the Irish had great respect for the feminine element within society. However, larger-than-life characters, such as Queen Medb, may lead one to assume that the Celtic women in Irish lore are nothing more than highly idealized depictions. This is something that Proinsias MacCana, in *Celtic Mythology*, considers: "We must ask whether a society which in its literature attributes such independence to its women characters as does much of the early Irish literature would on the other hand deny it or rigidly curtail it in real life."[66] MacCana's question is not without validity, especially when one observes the disapproval modern Irish society holds for its female element. Nevertheless, one reason that the mythological female characters represent the Irish cultural attitudes toward women is the fact that the female actions and positions in these myths are not contrary to the early Celtic laws and customs of the time. An excellent example of this would be Queen Medb and her relationship with her husband. So when considering Ireland's past, it is not just her mythology, songs and literature, that demonstrate more or less equal status between men and women, but also her laws — The Brehon Laws.

Ireland's Brehon Laws

It is one thing for a society to elevate women's status in myth and song, but it is completely another thing to do so with its laws: "One will find that women were regarded in the laws of early Ireland with a humanity which is refreshing. Whatever happened sometimes in practice is another matter. At least the law was always on their side."[67] The Brehon Laws[68] (in their *purest* form before the March Laws, which combined both English and Irish laws) are understood to have existed in ancient Ireland, and by "'ancient Ireland' [it] is understood to refer to the period from the dawn of history until the coming of the Normans in the twelfth century."[69] However, even with the coming of the Normans and the strength of the English Crown, the Brehon Laws were used in practice and continued to benefit women and her status up until the early 1600s:

> The Brehon Law remained the law of three-quarters of Ireland for several centuries after the coming of the English — was in fact adopted by a large portion of the English settlers themselves, to the exclusion of the Anglo-Norman code — and it may be said not to have gone out of existence as living law until the sixteenth Century.[70]

As mentioned before, Ireland's documented history did not occur until the coming of Christianity and, as tradition holds, St. Patrick. Hence, like the traditional Irish myths, there is little that is known about the Brehon Laws before the coming of St. Patrick and Christianity. It is known, however, that whatever face Christianity may have held in Romanized societies, it is not the same face worn by the Christian Irish people of ancient times. St. Patrick, when bringing Christianity to Ireland, did so in his own unique way, as Thomas Cahill explains: "Patrick's gift to the Irish was his Christianity—for the first de-Romanized Christianity in human history, a Christianity without the sociopolitical baggage of the Greco–Roman world, a Christianity that completely inculturated itself into the Irish scene."[71] Hence, as discussed above, Celtic Ireland continued to be Celtic Ireland, except now it also contained many elements of Christianity: "Indeed, the survival of an Irish psychological identity is one of the marvels of the Irish story. Unlike the continental church fathers, the Irish never troubled themselves overmuch about eradicating pagan influences, which they tended to wink at and enjoy."[72] Keeping this in mind, it is not surprising to find that St. Patrick and the Irish Catholic Monks are traditionally credited with saving the Brehon Laws from extinction.

Only about five volumes of the ancient Brehon Laws still exist, most of which are the *Senchas Már*, traditionally said to be St. Patrick's effort, and their ordinances, called the *Cáin Padraic* (the Statute Law of Patrick)[73]:

> When it is stated that in the ancient glosses upon the Senchus Mor citations are made from no less than fourteen different books of civil law; and that the Cormac in his later Glossary (about the tenth century) quotes from five law books only one of which is among the fourteen of the Senchus glosses, that also will give the reader a little idea of the multitude of law books that here must have been prior to the tenth century in which the scholar Cormac wrote.[74]

Further, considering the vastness of the original documented law, Kelly divides the *Senchas Már* into three parts: 1) the first third or the *train toísech*, the second third or the *train medónach*, and the final third or the *train déidenach*.[75] The laws that are still in existence throw a flood of light onto the intellectual and social conditions of early Irish civilization and how that civilization viewed their gender differences.

The Brehon Laws, Sex, Marriage and Ownership

During a time of history where the Romanized West denied women such basic rights as land ownership, education and independence, Patrick's Catholic Ireland granted women rights and opportunity in the Catholic Church, the law as autonomous beings, and land/wealth ownership rights. As Sjöö and Mor point out, women were "relatively free" because they had greater economic, social and even sexual "autonomy" than their counterparts in other parts of the Roman West. Further, they point out that the "early Celtic Christian Church was suspect to the Roman Catholic orthodoxy precisely because it was pro-women — women celebrated mass. Women priests, called *conhospitae*, administered the sacramental wine while male priests distributed the wafers."[76] This relatively progressive view of women's rights and status can also be seen through the Brehon Laws dealing with marriage, divorce, and the division/ownership of property. It is significant to remember that although unique women such as Queen Medb might have existed, the majority of women in early Ireland were wives and mothers — not queens. For this reason it is extremely important to examine the laws on marriage, divorce and dowries, provided for under the Brehon Laws, as they demonstrate how women and their worth were viewed by society.[77] Moreover, these laws offer a starting point from where it can be demonstrated which rights women lost with the destruction of the Brehon Laws and the institution of English Law. These laws also offer the understanding that no union between a man and a woman was to be considered lightly, and even though the Christian faith was well established, it must be pointed out that most unions were made under the Brehon Laws (focusing on marriage as a contract) and not through the Catholic Church (which focused on marriage as a spiritual contract).[78]

Lawful Relationships

Irish historians Patrick C. Power, in *Sex and Marriage in Ancient Ireland*, and Fergus Kelly, *A Guide to Early English Law*, offer an important overview concerning the Irish Brehon Laws detailing sex and marriage in ancient Ireland. Power points out that there were ten different types of *Lánamnas* (marriages), or sexual contracts, recognized by the Brehon Laws.[79] The first type of contract was a union of equal rank or "union of joint property" (*lánamnas comthinchuir*).[80] In this case the couple was equal in rank and property, "in which both partners contribute movable goods (*tinchor*),"[81] and it is considered the most ideal type of union by Celtic societal standards. The second *lánamnas* was that of a union between unequal ranked people, where a woman was supported on a man's property (*lánamnas mná for fertinchur*), because she comes to the union with little or nothing in ways of *tinchor*.[82] The third type of union, and a literary account of this kind can be found with Queen Medb in the *Táin Bó Cuailnge*, was when a man was supported on a women's property (*lánamnas fir for bantinchur*): "In this case it is stipulated that the man must do the work on the woman's property, such as tilling the land and tending the cattle."[83] Consequently, he was not a *kept man*. Also stipulated by the lawgivers, was when a woman was received in place of a wife—the concubine—whose status and rights as a person were recognized and safeguarded.[84] The fifth type of union legislated for what resembles a modern relationship, since it stipulates for when a couple does not live together permanently and also does not rely on each other for financial support.[85] The seventh type of union provided for was that of the wandering soldier and his wife: "Evidently this type of union had to be specifically recognized because all the other partnerships were between people who had a stake in the rural community. The soldier and his wife were footloose people who did not fit into the normal type of community in ancient Ireland."[86]

The next two unions legislated for dealt with relations established out of deception. In these cases, the law strove to right the wrongs of unions established through sexual deceptions that might also result in pregnancy and birth. The focus of these laws is not simply on the wronged man or women, but on the children. Regardless of how a pregnancy occurred, "the title implies that a man began the sexual partnership by some ruse such as having intercourse with a woman who was asleep. He incurred specific obligations to her and her child or children in this case."[87] The related ninth union specifically examined rape: "While the perpetrator was punished for the violence offered and the breach of honour to the girl and her kindred, any child or children born of the illicit union is recognized and the situation regularized."[88] The final type of union provided for under the law was the sexual relationship between "idiots or lunatics."[89] Finally, Kelly argues that the different types of unions were also complicated by the widespread practice of polygamy, which is substantiated by the fact that the law texts tended to distinguish and provide for two different ranking of wives: "a man's chief wife or *cétmuinter* (no doubt normally married to him in one of the first three forms of unions) and his concubine (*adaltrach* or *dormun*)."[90] Although the chief wife lived under the husband's rule, the concubine had the right to choose to live under her mate's, her kin's family, or her son's rule. However, the chief wife was worth more in terms of status since the concubine only received half the status of the first wife.[91]

It is important to note concerning all these types of legal unions that there was a custom that allowed for a one-year trial marriage, where either the woman or the man could walk away from the marriage on February 1, the *Feast of Imbolc*, "which meant that Irish marriages were renewable yearly, like magazine subscriptions or insurance policies."[92] Interestingly, the last recorded one-year marriage was in the mid–1500s with Granuaile (Grace O'Malley), the famous sea captain of Ireland. As Chambers recounts, toward the end of her first year of marriage to Richard Burke, Granuaile had taken over Burke's castle (Carraigahowley) and along with her warriors and followers, locked him out of the castle, and "from the ramparts [she] shouted down the words of divorce, 'Richard Burke, I dismiss you,' thereby at one fell swoop acquiring a castle and ridding herself of a husband."[93] As one can see, from the descriptions of law concerning marriages, the female element was both considered and respected. Power comments on the general civility of law toward women and children:

> The principal comment to be made on the ten cases quoted above is that there could be no such thing as an "illegitimate child." All children born to a woman, no matter what the circumstances of their conception, were legislated for and their right recognized. The lawgivers were not hamstrung by the idea of a single lawful marriage, the issue of which was alone "legitimate." All children were "legitimate." Victorian and modern English and Irish laws made maintenance orders against the putative fathers of children born out of wedlock, and that was all. The child was not recognized in his birth certificate as the offspring of his father. The column for that detail was left blank, as if the mother had conceived through parthenogenesis! Such a crazy situation did not exist in ancient Ireland.[94]

An interesting fact about the varying types of marriage is how they are contained not only in the Brehon Laws, but also in Irish mythology. The Great Saga of *Táin Bó Cuailnge*, as Squire recounts in *Celtic Myths and Legends*, starts off with Queen Medb and her husband comparing their wealth while sitting up in bed. The entire conflict, and reason for Medb's cattle raid on Ulster, was because Medb's husband claimed that the only reason she was worthwhile was because of *his* status. This statement enraged Medb, and she proceeded to prove to her husband why her status and wealth were higher than his — thus suggesting that theirs was a union of a man on a woman's property (*lánamnas fir for bantinchur*). First, Medb points out that she is the daughter of a King, the best of his daughters, and also the best warrior of them all. Furthermore, she has more fighting men that served under her then her husband has serving under him. Additionally, her followers were said to have served her outright because she is Queen of Connacht, made so by her father and not because she married into royalty. The final piece of proof she offers is the fact that it was she who chose him to be her husband because of his generosity, lack of fear, and lack of jealousy. In the end after the two had sized up their qualities, they found themselves on equal ground. So to settle the argument, they counted their cattle (again, the enduring symbol of Irish wealth). Medb owned more cattle than her husband. However, her most coveted bull would not stay with her herd because he could not stand to be owned by a woman. Angered by this realization, Queen Medb set out to own the most prized bull in all of Ireland, hence the Cattle Raid of *Cuailnge*.

Besides the issue of the cattle, it is important to point out that their marriage contract was one where the man was supported on the woman's property. Moreover, this particular saga corresponds with the laws and the social customs of the time. As pointed out with Queen Medb, personal wealth was a very important issue when settling a marriage contract.

The Marriage Contract

Wealth and possessions were a key element in all Irish contractual unions. Before a union could take place, the matter of the dowry had to be contracted for. The principal dowry paid for the bride was called the *coibche* (literal translation is "bride price"). The husband-to-be had to pay a *coibche* to the girl's father, who then divided it with the head of the kindred (*áige fine*, which loosely translated means "the head of the tribe").[95] The wife-to-be also received a *Tinól*, a type of a wedding present, which was given to the bride by friends and acquaintances. The *Tinól* usually consisted of cattle, and was divided between the bride and her father, who received one third. The third type of dowry was the *Tinchor*, which consisted of household goods and belonged solely to the wife-to-be. The final portion of the dowry was the *Tinnscra*, or bride-payment, which included silver, gold, copper and brass and was made to the father of the bride.[96] After a total of 21 years of marriage (the amount of time it took to pay off the entire dowry), a woman could accumulate a great deal of wealth in her own right, and if her husband should die or if a mutual divorce was had, she kept all that she had acquired throughout the years. Which brings us to the next legislation of unions — divorce.

Divorce

The Brehon Laws treated divorce (*imscarad*) quite fairly and, with the exception of one-year marriages, were provided for in an equitable manner for all concerned. One or both of the partners could obtain divorce for several reasons under Brehon Law, including no-fault divorce[97] and divorce when the wife was wronged by her husband.[98] For example, a woman could divorce her husband and retain rights to her full *coibche* or bride-price if it was found that she was rejected for another woman, if he tells false story about her (this stipulation reinforces the importance of stories in early Irish culture), if he tricked her into marriage by sorcery or if he strikes her causing a blemish.[99] Further stipulations include those covering sexuality such as if the husband was sterile, or is practicing homosexuality.[100] Compared to other societies at this time (and even "modern" twentieth-century Ireland), Irish women enjoyed considerable rights concerning her sex: choice of mate and freedom of divorce.

Additionally, it must be remembered that marriage in ancient Catholic Ireland was nothing more than a *legal contract*, so every aspect of this legal union (rather than spiritual or religious) was legislated, including marriage, divorce, and the division of property:

> Throughout the laws there is no talk of the sacred character of marriage. Any such character cannot really come from the formal binding together of a couple; it must grow. Marriage, therefore, was a relative thing. Its success depended on time, place and persons concerned. It was no absolute thing in the eyes of the Brehons, who were human beings legislating for human beings, and not idealists legislating like God.[101]

With concern to divorce, however, of vast importance are the laws that gave women rights to property after a divorce was obtained. This is an especially crucial issue, because most Romanized societies (and modern Ireland) denied divorce to women — only men could obtain divorce by means of proving their wife unfit in some way. Once divorced, the woman was offered no guarantee of property or maintenance whatsoever, unless specified for under the original marriage contract, and this mostly benefited those who belonged in the upper economic classes. However, it is important to point out that women in Ireland had no rights in regard to inherited lands. As Steven Ellis points out, a woman could not inherit land, but she could own land separately from her husband.[102] Power further demonstrates how land amassed during marriage was split between a husband, wife and others living on the land.[103] This counters Ellis' assertion that Irish women had "no entitlement to her late husband's property."[104] Ellis' statement becomes problematic, as it assumes that property gained during marriage solely belonged to the husband. By examining the Brehon marriage laws, this is clearly not the case, since land and property amassed during marriage was seen as *kin ownership* rather than an exclusive ownership (which was practiced in England).[105] Further, as Kelly points out, according to older commentary on the early law texts, although a daughter was not normally entitled to inherit her father's land, she was entitled to a share of her father's personal property (valuables), and if her father had no sons, his land as well.[106] Simply put and as discussed above, when there was a separation between equal partners, the wife was allowed to keep all she came into the marriage with. This included the entire dowry she had accrued up until the point of separation. As for the rest of the property that was accumulated throughout the marriage union, it was expected that the property would be divided up equally between all the parties involved. For example, if the couple's livestock had increased during their union, "one-third of the increase was left behind on the land, another third went to the owner of the cattle, and the last third was divided in three and given to the husband, wife and herdsmen in equal shares."[107] However, if it could be proven that the divorce was the fault of the wife, she then forfeited all dowries she had accumulated. Likewise, if the husband was at fault, then the wife kept her entire dowry, and she also had to be compensated beyond that, depending upon the severity of the crime the husband had committed against her. In the end, the laws concerning women and her most likely place in society were legislated for fairly under the Brehon Laws. Furthermore, these laws existed far into the end of the sixteenth century, when their final destruction occurred with a series of events that brought English rule into Ireland, along with the eradication of women's rights and status — opening a door for the later Magdalene laundries, and magdalenism.

Chapter Five

The Colonization of Ireland and Her Women

> On she went, and her maiden smile
> In safety lighted her round the Green Isle;
> And blest forever was she who relied
> Upon Erin's honor and Erin's pride.
> — Thomas Moore, "Rich and
> Rare Were the Gems She Wore."

If Ireland was allowed an historic continuation of her core values and laws outside of the influence of English rule and the Romanized Catholic Church, the Magdalene laundries might never have arrived in Éire. And if they did, they most likely would have remained philanthropic efforts rather than spiritual and state-sanctioned labor homes. Fundamental to this different focus regarding the homes, convents, laundries and asylums found between colonized areas such as Ireland and core market centers such as England is the question regarding autonomy in both rule and economics. Ireland's autonomy was taken when England colonized her. Once colonized, Ireland was reinvented to serve the economic and labor needs of the colonizer, England, and many institutions, including charitable ones, were reformed to help serve this purpose. Ireland, Australia, Scotland and parts of Canada found this to be true with the Magdalene convents, laundries, and asylums.

However, Ireland becomes a particularly interesting case study because there is a clear view of converging historical elements that allow a better view as to how the process of colonization reformed the Irish identity, as well as women's rights. Accordingly, this chapter will examine the colonization of Ireland and its later influence on women's rights and status as autonomous citizens.

Primitive Accumulation and Early Colonization

In Karl Polanyi's *The Great Transformation,* Polanyi states that most theories about the industrial revolution were wrong because they looked at societal transformation purely from the economic viewpoint.[1] By using deterministic modes of deduction, a reinforcement of abstraction occurs that limits the possibility of viewing real changing power relations. Likewise, Karl Marx in volume one of *Capital* (under "Fetishism of the Commodity and Its Secret") makes it very clear that the economic structure of a society, labor and production, is best viewed through social relations, and, therefore, he challenges Hegel's concept of a form, an object, as being abstracted from everyday life, experience, and action.[2] For Marx, and the later pragmatists, the true subjects of history are "'real, living individuals' themselves."[3] In order to avoid the fallacy of abstraction and deterministic analysis regarding colonization and the fall of women's rights in Ireland, following Polanyi and Marx, this chapter will examine the process of land enclosures and dislocation of the Irish from their means of production in an attempt to also demonstrate how this dislocation worked to destroy social Irish relations, law, and women's status — a process that starts with the concept of primitive accumulation, leads to land enclosures, and finally to the eradication of traditional Irish Law.

Primitive Accumulation and Agricultural Insistence

While examining primitive accumulation,[4] Marx states that the central point to the whole process of agricultural accumulation is the exploitation and eviction of the peasant from the land: "The history of this expropriation assumes different aspects in different countries, and runs through its various phases in different orders of succession, and at different historical epochs."[5] When examining the unique Irish case, what must be remembered is that unlike the feudal states that Marx focused on in his discussion regarding primitive accumulation and the rise of Capitalism, Ireland was neither feudalistic nor agriculturally structured. It could be argued that the difficulty of colonizing Ireland was linked to these two specific differences that radically distinguished Ireland from the rest of Europe, including such Celtic lands as Scotland. However, Marx's concept of primitive accumulation is relevant to Ireland, and, as Marx insisted himself, "Expropriation assumes different aspects in different countries."[6]

In "So-Called Primitive Accumulation," Marx traces the different ways in which peasant workers were displaced from communal land, "an old Teutonic institution which lived on under the cover of Feudalism,"[7] and made into wage workers: "The newly freed men became sellers of themselves only after they had been robbed of all their own means of production, and all the guarantees of existence afforded by the old feudal arrangement."[8] This redefinition of the peasant into the wage worker was promoted by state and capitalist's action to privatize land (by numerous forms of force) into the hands of a few rich landholders who often annihilated the land and also forced peasants to sell their labor to survive.[9] Fundamental to this process described by Marx is the eventual and total displacement of the peasant from the land. This theory, as explained by Araghi in "Global Depeasantization," is referred to as the "disappearance theory," which is in opposition to the "permanence theory," a theory that insists that peasant societies will adapt to new conditions because they have a "developmental logic of their own" that allows for continuity.[10] Araghi rightly argues that both of these theories are inadequate to explain the larger "peasant question," because neither theory has been proved completely correct. Indeed, Ireland in the late 1500s does not fit either one of these models, but falls somewhere in between.

English efforts to colonize Ireland began toward the end of the twelfth and the beginning of the thirteenth century,[11] and effectively ended after the Williamite War of 1689–1691 and with the Treaty of Limerick.[12] The first wave of invasion occurred in 1169–1171 under Henry II, and by the end of the twelfth century "most of Ireland had fallen under some semblance of English control in the form of Anglo-Norman barons who had been given titles to Irish lands, which they ruled as personal fiefdoms.[13] Irish Historian Katharine Simms, in "The Norman Invasion and the Gaelic Recovery," offers a detailed account of this process, which originally flourished in Eastern Ireland. Made on a military basis, feudal grants were offered to private individuals (termed the "Old English") who acquired large "underpopulated agricultural land in Ireland."[14] This process of colonizing land quickly moved from underpopulated to populated strategic locations where there was economic potential, as was found in the "larger ecclesiastical settlements of pre–Norman Ireland."[15] Once securely situated on the land, and creating a *borough* town, colonizers displaced local Irish citizens and imported tenants and laborers to help create a market for agricultural surplus. Importing labor and tenants became central, since most native Irish preferred to move to uncolonized territories rather than to live under this new system. However, this meant that Irish territories were quickly shrinking in the East, as well as other parts of Ireland, and Irish citizens were forced to live in the *peripheral*. This process of English colonized invasion continued off and on in relation to Irish resistance, which was constant.[16] Oddly, what became Ireland's downfall in the end was also the aspect of Irish institutional organization that originally hindered the English colonization efforts: namely, Ireland lacked a central government. Because of this, the English were forced to make treaties with individual clans and petty kings, but these treaties tended to only last as long as the Irish chieftain felt it was beneficial to their specific cause and, thus, was contingent upon perceived benefits. A second point of contention was that of conflicting institutional organization emphasis: agricultural versus pastoral lands.

Enclosing the Land: The Pastoralists versus the Agriculturalists

Polanyi insists that the process of enclosing land was only considered an improvement if "no conversion to pasture took place": "Where tillage was maintained, employment did not fall off, and the food supply markedly increased. The yield of the land manifestly increased, especially where the land was let."[17] Likewise, Marx, in his chapter on primitive accumulation, traces the English's systematic efforts of displacing the peasant from his or her means of production by, first, displacing them from the land. However, as discussed in the previous chapter, the Irish were not an agriculturalist people but a pastoral people, who understood wealth in terms of cattle. Agricultural practices, up through the 1600s, were mostly practiced in areas of Ireland that had been colonized by the Old English (the pale) because those lands were better suited for agricultural cultivation and, second, because the Irish were not traditionally an agricultural people.

Historian Nicholas Patrick Canny, in "Early Modern Ireland, c. 1500–1700," insists that the lack of agricultural practices among the Irish was not exclusively because of their pastoral tradition, but because "the technology of arable farming remained backward and was still primarily dependent upon the spade."[18] However, the emphasis this view offers is incorrect. Although Canny is correct about the lack of agricultural technology possessed by the Irish, it is not simply because of a "backward" technology lack that the Irish did not utilize agricultural potential; rather, it is because, traditionally, the Irish placed little importance on the widespread use of agriculture, as their institutions and social/political organization were based upon pastoral, not agricultural, organization and resulting social emphasis. Canny's view, indeed his choice of language such as "backwards," suggests an embedded logic of the superior nature of agricultural societies. Such assumptions regarding the "superior" nature of an agricultural culture is central to the process of colonization that embodies not only "accumulation and acquisition" but also "impressive ideological formations that include notions that certain territories and peoples *require* and beseech domination, as well as *forms of knowledge affiliated with dominations.*"[19] This could be why there is in Canny's work the prevailing insistence of "backward" agricultural technologies possessed by the Irish. It is helpful, then, to turn to Audrey Smedley's work *Race in North America*, where she traces the concept of modern racism, colonization, and slavery based on embedded assumptions of racial and organizational superiority found within the Eurocentric emphasis on agriculture.

The English attempts to invade and assume rule over Ireland were not only attempts to spread English civilization but, more importantly, attempts to acquire Irish land and exploit Irish labor — creating both a political and economic threat for Ireland.[20] Wallerstein argues that as a peripheral region, Ireland fought against two separate but coordinated trends: first, the strengthening of the English-British state (political), and second, the "triumph" of capitalism (economic threat).[21] Central to these two "trends" was a cultural conflict between the Irish (pastoralists) and the English (agriculturalists), which, Smedley argues, was a difference pivotal to the English's development of racism:

> The hostility between the Irish and the English ran much deeper. It exemplified an age-old struggle, symbolized in biblical times by the conflict between Cain and Abel, that has recurred repeatedly in many places throughout history: the clash between nomadic or seminomadic pastoralists and peoples who settled on the land as farmers and cultivated a sedentary way of life. This was a fundamental conflict between two very different lifestyles, two different views of the world, two different value systems, two different sets of problems and solutions for them.[22]

This fundamental cultural difference between the Irish (pastoralists) and the English (agriculturalists) conflicted because of ideological *lifestyle* assumptions particular to these two ways of living. In the end, this conflict and the pastoral versus agricultural relationship to the land have very different consequences that instilled an extreme hatred between the Irish and the English — cultural and rhetorical clashes. For example, whereas the English saw worth and wealth in terms of land, the Irish viewed wealth in terms of cattle. Hence, for the Irish, the worth of one unit of land or *cumal* (1,492,992 square feet) could only be understood in terms of livestock: "The value of a *cumal* of land ranges from 24 milch cows for best arable down to 8 dry cows for bogland."[23] As such, one of the underlying differences of lifestyles between the Irish and the English has to do with importance of land, specifically the English's view that by not settling the land, and enclosing the land, the Irish were *wasting* the land.[24] This "waste" could be seen, according to the English, in other aspects of the Irish lifestyle, such as the accused "laziness," "lack of cleanliness," "lawlessness," "promiscuity" and "lack of economic direction." Private ownership was of the utmost importance for the English, and as such was considered an improvement both economically and socially over a pastoral lifestyle. Consequently, Polanyi points to an official English document of 1607, a Privy Council memorandum that was prepared for the use of the Lords of the Realm:

"The poor man shall be satisfied in his end: Habitation; and the gentleman not hindered in his desire: *Improvement*." This formula appears to take for granted the essence of purely economic progress, which is to achieve improvement at the price of social dislocation. But it also hints at the tragic necessity by which the poor man clings to his hovel doomed by the rich man's desire for a public improvement which profits him privately.[25]

For the Irish, however, the concept of land ownership was constantly up for negotiation within the kinship, something that was reflected within the Brehon Laws.[26] Further, the idea of ownership and property, which would later be used by the English to consider certain "savages" as property, could also be seen through the different ways the Irish and English viewed women.[27] While demonstrating the "disdain for the customs and habits of the 'wild Irish,'" Smedley tells us of Edmund Campion's view: "Himself a Catholic, excoriated the Irish for their supposed cannibalism, their lewd marriage customs (they had trial marriages and sometimes engaged in polygamy and free sexual behavior)."[28] As Smedley's story illustrates, the desire for freedom and autonomy, which extended from the Irish pastoral culture, was reflected even in their marriage laws. Again, the Irish did have a "trial marriage" provision, which lasted for one year, and contracts were also available for men to take more than one wife (concubines), justified by the early Irish using the Old Testament. However, unlike the English marriage laws, which stipulated no provisions for women in terms of ownership and rights, the Irish had laws in place to protect women inside and outside of marriage, as was demonstrated in chapter four of this work. Another way in which the marriage laws reflected the nomadic nature of pastoral peoples is through their provision for a "no-fault" divorce, which could be secured if a "pilgrimage was being made by one of the parties."[29] A pilgrimage could be considered one of religious importance, but it could also be a result of the husband (and rarely the wife) going off to war; in either case a divorce could be obtained by the female — something that did not exist in English law.

The Rhetoric of the "Wild Irish"—Justifying Depeasantization and Marriage Laws

When considering the differing cultural ideologies and the corresponding efforts of Great Briton to usurp Irish land and law, while promoting the process of generalized *depeasantization*, it is important to once again glimpse the either/or rhetoric at the core of this issue, because similar rhetoric will later be used to justify imprisoning women into the laundries. Not unlike the rhetoric involved in distinguishing Mary Magdalene from the Virgin Mary, the English were working to justify their agricultural position, as well as the process of displacing the Irish from their own lands by generally defining their interest in opposition to the Irish — good versus bad, civilized versus uncivilized, advanced versus backward. As discussed in chapter two, Kenneth Burke defines rhetoric as identification, because essentially when people are being persuasive, they are working to convince others to identify with their actions and outlook. But identification is also closely related to the work of division. People define their selves by what they are not (such as the Magdalene is not the Virgin) — which causes strife and even (certainly in the Irish cause) War: "we found that this wavering line between identification and division was forever bringing rhetoric against the possibility of malice and the lie; for if an identification favorable to the speaker or his cause is made to see favorable to the audience, there enters the possibility of such 'heightened consciousness' as goes with deliberate cunning."[30] England worked hard to create identification and support for their cause of land acquisition and colonialization of Ireland partly by characterizing the Irish, and their relationship to the land, as wasteful, which in turn suggested that their culture was not only wasteful, but uncivilized. Smedley reminds us that the literature of the sixteenth and seventeenth century about Ireland is littered with such rhetoric: "Irish resistance throughout the sixteenth century enraged many Englishmen, who persisted in viewing the Irish as 'rude, beastly, ignorant, cruel and unruly infidels' (Liggio 1976, 8)."[31] But this rhetoric can find its roots much earlier in Irish history, going back to the first so-called comprehensive documentation of Ireland given by Giraldus Cambrensis (Gerald of Wales — ca. 1146–ca.1223) in his *Topography of Ireland*, ca. 1188, and *The Conquest of Ireland*.

In the *Topography of Ireland*, Cambrensis starts off with a positive discussion of the beauty found in Ireland's wildlife, vegetation and, importantly, the landscape. Here Cambrensis states that although the country is "uneven" and "mountainous," the soil is "friable and moist, well wooded and marshy; it is truly a desert land, without roads, but well watered ... the tillage land is exuberantly rich, the fields yielding large crops of corn; and herds of cattle are fed on the mountains ... but this island is more productive in pasture than in corn, in grass than in grain. The crops give great promise when in the blade ... [and] the fields are luxuriantly covered, and the barns loaded with produce. The granaries only show scantly returns."[32] This general description of the beautiful and certainly the agricultural potential of Irish lands is then followed by a rather dismal description of the people who live and work these "fertile" lands. In chapter XIX: "How the Irish people are very ignorant of the rudiments of the faith," Cambrensis writes:

> It is indeed a most filthy race, a race sunk in vice, a race more ignorant than all other nations of the first principles of the faith. Hitherto they neither pay tithes nor first fruits; they do not contract marriages, nor shun

> incestuous connections; they frequent not the church of God with proper reverence. Nay, what is most detestable ... in many parts of Ireland brothers (I will not say marry) seduce and debauch the wives of their brothers deceased, and have incestuous intercourse with them; adhering in this to the letter, and not to the spirit, of the Old Testament.[33]

Cambrensis continues in this rhetorical line of argument by suggesting that the Irish are treacherous in chapter XX, and never keep a pledge[34]; further, that this tendency toward treachery and violence can be understood by the fact that the Irish carry an axe and not a staff.[35] Other accusations abound in this text as well, including the argument that the Irish use religious excuses and covert cover in order to kill their kin,[36] and how they generally hate their blood brothers but love their foster children.[37] Toward the end of this text, Cambrensis' final verdict on the Irish People condemns them for their nature, for not following but rejecting the natural course toward agricultural civilization, and so, importantly, he scolds them for their lack of care and respect regarding how land *should* be used:

> The Irish are a rude people, subsisting on the produce of their cattle only, and living themselves like beasts — a people that has not yet departed from the primitive habits of pastoral life. In the common course of things, mankind progresses from the forest to the field, from the field to the town, and to the social conditions of citizens; but this nation, holding agricultural labour in contempt, and little covering the wealth of towns, as well as being exceeding averse to civil institutions — lead the same life their fathers did in the woods and open pastures, neither willing to abandon their old habits or learn anything new.[38]

By nature, then, the Irish are backward because they will not embrace an agricultural lifestyle: "The whole habits of the people are contrary to agricultural pursuits, so that the rich blebe is barren for want of husbandmen, the fields demanding labour which is not forthcoming."[39] Thus it is not only Cambrensis who notices this lack and barbarian nature of the Irish, but *the Island*, Éire, too, cries about this unjust nature. Here Cambrensis describes the land not unlike a milk-cow who experiences pain when not milked. The land is crying out for "husbandmen" to till her and nurture her (conquer her?), something that the treacherous Irish refuse to do, care for the land they live on. Indeed, this rhetoric demonstrates the division effect quite specifically. Cambrensis is English, and the English are portrayed here as a religious people who follow church rules on marriage, family inheritance of land, and power, but above all, the English have followed the natural, indeed God-given, evolution from the wilderness to the fields to cities and proper towns. In the end, Cambrensis and his English brothers and sisters are what the Irish are not: civilized.

Medieval English literature scholar David Wallace, in *The Cambridge History of Medieval English Literature*, examines Cambrensis' *Conquest of Ireland*[40] and finds in this document much of the same contempt for the Irish as the author displayed in his *Topography*. Further, Wallace points out how much of Cambrensis's rhetoric focused on justifying the invasion of Ireland by England and Henry II because the Irish people were "in his view, delinquent and in need of firm, moral leadership."[41] As Simms also explains, the English have discussed, since the rein of William the Conqueror and Henry I, the possibility of invading Ireland. However, it was not until the rein of Henry II did this project see the light of day. Between Henry I and Henry II, the difference hinged on a single event: the archbishop of Canterbury lost all rights in Dublin "when it became an Irish archbishopric in 1152": "The archbishop of Canterbury's secretary, John of Salisbury, was sent as an envoy of Henry II to the English pope, Adrian IV. As a result of his negotiations, the pope invested Henry II and his successors with the right to rule Ireland."[42] Originally, Henry II was not going to actively divert resources to concur Ireland, but the Dublin King, King Dermont MacMurrough (the English immediately demoted him in their literature to the rank of prince) asked for the Henry II's assistance with a local war. In Cambrensis's *Conquest*, the author writes as if he was witness to the events that occurred between the two kings, Henry II and Dermont MacMurrough:

> Meanwhile, Mac Murchard, submitting to his change of fortune, and confidently hoping for some favourable turn, crossed the sea with a favourable wind, and came to Henry II., King of England, for the purpose of earnestly imploring his succor. Although the king was at that time beyond sea, far away in Aquitaine, in France, and much engaged in business, he received Murchard with great kindness, and the liberality and courtesy which was natural to him ... granted him letters patent to the effect following: "Henry, king of England, duke of Normandy and Aquitaine, and count of Anjou, to all his liegmen, English, Normans, Welsh, and Scots, and to all other nations subject to his dominion, sendeth greeting. Whensoever these our letters shall come unto you, know ye that we have received Dermitius, prince of Leinster, into our grace and favour,— Wherefore, whosoever within the bounds of our territories shall be willing to give him aid, as our vassal and liegeman, in recovering his territories, let him be assured of our favour and licence on that behalf."[43]

Wallace notes that although Cambrensis is careful to paint King Dermont MacMurrough in a good light, being that Dermont had the good sense to seek the English out for help, the rest of the Irish were still a "backward race" in need of proper guidance. This, Wallace notes, is a sentiment carefully placed in the character of Dermont as well, who views the English soldiers granted to him by Henry II as powerful and goodly:

He always stresses the valour of the English soldiery, sometimes through the eyes of Diarmait: "Macmoro3w3ch sawe the englysshe-men so stalwart that no power might ham wythstond" (p. 28, II. 1–2). Diarmait's opinion is crucial to comprehending the English attitude to their invasion of Ireland: he triggered off the whole sad story, and Giraldus's subtle portrayal of him as a victim of his own countrymen is designed to justify the English presence in Ireland.[44]

In the end, a long history of division rhetoric is presented between the Irish and the English, which will continue well into the sixteenth and seventeenth century. Indeed, the notable figure of William Thomas and his 1546 publication of *The Pilgrim* is a prime example; using the rhetoric of division, Thomas describes the Irish as being "wild" and barbaric in nature as compared to the civilized English:

> You must understand that the Kings of Ireland have had dominion over a great part of Ireland these 300 years and more, by reason whereof both the country and nation hath been divided into two sundry parts — that is to say, the English pale and the Wild Irish; and like as they of the English pale always used the self-same religion, customs, laws, and manners of civil living that we used in England, so contrariwise they of the wild Irish, as unreasonable beasts, lived without any knowledge of God or good manners, in common of their goods, cattle, women, children, and every other thing.[45]

Central to Thomas' rhetoric was, again, Cambrensis's observation that the Irish wasted the land and the resources of nature. Thus, the good and generous English must help the "backward" Irish in order to learn the ways of civilization, whether the Irish liked it or not, because *the land* demanded it. This rhetoric worked to justify the eventual colonization of Ireland, her lands, her laws (especially the Brehon marriage laws that the English held in such contempt), and later her women. This was a process that started with depeasantization, sending the Irish even further in to the peripheral social, political, and economic spaces.

Disappearance Theory versus Permanence Theory or Somewhere in Between

As briefly explored above, Farshad Araghi, in "Global Depeasantization, 1945–1990," explores the "disappearance theory,"[46] which is in opposition to the "permanence theory" concerning the process of depeasantization. The disappearance theory, linked to Marx, suggests that through colonization, there occurs an eventual and total displacement of the peasant from the land. This is contrary to the permanence theory's insistence that a peasant society will develop their own means of logic to guarantee their survival, as well as their survival of reproduction.[47] As stated above, the early Irish case falls somewhere in between. Closing onto the late 1500s, English colonization became more prevalent since the younger sons of English nobles, those who did not have the opportunity to inherit their father's estates, looked to Ireland to obtain their fortunes with the aid of Irish labor. Yet as was seen in the late twelfth and thirteenth centuries, it was almost impossible to force Irishmen to take to agrarian practices; so "when the English met their intransigence by confiscating and destroying [the Irish] cattle, the Irish fled into the forests and let it be known that they preferred starvation to life as forced laborers on English farms."[48] This unilateral action of destroying and confiscating cattle, Irish wealth, became fundamental to the English's ability to usurp Irish land for agricultural purposes. With the cattle destroyed by the middle to late 1500s, the Irish abandoned much of the central land of Ireland for the peripheral. However, this change in location did not create a disappearance or a permanent stance for the Irish victims of English domination. Rather, this process not only converted many Irish over to the English way of things; it also created a resistance movement that continues to this day in Northern Ireland. This is an early example of what sociologist Gay W. Seidman later discovered and explored regarding the modern South African and Brazilian resistance movements in his work *Manufacturing Militance*. What Seidman noticed was that Brazilian and South African unions worked to have labor resistance movements situated more in terms of a *broad class* rather than the limited terms of *labor*— thus involving the larger peripheral community as well.[49] Although Ireland in the late 1500s to 1600s is an entirely different situation, there is evidence that the Irish in the peripheral worked to overcome their clan differences and engage in *united* action against English domination; thus, like the Brazilian and South African movements, Irish movements worked to expand resistance possibilities by redefining resistance from isolated clans to united fronts. If it may be recalled, one aspect regarding Irish civilization that hindered the English's process of unilateral domination was that Ireland lacked a central government. Furthermore, this lack of central government also worked against the Irish, since Irish clans were known to constantly fight among themselves, allowing the English to pit one clan against another, weakening the potential for a united Irish front. However, confronted with a common threat and the extinction of a way of life, the Irish launched several united campaigns that transcended individual interests. For example, Anne Chamber recounts an historical event, originally recorded in *The Annals of The Four Masters*, where the petty king title of MacWilliam, in Mayo Ireland, was redefined for English benefit but later, through a united Irish movement, was retranslated back to Irish Law.[50]

In 1571, MacOliverus Bourke was elected to the *tí túaithe*, petty king position titled the MacWilliamship. In 1575, Sir Henry Sidney, the English lord deputy at the time, called on the Irish chieftains and the lords of Connaught to surrender to the queen and English law in exchange for royal appointments and a return of land holdings. Originally MacWilliam refused to obey, and so Sidney, under Queen Elizabeth's policy of "divide and conquer," worked to divide MacWilliam's political and military support by seducing away MacWilliam's Clandonnel gallowglass (an armed retainer or mercenary in the service of an Irish chieftain). Once this was accomplished, MacWilliam lost his power base and was forced to submit to the English in order to save what little power and land he still possessed:

> Together with his sub-lords of Mayo, including the O'Malley, [MacWilliam] went to Galway. Sidney recorded his encounter with MacWilliam — "I found MacWilliam very sensible, though wanting the English tongue, yet understanding the Latin, a lover of Quiet and Civility" — who impressed him with, as Sidney claims, his desire "to hold his Lands of the Queen and suppress Irish Extortion and to expulse the Scots, who swarm in those quarters."[51]

When submitting to English rule, MacWilliam agreed to uphold English Law, to pay 250 pounds a year in rent to the crown and to furnish the English governor with a force of two hundred soldiers for two months each year. In return, Sidney conferred upon MacWilliam "'his country ... by way of Seneschalship.... The order of Knighthood I bestowed upon him ... and some other little trifles' ... including the imposition of a sheriff in his territory."[52] Thus, MacWilliam was no longer an independent Gaelic chieftain but *indentured* English knight. This event had devastating consequences for Irish Law and tradition, because now the MacWilliamship could no longer be an *elected position* stipulated for under Early Irish Law but, concurrent to English law, a *heredity endowment*. In the late 1580s, when the MacWilliam died, Bourke's brother, Richard, was prepared to assume the position because he was deemed the Heir by English law. However, Grace O'Malley (Granuaile), along with her husband, Richard-an-Iarainn, who by Irish custom should have assumed the position, was able to cross clan lines and amass a huge army of 1,200 gallowglass, 700 Scots, 300 kerne (soldiers), and 200 horsemen.[53] They were also able to gain the support of the Mayo chieftains, as well as the Earl of Clanrickard's sons, to show unilateral undivided support for traditional Irish law and Richard-an-Iarainn's claim to the MacWilliamship. This is only one example where original division of Irish interests were overcome and reinterpreted into a broader frame of resistance. Historically situated, this is not an either/or situation of disappearance or permanence, but a continued struggle between dominance and independence — a struggle that can still be witnessed today between England and Northern Ireland. However, as the struggle continued, England's policies embraced, first, a hegemonic stance that worked to gain Irish consent and, failing that, England converted to pure domination tactics that would ultimately, for a time, transfer Ireland to English control.

Colonial Policy of Henry VIII to Queen Elizabeth I: From Hegemonic to Domination

As discussed in part one, chapter two, Gramsci, in his *Prison Notebooks*, offers the concept of "hegemony" where the idea of state is enlarged to include all the workings of civil society. However, as Buci-Glucksmann points out, Gramsci's concept of hegemony is often misused.[54] Hegemony is "primarily a *strategy* for the gaining of the active consent of the masses through their self-organization."[55] Hegemony then depends on the *active consent* of domination where the dominated party feels that they are receiving some type of benefit from the agreement. Max Weber defines domination as:

> The probability that certain specific commands (or all commands) will be obeyed by a given group of persons ... domination ("authority") in this sense may be based on the most diverse motives of compliance: all the way from simple habituation to the most purely rational calculation of advantage. Hence every genuine form of domination *implies a minimum of voluntary compliance*, that is, an *interest* (based on ulterior motives or genuine acceptance) in obedience.[56]

Central to the English invasion of Ireland became the need to get Irish men and women to consent to, and agree with, English domination. Under the English rule of Henry VII, 1494, Henry VII's policy was that of forced colonization, which, in the long run, failed miserably. However, Henry VIII took a more hegemonic approach, since he preferred to "provide mechanisms by which the Irish would *voluntarily* submit to his rule."[57] Although a complete hegemonic approach, one which encompasses all apparatuses of civil society, was not fully realized in the late 1500s, an early attempt at an hegemonic policy can be glimpsed with Henry VIII's policies in Ireland where he worked to gain active consent for English rule from the Irish leaders, and thus, the Irish people. It is through Henry VIII's efforts that there are significant changes in the Brehon Laws, as well as Irish culture.

The Brehon Laws changed little up until the end of the 1500s. With each invading people (especially the coming of Christianity in the fifth century, and later, that of the Normans in the twelfth century) there were small changes to the early Irish laws. For the most part, each differing societal invasion adapted to the Irish laws and customs:

> Adaptability of the law and its practitioners is a marked feature in all parts of Ireland down to the later sixteenth century. Relatively soon after its establishment in the twelfth century, the colonial government had begun to recognize the use of Brehon Law among the Gaelic Irish. Anglo-Norman magnates adapted features of the Brehon Law to the common law in a hybrid system known as "March Law."[58]

This hybrid system (March Law) was accepted by most people in Ireland, and by the early sixteenth century, a balance was struck in the Irish legal system where "even colonial shire areas [were] employing Brehon Law but the Pale and towns [were] abiding by the common law."[59] At this point in history, English power was mostly confined to Dublin and the Pale, a small area stretching north, south and west of Dublin proper. Steven G. Ellis specifies Dublin and its hinterland, lowland parts of Leinster and Muster.[60] As for the original Anglo-Normans, it seems that by the early 1500s they had become more Irish than the Irish, accepting the customs and social mores of the Irish people. All this started to change, however, with Henry VIII in 1537. Until this time, Henry's main concern was with the Reformation, his continuing marital problems, and attempts to sire a male heir. However in 1537, the House of Kildare, which had been loyal servants to the crown, revolted against English rule. As a result, the entire house was put to death: *The Annals of the Four Masters* recorded this account as a great loss to Ireland:

> Thomas, the son of the Earl of Kildare, the best man of the English of Ireland in his time, and his father's five brothers, whom we have already mentioned, namely, James Meirgeach, Oliver, John, Walter, and Richard, were put to death in England on the 3rd of the Nines of February; and all the Geraldines of Leinster were exiled and banished. The earldom of Kildare was vested in the King; and every one of the family who was apprehended, whether lay or ecclesiastical, was tortured and put to death. These were great losses, and the cause of lamentation throughout Ireland.[61]

After the revolt, King Henry decided to install what is known as the "surrender and regrant" policy of colonization: "On submission to the King, the chieftain or lord would receive back his lands, in the King's name, provided that he agreed to rule by English law and attend the King's parliament in Dublin. In return, he would receive an English title suited to his rank."[62] This "surrender and regrant" policy started the process of outlawing the Brehon and March Laws in Ireland, compelling Irish chieftains and citizens to observe English law instead of Irish and, eventually, destroying what equality was granted to Irish women. However, most people in Ireland tended to submit only when it suited them, using the English law when it benefited them and the Brehon laws when they seemed beneficial. Nevertheless, Henry VIII's policies helped build defensive forts and also to establish a standing army in

Ireland "with the intention of ridding the fertile areas of all those who refused to submit to English Rule."[63] Smedley rightly insists that this policy established by Henry VIII was continued by his successors,[64] but what she does not mention was that this policy was dramatically changed by Queen Elizabeth I, who would abandon the hegemonic approach for a decidedly more violent scheme.

Queen Elizabeth continued with her father's policies toward Ireland while she tried to extend English power into Chonnacht (c. 1564). Until this time, Chonnacht had stayed extremely Celtic, because English rule had not extended that far. As Ellis explains, the balance of power between the English and the Irish had not changed by the time Queen Elizabeth I assumed the throne. What had changed was the nature of the English state. Becoming more centralized and uniform, England was able to create fairly stabilized political and cultural centers in colonized areas — that is, except for Ireland:

> Thus by the 1560s the characteristically Tudor pattern of state formation by political centralization, administrative uniformity and cultural imperialism seemed to be making good progress in taming the wild borderers and fostering a more civil society among degenerate English settlers in outlying parts of the Tudor state. These changes had ensured that, over the previous 30 years, the crown's awareness of its Irish problem had greatly intensified, and long-term developments outside Ireland had substantially altered its view of the nature of the program.[65]

Frustrated that little to no progress had been made in Ireland, Elizabeth I abandoned the hegemonic policies adopted by her father and opted for a more aggressive approach. Thus, the extension of English power and domination into Gaelic areas of Ireland launched a series of events and revolts against English rule that would, ultimately, convince Queen Elizabeth I to change her policy toward Ireland. The main trigger event involved a minor chieftain of the O'Flahertys, Murrough-na-dTuadh. He launched a campaign to extend his own power into mainly English territory when he attacked the English Earl of Thomond just two miles west of where the English held Galway:

> This incident was too serious to be overlooked by the English. To overcome Murrough by force would prove too costly, given his undoubted strength and the remoteness of his territory. If, however, he could be persuaded to become loyal to the crown, it would prove an advantage in spreading the Anglicization policy further west. The Queen issued Murrough with a pardon and appointed him lord of all Iar Chonnacht. In return, Murrough promised, "to observe the Queen's peace, to appear and answer at all sessions within the province ... to satisfy the demands of all the Queen's subjects." ... The appointment was a repudiation of Brehon Law.[66]

The O'Flaherty's action and the English's reaction was the first example of a new policy adopted by Queen Elizabeth called the "divide and conquer" policy, which abandoned any real hegemonic attempts of active consent and, instead, resorted to dominating conquering policies. As Ellis suggests, this move also represented the new approach and policy of English state formation:

> From the late 1580s, there was a growing disillusion in government circles with traditional Tudor [Henry VIII] reform strategy and increasing support for the idea that English aims could only be achieved by a massive reassertion of English armed might so as to break Gaelic resistance by military conquest and extensive plantations. Thus, in the wider context of state formation, Elizabeth's reign marks a traditional phase between the classic Tudor pattern of expansion and the emergence in the 1590s of a more aggressive colonialism which was the chief legacy of late Elizabethan Ireland to English colonization in the New World.[67]

By playing clan against clan, and chief against chief, Elizabeth I could easily bypass Brehon Laws, get the Irish to fight each other, dividing loyalties, which allowed the English to militarily overcome smaller resistance units. In this present example, by ignoring the traditional Brehon Laws, Elizabeth had promoted *a minor chieftain* to a *Celtic King's position*, disregarding the traditional Irish social and political system. Furthermore, the "divide and conquer" policy effectively ended Gaelic power, outlawing the Brehon Laws entirely by the 1600s. Effective in its use, this policy pitted Irish against Irish, appealing to the Irish passion for petty kingdom power. Again, as observed above, both a grace and a hindrance to the Irish was the lack of a political organization. With the successful end of the Irish political and legal system in the early 1600s, the Irish people had no legal system of their own and were forced to try and understand a foreign law that did not work in their favor. Furthermore, the Irish were illiterate by English standards, as many documents signed by chieftains, and other Irish lords surrendering their lands and rights to the Crown, were signed with their "mark." There is no true way of knowing if the Irish lords or chieftains knew what they were signing, what rights they were giving up, or property they were surrendering. As for women's status as recognized citizens, all was lost with the destruction of the Brehon laws.

Irish Women's Loss of Rights and Citizenship Status

Evelyn Nakano-Glenn, professor of Asian American Studies, in *Unequal Freedoms*, looks at both labor and citizenship in relation to gender relations in the United States. By viewing modes of citizenship, Nakano-Glenn is able to view lines of power relations in relation to who is and who is not considered a citizen: "Citizenship has been used to draw boundaries between those who are included as members of the community and entitled to respect, protection, and rights and those who are excluded and thus not entitled to recognition and rights."[68] Likewise, social theorist T.H. Marshall points out, "Citizenship has itself become, in certain respects, the architect of legitimate social inequality."[69] In exploring this line of argument, Marshall, in "Citizenship and Social Class," divides citizenship into three parts: civil, political, and social. Civil citizenship is often ruled under the courts of justice and is "composed of the rights necessary for individual freedom — liberty of the person, freedom of speech, thought and faith, the right to own property and to conclude valid contracts, and the right to justice."[70] Political citizenship is the right to "participate in the exercise of political power."[71] Finally, social citizenship encompasses the "whole range from the right to a modicum of economic welfare and security to the right to share to the full in the social heritage and to live the life of a civilized being according to the standards prevailing in the society."[72] Concerning all aspects of citizenship then, Irish women lost citizenship status (civil, political, and social) once the Irish Brehon Laws were replaced by English law and property rights, as well as corresponding reinforcement of patriarchal hierarchy under the Catholic religion. In order to understand the latter, it is helpful to examine Friedrich Engels' influential essay, "The Patriarchal Family."

Although R.W. Connell in *Gender and Power* is correct to criticize Engels, as well as contemporary gender analysis, for assuming the "naturalness" within the categories of men and women,[73] Engels is still, nevertheless, helpful since his analysis demonstrates "the idea of relationships between men and women as a social system with a definite historical trajectory."[74] And considering Ireland in the 1500s to 1600s, it is this "historical trajectory" that is of great importance. In "The Patriarchal Family," Engels traces the development from communistic households, not unlike those in Brehon Ireland, to the "Pairing" family, or the patriarchal family, as seen throughout Christian Europe. Originally, according to Engels, the communistic household was ruled by the woman and not the man:

> But the communistic household implies the supremacy of women in the house, just as the exclusive recognition of a natural mother, because of the impossibility of determining the natural father with certainty, signifies high esteem for the women, that is, the mothers. That woman was the slave of man at the commencement of society is one of the most absurd notions that have come down to us from the period of Enlightenment of the eighteenth century.[75]

The communistic family changed into a patriarchal family because of increase in wealth. This, in turn, gave the male more important status and "strengthened position in order to overthrow the traditional order of inheritance in favour of his children."[76] Engels suggests that this change of power happened without causing a great upheaval in society, as everyone in the household kept his or her place; however, the concept of inheritance is what changed things:

> The simple decision sufficed that in the future the descendants of the male members should remain in the genes, but that those of the females were to be excluded from the genes and transferred to that of their father. The reckoning of descent through the female line and the right of inheritance through the mother were hereby overthrown and male lineage and right of inheritance from the father instituted.[77]

Engels locates the transition from matriarchal to patriarchal rule in "prehistoric" times and further suggests that this move was the death of women's rights as a free person: "The overthrow of the mother right was the *world-historic defeat of the female sex*. The man seized the reins in the house also, the woman was degraded, enthralled, the slave of the man's lust, a mere instrument for breeding children."[78] Furthermore, what happened to women can be seen as an example of what happens to any subordinate group within society:

> Slavery was the first form of exploitation, particular to the world of antiquity; it was followed by serfdom in the Middle Ages, and by wage labour in the modern times. These are the three great forms of servitude, characteristic of the three great epochs of civilization; open, and, latterly, disguised slavery, are its steady companions.[79]

As social and gender theorist Deniz Kandiyoti states in "Bargaining with Patriarchy," different historical forms need different applications of theory.[80] When viewing the Irish situation of the 1500s to 1600s, traditional patriarchy (that is, men's domination over women in social, political, and civil law) appears to have asserted itself with little resistance from Irish women. So it is that Kandiyoti observed this "classical patriarchy"[81] was aided by women actually accommodating the spiritual insistence led by the Irish Catholic Church in reaction against English Protestant law. From the 1500s to 1700, in both Ireland and England, a strengthening of patriarchal ties and hierarchy was experienced.[82] Of course, because of the destruction of the Brehon Laws, this transition was more acute for Ireland, and, unlike Engels' pinpointed time of "prehistoric" times, the complete transition to a patriarchal inheritance system was not felt in its entirety until the later 1600s. Nevertheless, as Stone points out, the strengthening of patriarchal ties occurred because, first, importance on the nuclear family increased and, second, "the importance of affective bonds to tie the conjugal unit together began to increase."[83]

Both these factors were further reinforced by the decline of kinship and clientage, the rise and power of a centralized state, and finally assisted by Protestant reforms. In Ireland, however, it was not only the rise of powerful English state that changed women's status as citizens, but it was also Protestant and Catholic reforms that occurred in *reaction to* state and law reconfiguration.

One of the most important aspects condemning Irish women at this time, besides not having the Irish laws on their side, was the fact that they were Catholics living under Protestant rule. As early as the late 1400s, Catholic churches and clergy members in Ireland were no longer independent institutions, but were firmly under secular landowners rule — both Irish and English loyalty.[84] As the English under Henry VIII, and later under Queen Elizabeth I, employed more drastic colonization techniques, monasteries and churches increasingly found their property taken away and given over to new English lords. Thus, as Marx points to in England, Catholic land and rule in Ireland as well was quickly disappearing:

> The process of forcible expropriation of the people received a new and terrible impulse in the sixteenth century from the Reformation, and the consequent colossal spoliation of church property. The Catholic Church, was at the time of the Reformation, the feudal proprietor of a great part of the soil of England. The dissolution of the monasteries, etc., hurled their inmates into the proletariat. The estates of the church were to a large extent given away to rapacious royal favourites, or sold at a nominal price to speculating farmers and townsmen, who drove out the old-established hereditary sub-tenants in great numbers, and threw their holdings together. The legally guaranteed property of the poorer folk in a part of the church's tithes was quietly confiscated.[85]

Displaced from traditional areas of Ireland, the friars and priests pressed for spiritual reforms within the peripheral areas where the Irish still maintained power. This counterpush by the Catholic priests in Ireland insisted on patriarchal and spiritual reforms that would counter the traditional Brehon civil laws and contracts dealing with marriage. Furthermore, this spiritual push for Catholic unity among the Irish worked, since they saw it as another way in which to resist Protestant English rule. Thus, in 1588 the Irish voiced their support for the Spanish Invasion of England and King Philip's "planned crusade against his 'heretic' sister-in-law."[86] Nevertheless, by aligning the Irish cause with the Catholic cause, Irish women found their role in society diminished by both law and spiritual insistence. Thus, when English protestant law gained strength in Ireland, so too did Romanized Catholic spiritual law gain power over the Irish people — leaving Irish women caught in the middle. Most marriages in Ireland now became unions under Christian law, since the Brehon Laws no longer existed, and although divorce was allowed in England, once married under Catholic law, no one could get a divorce.[87] Even if an Irish woman was able to obtain a fair judgment within English law, she was hindered because English laws concerning sex and marriage were never as liberal, or fair, to women as were the Irish Brehon Laws. Because of this religious push and pull between Catholic and Protestant influence that dictated social relations, Irish women's social citizenship was effectively distinguished.

Under the Brehon Laws, as may be recalled, Irish women were entitled to property before and after marriage, whether marriage ended in the death of a spouse or in divorce. Of course, the amount of property awarded was dependant upon the contingent circumstances. However, most divorces in Brehon Ireland were of the "no-fault" variety, and thus all members of the household (not only husband and wife) left the union with property possessions. Once the Brehon Laws were outlawed, according to English law, all possessions belonged solely to the husband no matter what the circumstances. It became an issue also of private over communal or familial ownership. If divorce was obtained, then all property rights remained with the husband. If the husband was deceased, then the property rights reverted to the next eldest male in his line. Under the new English law, now the only option left for Irish women outside the Catholic Church, women had few legal rights to ownership of her own personal property after marriage:

> At this time a woman's legal right to hold and dispose of her own property was limited to what she could specifically lay claim to in a marriage contract. By marriage, the husband and wife became one person in law — and that person was the husband. He acquired absolute control of all his wife's personal property, which he could sell at will. By a judicial interpretation, a husband's debts became by law a prior charge on his wife's jewels and other personal property.... A husband always had full rights during his lifetime over his wife's real estate, and by an act of 1540 he was empowered to make long leases for three lives or twenty-one years and to pocket the fines.[88]

These new laws directly contradicted the early Irish laws. No longer was the husband required to discuss all selling and trading of property with his wife, something required by Brehon Laws, no longer could she own property of her own; indeed her entire dowry was paid directly to her father, while she saw none of it in her lifetime. These new laws took away a woman's civic and political citizenship, as now she was defined specifically as *a thing* to be *owned*— property of her father, brother, or husband. Because the law deemed the female as an object, she could easily be magdalenized later, dehumanized as a sexual thing that works. Moreover, if her spouse happened to be a bad husband, there was little she could do, because no recourse was offered to her under the new English laws. As for divorce, under the stronger Catholic hold of Ireland, there was no possibility. However, if the Irish (and English) male wished a divorce, and happened to be extremely well off, he could obtain one:

> In the late seventeenth and eighteenth centuries, therefore, full divorce and remarriage were possible by law for the very rich and by folk custom for the very poor, but impossible for the great majority in the middle who could not afford the cost of the one or the social stigma and remote risks of prosecution of the other.[89]

Mostly, instead of civil separations, there was a rash of abandonments in Ireland, and if it is believed, an unbelievable number of prostitutes reported in Ireland in the eighteenth and nineteenth centuries (discussed in chapter six); a repeat of the medieval pattern can be seen where strict and narrow regulation and definition of marriage has the unexpected effect of creating a market for prostitution, abandonments, and extramarital affairs. As such, if abandonment was not an option, then bigamy was another alternative "which seems to have been both easy and common."[90] A third alternative, which was practiced both in England and in Ireland during the 1600–1700s was a "folk custom"—the selling of the wife:

> The husband puts a halter about her neck and thereby leads her to the next market place, and there puts her up to auction to be sold to the best bidder, as if she were a brood mare or milch-cow. A procedure was based closely on that of the sale of cattle. It took place frequently in a cattle-market like Smithfield and was accompanied by the use of a symbolic halter, by which the wife was led to market by the seller, and led away again by the buyer. The transaction sometimes even included the payment of a fee to the clerk of the market. In the popular mind, this elaborate ritual freed the husband of all future responsibility for his wife, and allowed both parties to marry again.[91]

The selling of the wife, this fetishized abstraction of magdalenism was often prearranged, where the buyer intended to be the wife's new husband. However, one can see how the women of Ireland became nothing more than a "milch-cow" under the new English law. She was no longer seen as a person, but a non-citizen, and, often, considered barely human, because, being "barely human," like the land she could also be "enclosed" behind fortified walls.

Conclusion and into Modernity

By the late 1700s, Irish women had lost so much status in the social order that state, society, and the Catholic Church felt justified in removing unwanted women from society, and placing them into convents, Magdalene laundries, where they were put to forced servitude washing laundry and doing other menial jobs for life, without any hope of escape. At first this movement was an altruistic effort to help former prostitutes, unwed or abandoned mothers and was often a better place to live than the Lock Hospitals also available to these women. However, as English and later modern Irish laws, as well as the Irish Catholic Church, marginalized the Irish woman within society, she often found herself rejected by society, and by her own family, for a number of offenses: being an unwed mother, staying out too late at night, being born too pretty, orphaned, as well as many other offenses often not of her own making. Regardless, it is quite clear that the laundries and asylums would have never occurred if it were not for the fundamental changes that took place in Ireland in the 1500–1600s. The colonizing efforts of Ireland by England set off a domino effect where imposing factors such as primitive accumulation, displacement, and resistance, as well as rhetorical and religious influences, merged and worked to dismantle traditional organizational structures within Irish society. With the customary structures of organization (including the Brehon Laws, family organization, and traditional gender relations) destroyed, Irish society de-evolved in its relatively liberal view toward women's rights and citizenship status. Once citizenship status was reinterpreted for Irish women, they found themselves without legal or spiritual recourse when threatened or wronged. Finally, it is interesting to note that this lack of citizenship status has continued in Ireland up through the twentieth century and that the final Magdalene laundry was not closed in Ireland until 1996. Thus, even decolonized Ireland, since winning its independence in 1929, still carried with it the cross it bore as a result of converging factors occurring in the 1500–1600s.

Chapter Six

The Rise of the Irish Magdalene Laundries

It is not all uncommon, therefore, to find that the yellow and foul water from the row of tanks or washing machines at one end of the wash-house flows all across the floor and over the feet of the workers before eventually reaching the drain (1900, 385). Very often on entering the washing-house the whole place is so pervaded with steam that I cannot see the workers. A great deal of this steam comes from the coppers, of which there are generally two or three. The provision of hoods would to a great extent remedy matters, but in the greater number of cases these are conspicuous by their absence.[1]
— Annual Report H.M. Chief Inspector of Factories, 1900, p. 385, and Principal Lady Inspector of Factories for 1899, p. 257.

Before examining the rise and history of the Magdalene asylums and laundries as they developed and evolved in Ireland, one of England's periphery states, it is helpful to look briefly at the context in which these new and different asylums arose.[2] Whereas the convents in the Middle Ages were also state- and church-sponsored institutions, it must be recalled that most of the Magdalene houses and convents were municipally held and sponsored, and they functioned more in the vein of halfway homes for retired, municipal-approved prostitutes to retransition into society through marriage, or another means, when their career as a prostitute was over. Further, although women other than former prostitutes entered the medieval Magdalene convents, such as the abandoned wife, these institutions were mostly meant for former prostitutes only, an important difference when examining the Magdalene institutions and asylums from the eighteenth century on. Although originally structured as institutions to reform prostitutes, the Magdalene asylums in this period housed a larger section of society — marginalized women from all walks of life. Thus, society *widely* defined the prostitute as the "fallen" woman, ruined because of loss of virginity outside of marital vows, or ruined reputation (regardless of her virginal state). Any woman, whether she freely gave herself or was violated, could be considered a fallen woman and placed in the same category as a prostitute. This wider definition of the prostitute and the fallen allowed for women from mostly the middle and lower classes to be incarcerated in virtual workhouses and, for all intents and purposes, used as indentured servants doing laundry, needlework, and other female-approved modes of labor. How did this occur? Who ran these establishments, and how were they funded? To answer the second question first, most of these institutes were run by different orders of the Catholic Church (Sisters of Mercy and the Good Shepherd Sisters) and funded by the state as well as the labor of the inmates. There has been a good deal of anger at the Catholic Church, the nuns and priests, and their facilitation of these workhouses. Indeed, this work agrees that the Church has much to answer for, including the horrible treatment of the inmates left in their care. The promotion of magdalenism and the subsequent inhumane treatment of the women incarcerated (including working the women up to 19 hours a day, changing their name, hiding them from their families, poor working conditions, and neglect of education) has been documented in several books, including Frances Finnegan's *Do Penance or Perish*,[3] James Smith's *Ireland's Magdalene Laundries and the Nation's Architecture of Containment*,[4] movies such as *The Magdalene Sisters*,[5] and documentaries such as *Sex in a Cold Climate*.[6] Although the final section of this book will briefly document the history and treatment of the women in these institutions, the main purpose is to better understand the motivation, that is the *why* of modern magdalenism, and to pinpoint how these institutions generally differed in how they functioned and treated the women in the peripheral/colonized Ireland as compared to the Magdalene laundries and asylums found in the core market center of England. As such, although the Catholic Church and the nuns who ran these workhouses have much to account for, this work argues that placing blanketed blame on the Church is misleading. Indeed, the very fact, as will be demonstrated, that the laundries, asylums, and houses functioned and evolved differently in different parts of the world should inform us that different converging influences in different states worked to determine how magdalenism and these institutions worked within each social situation. Although it appears that the washing of laundry, needlework, and other approved "female labors" were used by most of these institutions across-the-board, the fundamental difference between core and periphery Magdalene laundries lies with the following factors: How were concepts of nation building, capital, labor, female worth and sexuality understood within the growing core versus peripheral/colonized state? These considerations determined other practical conditions in the laundries such as: (1) were the women allowed to leave after learning a new skill, or were they encouraged and forced to stay for life? ((2) Was there an active attempt to find women suitable employment or marriage after leaving the laundry? (3) Was there an attempt to provide an education to help the Magdalene learn new marketable skills and facilitate a more autonomous existence? For the most part, these three elements were mostly attempted in the core market state of England, but not in colonized state of Ireland. The difference lies with the convergence of several factors including how the rise of the state worked to facilitate not only a capitalist world economy, but also the formation of classes, national identity, and corresponding social attitudes toward certain classes, now determined by labor rather than the feudal hierarchy. These factors are seen, for example, through the *Poor Laws* of England and Ireland, as well as the *Factory Laws* that exempt religious laundries from having to follow any labor regulation in regards to the treatment of the worker and the condition of the facility.

As has been shown, the rise of the capitalist world system in the late sixteenth century coincided with long-distance trade, a marketable change in division of labor between core states, and the colonized, captured areas or what is termed the *periphery*.[7] As political theorist David Held reminds us regarding Wallenstein's keen observations apropos the rise of capitalism, along with the rise and formation of the state (and national identity), there is a distinction between world empires and a world economy. Whereas world empires are inflexible entities that work to control all elements of socialization including economics, a world economy transcends the boundaries of all political structures and the modern state specifically rose to accommodate this process.[8] Thus, Wallenstein writes about this world economy as a world system:

> It is a "world" system not because it encompasses the whole world, but because it is larger than any juridically-defined political unit. And it's a "world-*economy*" because the basic linkage between the parts of the system is economic, although this was reinforced to some extent by cultural links and eventually ... by political arrangements that even confederal structures.[9]

Within this process, global capitalism creates unequal economic and political power between different areas of the world and particularly between the core states and "her" colonized peripheral counterparts. As such, peripheral markets are working for the core markets, affecting both trade and labor in the colonized states as well as social relations. As Held further points out, it is important to make a distinction between how a world system affects not only market expansion but also social/labor relations:

> It is useful to make a distinction (which Wallenstein fails to do) between the expansion of capitalist market relations based on the desire to buy, sell, and accumulate mobile resources or capital, and the formation of industrial capitalism involving highly distinctive class relations — based on those who own and control the means of production and those who have only their

Stairs leading up to the Good Shepherd convent, laundry and orphanage at Sunday's Well, Cork, Ireland. In 1903, Michael John Fitzgerald McCarthy writes briefly about the institution in *Priests and People in Ireland*: "The Sisters of the Good Shepherd have a palatial collection of buildings at Sunday's Well, including an 'industrial' school, for which they draw £3157, 17s. 1d. per annum from the State" (p. 511). Photographed by and reproduced with permission from Mark Davis.

The Good Shepherd convent at Sunday's Well, Cork, Ireland: "It is built in the Gothic style, of brown stone, with bright coloured limestone quoins, windows, and door-ways, and is a beautiful and picturesque building" (Taylor, 1867, *Irish Homes and Irish Hearts*, p. 153). Photographed by and reproduced with permission from Mark Davis.

Arched in dignity. "To the [...] is committed the charge of the Magdalen Asylum,—an onerous duty, not at all to their liking, said the holy mother, and apparently not much to that of the penitents themselves; for recently something like a rebellion, ending in a secession, broke out amongst them" (Manners, 1881, *Notes of an Irish Tour*, p. 98). Photographed by and reproduced with permission from Mark Davis.

Rear aspect of the fire-damaged Shepherd convent and orphanage. In 2003, the convent, orphanage and laundry were destroyed in a devastating fire. Photographed by and reproduced with permission from Mark Davis.

laboring capacity to sell. "Capitalists," under the latter conditions, own factories and technology, while wage-laborers or "Wage-Workers," are without ownership in the means of production.[10]

Both England and, by default, Ireland hegemonically helped accommodate the expansion of capitalist market relations by creating laws that regulated distinct class relations in regards to labor. This, as well as corresponding social attitudes, had a direct effect on the Magdalene asylums and laundries. As the famous economic and political theorist Karl Polanyi points out in *The Great Transformation*, the free market and the world economy was assisted in a large part by "centrally organized and controlled interventionism."[11] This state interventionism included the creation of laws, such as the *Poor Laws* in England and Ireland, as well as the later *Factory Laws* that fashioned the conditions for forced labor, which was to exist in Ireland well into the twentieth century. Because the *Poor* and the later *Factory Laws* (discussed below) worked to allow an opening for the Magdalene laundries, it is important to see how they rose and functioned in English and Irish society.

The Poor Laws 1601–1834

The Poor Law Act of 1601, also called the *Elizabethan Poor Law*, was the first attempt by Great Britain to comprehensively address and provide for the poor. As Marjie Bloy[12] points out in her article "The 1601 Elizabethan Poor Laws," traditionally the care for the poor and the infirmed fell upon the parishes and a prevailing belief in the Christian Duty to care for the *least* in society. Upon the formation of the state, the Reformation and the establishment of the Church of England, an effort was made to legislate the problem of poverty. First, in 1552 parish registers were required to keep a record of the poor they administered to. In 1563, official state collections, collected by the Justices of the Peace for the poor was enacted, and, importantly, at this time the poor were separated into three separate categories:

- *Those who would work but could not*: these were the able-bodied or deserving poor. They were to be given help either through outdoor relief or by being given work in return for a wage.
- *Those who could work but would not*: these were the idle poor. They were to be whipped through the streets, publicly, until they learned the error of their ways.
- *Those who were too old/ill/young to work*: these were the impotent or deserving poor. They were to be looked after in almshouses, hospitals, orphanages or poor houses. Orphans and children of the poor were to be given a trade apprenticeship so that they would have a trade to pursue when they grew up.[13]

In 1572, a tax was installed to care for the poor. In 1576, poor workhouses were first suggested but not adopted, and in 1601 the *Elizabethan Poor Law* was approved.[14] Also known as the *Old Poor Law*, this provision levied a poor rate (tax) on each parish, created overseers to maintain the effort, legislated for the poor to work and supervised the poor house.[15] Two basic types of relief were included in this act: First was the outdoor relief where a "dole" of money, as well as food and clothing, was provided to the poor so that he or she could continue living in their own home.[16] Next, "indoor relief" was offered in the form of almshouses, hospitals, orphanages and workhouses for the "idle poor."[17]

These *Poor Laws* were maintained and augmented until their reform in 1834. Of particular interest regarding added legislation before the 1834 rewriting of the *Poor Laws* include the 1662 *Settlement Laws* that attempted to stop the poor from relocating to richer and more generous parishes, thereby taxing the system in any one parish:

> That whereas by reason of some Defects in the Law, poor People are not restrained from going from one Parish to another, and therefore do endeavour to settle themselves in those Parishes where there is the best Stock, the largest Commons or Wastes to build Cottages, and the most Woods for them to burn and destroy; and when they have consumed it, then to another Parish, and at last become Rogues and Vagabonds, to the great Discouragement of Parishes to provide Stocks, where it is liable to be devoured by Strangers.[18]

Unfortunately, this law had the unforeseen adverse effect of "limiting the mobility of labor and discouraged the unemployed from leaving the parish of their birth in order to find work."[19] There was also the rather harsh legal addition of the *Workhouse Test Act* of 1723 that required anyone looking for relief to "enter the workhouse where s/he would be obligated to undertake set work in return for relief. The principle was that entering the workhouse should be a deterrent to casual in irresponsible claims on the poor rates."[20] This act will later influence the Magdalene institutions, other workhouses, as well as magdalenism. In 1785 came *Gilbert's Act*, an attempt to offer a kinder helping hand to the poor than what was provided with the *Workhouse Test Act* by excluding "able bodied" paupers from the workhouses and allowing them to receive outdoor relief, as well as obtaining employment near their own homes. Part of the pragmatic necessity of *Gilbert's Act* came about because of the process of agricultural enclosure and the resulting low wages that created a higher unemployment rate, overwhelming the existing workhouses.[21] According to Polanyi, *Gilbert's Act* was helpful because as long "as outdoor relief and aid-in-wages were merely subsidiary to positive social legislation, they need not have been fatal to a rational solution."[22] However, what effec-

Labyrinth. The south tunnel entrance, leading underground to the convent property. Photographed by and reproduced with permission from Mark Davis.

Gallery. "In the Cork asylum, as elsewhere, the penitents have to work for their own support. There is a large workroom, and magnificent laundries" (Taylor, 1867, *Irish Homes and Irish Hearts*, p. 153). Photographed by and reproduced with permission from Mark Davis.

Labor of love. Sinks. Photographed by and reproduced with permission from Mark Davis.

tively made the *Elizabethan Poor Law System* ineffective, and in conflict to the rise of capitalism and labor completion, was the *Speenhamland System* (1795) that essentially erased the traditional distinction between the workhouse and the poorhouse poor, as it provided *generally* for all. In 1793, England was involved in the French Wars (1793–1815), which created a shortage of food imports followed by an increase in the price of bread. Because of this hardship, it was felt that additional assistance was needed to help the poor, by establishing income supplement scaled to the price of bread. Polanyi recounts: "The Justices of Berkshire, meeting at the Pelican Inn, in Speenhamland, near Newbury, on May 6, 1795, in a time of great distress, decided that subsidies in aid of wages should be granted in accordance with a scale dependent upon the price of bread, so that a minimum income should be assured to the poor *irrespective of their earnings*."[23] This system became adopted as the law of the land, and until it was abolished in 1832, "it effectively prevented the establishment of a competitive labor market" because workers no longer had an incentive to work harder for his or her employer because whether employed or unemployed, indeed irrespective of their earnings, all individuals were basically guaranteed a living wage: "Hence, no laborer had any financial interest in satisfying his employer, his income being the same whatever wages he earned."[24] As the *Speenhamland System* basically halted the effectiveness of market competition and competitive labor sources, it was abolished in 1832, and in 1834 the *New Poor Laws* were enacted (followed by the *Irish Poor Laws* in 1838).

The *New Poor Laws* of 1834 enacted a system of dealing with the poor almost entirely around the concept of a workhouse, taking its inspiration from the former 1723 *Workhouse Test Act*. Dismantling the *Old Poor Laws* and any real humanitarian aid to the poor, *The New Poor Laws* were constructed under the guise of *if you make the receiving of aid so horrible and almost pointless to obtain, you will not see the poor seeking aid and instead they will seek a wage earning job!* This approach can be seen in the overall stipulations of the *New Poor Laws* that allowed workhouse conditions to be intentionally worse than those found in the lowest paying jobs, and in private industry. Further, the *New Poor Laws* did away with outdoor relief (instituted with the earlier *Gilbert's Act* of 1785), segregated the classes of the poor, separated spouses and children from their families and finally abolished the "rate-in-aid" stipulated for by the *Old Poor Laws* that helped those earning very low wages.[25] In 1838, Ireland also enacted a *Poor Law Amendment Act* that extended the *New Poor Laws of England and Wales* to Ireland.[26] These acts allowed the Board of Guardians to collect a poor rate or tax in order to support local parish union workhouses.[27] Few poorhouses had existed in Ireland, mostly because aid to the poor remained a religious or spiritual domain. Thus these new laws aided in the development of parochial workhouses, which directly informed the development of the laundries. The *New Poor Laws* in effect not only aided the capitalist world system by creating state laws that promoted division of labor, labor classes, and the expansion of labor markets, but they also did so from the point of view of a central authority of governmental administration that supported and encouraged parochial workhouses in England, but especially in Ireland. Finally, aspects of the *New Poor Laws* served as inspiration and precedence for Ireland's later mother and daughter homes, Magdalene laundries, as well as the social/labor conditions found and promoted in these institutions (for example, separating mother and child, segregation by class and religion, and allowing for substandard working conditions).

Ireland's Early Magdalene Laundries

Lady Arbella Denny,[28] who originally was involved in reforming Dublin's Foundling Hospital, established the first Protestant Magdalene Asylum in Ireland in 1766.[29] Her work with the Foundling Hospital introduced her to the dreadful plight of women (prostitutes and single mothers) abandoned by their families, forced to give up their children, and then discarded by society. At this time in Irish History, the only government institution for prostitutes and other *fallen* women, besides prison, was the Lock Hospital, opened originally in 1755, in Dublin. Lady Denny's concern for these forgotten women prompted her to convince wealthy friends to contribute to a charitable fund that would provide for the *fallen* and rejected women of society, and on August 17, 1797, the first inmate was accepted.[30] In 1825, writer and clergyman George Newenham Wright (1794–1877) described the asylum as a brick building in Lesson-Street, and the inmates as "objects," who, the reader is told, receive some financial return for their labor: "The produce of the penitent's labour is partly bestowed upon them, as an incentive to industry, and a part is reserved for donations upon their being restored to moral habits, and permitted to quit the asylum."[31] Although it is clear from the early literature that Lady Denny was a committed philanthropic and well-loved woman, her decision to run a Magdalene asylum was likely influenced in part by the success of England's Magdalen-Home (the first one established in Whitechapel, 1758), which inspired a 1767 circulated letter calling for the establishment of a Magdalene asylum in Dublin: "Here, instead of loathsome disease these reclaimed individuals will enjoy the blessings of health. They will exchange gross ignorance for useful knowledge ... the base drudgery of prostitution for profitable employment in innocent recreations.... In short, instead of Devils, they will become Christians."[32] The Lesson-Street Magdalene Asylum was a success, receiving 60 penitents in 1846 alone,[33] and then was followed by mostly

Divine light. Likely, sleeping quarters. Photographed by and reproduced with permission from Mark Davis.

Fireplace in sleeping quarters. This former convent, laundry and orphanage will become the site of redevelopment as 200 plus high-end homes will be built on the location. Redevelopment approved by *An Bord Pleanála*. Photographed by and reproduced with permission from Mark Davis.

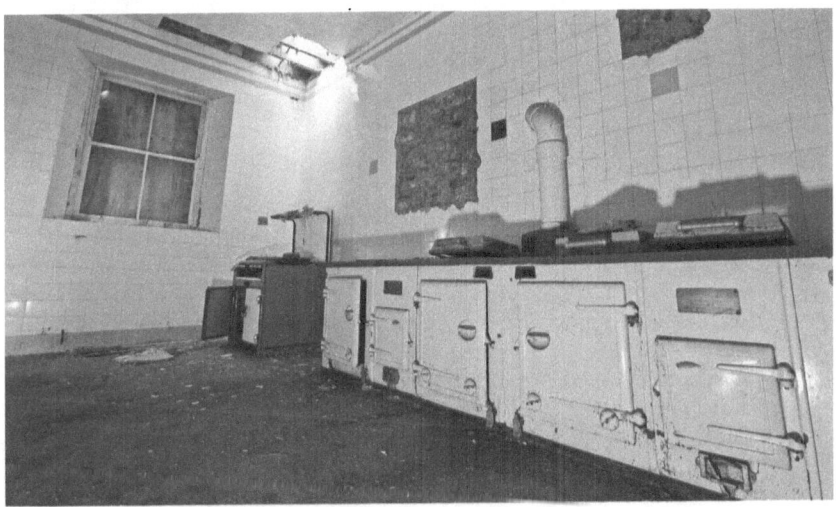

Free range. The kitchen. Photographed by and reproduced with permission from Mark Davis.

Baker's oven. Photographed by and reproduced with permission from Mark Davis. Taylor, in *Irish Homes and Irish Hearts* (1867) consider the food conditions for children in public workhouses: "Children in the workhouse never, or very rarely, see the commonest articles used in a kitchen [...] beef, mutton, poultry, fish, &c., were all things they read of or saw in pictures.... Soup or porridge they could understand — it was their daily food — but if they were starving, and given the materials to make them, they could not do so" (pp. 157–58).

Catholic Institutions throughout Ireland. In 1797, the First Catholic Magdalene asylum in Ireland opened on Townsend Street, Dublin, by Mrs. Bridget Burke. Writer and novelist Fanny Taylor (1832–1900) in her highly sentiment 1867 publication *Irish Homes and Irish Hearts*,[34] offers her rather imaginary description on the founding of Bruke's Magdalene asylum:

> Bridget Burke was a poor widow, who after her husband's death became a domestic servant. While in this employment she began to take a lively interest in the fallen of her own sex, and rescued one after another of them from evil courses. A good man about the same rank in life as her helped her, and at last proposed to her that they should take a house in which to receive penitents. "But," exclaimed Bridget, "sure we have no money."— "Let us have confidence in God," he answered; "let us place it under the protection of the Blessed Trinity." They knelt down together and prayed. On rising, Mr. Quarterman said, "Here is a penny." Bridget gave another; a third was contributed by her daughter, and with this sum they commenced their undertaking; they began to collect, and most of their funds came from the poor, chiefly domestic servants, and so the work prospered and grew into its present form.[35]

Like the Lesson-Street Magdalene Asylum, the Townsend Street Asylum trained the inmates in laundry and needlework as well as other skills that would help the inmate support herself when she left the asylum either for marriage or employment.[36]

In 1798 the General Magdalen Asylum of Donnybrook Green was established and run by the Sisters of Charity.[37] Taylor describes the asylum as being a peaceful place just outside of Dublin on Stillorgan Road. Offering a bit of historical ethos and pathos to her description, Taylor tells how the asylum was built upon a site famous for an annual fair where once a great riot broke out and "an Irishman in all his glory was there, with his sprig of shillelagh and shamrock so green," met with a "disastrous" ending. But, the fair was soon abolished and upon the site was built a beautiful church and Magdalene asylum run by the Sisters of Charity.[38] Unlike the earlier Magdalene asylums, the Sisters of Charity started the *tradition* of maintaining the Magdalene inmate for life. Further, unlike the late medieval institutions where former prostitutes retired for life, these institutes did not allow for autonomous existence, because the "Magdalenes" were ruled over by the Sisters of Charity, creating not so much a community as a reformatory. Taylor recounted a conversation with the Mother Superior regarding this hierarchal arrangement: "The wish and intention of the Sisters is that their inmates should remain with them for life.... The Sisters believe that very few of these who have lost their good name, and, generally speaking, have contracted habits of intemperance, idleness, and other vices, will be able to resist temptation if exposed to the rough contact of the world again."[39] This is an important rhetorical and social ideology regarding the Irish Magdalene as compared to the English Magdalene. Although both the Irish and the English believed that salvation could only be found through hard work, prayer, and religious contemplation, the English reformer sought to help the Magdalene "realize her economic potential,"[40] while the Irish institution felt that it was impossible to allow such a woman back into society without the expectation that she would again fall. Both in England and Ireland, it was suggested that the labor market and all its pitfalls including the desire for "goods and luxury," as well as the difficulty to compete as a female laborer in a free market, caused women to fall.[41] If labor markets were the *catalyst* for prostitution and immoral behavior, then placing the Magdalene inmate back into that mix was just setting her up for failure, according to many of the nuns who ran the Irish Magdalene asylums. In England, however, it was felt that although labor markets might have caused the woman's initial fall, it did so because she did not have adequate skills to support herself and compete in the job market; thus, if you offer the Magdalene expertise, including industry skills and the ability to read and write, the reformed inmate had a fighting chance to survive with her dignity intact.[42] The difference between these two attitudes is imperative, because it appears that in core market centers (England and later the United States), a "fallen" woman's reforming process was also a process of learning the skills to realize her "economic potential," thereby becoming a vital citizen and helping promote the English (or U.S.) nationality.[43] In the case of the peripheral market centers, on the other hand, it appears that the core understanding of "economic potential" of the inmate was only promoted within and for the laundry asylum itself. In this situation, the inmates were "children" who lacked strength and common sense and needed constant labor structure to occupy their time. As the Mother Superior of the Donnybrook Green asylum explained to Taylor, the peaceful Magdalene inmates were the ones who had been in the laundry for a very long time, suggesting that time, physical space, and labor were the only saviors for these women: "There had been time for the fierce passions to be subdued, and the wild history of the past to fade out of the mind."[44] Further it was felt that education would be wasted on such women who, like children, had little capacity to reason anyway. In the end, most of the Irish Magdalenes could not read or write, nor were they instructed to do so: "Education, particularly in Convent Magdalen Asylums, hardly existed — an omission revealed in the Rules for the Direction of the Classes and demonstrated in the 1901 Consensus.... This source indicates that in spite of having spent years, sometimes even lifetimes in the Homes, many Good Shepherd penitents were unable to read or write."[45] Withholding education worked to aid the promotion of magdalenism by keeping the inmates ignorant and therefore dependant on their keepers. This attitude and rhetoric

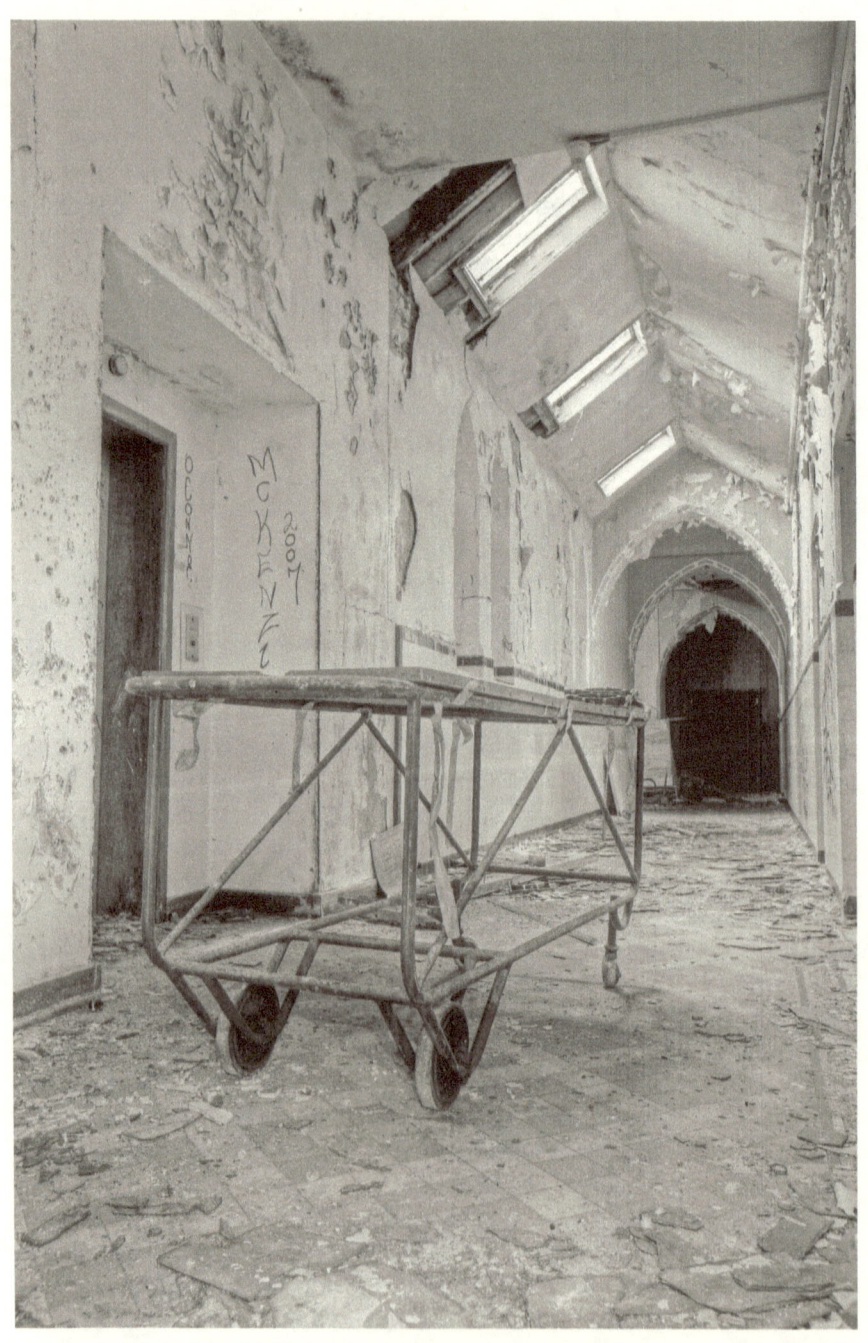

Abandoned. A forgotten trolley: "A number of orphans and deserted children are always found in the workhouse school; when they become old enough to go out to service, they are sent to it..." (Taylor, 1867, *Irish Homes and Irish Hearts*, p. 154). Photographed by and reproduced with permission from Mark Davis.

Close-up of the baker's oven. Photographed by and reproduced with permission from Mark Davis.

Loft. "The penitents attend Mass in a chapel separated from the main chapel by a wall of Venetian blinds; so that no one can see them while at their devotions" (Manners, 1881, *Notes of an Irish Tour*, p. 98). Photographed by and reproduced with permission from Mark Davis.

regarding the helpless nature of the Magdalene, although not shared by all of Ireland's early laundries, became prevalent as the institutions move into the late nineteenth and twentieth century. This is pointedly seen with the orders of the Sisters of Mercy and the Sisters of the Good Shepherd. Now, both of these organizations have become synonymous with widespread abuse occurring in their laundries and industrial homes.

Later Irish Magdalene Asylums

During the 1800s, Magdalene *Refuges*, as they were deceptively referred to, became more numerous and were at first privately funded, run by women for their fallen sisters in society: prostitutes, unwed mothers, elderly and the handicapped. Originally, private management and committees controlled most of these institutions, because such work was considered properly women's vocation.[46] Besides Lady Denny's efforts, Miss Lynch's philanthropic endeavors established an asylum in Galway City (1832), which was eventually left in the care of the Sisters of Mercy upon her death in 1847[47]: "the Sisters of Mercy have a large convent in Galway, from whence the religious who serve the infirmary are sent out; they have two branch houses, one an orphanage, the other a Magdalene asylum."[48] Additionally, Irish historian Frances Finnegan recounts the story of Miss Reddan, who in 1826 founded a *refuge* for former prostitutes in Limerick, and a laundry used to support them on a bit of land next to the Provincial monastery of the Congregation of the Good Shepherd.[49] According to both Finnegan and Taylor, Miss Reddan had always wanted to enter the Good Shepherd Sister's Order, and insisted that they should take over her efforts with the penitents: "A successful application was made to the Angers Mother House, and on 18th February 1848, three sisters — the Foundresses of the Good Shepherd Mission in Ireland — arrived in Limerick."[50] An important event since it is under the Good Shepherds and the Sisters of Mercy that the Irish Magdalene movement and laundries were directed for a hundred and fifty years.[51] Regardless, because private individuals and charities did most of their charity work out of the public eye, there is little information on many of the early institutions. Likewise, there is little information of the later institutions at the turn of the century run by the Catholic Church, because records were not kept; indeed, Irish and English law did not require the Churches and other charitable institutions to keep records — and most did not. As Finnegan discusses regarding the New Ross Home: "The records contain little evidence regarding penitents' daily routine, hours of work, and time allowed for recreation. However, there are indications that they labored in the laundries for most of the day, that many were exploited in this respect, and that other aspects of their "training" and welfare were sacrificed to this important rule."[52] However, by the 1800s there were more Magdalene asylums in Ireland than England. What is so strange about this fact is that the problem of prostitution was not as prevalent in Ireland as it was in England. As such, historian Maria *Luddy* points to an 1835 exchange between Monsignor Kinseley of Kilkenny and Alexis de Tocqueville. The Monsignor admits that "twenty years in the confessional have made me aware that the misconduct of girls is very rare, and that of married women almost unknown. Public opinion, one might almost say, goes too far in this direction. A woman suspected is lost for life."[53] In Dublin alone, where the highest number of arrested prostitutes existed, there were only 3,255 arrests in 1870, a number that declined so continuously that by 1900 there were only 431 prostitutes arrested.[54] This number was partly reduced by the appearance of Magdalene asylums, which popped up in numerous places around Ireland and especially in Dublin. As Finnegan observes, some of the early homes included "the Liverpool Female Penitentiary founded in 1810; the Hull Home of Hope, 1811; the Glasgow Magdalene Asylum, 1815; the Devon and Exeter Female Penitentiary, 1819; the Leeds Guardian and the Gloucester Magdalene Asylums, both opened in 1821; and the York Refuge, and the Manchester Asylum for Female Penitents, each established in 1822."[55]

Early on there was a great deal of interest from the public as the first such asylums appeared all over Ireland, after which public financial support and interest began to wane. To counteract this financial problem, the women penitents were made to do needlework and laundry to earn their keep, often forfeiting even token pay. Such additional work is ironic when reflecting on the fact that laundresses used to have to supplement their income by prostitution. Still, enough money could not be generated to keep these institutions private. This dire financial situation was even noted in a sermon preached by the rector of Fethard, the Rev. Henry Woodward, M.A., for a Magdalene Asylum (February 20, 1825, Sermon XI), where Woodward specifically discusses such funding problems: "That there is ample room in this establishment for more accommodation than its funds enable it to supply; 2nd. That a considerable diminution, of even its ordinary funds, has been occasioned this year by the death of some of its best supporters."[56] Eventually all the privately owned Magdalene asylums were adopted into Irish Catholic Convents and partially supported by the state, but this did not occur until after the *Contagious Diseases Acts* (1864), which allowed women to be checked for sexually transmitted diseases in Ireland and England, and then to be *forcibly* retained in lock hospitals, laundries, and penitentiaries. It is with the *Contagious Diseases Acts* that modern magdalenism is really born. Promoted by state and church, the profit motive was sought under the guise of social health and spiritual reform, dropping any illusions to the creation of a hegemonic rela-

Cemetery gates. Photographed by and reproduced with permission from Mark Davis.

Cemetery. Photographed by and reproduced with permission from Mark Davis.

Six. The Rise of the Irish Magdalene Laundries

Little Nell (Nellie Organ 1903–1908). "This saintly child was the daughter of humble Catholic parents whose only inheritance was a sterling Irish faith. The youngest of four children, Nellie was not four years old when her mother died and she, with her sister was placed in the Industrial School of the Sisters of the Good Shepherd, at Sunday's Well in 1907. It was soon discovered that she was suffering from phthisis and curvature of the spine. As her frail little body wasted away her heart and soul opened to the love of God and the illumination of His grace in an extraordinary degree" (*The Catholic Encyclopedia*, edited by Edward Aloysius Pace, supplement 1, vol. xvii, 1922, p. 563b).

tionship between labor and capital, fallen and the religious, where those forced to do the labor in the Magdalene laundries found that they were no longer getting something out of the arrangement.[57] In *Do Penance or Perish*, Finnegan recounts how 20 prostitutes in 1876 were forced out of brothels by their local priest and then installed into Cork's Magdalene Asylums[58]: "It was further alleged that thirty more of their number joined them over the next few days. This 'celebrated' incident, much exaggerated, was reported in the Convent's annals and in the local press. It was submitted as evidence before the Select Committee on the *Contagious Diseases Act* in 1881–82, and described (mostly embellished) in both the 1895 and 1933 biographies of the Order's Foundress."[59] Regarding the forced incarceration as a result of the *Contagious Diseases Act*, it appears that the new Magdalene inmates did not take to their situation well. Between the period travel writers Taylor, *Irish Homes and Irish Hearts*, and also John James R. Manner (1818–1907, 7th Duke of Rutland), *Notes of an Irish Tour*, there are two very different images of this particular workhouse asylum. Writing in 1867, Taylor reports that "in the Cork asylum, as elsewhere, the penitents have to work for their own support. There is a large workroom, and magnificent laundries. We were much struck by the quiet manner and modest demeanour of many of the women, giving evidence of the improvement which had been wrought in their characters."[60] Manner, writing in 1881, at the time of the forced incarnations discussed by Finnegan, offers a different picture, one in which the Magdalene inmates were not "quiet" or "modest," but actively rebellious in regard to the treatment they were receiving: "To the sisters of Charity, of Cork, is committed the charge of the Magdalen Asylum,—an onerous duty, not at all to their liking, said the holy mother, and apparently not much to that of the penitents themselves; for recently something like a rebellion, ending in a secession, broke out amongst them."[61] As the Cork situation demonstrates, The *Contagious Diseases Act* and a corresponding issue with sexually transmitted diseases created an increase in government interest concerning the problem of prostitution in Ireland. With the *Contagious Diseases Acts*, more Lock Hospitals were established throughout Ireland, and women were shifted from Lock Hospitals to the Magdalene asylums, from (the later) mother and child homes to Magdalene asylums, and from orphanages to Magdalene asylums, making these institutions religiously run and state endorsed.

Prostitution and sexual immorality became convoluted with anything associated with sex including unwed motherhood, rape, and incest. Once again the great divide between the Mother Mary (the ideal images held for the female in Irish society) and the fallen Magdalene was conjured. But this time, repentance for the Magdalene and her imagined crimes could not be found in her solitary cave, but through hard and mostly free labor: "These attempts subjected the women to a repressive moral regime while making money from their labour. The patients wore uniforms and were placed in separate wards; *fallen women* were segregated from married women, who had to prove their marital status by producing their marriage certificate, and Protestant was separated from Catholic."[62] This segregation of the good from the fallen in the general hospitals and workhouses created a horrific stigma, which again reinforced and either/or dichotomy between the sinful and the sinless, the Virgin and the Whore, the Magdalene and the Mother Mary. However, in the Magdalene laundries, there was no real distinction between women and their so-called crimes. Even if a woman was placed there to stop her from "falling," she was seen as fallen once she stepped inside the laundry — all sin, including potential sin, equated a fall: "The real evil lay in uniformity of treatment — an unavoidable consequence of such a system. Punitive measures, designed to control the most depraved of women, were applied indiscrimi-

Close-up of cemetery grounds. Penitents and nuns were not buried in the same cemetery but kept separate from each other, with the sisters' final resting ground far outshining that of the orphans or penitents. Fanny Taylor (1867) was very fond of convent cemetery grounds and spoke of them often in her publication *Irish Homes and Irish Hearts*: "After Benediction, we walked through the new grounds, and visited the nuns' cemetery, a pretty, peaceful spot. The names and ages of all the departed are inscribed on a stone tablet [...] we observed that many of the Sisters had attained great ages; none had died young..." (p. 82).

nately to all."[63] Such a misguided rule-utilitarian approach to action and thought did not promote the greatest good, but instead made everyone, prostitute, rape and incest victims, and the single mother, all the same — sinners of the lowest kind. In addition, it was no longer prostitutes and single mothers that were placed in the laundries, since the authorities, the church, and family members enrolled any woman who stood outside the fold — creating a ripe environment for extreme gender discrimination and magdalenism. The reason? Partly it was the Irish identification with the Catholic Church and concepts of immorality; however, economics plays a heavy role as well, especially considering the great Irish Famine (*An Gorta Mór*) between 1845 and 1852, which filled the poor workhouses and laundries to capacity, while reducing the Irish population by almost a quarter. Since food and employment became almost nonexistent, more women turned to prostitution as a way to survive. Further, women and children were also abandoned by their husbands, who were often hopeless because of the lack of work and a corresponding inability to provide for their families. All these conditions added to the popularity of the laundries. Of course, England wanted little to do with the burden that the Famine and the so-called *Irish Question* presented to them. England attempted to simply get rid of the perceived problem of the fallen Irish female by shipping her to Australia as a servant after she had stayed a year in the Irish workhouse. But upon arrival in Australia, and finding that many of these women lacked the skills and education for such work, employers turned many of these women out into the streets to endure on

Sister of Mercy Magdalene Asylum Steam Laundry advertisement, ca. 1897. Reproduced from the British India & Queensland Agency Company's *Handbook of Information for the Colonies and India.*

their own, where they turned to prostitution to survive — again, creating a continual need and environment for the rise of Magdalene laundries in Australia as well.[64]

Ireland and the Early Factory Laws

Another economic consideration can be found in the free labor the Magdalenes provided for the convents, and how this labor was unregulated. Indeed, after the establishment of the 1895 *Factory Laws* (fully discussed in chapter seven) and their minimal regulations on working hours as well as working conditions, the religious laundries were allowed to work women sometimes 19 hours a day.[65] As the Fabian Society noted in their publication, *Life in a Laundry* (1900), most laundries were exempt from following the *Factory Laws* and subsequently from following legislated protections for the laborer and regulations regarding working conditions. Furthermore, they were also exempt from receiving inspections, random or prearranged. The *Factory Bill* of 1895, which extended well into the twentieth century, held the following exemptions:

(a) Inmates of any prison, reformatory or industrial school, or any other institution for the time being subject to an inspection under any other than the Factory act; or

(b) Inmates of an institution conducted in good faith for religious or charitable purposes; or

(c) Members of the same family dwelling there, or in which not more than two persons dwelling elsewhere are employed.[66]

Further, the report noted that when the question of regulation and inspection regarding religious laundries were discussed in Parliament, it was the objections of the Irish Parliament members that halted reform from 1895 through to 1907.[67] One of the main arguments against the Magdalene laundries having to submit to random inspections and factory regulations was that they were not in the laundry business for profit, but for spiritual reform. However, many records show, including the Annual Charities' register for 1901 below, that these institutions were making a great deal of money[68]:

Name of House	Income from Laundry £	Income from Other Sources £
Magdalen Home, Edgbaston	631	237
Home of Good Shepherd, Malvern	703	287
Asylum for Penitent Females, Dublin	1,046	225
Edgar Home, Belfast	1,132	144
Edinboro' Industrial Home for Fallen Women	1,649	158
Magdalen Asylum, Edinburgh	5,847	493

This profit motive can be seen in McCarthy's 1903 account of the Convent at Mercy's Laundry at Wexford.[69] Examining the coast county of Wexford (the towns of Wexford, Enniscorthy, New Ross and Gorey), McCarthy recounted a meeting of the Poor Law Union and District Council, who were to decide on a proposal to send children to work in the Convent laundry:

> The Convent at Mercy at Wexford is a profit-making institution, receiving £2063 of public money yearly for 105 vagrant children in its industrial school. The nuns, in this letter, propose to employ the poorhouse children at the lucrative employment of laundry and "cookery, &c., &c.," to quote the Superioress's expressive abbreviations. They ask the guardians to provide an outfit. They expect the labour of the children free, and, in addition, to get a pension of £9 per annum for each child out of the rates.[70]

Although the ladies of council tended to support the proposal, Councilman Mr. Lambert argued against it, stating that the training at the convent was poor, and that the convent was already putting people out of work: "*The Convent of Mercy was the means of taking work out of the hands of many honest laboring families in Wexford.... The Convent of Mercy had put as many people out of work as they had in the House of Mercy at present*, and the people that formally did the laundry work were the most useful members of the community."[71] Thus for Mr. Lambert, the question was also one of unregulated competition.

True to form, regular laundry businesses were very angry about such unregulated competition because the religious institutions could work the women (and children) unregulated hours, without paying the workers (indentured servitude induced by market conditions), and therefore pricing "business" (as opposed to religious or reform) laundries out of the industry. Indeed, this very situation was reported in the Annual Report of Chief Inspectors of Factories in 1898, and again in 1900: "Again I must record that the exemption of the present domestic laundries and charitable institutions causes great dissatisfaction to the other laundry proprietors. They complain bitterly of the competition of places which are allowed to work 'all hours of the night,' and I must say I think they are fully justified in their complaint."[72] Yet what make these exceptions from labor laws acceptable, as well as the promotion of magdalenism, were the rhetoric of God, morality, and the evils of female sexuality. In a sense, the ideas that hard labor was a cure for a wayward and sexually charged soul helped justify labor practices encouraged by a partially regulated market. What must not be underestimated here was the palatable fear of female sexuality and the ability to use that fear to substantiate and justify a partially unregulated market. Regardless of her early traditions, Ireland and other "religious" peripheral market centers used and promoted the fear of women's sexuality for both national identity building[73] and profit making—

combining capital with moral righteousness. Again, this moral profit motive can be viewed with how the workers in these religious *retreats* were unregulated and worked to their physical limits: As the Rev. Arthur Brinckerman, Assistant Chaplain at St. Andrew's Home in Edinburgh as well as the Chaplain for the St. Agnes Hospital for the fallen, stated: "I have known girls far advanced in consumption in the laundry working long after they ought to have been elsewhere, or in hospital. Self-supporting homes need extra inspection, the temptation being to overwork the girls. After more than 30 years' close connections with hospitals, sisterhoods, homes and refuges, I feel the need of inspection most strongly."[74] Finally, whenever public protest occurred in defiance of the Magdalene laundresses, although labor and capital was an issue, there were several other legal, social and rhetorical sources of defense offered: The 1861 *Offenses Against the Person Act*, the *1885 Criminal Law Amendment Act,* the *Carrigan Committee Report, Criminal Law Amendment Act* of 1935, and the British and Irish *Catholic Cannons Laws,* all of which will influence the *Irish Constitution, 1937.*

Offences against the Person, Criminal Law, Catholic Concepts of Immorality, and the Irish State

In order to understand how it is charitable institutions at the turn of the century became virtual prisons in modern-day Ireland, it is important to follow the establishment of a series of laws. Just as was demonstrated regarding how the Brehon Laws mutated into the March Laws, and finally into English law regulating poverty, sex, property ownership, and morality, the laws of "modern" Ireland would follow a similar direction from English law, to Catholic law, to the establishment of the *Irish Constitution* that solidified Irish National Identity with that of Catholic morality. The *Contagious Diseases Acts* and how they allowed for *suspected* prostitutes to be inspected for venereal diseases and then instilled in Magdalene homes, penitentiaries, Lock Hospitals and laundries has already been discussed. When these acts were combined with the earlier *1861 Offenses Against the Person Act*, many girls and women, prostitutes or not, found themselves ostracized by society through laws that regulated sex and sexual crimes. For example, the 1861 *Offenses Against the Person Act* cited the age of sexual consent as being as young as twelve years of age,[75] and made it a felony to have sexual (carnal) relations with a girl under the age of ten, and a misdemeanor between the ages of ten and twelve. Thus, while having sex with a young girl worked to ruin that girl for life, the penalty for the male was not different than the penalty for public drunkenness. These laws favored the male, while providing almost no real protection for the female. Nevertheless, *The Offenses Act* was slightly amended with the *Criminal Law Amendment Act* of 1885, where consent was raised to 16 years of age,[76] and the new law deemed that carnal knowledge with a girl under the age of 14 a felony (under 17 a misdemeanor),[77] but that conviction of breaking these laws relied upon the availability of witnesses: "No person shall be convicted of an offence under this section upon the evidence of one witness only, unless such witness be corroborated in some material particular by evidence implicating the accused."[78] Because there was (and is) rarely witnesses to such sexual assaults other than the person being assaulted and his or her attacker, few convictions were made. Further, it is important to note that the *1861 Offenses Against the Person Act* also held a provision against the procedure of abortion, laid out in section 58 of the Act. Although the free Irish State of the twentieth century will be discussed more fully in chapter eight, in 1937 with the founding of the *Irish Constitution*, section 58 of the *1861 Offenses Against the Person Act* became one with Irish law under Article 40:3–3 regarding personal rights: "The State acknowledges the right to life of the unborn and with due regard to the equal right to life of the mother, guarantees in its laws to respect, and, as far as practical, by its laws to defend and vindicate that right." Further, under Personal Rights in the *Irish Constitution*, and directly relating to the *Catholic Cannon Laws* for Britain and Ireland, is a clause regarding public morality: "The State guarantees liberty for the exercise of the following rights, subject to public order and morality."[79] This idea of "public order and morality" continues as the *Irish Constitution* defines the role of women within the Irish state, as being limited to that of housewife and mother:

> 41.2.1 The state recognizes that by her life within the home, women gives to the state a support without which the common good cannot be achieved,
> 41.2.2 The state shall, therefore, endeavor to ensure that mothers shall not be obliged by economic necessity to engage in labor to the neglect of their duties in the home.[80]

Although these laws within the *Irish Constitution* appear harmless enough (recognizing the rights of the unborn child, the mother, societal order and provisions for the housewife), when these laws are reinforced with the *Catholic Cannon Laws*, they create strict rules on how and where a woman can exist in Irish Society. In part two of *The British and Catholic Cannon Laws* ("Penalties for Particular Offenses"); Title One ("Offenses Against Religion and the Unity of the Church"), penalties are stipulated toward anyone who disrupts the morality of the Catholic community: "A person is to be punished with a just penalty, who, at a public event or assembly, or in a published written, or by otherwise using the means of social communication, utters blasphemy, or gravely harms public morals, or rails at or excites hatred of or contempt for religion or the church."⁸¹ From the above provisions, any woman who acts outside the allotted legal and moral roles legislated for her was harming public *morals*: the prostitute, the single mother, the abandoned wife, the unruly daughter, the woman sexually assaulted or raped — and yes, the daughter born too pretty — all were deemed a danger to moral society. Further, these same women were being pitted against one another, since it was the woman's responsibility to uphold moral standards in Irish Society, literally disavowing the male his responsibility regarding sex and illegal sexual acts such as rape.⁸² In order to maintain proper morality, these Catholic and Irish state laws came together, forming a type of legal church and state marriage that allowed the state and local churches to place any women they felt were fallen, or might cause moral damage to the community, into Magdalene laundries. No longer were these institutions an opportunity for change and hope. In the same way Mary Magdalene went from being an independent woman of means to a repented prostitute, these institutions (intertwined within the Irish system) became a virtual prison for any woman who gave the wrong impression. In the end, there is a confluence of laws and regulations (from the *Poor Laws*, to being exempted within the *Factory Laws*, to the *Contagious Diseases Act*, and *Offenses Against the Person Act*, to the *Catholic Canon Law* and the Irish Constitution) all converging within a domino effect — piling upon the Irish Female to create legislated discrimination, as well as arranging for a cheap labor force. Although not quite slavery in the sense it is often talk about it, certainly a form of slavery was legislated for under this convergence of bureaucratic tangles that undoubtedly helped, if not specially meant to, inform and promote a market economy. So it was that many women in Ireland became second-class citizens. This series of law transmutations starting from the Brehon Laws to the constitution of Ireland seem almost surreal, because one would expect Ireland, like many Anglicized societies, to have evolved in its thinking about women and women's rights. It is also a bit strange that the new Irish government of 1921 did not try to regain any of their ancient roots (culture and laws) after English invasion and rule. As Power rightly laments, "When one looks at the declared aims of this and later governments to Gaelicise the country, one can only comment on the shallow hypocrisy of it all. Indeed a law forbidding divorce was passed by that first government and a kind of sub–Victorian state, in the most pejorative sense of the term, emerged to reach the dead years of the 1950's."⁸³ This observation becomes more bewildering because one aim of the Easter Rising of 1916 (Ireland's fight for independence) was to reclaim Irish culture and law that existed before the English had seized Ireland. In fact, many women's group formed to help in this effort looked to the Brehon Laws as a form of inspiration and hope.⁸⁴ Furthermore, the Declaration of the Provisional Government of the Irish Republic, posted during the Easter Rising, relied on these ancient laws while declaring the intent for true equal rights between men and women:

> The Republic guarantees civil and religious liberty, equal rights and equal opportunities to all its citizens, and declares its resolve to pursue the happiness and prosperity of the whole nation and of all its parts, cherishing all the children of the nation equally, and oblivious of the differences carefully fostered by an alien government, which have divided a minority from the majority in the past.[85]

However, when the Irish Republic was finally free from English rule, instead of looking toward their heritage for inspiration, they looked toward the Roman Catholic Church, creating a constitution that limited women's rights to the *Canon Laws* held by the Catholic Church. Indeed, by inserting articles 41.2.1–2 into the *Irish Constitution*, the government, with the Catholic Church at its side, has legally forced women into a role of citizenship that is designed to coincide with a concept of national, Catholic, identity that started with the death of the March Laws in the 1600s, the colonization of Ireland by England, and which gained considerable momentum with the Catholic emancipation in 1829.[86] As Smith correctly argues in *Ireland's Magdalen Laundries*: "Catholic morality became at once a hallmark of Irish identity, differentiating the national community from its near neighbors, and an emblem of the uncontested political territory."[87]

Catholic Morality, Single Mothers, and the Process of Legal Concealment

In *Ireland's Magdalen Laundries and the Nation's Architecture of Containment*, Irish Historian James Smith argues that Ireland can trace the laws and ideology that guided the later Irish Magdalene laundries back to *The Carrigan Report* with its focus on the problems of juvenile prostitution, as well as a series of laws including the *Criminal Law Amendment Act* (1935) and the establishment of the mother and child homes, first seriously proposed in 1922 and well established by 1933. Although this work traces the economic and resulting social motivations that influenced the different development of the Magdalene asylums in different market centers, Smith's argument regarding the legal efforts behind Ireland's effort at nation building, citizenship, and the defining of social roles through Catholic morality is crucial. Be it that the most respected and admired image of womanhood in Ireland was the celibate nun,[88] most Irish women could only find sanctioned citizenship through perceived domestic worth as an "approved" mother and homemaker.[89] This realization of female citizenship, of course, will become crystal clear with the *Irish*

Constitution, as discussed above. Regardless, the Irish female as a domestic citizen was narrowly defined within the confines of Catholic morality, legitimate marriage, and motherhood. Single mothers and other women deemed sexually immoral could not be tolerated as legitimate, cogent, citizens, and so a system of "containment" was developed that "empowered the decolonizing nation-state to confine aberrant citizens, rendering invisible women and children who fell foul of society's moral proscriptions."[90] Fundamental to efforts at segregation and confinement were the mother and child homes financed by the state, the inmate's labor, and private donations, while being run by Catholic nuns. Growing with the newly freed state of Ireland, these mother and child homes were part of a two-tiered system that divided the "first fallen" women from the habitual "repeat" offender: "Here the unmarried mother was guaranteed a safe environment ... [while the] nuns arranged a 'situation' for the mother after her release. She could continue to visit her baby, and she was expected to 'pay out of her earnings' for the child's upkeep."[91] If the woman was a repeat offender, she was urged to "voluntarily" submit herself to a Magdalene laundry. In this case, she was offered a "choice," either enter the laundry or the penitentiary system. Because the illusion of "choice" was often given to the women who spent their lives in the Magdalene laundries, the state to this day considers these institutions as voluntary asylums.[92] Consequently, as Smith concludes, there were two types of female offenders in Ireland: (1) those who still had the potential to reform, the so-called first fallen, and (2) the hopeless cases sent to prisons or, more often, the laundries.[93] The problem was there were more women in the second category to contend with than the first — repeat offenders who, because of poverty, lack of education or sexual crimes committed on them, found themselves pregnant out of wedlock more than once.

Several other elements converged to create these conditions: lack of sexual education, the unavailability of contraceptives, and laws that took away the male culpability for sexual crimes, and allowed children to be taken from their parents under the guise of "moral danger." However, it is also important to reflect back on the Victorian utilitarian insistence of acquiring practical working skills as a solution for ending poverty. As the Commission to Inquire into Child Abuse (Ireland) 2009 states in the introduction of their final report, industrial schools and other reformatories that cited the instilment of skills were also designed to drive the industrial revolution[94] and, as argued above, a world-capitalist economy. What Smith coins an "Architecture of Containment" was essentially a system of mother and child homes, industrial and reformatory schools and laundries — all of which were ancestors of the earlier poor laws and workhouses discussed earlier in this chapter,[95] and all of which helped drive a capitalist economy and industry under the rhetoric of moral reform. This system of "containment" became interwoven because of the rhetoric of illegitimacy in Irish Society. Again, prostitution became associated with any woman who became pregnant outside of the bonds of marriage in Ireland. Further, prostitution was not longer discussed in regards to the Magdalene laundries, but the focus changed to unmarried mothers.[96] This, Smith argues, is the legacy of *The Carrigan Report* that ignored the sociological truths regarding lack of sexual education, poverty, the influence of industry, and other social realities of the time.[97] As immorality was directly associated with illegitimacy, the laws allowed any child who was deemed in *moral danger*[98] to be taken away from the mother (or family) and placed in the industrial and reformatory institutions.[99] After the birth, single mothers (both first and repeated offenders) often found themselves placed in the Magdalene laundries when better situations could not be found, while their children were placed in fosters homes or, as was the usual case, "charitable" and religious industrial schools — by 1952, Ireland's *Adoption Act* allowed for these children to be taken out of the country and adopted by approved Catholic families.[100] This interwoven system of concealment and confinement lasted until 1996, with women still being sent to the laundry asylums in the 1980s.[101]

Conclusion and Convergences

It is important to remember that Ireland was not the only state harboring such contempt for women in the name of morality and, importantly, profit. Truly, these laundries existed in England, Scotland, Australia, Canada, the United States and elsewhere as well. Like other peripheral/colonized states (Australia and Scotland for example) these institutions lasted well into the twentieth century and also relied on a particular interconnected system of reformatory and industrial schools for the female sex.[102] Just as England offers the paradigm for the Magdalene laundries found in the core market center of the rising world economy, Ireland is the exemplar example of these peripheral Magdalene laundries, because a domino effect of circumstances, convergences, and conditions that all eventually lead to the legal confinement of women to labor houses well into the late twentieth century can be clearly viewed. What will be demonstrated with the English example is how there is a remarkable difference in how women were viewed in the core market center in relation to industry, nation building efforts, and citizenship. Indeed the question becomes: what constitutes a wanted citizen through law and society? Although religion is an aspect in determining the early answer to this question, it is not strictly a Catholic versus Protestant outlook, but an outlook that relies on the convergences of events leading to industry and the development of a world economy.

In defense of the many convents that housed the Magdalene laundresses, the expectations placed upon the nuns were unreasonable and demanding. Niall McElwee (director in Applied Social Studies at the Waterford Institute of Technology in Ireland) expressed this opinion in an article regarding the modern tragedy: "The nuns who were the guardians of the 'penitents' living in these institutions were expected by the society of the time to operate as both [care givers] and gaolers [jailers]. They were hardly compatible tasks."[103] However true this may be, the idea that society had no tolerance or place for these women outside of the laundries is a sentiment easily spouted and accepted, just as Pope Gregory I and others blindly accepted Mary Magdalene as a prostitute. Sister Meta Reid offered her opinion of the situation: "Society didn't want these women. Their families didn't want them. There was no place else for them to go. Yes, we were unjust, but we were unwittingly facilitating a system that was unjust."[104] This unjust attitude could also be traced to a tradition of high distrust and disgust held for the Magdalene penitent. As Finnegan recounts about the general attitude that many of the sisters had for the Magdalenes in their care (from the *Conferences and Instructions of the Venerable Mother Mary of Saint Euphraisi Pelletier, Foundress of the Generalate of the Congregation of Our Lady of Charity of the Good Shepherd of Angers*, chapter IV): "I warn you to be on your guard against their wiles, to fear them, as you would the snares of the serpent."[105] This unjust treatment toward the penitents was increased as the Magdalene women, although originally "free" to leave the convents at any time, were constantly reminded of their unworthiness, locked up at night, and "encouraged" to stay for life.[106] Indeed, life within the Irish Magdalene laundries, and the promotion of magdalenism, was ultimately physiologically and physically abusive.

Chapter Seven

The Rise of the English Magdalenes and the Magdalen-House

> *I am not almost ready to think with the psalmist, that it is good for me that I have been in trouble, that I may learn the statutes of my Creator; for in this blessed Asylum, I have the best opportunity I ever had of improving myself in the principles of religion, which is advantage of a most weighty importance.*[1]
> — Letter IV. From M — to her Father, Magdalen-House, Perscot-Street, Goodman's Fields, December 27, 1759

The difference between the Irish and the English, the core and peripheral Magdalene is found in several different functional and ideological aspects including the rhetoric used to describe the fallen woman, the consideration of whether such a woman could be rehabilitated to reenter society, where and how her labor and economic worth should be directed, and finally how a fallen woman was understood in relation to nation and citizenship. By the nineteenth and early twentieth century in England and Ireland, there was a great divide between these considerations, which can be viewed through the literature and art regarding the fallen woman (romantic, political, and fictional), the Magdalene institutions themselves, and the labor laws within the factory acts as they applied to the religiously run laundries. What will be revealed are the ideological and functional differences regarding the image of the fallen woman, female division of labor, nationhood and citizenship. For example, whereas the first Magdalene Asylums in Ireland were founded within a sexually repressive environment by women and quickly converted to a state-supported and religious-run institution, England's first Magdalen-Home was founded by wealthy male merchants, during the middle of a sexual revolution, where the Magdalene was romanticized and celebrated as sexual potential for erotic art. Indeed, the social attitudes between the two countries could not have been more different even as women shared some of the same hardships regarding labor issues. This great divide between England and Ireland's approach to magdalenism will have major repercussions for women's rights in modernity and for the modern Magdalene.

The 1670 to 1810 Sexual and Countersexual Revolutions in England

The first Magdalen-House in England was established in 1758 with the aim of rendering "the inmates happy in themselves and useful to others. To this end the home, first opened in a house that had been the London Infirmary, was organized as a place of industry. It was not to appear as a House of Correction, and the inmates were to be treated with all delicacy. Wherever practicable they were to be put to service, restored to friends, or allowed to marry."[2] As the philanthropy and social policy historian Benjamin Kirkman Gray (1862–1907) discusses in his history of *English Philanthropy*, although the overall wish was to save a woman before she "fell" or turned to prostitution, it was found that many women were either violated or forced into prostitution for the sake of survival. Further, as was seen regarding the Middle Ages, sexual expression, and with it prostitution, saw several trends from the late sixteenth century to the late twentieth century in England as elsewhere. Lawrence Stone demonstrates the general acceptance and toleration for sexuality up to the late sixteenth century until, as discussed in chapter three, a new sense of sexual repression occurred from around 1570 to 1670.[3] This was followed by a sexual revolution, not unlike what was experienced in the 1960s, where sexual acceptance, what Stone calls "permissiveness, even licence," occurred from 1670 to 1810. However, a general backlash and restoration to sexual repression started to occur by 1770,[4] right around the time Magdalene homes and asylums became popular again throughout Europe. Although there were renewed calls to end prostitution and to save the fallen women (dated from at least 1758 on), there was a corresponding thriving business selling sex. In fact, condoms, sexual toys and written material, as well as prostitution were actively and openly publicized, advertised and promoted in England. Stone points to various publications including the *Covent Garden Magazine, Amorous Repository, The Ranger's Magazine,* or the *Man of Fashion's Companion,* all of which ran advertisements for prostitutes and brothels — "five shillings 'for a temporary favor,' and half a guinea 'for a night's lodging.'"[5] Of particular interest was *Harris' List of Convent Garden Ladies,* which was an annual publication that listed, rated, and described prostitutes, their services, their appearance as well as side stories related to the women and their paying companions. Katie Hickman in her book *Courtesans* lists some of the more interesting examples of these stories:

Miss B-nf-ld, at 9 Poland Street, was "frequently mounted à la militaire, and as frequently performs the rites of the love-inspired queen according to the equestrian order, in which style she is said to afford uncommon delight." Mis B-lm-t of 32 Union Street, on the other hand, while not at all pretty, compensated for her lack of looks by her mouth, which seemed "by its largeness, prepared to swallow up whoever may have courage to approach her."[6]

Further proof of sexual permissiveness, and something rather repressed in Ireland, was the importation of sexual toys and condoms, which "London and Paris were said to have been the only capital cities in Europe in the second half of the eighteenth century where these devises, then used for prophylactic rather than contraceptive purposes, were openly manufactured, advertised, sold and used."[7] Pornographic literature and pictures also started to be produced in England at this time, and indeed this has a direct link to the image of the Magdalene.

In Italy, in the beginning of the sixteenth century, Mary Magdalene became not only a figure of repentant beauty, but also a Venus figure. Ideas of love, beauty, and passion were being reexamined and compared to those theories put forth by the neoplatonists and, of course, Plato himself. What is beauty? What is passion? And how can the ethereal ideas of passion and beauty combine with those things found in the earthly realm?[8] The combination of beauty, women and Greek ideals came to play an important role—a role that Mary Magdalene and, not surprisingly, the fallen women taking on the mantel of the "Magdalene" would not escape. If women were an important source of love, platonic love being the most precious, then Mary Magdalene and her love for Christ was the perfect illustration. Women, in general, were now said to be the sex that awakened our senses, our empathy, our minds and kept us grounded both in the physical and the spiritual world, as long as she never stepped over the line between sexually appealing and sexually active. Mary Magdalene was the exemplar of this newly understood power in women. As a result, she became the sexy Venus figure, the repentant, and the pious religious example—the whole perfect woman. This period also found renewed interest in the classic female nude—another influence from the Greeks. Mary Magdalene not only became a Venus figure, but once again a *nude* Venus figure, representing what the renaissance saw as the perfect female body. But by the late seventeenth and eighteenth centuries,[9] a new trend emerged: portraying your friend, relative, or mistress as your favorite saint. Again, Mary Magdalene led the way[10]:

> She reappeared in a new genre of painting, the "saintly" portrait, known primarily in England and France, created by and for courtly circles. Indeed, from this period, her image and significance became entirely secularized,

adhering, firstly, to the tastes of monarchs, princelings and minor aristocrats and, secondly, to the context of the establishment in mid-eighteenth-century England of reformatories for women called "Magdalen-houses."[11]

Along with the new trend of pornographic literature, suggestive Magdalene paintings were the fashion and in vogue. Four mistresses of Charles II had themselves painted as Mary Magdalene. One of his mistresses, Louise de Kéroualle, Duchess of Portsmouth (1649–1734) was the penitent reclining in her grotto. She is naked to the waist and draped in a deep blue cloak with her long hair flowing over her shoulder.[12] The court of Charles II saw a lot of these Magdalene paintings in general. One of Charles' court painters (Godfrey Kneller 1646/9–1723) painted several of the court ladies as Mary Magdalene, including Henrietta (duchess of Marlborough), Martha Blount (Lady Wyndham) and Elizabeth Villiers (The Countess of Orkney). He also painted his own illegitimate daughter as a Magdalene—this time, however, she is very clothed.[13] Not to be outdone by England in either the condom industry or the Magdalene painting industry, it should be noted that France also enjoyed this Magdalene print fad. Yet by the end of the eighteenth century, this trend died out with the new turn toward sexual conservatism, and a concern for the fallen woman. Mary Magdalene's image changed once more, from being a fashion statement to a real problem in need of attention.

England's Prostitution Problem and the Common Fallen Girl

Prostitution became a very large problem during the eighteenth and nineteenth centuries in England. As eighteenth-century scholar Jennie Batchelor points out, in "'Industry in Distress,' Reconfiguring Femininity and Labor in the Magdalen House," the most common reasons given for this rise of prostitution were a woman's weak constitution and a corresponding desire to own beautiful things.[14] However, a more realistic outlook regarding a cause of prostitution could be found in what was known as Place's Law, the realization that for women "chastity and poverty are incompatible."[15] Regarding the first cause, Batchelor points to Robert Dingley (the founder of the first Magdalen-House and discussed more below), Jonas Hanway (discussed below), and Saunders Welch, a Justice of the peace and once High-Constable of Holborn (serving under Henry Fielding in 1749), all of whom linked prostitution to a desire for the better things in life: "Welch, for example, highlighted 'the pride and idleness' of girls and young women who set their sights on fine clothes and impossible marriages, which inevitably augured their moral decline; and he, Dingley, and Hanway stressed the need to channel the penitents' desire to emulate their fashionable social superiors into a desire to emulate a Christian model of piety and prudence."[16] A stronger argument, however, can be found in the realities of eighteenth- and nineteenth-century life, where the growth of prostitution can be better linked to poverty, the rise of industry and, as discussed above, a sexually promiscuous culture.[17] In regards to industry and "Place's Law," it was recognized by many at the time that industry and labor laws made and broke women. When fighting against the *Factory Law Acts*, for example, "feminists" of the time highly objected to the law's proposal to limit the working times and hours for women, because these limits made it impossible for most women, unskilled workers, to make a living. In 1896, writer Emilia Boucherett argues this point, in *The Condition of Working Women and the Factory Acts*, by first reviewing the general wages earned by women working in different professions: dressmakers made no money for the first year, but after training they could become an "improver," earning 3s. 6d., upwards to 10s., a week as an assistant.[18] In the same profession, a "cutter-out" or "forewoman" could make as much as £40 to £70 a year.[19] Laundresses earned 2s. 6d. a day, ironers 3s. a day, and general unskilled workers earned approximately 10s a week.[20] Boucherett then compares these general wages to the cost of living off 14s. compared to the more standard 7s. 6d. a week:

Table of Expenditure of Girl Earnings [sic] 14s. a Week.[21]

Double-bedded Kitchen[22]

Rent, 9s. 2d. a month, or £5 5s. per annum.*
Coals, 10d. per week.
Gas, 4s. 4d. for six months.
Food, about 6s. a week.

Breakfast		*Dinner*	
Porridge and milk	1d.	Potatoes and stew	2d.
Ham or an egg	1d.	Sugar "cookie"	½d.
Cup of tea	½d.	Cup of tea†	½d. = 3d.
Roll and butter	1d. = 3½d.		
Tea			
"Kitchen"‡: haddock	1½d.	Sunday dinner	
Or morsel of meat	2¼d.	(leaving something for Monday):	
Or sausage	1½d.	1 lb. boiling beef	6d.
2 oz. of tea (lasting two days)	3d.	Potatoes and other vegetables	2½d.
1 lb. of sugar (lasting a week)	2d.		

*In London rent would be higher.
†Breakfast and dinner on week-days were taken at a cheap restaurant.
‡"Kitchen" means meat or fish.

(*Table of Expenditure ... 14s. a Week*, continued)

Clothing

1 dress (lasting probably two years), £2 10s. or thereabouts.
2 hats a year (price could not be estimated).
Boots, two pairs a year, at 6s. 6d. each pair.

Table of Expenditure of Girl Earning [sic] *7s. 6d. a Week.*²³

Rent*	1½d.	per week
Coals	9d.	"
Butter	6d.	"
Sugar	3d.	"
Tea (no milk used)	4½d.	"
"Kitchen"†	1s. 6d.	"

As Boucherett argued in 1896, these figures offer a disturbing picture regarding labor worth and women's ability to live as an unskilled worker — which the majority of women in poverty were. Thus, the organizers of the first Magdalen-House in England, such as Hanway, argued that the labor market was certainly part of the reason prostitution was growing. This argument in relation to reform and industry caused a problem for the organizers of the first Magdalen-House. The question they faced was: why reform a woman to reenter a market that might, once again, push her toward prostitution?²⁴ The solution? Make the unskilled woman a skilled woman with the potential of realizing her economic worth. With this goal in mind, plans for the first Magdalen-House started in the mid–1700s, but efforts to deal with the problems around prostitution started much sooner.²⁵ For example, in 1724 Bernard de Manderville, while lobbying against the *Society of the Suppression of Vice*, suggested that instead of shutting down the brothels and forcing them into the shadows and back alleys of life, there should be a state-run operation, not unlike the municipal brothels in the high Middle Ages: "His solution was the establishment of publically licensed and medically supervised brothels under state control, with different classes of girls and houses catering for different social groups, the cost varying from two shillings and sixpence to one guinea."²⁶ Manderville's progressive proposal was rejected, while the more conservative proposal for the establishment of the Magdalen-House was put forth successfully by several gentlemen and merchants. Fundamental to these efforts at establishing the Magdalen-House were plans put forth by Robert Dingley, Jonas Hanway, Sir John Fielding, Joshua Reynolds and the some-

---

*In London rent would be higher.
†"Kitchen" means meat or fish.

what tragic figure of the institute's preacher — Mr. William Dodd, who ironically, was the last man be hanged at Tyburn for forgery in 1777.[27] These men and others formed a group to help reform prostitutes, approximately 8,983 women, within an institution that lasted 150 years, until around 1860.

England's First Magdalen-House, the Organizers, Its Priest, and the Women

Core to the effort of establishing the Magdalen-House was Robert Dingley, a London silk merchant who placed a call in the *Rambler*, no. 107, in March of 1751: "Proposal for establishing place of Reception for penitent Prostitutes." As later published by the Institution's Handbook, *An account of the Rise, Progress, and Present State of the Magdalen Charity*, Dingley proposed the following:

> Noble and extensive are the charities already established in this Metropolis; unfortunate Females seem the only objects who have not yet cached the attention of public benevolence ... and it is obvious to every mind, from its own experience, that there cannot be greater objects of compassion, than poor, young, thoughtless Females, plunged into ruin by those temptations, to which their very youth and personal advantages expose them, no less than those passions implanted in our nature for wife and good ends.... Abandoned by the seducer, deserted by their friends, contemned by the world, they are left to struggle with want, despair, and scorn.... What act of benevolence, then to give these real objects of compassion an opportunity to reclaim, and recover themselves from their otherwise lost state; an opportunity to become, of pests, useful members of society, as it is not doubted many of them may and will?[28]

A Magdalene in her uniform, ca. 1776. Reproduced from *An Account of the Rise, Progress, and Present State of the Magdalen Hospital*, by William Dodd, C. Chapman, and Charlotte Smith.

Dingley's passionate proposal was picked up and championed by Jonas Hanway, who became a force in the effort to get the Magdalen-House up and running.

Jonas Hanway (1712–1786) was born in Portsmouth, and moved to London after his father's death. With a career in the merchant trade, Hanway traveled all of Europe, was robbed by pirates, ill with exotic diseases, and had lived through enough unusual and dangerous adventures to write a book about it in 1753, *An Historical Account of the British Trade Over the Caspian Sea*. This autobiography demonstrates that Hanway was not unaware of how women were used as sexual objects when he reminisces about being offered women in exchange for payment, while trading in Turkey: "In a visit I made Behud Khan, he demanded, for the second time, if I would take part of my payment in the women who were to be sold as slaves."[29] In the light of such accounts, his work and life made him a man to know in English society. An eccentric, Hanway was soured on the habit of tea drinking[30] and created what would later be a fashion trend by being the "the first man who ventured to dare public reproach and ridicule by carrying an umbrella."[31] Regardless, Hanway was a stylish man who always sported dress clothes, carried a large French bag, a hat with a gold button on it, his umbrella of course, and a neatly groomed wig. It is partly because of his notoriety and eccentric self that he was able to raise so much enthusiasm for the Magdalen-House and other causes. Hanway championed the downtrodden of society. One of his most important and first efforts were for children. As writers Inwood and Porter mention in *A History of London*, between the 1740s and 1750s there was a strong movement to save unwanted children from starvation and vice,[32] and in 1767 Hanway was able to persuade Parliament to pass an act that required children to be sent to private foster parents who would receive a reward if the children lived. *The Hanway Act*, as it was called, was so successful that the number of children buried in London fell by 2,240. But providing incentives to keep children alive was not enough. Something had to be done about the number of unwanted children being born, and a good place to start would be with the prostitutes. In the introduction to the Magdalene Rulebook used by the first Magdalen-House, Hanway writes:

> There cannot be greater Objects of Compassion, than poor, young thoughtless Females, plunged into ruin by those Temptations to which their very youth, and personal advantages expose them.... And once seduced, how soon to their golden dreams vanish! Abandoned by the Seducer, deserted by Friends, contemned by the World, they are left to struggle with Want, Despair, and Scorn, and even in their own defense to plunge deeper and deeper into sin, till Disease and Death conclude a human Being.[33]

Being so moved, Hanway lent his voice to Dingley's proposal, calling for an establishment of a Magdalen-House.[34] However, as Haskin notes, Hanway objected to the name of *Magdalene*, because he found no biblical proof that the Magdalene was as a prostitute: "It does not appear to me that Mary Magdalen was deficient in point of chastity, as is vulgarly understood. I rather imagine that she was not."[35] Nevertheless, he noted that as a "lady of distinction," the Magdalene inspired reform and so the name was fitting one: "Your charity requires a zeal like hers: you are her *disciples*, and the dedication of your institution to her *memory*, is entirely consistent with the honor due to her *character*; and in this light, no name more proper could be given it."[36]

The final strong advocate for the establishment of the Magdalen-House was Sir John Fielding, a real-life hero as well as a fictional one celebrated widely through mystery novels. Born in 1721, John's younger half-brother was the famous English novelist Henry Fielding, who wrote *The History of Tom Jones* (1749) and *Amelia* (1751). John, however, took a different path and joined the Navy when he was young. Unfortunately, a horrible accident cost him his eyesight and military career. Once John left the military, his brother Henry taught him the law and both acted as local magistrates out of their home in Bow Street, which became a police headquarters of sorts,[37] and home to the famous "Bow Street Runners." After Henry retired in 1754, John, now known as the *Blind Beak*, was appointed the new chief of metropolitan police. With this new office, John revolutionized law enforcement, making it a public rather than a private institution, and promoted reformatory efforts over simple punishment and imprisonment. In Industrial England, crimes such as stealing were punishable by death, but John Fielding felt that a great deal of crime existed because of poverty and lack of general education. Thus, while other magistrates were hanging young children for stealing a loaf of bread, John was sending these young men out to sea with the Royal Navy as cabin boys, offering an opportunity to learn a skill and to escape crime. He took the same stance toward those entering the oldest profession, sending women to the newly minted Magdalen-House for training and reform. Without John Fielding, the Magdalen-House and other reform institutions like it would not have been as successful as they were in England. He endorsed their effectiveness and encouraged other men of means to financially support these reformatories, rather than giving credence to lifetime incarceration.

With such endorsements and financial support, it took little time to collect over £3,500, and open the Magdalen-Home to initially eight women and then "one hundred and forty to one hundred and fifty subscribers in the year (1758)."[38] Timbs, *Curiosities of London: Exhibiting the Most Rare and Remarkable Objects of Interest in the Metropolis, with Nearly Sixty Years' Personal Recollections,* recalls the effort it took to establish this home[39]:

> St. George's Fields, for the relief and reformation of unfortunate women and penitent prostitutes, was projected by Robert Dingley, Jonas Hanway and a few others, in 1758; and opened at a house in Prescot-street, Goodman's fields, when eight unhappy objects were admitted; and from thence to Feb. 26, 1761, there were received into "Magdalen-house" 281; of a hundred inmates, not a seventh were 15 years old.[40]

The aim of this first Magdalen-House was to help, reform, and restore the fallen to the community. Although preference was given to "the more innocent among the girls, chiefly to those who had suffered seduction, and might be saved from worse,"[41] many women from different circumstances were admitted once a month.[42] According to the period travel writer John Feltham (1803), on the first Thursday of the month women were allowed to petition for entry. Interested women would apply with a clerk at the door, receive a petition, and then went before the Board in order to prove their "sincerity of their professions, and to ascertain the truth of their assertions."[43] The Magdalen-House saw great success and in 1776, William Dodd noted the following successes and failures in the Institutions' annual publication[44]:

From that time to Christmas 1775, there have been received into the house,	
Of these several were very young: shocking to think, even under fourteen years of age! And several, objects of such complicated distress, that no man could hear their piteous complaints, or behold their deplorable miseries, without the tenderness emotions of compassion!	1,637
The conductors of the charity have had the happiness to see of these, reconciled to, and received by their friends, or placed in services in reputable families, and to trades,	943
Proved lunatics, and afflicted with incurable fits, who have been sent to St. Luke's hospital, or their own parishes,	44
Died with all the marks of unfeigned contrition,	43
Dismissed, at their own request, and upon reasonable views of advantage, or uneasy under confinement, through otherwise not blamable in their conduct,	204
Never returned from hospitals, to which they were sent to be cured,	52
Dismissed for irregularities, among which want of temper has been the common evil,	255
In the house,	96
In the whole	1,637

Unlike a regular "convent" or other religious reformatories of the times, this Magdalen-House was meant to be a place where fallen women could acquire a different occupation, while reforming their morals and remaking their reputations. This halfway house allowed women to reform by giving them a moral and practical education.[45] The women attended church, kept chaste and were instructed in how to mend linen and lace, make artificial flowers, toys, gloves, and learned the art of weaving hair for wigs — all considered skilled jobs in the marketplace. The women were also encouraged to read and learn how to read. Haskins points to some of the required reading as including Hanway's *Instruction for the Conduct of Women*, and *Virtue in the Humble Life*. There was also the selection of *Knowledge and Practice of Christianity — An Essay towards the Instruction for the Indians* by Bishop Wilson, and the anonymously written *Exhortation to Chastity*.[46] Yet it was the services and crafts that the women worked at that helped provide support for the house, and in turn the women received a small sum of money for their work. It is interesting and important to note that the topic of paying the women for their work (outside of room and board) created much debate. The fear was that pocket money would ignite the Magdalene's natural desire for the "good things" in life, such as fancy clothing and hats. Welsh and Dingley both worried about this issue and struggled for different options on rewarding the women. Dingley suggested everything from offering the *better behaved Magdalene* nicer clothing (a white apron, silk handkerchief, a Knot or laced cap), better food, or potentially a "closet" to retire with; regardless, most of the managers and originators of the Magdalen-House agreed that the Magdalenes should receive some practical reward for their efforts.[47] This reward and the maintenance for the home was financed though the items the Magdalenes made, as well as subscriptions that were often obtained through advertisements and, interesting enough, the display of the Magdalenes themselves. Fascination with the reforming fallen woman, combined with the upper classes' somewhat morbid need to observe the lower classes, and thereby to maintain their hegemonic positions, made the Magdalen-House a place of entertainment. The class and social differences that existed between the "good" woman and the "fallen," the poor and rich, was extreme. The upper classes may have said they wished to help these poor victims, but only as long as they kept them at several arms length. This is one of the major problems inherited with the Magdalene Asylums, since the inmates (almost always referred to as inmates, children, or objects) were second-class citizens — even after they reformed. Rhetorically referring to these women as "objects," "children" and "inmates" allowed a process of objectification where a woman became much less an autonomous individual, and more akin to an inanimate object in need of care and show. As such, first mention of the Magdalen-House as a place for entertainment is found in a letter from Horace Walpole.

Walpole (1717–1797), another fascinating character in the list of the Magdalen-House supporters, was the youngest son of England's longest-ruling Prime Minister, Robert Walpole, and was schooled in Eton and Cambridge. Later, he traveled for two years with Thomas Gray (the famous English writer), and then returned to take a seat in Parliament (1741). In 1747 Walpole bought a house near Twickenham outside London, which, over the course of his life, he turned into a fantastic neo-Gothic castle called Strawberry Hill. There he housed one of the most extensive and eclectic collections of art in England,

Seven. The Rise of the English Magdalenes and the Magdalen-House

and set up a small private press, publishing works by Thomas Gray, Hannah More, and Joseph Spence; but he is best known for writing the first Gothic novel, *The Castle of Otranto* (1765). Walpole traveled in only the finest of circles, attracting artists, writers, and royalty to share in his "entertainments," one of which was the Magdalenes at the Magdalen-House. Not unlike how scientists observe animals in their *natural* setting, the rich in this case observed the poor and the fallen. A sense of "pity" was felt for the lower classes, but one also imagines that with that pity came a corresponding feeling of excitement, *right* and *might*. There was of course social duty involved with such entertainment. Many of the upper classes donated a great deal of money to charity houses and they wanted to make sure that their money was being well spent. The new Magdalen-House was no exception. One very cold afternoon in January, Walpole and several important English citizens, including Prince Edward, visited the Magdalen-House as their afternoon's amusement. Walpole documented the outing in a letter to his friend, George Montague, on January 28:

> As you seem amused with my entertainments, I will tell you how I passed yesterday. A party was made to go to the Magdalen-House. We met at Northumberland House at five, and set out in four coaches; Prince Edward, Colonel Brudenel his groom, Lady Northumberland, Lady Mary Coke, Lady Carlisle, Miss Pelham, Lady Herford, Lord Beauchamp, Lord Huntingdon, old Bowman, and I.... We were received by—Oh! First, a vast mob, for princes are not so common at that end of town as this. Lord Hertford at the head of the Governors with their white staves met us at the door, and led the Prince directly into the chapel, where before the altar was an armchair for him, with a blue damask cushion, a *prie-dieu*, and a footstool of black cloth with gold nails.... The chapel is small and low, but neat, hung with Gothic paper and tables of benefactions. At the west end were enclosed the sisterhood, above an hundred and thirty, all in grayish brown stuffs, broad handkerchiefs, and flat straw hats with a blue rib and, pulled quite over their faces. As soon as we entered the chapel, the organ played, and the Magdalens sung a hymn in parts; you cannot imagine how well.... Prayers then began, [and] ... one Dodd ... apostrophized the lost sheep, who sobbed and cried from their souls—so did my Lady Hertford and Fanny Pelham, till I Believe the City dames took them both for Jane Shores.[48] ... In short, it was a very pleasing performance.... From thence we went to the refectory, where all the nuns, without their hats, were ranged at long tables ready for supper. A few were handsome, many who seemed to have no title to their profession, and two or three of twelve years old: but all recovered, and looking healthy. I was struck and pleased with the modesty of two of them, who swooned away with the confusion of being stared at—one of these is a niece of Sir Clement Cotterel. We were showed their work, which is, making linen, and bead-work; they earn ten pounds a week. One circumstance diverted me, but amidst all this decorum I kept it

to myself. The wands of the governors are white, but twisted at top with black and white, which put me in mind of Jacob's rods that he placed before the cattle to make them breed. My lord Hertford would never have forgiven me if I had joked on this; so I kept my countenance very demurely, nor even inquired whether among the pensioners they were any novices from Mrs. Naylors.[49]

This odd idea of entertainment was not limited to Walpole, and the practice sparked an ingenious if not somewhat disturbing idea on how to raise more money for the growing Magdalen-House; namely, having the Magdalenes stared at rather like zoo animals. Even a hundred years later in several fashionable tourist guides, including the 1844 and 1848 Mogg's *New Picture of London and Visitor's Guide to its Sights*, the Magdalen-House was celebrated as a *must-see* tourist site.[50]

Peter Cunningham's *Hand-book of London: Past and Present* (1850) mentions the house and its founders, as does the earlier guidebook to entertainments and amusements, *The Picture of London, for 1803: Being a Correct Guide to All the Curiosities, Amusements, Exhibitions, Public Establishments, and Remarkable Objects, in and Near London; with a Collection of Appropriate Tables* by John Feltham, who claims how "no young woman, who has behaved well during her stay in the house, is discharged unprovided for."[51] Being an entertainment for the rich and a tourist trap for the curious helped the house survive financially. The plan was to have tours of the convent and house where wealthy patrons could feel their heart strings being tugged at, while observing the penitents. This in turn would encourage those with money to spare to dig deeper into their pockets, donating generously. Ample donations were something the organization desperately needed since the Magdalen-House became so popular that it had to move to a larger building, in St. George's Fields — a move that was overseen by the infamous figure of the Magdalen-House Chaplin, Dr. William Dodd:

> In 1769, the charity was incorporated and the institution declared extra-parochial: the present Hospital was commenced, 6 acres of St. George's common fields having been purchased by the governors. Attached to the Hospital is a chapel, rendered attractive by the singing of the Magdalens, screened from the congregation; and the donations at the chapel doors are very productive to the hospital funds: formally, the admission on Sunday evenings was by ticket. Queen Charlotte patronized this charity 56 years. Queen Victoria became patroness in 1741.[52]

By the nineteenth century, women took over the majority of reform work once conducted by men such as Dodd, Fielding, Welsh, Dingley and Hanway. As Haskins observes, the Cult of the True Womanhood ushered in a return to not only conservative sexual beliefs by the middle class, but a sense of social outrage regarding what was now called the "Great Social Evil," or prostitution.[53] As also happened in Ireland, the *Contagious Diseases Acts of the 1860s* stirred public concern regarding prostitution and the spread of sexually transmitted diseases, which became quite common among not only the military, but also the poverty stricken English citizens and women who supplemented their income with prostitution: "Any woman deemed to be a 'common prostitute' was registered by the police and made to undergo periodic, and sometimes extremely brutal, medical examinations."[54] This concern was met in part by women who now felt it their right of *womanhood* to save and correct those involved with prostitution. Philanthropy became a female activity in England, especially when it came to saving the souls of other women in the name of Christ. Subsequently, as the backlash to the sexual promiscuity of the eighteenth century ensued, several new charitable and religious Magdalene asylums and laundries sprouted throughout England. Many of the institutions in the late 1800s resembled penitentiary work-houses and were nothing like the original Magdalen-House discussed above. However, England, unlike Ireland, seriously forced the issue of labor regulation and site inspections of the religious "Magdalene" laundries facilities, because many people saw them as commercial workshops and factories. So it is that even before the 1907 laws requiring all laundries and workshops to be inspected and to adhere to current labor laws, England's religious Magdalene asylums and laundries submitted to voluntary inspection, whereas most of the Irish laundries continued to fight inspections, since many in Ireland considered the inspections as an intrusion on the institutions and harmful to the business of reform. Indeed, here is another great divide between the English and Irish Magdalene asylums and laundries. This is not to say that many Magdalene Laundries in England did not abuse the women, the workers, employed there — they did, as a review of the *Factory Laws* below will demonstrate. The difference, however, lies in how these asylums were defined and conceptualized by the state and by society. What is revealed by examining the long debate surrounding the Magdalene laundries and their place in the *Factory Laws* is that concepts of labor, reform, and the rights of the fallen woman in relation to profit, nationhood, and citizenship were received in drastically different ways between the Irish and English Parliament members.

The Factory Acts, Exemptions, and the English/Irish Divide

Up until the turn of the twentieth century, religious Magdalene laundries, no matter where they resided (France, Ireland, England, etc.) were, more often than not, labor abusive institutions organized under the rhetoric of spiritual reform, but run under the realities of material profit. As the turn of the new century arrived, an interesting split occurred between the core and peripheral nations of England and Ireland — two countries forming their national identity in the face of capitalism as well as Ireland's bid for independence. With regard to the Magdalene asylums, national identity was a core issue for each nation. As Batchelor points out, many of the early English advocates of the first Magdalen-House linked the need for the asylums to concepts of citizenship, nationality, and nation building. For example, Daniel Defoe and John Fielding wanted to rescue fallen women so that they could be reformed into useful citizens, "useful not only because they would supply the country with the men who collectively assert the nation's imperial might, but because they would strengthen the national economy through their work in 'Manufactures' and as 'servants.'"[55] Rehabilitating the prostitute meant working for the nation; as such, it was a task of building both a nation and nationality, which is why most of the "Magdalen pamphleteers" related these efforts with national reform. If, for example, prostitution was a blight on society that spread disease, hampered the workforce, and lowered morals, than rehabilitating the prostitute by showing her legitimate ways in which she could realize her economic potential would serve and promote national interests. For England, then, a woman was seen as wife, daughter, mother and *wage earner*. A similar but vitally different emphasis can be viewed with the Magdalene convents and asylums in Ireland. As discussed in chapter six, a key element to Ireland's effort at national identity throughout and after colonization was relating nationhood and citizenship to the spiritual and legal teachings of the Roman Catholic Church.[56] In Ireland, Catholic morality became wed with both national identity and the economy, which in turn informed the Magdalene laundries. By wedding national identity and the work of nation building so closely with the social attitudes of the Catholic Church, there ends up being a totally different understanding of the fallen woman and her place in the nation. Unlike the suggestion that the prostitute needs to realize her legitimate economic potential in society, there is the insistence that a good woman will stay in the home and thereby serve the nation. In this image, she is wife, mother, and sister but not wage earner (not legitimately). Because she can only understand her "economic potential" within the home serving family, once she falls (for whatever reason), she must also fall of the grid, because there is no longer any room for her in society. Hence a central difference between England and Ireland is how each social order defined a woman's place in society in relation to the market, family, and citizenship. England had a broader understanding of citizenship for women compared to Ireland. Accordingly, at the moment where England and other nations were liberating women from laundry confinement, Ireland was doing precisely the opposite: "Consequently, at precisely the time when their foreign equivalents were closing their doors or reforming their mission to become more vocational in orientation, the Irish asylums were progressively more secretive and opposed to public scrutiny."[57] The best place to view this great ideological divide is in the Parliament Debates of Great Britain between 1895 and 1907, and the discussion regarding religious laundries' exemption from factory inspection and regulation.

The Parliament Debates on the Factory Act

The *Factory* and *Workshop Acts* have a long an interesting history of regulation regarding the new industrial workplace, working hours for laborers, as well as working conditions. The laws were a slowly evolving effort that would have a defining impact on the laundries, many of which were exempt from inspection. *The Factory Acts of 1816* restricted child labor in the textile industry, but was found ineffective because of the lack of corresponding apparatuses needed to enforce the provisions.[58] In 1819 there was another effort to protect children laborers with *Hobhouse's Act,* by disallowing night work for anyone under the age of 21. Further limitations on child labor were enacted with the *Factory Acts of 1833,* which outlawed child labor under the age of nine in the textile industry.[59] Other provisions required that 9- to 13-year-old children be limited to a working day of nine hours, with two of those hours dedicated to education.[60] In 1844, legislation limited the workday of children to six and a half hours, and also those of women to 12. These hours were further reduced (1849) to 10 hours a day for women and teens, 13 to 18 years old.[61] Further refinements were made that included limiting the times of working hours in the *1850 Factory Acts* for both women and teens (13 to 18 years old), limiting working hours to either 6 A.M. to 6 P.M. or 7 A.M. to 7 P.M. The hours one could work was raised from ten to ten and a half hours a day.[62]

It is important to note that the problem with the *Factory* and *Workshop Acts* was that they made little technical difference between the concepts of "factory" versus "workshop," which will later have ramifications for the Magdalene laundries. As was argued in 1892, the distinction between the two was arbitrary: "There might be two working places close together, absolutely identical in all other respects save the number of operatives, and one business would have to be conform to the Factory Act, the other would be practically free, because the Workshop Act was really a dead letter till 1871."[63] In 1871, the *Workshop Act* was given over to factory inspectors, but the same poor difference between the two entities was maintained in law. In 1878, the *Consolidation Act* worked to close this gap; but the ambiguity continued to exist with so-called domestic industries and workshops that mostly employed women and children: "But these last three classes are almost entirely free from control."[64] This distinction between workshops and factories is important because the *1895 Factory and Workshop Act* continued to leave much of industry unregulated including the religious laundries and smaller "family" operations that did not employ steam equipment. In 1895 there was an attempt by the Home Secretary to have religious laundries inspected, but the effort was blocked by the Irish members of Parliament under the arguments that such inspections would interfere with the nuns' authority over the fallen women, and further that the religious institutions were not being run for profit but for spiritual reform, and finally that the nuns, being women of God, could be trusted to do the right thing. At the heart of the matter economically was the second argument: the religious laundries were not being run for profit. As chapter six demonstrated, this was not true. Malcolmson, in *English Laundresses: A Social History, 1850–1930*, demonstrates how commercial laundries were particularly upset regarding the unregulated competition from Magdalene laundries. In England, complaints from the "commercial" industry originated in Liverpool where the religious laundries were competing for large shipping contracts: "While these launderers' fears may have been exaggerated, there were at least ten institutional laundries there in 1902, and the Liverpool Magdalen Institution announced in its 51th Annual Report that it had updated its laundry with modern machinery 'to undertake the washing from ships, steamers, factories, hotels, cafes and hospitals, both promptly and efficiently.'"[65] Much of the debate had on the Parliament floor in 1895 regarding inspection of religious laundries were duplicated in 1901 where additional efforts were made to include the religious institutions in inspections.

Factory Act *Debates 1901*

By 1900 there were over 300 Magdalene Asylums in England[66] working outside of factory regulation; thus in 1901, the following amendments were proposed to the *Factory and Workshop Act*[67]: that all profit-making laundries had to be regulated by the Factory Laws. Further amendments including working hours for women being limited to 14 hours a day, 13- to 18-year-olds were limited to 12 hours a day, and children to 10 hours "in any consecutive twenty-four hours; nor a total for women and young persons of sixty hours, and for children of thirty hours, in any one week, in addition to such overtime as may be allowed in the case of women."[68] Besides proposals requiring work breaks and holidays,[69] the 1901 Act also provided for health and safety measures that included notices of law, power of inspectors, fines and other legal provisions meant to enforce the amendments in all laundries[70]: "This

Act shall have effect as if every laundry in which steam, water, or other mechanical power is used in aid of the laundry process were a factory, and every other laundry were a workshop, and as is every occupier of a laundry were the occupier of a factory or of a workshop."[71] Provisions for pregnancy[72] and overtime were also made, limiting overtime to the following conditions: "(a) A woman must not work more than fourteen hours in any day; and (b) the overtime worked must not exceed two hours in any day; and (c) overtime must not be worked on more than three days in any week or more than thirty days in any year; and (d) the requirements of section sixty of this Act with respect to notices must be observed."[73] These amendments would have provided much-needed protection for workers in the laundries if it was not for the fact that the exemptions originally in the 1895 bill remained in the 1901 bill:

> (4) Nothing in this section shall apply to any laundry in which the only persons employed are — (a) Inmates of any prison, reformatory, or industrial school, or other institution for the time being subject to inspection under any Act other than this Act; or (b) Inmates of an institution conducted in good faith for religious purposes; or (c) Member of the same family dwelling there, or in which not more than two persons dwelling elsewhere are employed.[74]

Although then — Home Secretary Ritchie favored including religious institutions under the act, in the end he argued that because these issues were brought up so late in the parliamentary proceedings, it was better to leave the exceptions in rather than risk losing the entire bill by those who would then vote all efforts down. In an effort to take the focus off the Irish members who

An English Magdalene laundry — site unknown.

categorically opposed the inspection of religious laundries, Ritchie stated that he had heard from many others who also felt that inspection of these institutions were not necessary or advised.[75] Several members of parliament, including Sir Charles Dilke and H.J. Tennant, criticized Ritchie's position and argued for inspection. It also becomes very clear in the debate transcripts that the only members truly opposed to the regulations were the Irish M.P.s, including John Redmond of Waterford.

Among those supporting the inspection of reformatory and religious industry was Mr. Asquith from Fifeshire, who felt that no good argument had been presented against regulation and inspection. With what was considered the positive addition of lady inspectors (it was felt that women inspectors were needed for the more feminine labors), Asquith felt that there should be no interruption or harm of inspections in religious intuitions at all.[76] Mr. Talbot from Oxford University agreed with Asquith's remarks, but he also understood the Irish M.P.'s claims: "Ordinary inspection of laundries is inappropriate to institutions which are of a reformatory character.... But it is a long step to say that because you object to a particular form of inspection then you must object to all inspections."[77] Trying to create a compromise between both factions, Mr. Talbot suggested a different type of inspection for the religious laundries than those for commercial laundries. He further felt that the Irish M.P.'s categorical rejection to inspection was suspect, stating that such an attitude suggested the need to hide something.[78] However, it was Mr. Tennant from Berwickshire who brought some of the most passionate pleas for inspection. Citing the Good Shepherd Religious Magdalen Asylums in France, Tennant plainly argues that abuse of workers can occur in any plant that is not regulated by law and inspection:

> It might be argued that nothing could be said against the convent laundries of Ireland, but a great deal of fault had justly been found with the convent laundries in France. Great scandals had been brought to light in connection with these laundries owing to an application to them of the law; and [I desire] to know what guarantee the House had that like institutions in this country were not being carried on in an equally disadvantageous way as those in France. There was no guarantee, and if there was any great eagerness to avoid inspection, such keenness to avoid inspection must inevitably give rise to the suspicion that here was something to conceal.[79]

Reading from the inspections reports from France, Mr. Tennant went on to describe the harsh working conditions, including the hard labor of children, the working of girls only four years old in the Good Shepherd Laundries, as well as questionable working conditions.[80] He ended his time on the floor by citing a newspaper item that told the story of two women who sought to escape a Good Shepherd House in Sheffield, England:

Two girls, named Maggie Gaffey, aged fifteen, and Minnie Hober, aged sixteen, made their escape from the convent of the Good Shepherd at midnight last night. They dropped twenty feet from a window on the fourth storey to the roof of another building, and then scaled the convent walls, from which they descended to the street. Hober sprained both her ankles, and the girls, being unable to run away, were arrested. The girls tell stories of starvation, hard work, and cruel treatment, and threatened to kill themselves if they are sent back.[81]

Upon hearing the news article, an outraged Mr. Dillon (from Ireland) interrupted Mr. Tennant, asking where and on what authority the news article was founded. An argument ensued between Tennant, Dillon, and Mr. John Redmond from Waterford, Ireland, regarding what Redmond called the "slandering [of] a religious community on the authority of a newspaper paragraph!"[82] Dismissing the ethos of the report based on the medium (newspaper report from the *Sheffield Independent*), it was suggested that Tennant was making up the report. Further, Mr. James Hope from Sheffield claimed that he never heard of such an event, further questioning the validity of the report.[83] Not to be deterred, Tennant ends his speech by stating that at least in England, many managers of religious laundries and homes desire inspection, including the Archbishop of Canterbury himself.[84]

What is interesting about the arguments for inspection is the connection that can be made back to concepts of "nationhood" and "citizenship." There is no disagreement among all the M.P.s in support of inspection of religious institutions that the women working in these places need hard work and a firm hand in order to reform — regarding this perceived truth, all members were in agreement. However, the English M.P.s rhetorically promoted a connection between nationhood and citizenship with the individual rights of a worker, regardless of *her* moral standing. That is not to say that the rights of the worker should necessarily trump the rights of "free enterprise." As discussed above, a large complaint as to why the religious institutions should be inspected was one regarding unfair competition. In a later exchange between the Irish and Welsh M.P.s in support of exemption for religious laundries and reformatories, Mr. Dillon (East Mayo) and M'Kenna, and the English Members in support of inspections, Mr. Renshaw and Tennant, is the question of whether the religious laundries constitute unfair competition to the regulated/commercial laundries. Renshaw states that he disapproves of the exceptions in the Act because it promotes unfair competition. Mr. M'Kenna of North Monmouthshire stated that "I deny that the increased restrictions under the Factory laws cause any additional expense [for the business laundries]."[85] Dillon concurred with M'Kenna, further adding, "Where then, if there is no increased cost, does the undue completion come in? The whole thing is ridiculous."[86] Dillon furthers his argument somewhat illogically by stating that "the nuns charge higher prices for the work done in order to avoid as far as possible competing unfairly with ordinary laundries."[87] Thus, even with the question of competition, there emerges the ideological divide regarding nationalism, reform, and religious sensibility. England does not equate religious morality with labor law, female reform, and nationhood, whereas Ireland does and this becomes clearer when examining the Irish argument more closely.

Speaking for Ireland and in support for the exemptions, the Irish M.P.s demonstrate the ideological difference between these two nations. Mr. Dillon of Mayo and Mr. Leamy of Kildare best represented the Irish argument since they speak at length regarding why the religious institutions should be exempt from inspection and regulation. Mr. Leamy argued the nuns in Ireland constantly welcome visitors and those who wish to tour the convents and laundries. Further, inspections, in his opinion, would harm the authority of the nuns and hinder their work with the penitents.[88] These women, it was argued, were hopeless "creatures" and "objects" who must be kept working, without undue interruptions, for their own good: "The nuns had learned from sad experience that if the girls went out after being a short time in the convent they descended to the abyss from which they had been taken. The nuns believed that they were actually responsible to Christ for the care of the girls, and they did their utmost to prevent them from straying again."[89] This plea was followed by the insistence that the girls could leave at any time, but they never did because of the love, compassion, and devotion of the nuns. Leamy, utilizing a rhetoric so far unexplored in this debate, proclaims miracles and divinity: "It was esteemed a miracle if a fallen woman turned round and altered her life, but that work of reform was being carried out week after week in the Irish convents. [Do not] weaken the hands of those by whom this miracle was being wrought."[90] Further, government inspectors were not needed because the Catholic Church inspects its own: "It should be remembered that the convents in Dublin were inspected yearly by Archbishop Walsh; then there were the hospital inspectors, and ladies of society where constantly going in to visit them."[91] Leamy's ending appeal for no inspections was made in the name of the fallen women themselves, the poor girls who were unwanted by all: "[I] ask that the Legislature would not interfere with the work of the nuns who, day after day and night after night, bestowed constant care, anxiety, and affection on these miserable creatures.... Some of these poor girls were the victims of men's passions, and some of their own folly; but could there be any more beautiful or touching sight than that of these women, who had been in the convent since they were only ten or eleven years of age, taking to their hearts women from the streets who came to them for help."[92] In

Leamy's argument, there is a decidedly different rhetoric at play, one that relies heavily on pathos rather than evidence (the ethos of inspections and news articles), or firm logic. Further, there is the suggestion that it is a church and the state arrangement that will offer the best care for these women. However, the state, although a financial supporter of the institutions, needs to be a silent partner in this arrangement. For the Irish argument, nation must give way to church. This argument is furthered by Mr. Dillon of Mayo, who, as was demonstrated, even linked the economic necessity of higher prices charged by the religious laundries to the church's desire to take themselves out of competition with commercial laundries.

Mr. Dillon also objects highly to any suggestion at all that anyone (fallen woman) would wish to escape the institutions by jumping out a window, as was suggested by Mr. Tennant. Indeed, for Mr. Dillon, it is almost as if once you take the oath of a priest or a nun for the Catholic Church, you divinely transform from fallible human to semi-divinity:

> Women who have turned their backs on all that makes life dear to the ordinary human being, and who devote their whole lives, without hope of reward, to one of the most painful, most difficult, and distressing occupations anyone in this world could understand, whose convents in Ireland are the objects of admiration and sympathy of everyone acquainted with their work and record, no matter what his religious belief may be, and I have known thousands with no religious beliefs at all who have admired them as much.[93]

Interesting enough, the more Dillon denies that he is championing the Irish Catholic Institution, the more he returns to the theme. Returning to his outrage on the article from the *Sheffield Independent,* Dillon states that the example was an "indictment of all the Catholic Convents," whose work with the fallen poor girls are of the holiest mission.[94] Dillon also believes, without offering evidence, that the charge against the French convent nuns is false: "I will not deal with what the Hon. Member said about the French convents. The shameful charges made against them by some newspapers in this country I believe to be base, contemptible, and lying charges."[95] For Dillon, nuns can do no harm; they are above question, which is why they do not need to be inspected. State and statesmen might be corrupt, but not the church— therefore, they do no harm and no labor abuse occurs in the religious laundries. Like Leamy before him, Dillon also argues that inspections will interrupt the good work being done by the nuns, but goes further in stating that female inspectors are worse than male ones since they would be "detrimental to the discipline of these institutions.... Well I had a letter the other day from the Superioress of one of these institutions, in which she said, 'for God's sake save us from inspection if you can, but if we are to be inspected at all, let us have a male Government inspector.'"⁹⁶ Unfortunately, it is never really explained why female inspectors are worse than male ones by any of the Irish M.P.s or the religious institutions, but this argument is consistently offered.⁹⁷ Further like his colleague Leamy, Dillon again explains how fallen women cannot handle outside inspection because of their particular (delicate?) state. To limit their hours or offer them breaks at work is to actually add to their torment, because the work distracts their minds from the reality of their wicked past: "The work they perform, although no doubt it is an assistance towards maintaining the institution, is mainly intended as a means of distracting the minds and occupying the time of the inmates. These are the grounds, and the only grounds, upon which we claim this exemption."⁹⁸ In the end, the difference between the religious laundries, labor, and issues of citizenship in connection with nationhood is whether the understanding of nation and citizenship must be located first within the spiritual teaching of the church and, second, of the state, or vice versa. Once Ireland obtains her freedom, she will ground her nationhood, and her constitution, within the teaching of the Catholic Church. England will define nationhood not through the Church of England, but through a statehood that respects but is not ruled by its church. Certainly one could suggest this divide occurred with Henry VIII and his separation from the Catholic Church. Ireland never made this stand and instead determined its identity through the Roman Catholic Church once it strove to create an image of itself outside of *mother* England.

Turning the Tides of Inspections

From 1901 to 1906 the debate on the exemption of religious institutions continued, with mostly the same arguments presented by many of the same players. Core to the arguments against inspection was that inspecting the religious institutions would somehow impede the nuns from doing their reform work. As P. Malcolmson observes, this argument was finally combated by convincing many religious laundry asylums to voluntarily submit to inspections, and by demonstrating the overall benefits of having inspections performed regularly. This effort was taken on by Adelaide Anderson. Anderson was one of the first four lady inspectors and was appointed the position of principle lady inspector of factories from 1897 to 1921.⁹⁹ In her publication, *Women in the Factory*, Anderson remembers: "It was about the year 1899 that we began, as a branch Inspectorate, to come in touch with certain convent or religious institutions industries; first, through the complaints of the ordinary trader that they were in an unfairly favoured position, and, secondly, through the research of Miss Deane and Miss Squire in Ireland, into convent industries really carried on by the way of ordinary trade."¹⁰⁰ After the debates of 1901,

Anderson took it upon herself to inspect religious laundries in France, Belgium, and Germany, and found that only England and her colonies demonstrate reluctance toward inspection[101]: "It was the discovery that in these countries, and most completely in France and Germany, the general hygienic and safety provisions of their industrial laws applied to the religious, charitable, and reformatory workplaces equally with ordinary industrial establishments, and were enforced by the same administrative methods."[102] Anderson's work demonstrated that the laundries had nothing to worry about in relation to interfering with reformatory work. Further, Anderson was able to demonstrate the benefits of having a professional inspector who also offers advice on how to better run the business aspect of the laundry.[103] These actions went a long way in alleviating and nullifying many of the arguments against inspections. However, there were some institutions, particularly in Ireland, that felt that moral reform required firm discipline and constant work, and so they continued to reject efforts at reform and inspection: "Some institutions maintained rules of silence, provided little exercise, few if any holidays, and deliberately prolonged work to keep inmates from mischief and ensured a monotonous routine and drab clothing in the cause of subduing evil and reforming character. The managers of these laundries believed that factory hours would undermine their efforts at reclamation."[104] In England at least, attitudes regarding discipline started to change greatly because of the efforts of Adelaide Anderson and others. By the 1906 Parliamentary Debates, Robert Bulwer-Lytton, the first Earl of Lytton, was able to successfully lobby Parliament to bring up and officially deal with question of exemptions, one way or another, during the 1907 session of Parliament:

> My Lords, my object in placing upon the Order Paper the Notice which stands in my name ... is considered of considerable importance, not only by the laundry interest as a whole, but also by a large number of people who take an interest generally in factory legislation; and *secondly to try and elicit some definite statement from his Majesty's Government as to their intentions in the matter.*[105]

In the 1906 debates, the focus was less on the issue of inspectors interfering with reform efforts, because there was now ample proof from those who had voluntarily submitted to inspection that no interference existed. Contrary, the debate focused on the problems of commerce and competition. The Earl of Lytton was able to offer documentation that many of the religiously run laundries did indeed make a profit, contrary to older objections, and therefore promoted unfair competition to the regulated laundries:

> It is particularly unfair when the branch of the industry is exempt starts with the advantage of not having to pay any wages. It is perfectly true that instead of wages they provide board and lodging for their workers which is

not done by the ordinary commercial laundry; but I would point out that the provision of accommodations is *qua* home and not *qua* laundry, and that the provision would be made whether the laundry was conducted as part of the institution or not.[106]

In 1906, there was little objection to inspection and regulation left, and by 1907, "An interdenominational deputation from charitable institutions in which laundry work was undertaken, headed by the Bishop of Stepney, presented the Home secretary, Mr. Herbert Gladstone, with a number of proposals for bringing institutional laundries under inspection corresponding to that to which commercial enterprises were subject."[107] Unfortunately, as might be recalled from the 1901 debates, a *different* type of inspection was thought appropriate for the reform and religious institutions. Consequently, special provisions were built in that gave these institutions more leeway involving announced rather than surprise inspections. This leeway, in the end, would allow Ireland to maintain a harsher and more closed-door policy with the laundries than what ended up existing in England. Further, with Ireland's later *Criminal Amendment Acts* (1880–1885 and 1935), as well as her constitution, there was a marriage between church and state, with the Irish state committing to the Catholic Church's stance on women and morality. This "moral" stance left no room for difference and legally allowed difference to be punished through forced labor in the laundries and other industrial institutionalized settings. Here is the core difference between the Irish and the English institutions, and, in the end, states. But a final divide exists as well—the rhetorical divide. Whereas the Irish actively sought to hide away the unwanted woman in society, ashamed of her story, the English tended to see the same woman not necessarily as an unwanted figure, but romanticized her as the tragic heroine and example for potential moral reform.

The English Magdalene Narrative

The plot is unmistakable, passionately wretched and predictable; the romanticized fiction of the fallen Magdalene can be linked to a template for the modern-day romance novel. A young woman, a delicate flower with beauty to rival that of Aphrodite, is our hero. She is a tragic hero who finds herself in moral and physical danger. She might have been born into a family of money but, when she was very young, a horrible accident took her parents away from her. She is alone in the world and no longer well off. Maybe there is a cruel distant relative forced to take her in, or she is placed into an orphanage. Now she sees how horrible the world can be without money. She finds herself being ruined early on. Maybe it is the rich aristocrat who promised her marriage and family as soon as he could secure the blessings of his family. Maybe it is the master of the house that she now serves as a scullery maid. Regardless of the man, she is deflowered and ruined. Pregnant, she finds herself out on the street. She begs, and when that produces not enough income, she offers her body in an exchange for money or shelter, food or clothing. Most of the men she encounters gladly take of her body but forget payment. Our flower wilts lower until a kind gentleman, surely sent by God, lifts her up out of the gutter. Scared, uncertain, and untrusting, she keeps her sordid past to herself once she surprisingly finds herself in good care. She has lost her child (as most stories tell it), but her health is being restored. This kind gentleman savior slowly and cautiously woos our flower. First he offers a friendly shoulder to lean on. Next he takes long walks with her in order to strengthen her. His friendship touching her heart, she is unable to keep the horrible secrets of her life to herself. She tells this man everything. But our wilting flower is scared that her confession will frighten away the kind gentleman she is now deeply in love with. But our man is nothing short of an angel and an upright Christian. He hears her story with complete compassion, and when she finishes, he reminds her of God's mercy and love. He will forgive her past because he loves her. Still our flower, our Magdalene, fights her love for this man. She is, after all, damaged goods — and like the Magdalene in the stories of old, finds herself reliving and repenting her past over and over again, disgusted by the skin she inhabits. But our gentleman will wait her out, and finally the two unite in holy matrimony, with the knowledge that soon they will have a child. Such a recognizable plot is this Magdalene saga, and one of many similar versions. Sometimes the Magdalene gets the man and the marriage, but if not, she must wither away, indeed die a tragic death for her sins. This romantic literature has been repackaged and remarketed over and over again through the history of creative romance literature, but during the industrial age, it was almost always the Magdalene that starred in these tragic fiction and nonfiction epics.

Popular Magdalene literature was wide and varied. There were the basic manuals for the fallen woman filled with house rules, hymns, prayers and helpful hints for a wise and wisdom-filled life.[108] One of the most popular of these manuals, written by John Dryden, was *The Second Collection of Psalms and Hymns Used at the Magdalen Chapel*. Not to be left out, several Magdalenes themselves (mostly fictionalized Magdalenes) wrote about their lives, creating popularity for sentimental "nonfiction." One of the most famous of these was Hugh Kelly's epistolary publication *Memoirs of a Magdalen: or, the History of Louisa Mildmay* in 1767: "I should have told you that Butler, a very sensible fellow, who is servant to the colonel, has been sent away to London to make a minute enquiry at Mrs. Darnel's, in relation to Louisa — God grant the honest man may succeed; for, if friendship is liable to be attended with such anguish as I feel upon this dear but unfortunate girl's account."[109] Working prostitutes and victims of sexual assault wrote about their experiences of seduction, sin and salvation, and the famous author, Daniel Defoe, wrote *Some Considerations upon Streetwalkers* (1726). However, it was the romantic and sentimental novel that really took center stage, with Defoe taking the lead.

Daniel Defoe (1660–1731) was fascinated by the plight of the unwanted woman who turns to prostitution in order to survive. Besides his pamphlets endorsing the Magdalen-House, his famous novel, *Moll Flanders*, is still popular today. *Moll Flanders* not only is a reflection of the times but also foreshadows a time to come, since Moll is a very strong female character that appeals even to our modern sensibilities. As the story has it, Moll was born in Newgate prison to a single mother, only to be abandoned six months later. Alone in life, Moll struggles to live in spite of horrible experiences of incest, adultery, bigamy, prostitution and a short career as a thief. Never truly deterred, however, Moll's character wins out because she sins, repents, and then becomes self-made and self-reliant. In many ways, Moll morphs into a modern woman, but most of the women in the Magdalene-themed novels are not as lucky, but held down by the morals and prejudices of the time, such as the main characters seen in Wilkey Collins novels. Collins (1824–1889) found the plot of the fallen woman attractive. In 1862, his novel *No Name* debuted to great controversy.[110] Cited as an immoral publication by his critics, *No Name* shows a great deal of social insight and reality surrounding the poor unmarried woman in England. The story of Mr. Vanstone's daughters who become *nobody's children* because their father and mother were not legally married when they were conceived is told. The daughters, Magdalen Vanstone and her sister Norah, are struck by the harshness of life after both their parents die in an accident and they are left without a legal name or claim to the family property or fortune. Disinherited by the law and finally thrown out of their childhood home, Combe-Raven, the two sisters have to fend for themselves. Norah chooses the noble path and becomes a governess; however, her high-energy sister, Magdalen, follows a different road. As if possessed by her namesake, Magdalen must fall before she is lifted up. Determined to regain her rightful inheritance at any cost, Magdalen uses her uncanny beauty and talent to get her way, considering marrying a man she hates in order to claim what is hers. In Collins' novel, *The Moonstone*,[111] 1868, another fallen woman is depicted, and in *The New Magdalen* (1873), the story of Mercy Merric is told. Merric is a former prostitute who takes on the identity of a woman she met while nursing and whom was now presumed dead. Seeing an opportunity to create a new life for herself, against her better judgment but feeling boxed in without opportunities for a better life, Merric take the identity of Grace Roseberry, who was an impoverished gentlewoman on her way

Seven. The Rise of the English Magdalenes and the Magdalen-House

to employment as a companion. Ultimately, Merric's decision to take this drastic step is because she feels there is no other way back into society. As Merric observers, even though society sets up so-called refuges for fallen women, it will not truly accept these fallen ones back into the fold. They are, in a sense, always an outcast, reformed or not. Collins also used the idea of the Madonna verses the Magdalene in two other novels: *Armadale* (1864) and *Basil* (1852). Yet his use of the Magdalene as character "designate[s] the outcast woman for whom there was no place in society."[112]

In these novels by Collins and others, the lower- and middle-class women fall because of circumstance, ignorance, promises of a better tomorrow and marriage. Left to fend for herself, she then turns to prostitution to survive. Eventually she emerges as the repentant woman, reclaiming herself, if not always being reclaimed by society. In some instances, the fallen woman does the "noble act" of killing herself, or else she wastes away, contemplating her sinful past. This was an appropriate way to behave if you were a sinful woman who truly wanted to repent, and it was a characteristic endorsed in such works as Rousseau's *Julie, or the New Heloise: letters of two lovers who live in a small town at the foot of the Alps* (1761). Rousseau's writings argue that a woman's character should always be under suspect, since women would use their sexuality to get whatever they wanted. This prevailing belief was rejected by writers such as Wollstonecraft, Mary Hays, Priscilla Wakefield and Hannah More, all of whom wisely connected circumstance, lack of education and poverty as being the causes of prostitution and single motherhood. The solution, as Wollstonecraft's writings argued, was to truly educate women and prepare them for life. As Wollstonecraft and others had hoped, reform for women and for the Magdalene laundries were to come in England, as it did for other core countries such as the United States. However, just as opportunities for women were to open up in the twentieth-century core market sites, the doors were closing in the peripheral centers, including those in Australia and especially Ireland. Thus, as the Magdalene because a shadow of a memory in England, she continued to be very real indeed in Ireland through, it is hard to believe, the 1980s. Sixteen years later, in 1996, the bottom would fall out, and public outrage for the Magdalene as the victim would be had. The new call? Justice for the Magdalene.

Chapter Eight

The Twentieth Century Magdalene Laundries

*The first day I was shown the laundry and the next day I was put in it....
I did starching, I did Priests' cloaks, you know the long white things they
wear? I did collars, you had to keep ironing them until they become real
stiff. There was a little wooden thing you could stand on.... There was a
little bit of relief that you got a night's sleep ... but you knew it was wrong
that I wasn't going to school.*[1]

*Down in the laundry you slaved all day. Most of the day was strict
silence.... Sr X ... would sit on the throne and God help you if you broke
your silence. She would report you to Mth ... Y ... and you would have
to stand when you went in for your food, your chair was taken away and
you ate on the floor.... After 3 days you would have to kneel in front of
Mth ... Y ... and you would have to say these words, I will never forget
them: "I beg almighty God's pardon, Our Lady's pardon. Pardon, my
companions, pardon for the bad example I have shown." I would then
take a bow and ask her could I have my seat back.*[2]
— CICA, *Investigation Into Child Abuse*, Volume III, 2009.

Frances Finnegan suggests that the Irish Magdalene Laundries started to close in the later part of the twentieth century not only because of changing attitudes regarding sexuality and women's status, but also because they were simply no longer profitable: "Possibly the advent of the washing machine has been as instrumental in closing these laundries as have changing attitudes."[3] Although the introduction of washing machines might have been central for the end of the Irish laundries, it was the application of labor regulations, as well as the social belief that the "Magdalene" was not the same as a criminal, that helped end their tenure in England. As chapter seven demonstrated, the collective efforts to include the religious laundries within the *Factory Acts* and labor regulations started to change the overall ideology sustained within the English Magdalene system, but not the Irish institutions: "Whereas in twentieth-century England, the Magdalen asylum went the way of the Dickensian workhouse, the Irish Magdalen Laundries prospered under the supervision of Catholic nuns."[4] Although concepts of reform were still associated with the benefits of hard labor (well into the twentieth century), most fallen women in England were also seen as victims in need of a temporary helping hand and of education.

This final chapter will examine the modern fallout associated with the Magdalenes as well as related and interconnected reformatory institutions and schools in Ireland. Indeed, toward the completion of writing this book, the highly controversial and deeply disturbing *Ryan's Report* (the Commission to Inquire into Child Abuse Report)[5] was finally released in Ireland. Although this report deals only partly with the laundries, it offers a clear and overwhelming picture regarding the extensive abuse (physical, sexual, and emotional) suffered by many who found themselves caught in the clutches of Ireland's institutional system. Even though many elements of *Ryan's Report* are disturbing, what is of particular interest to this project is the fact that inspections of the laundries and other reformatory and charity institutions continued to be little more than ceremonial acts in Ireland. Indeed, no real effort was made to regulate these institutions, or to guarantee that the "inmates" were treated with respect and care. Just like the laundries in Ireland and England in 1895, the modern institutions continued to fight regulation and inspection in the name of moral reform and, as was often the case, profit. Further, it will be noted that in order to avoid being investigated for abuse, both abusers and victims who spoke up regarding abuse in the various institutions were constantly and specifically shifted from one institution to another in order to evade sustained suspicion or detection. This allowed the apparatus of containment to keep victims silent, while it perpetuated and provided additional avenues of abuse for known repeat abusers. In a sense, this apparatus of institutional containment (as Smith rightly terms the situation in his investigation on the Magdalenes),[6] was self-maintaining and protecting. Not unlike Jeremy Bentham's theories behind Panopticon Penitentiary, movement and silence maintained the classes, separated the population and allowed for the gaining of profit through a form of approved slavery (by the silence of an aware citizenry) in this network of institutions.

It is important to note that to date, there has been no formal investigation into the notorious Irish Magdalene laundries specifically. Kept in the silenced peripheral, the laundries are still being actively swept under the carpet. The rationale for this quite cognitive action of silence is simply because the laundries were considered *voluntary* institutions.[7] As such, it might be argued, behind closed doors, that the women allowed themselves to be exposed to the conditions of the laundries. This, of course, seems absurd, but by insisting that these laundries were voluntary and by refusing to investigate them and to redress the victims of laundries specifically, religious institutions and the state of Ireland have basically endorsed this view. What will become apparent in this final chapter is that *forced submission* is not the same as a *voluntary action*. Freedom of action can only exist in a true free society, which did not exist for many women and children of single mothers in Ireland. As long as illegitimacy and sex were seen as crimes, freedom of choice was not present for many who found themselves in the long-maintained institutional system in Ireland.

Magdalene Laundries Controversy Unearthed

As briefly discussed in the introduction to this work, in September 1993, a city convent in Dublin's High Park (the Sisters of Our Lady of Charity) sold off a good portion of their land to a real-estate developer for one million pounds, and although such a transaction is not unusual, this business deal came with a much higher price — that of human lives. Beneath part of the land sold by the city convent lay 133 bodies of Magdalene laundresses — women who were considered a threat to the moral code: "For more than 150 years, until the early 1970's, thousands of Irishwomen, ... were relegated to lives of unpaid servitude in Catholic convents, working as laundresses. They were hidden away — unwed mothers, daughters of unwed mothers, prostitutes, orphans, nonconformists."[8] The High Park Magdalene Asylum, run by the Sisters of Charity, was established in 1853 for Magdalene penitents, who earned their keep by doing laundry. The early descriptions of this asylum are romantic and misleading at best. Taylor (1867) describes the institution (and she emphasizes this fact) as being a *retreat* containing "*voluntary prisoners* who, knowing their own degradation, and having tasted the bitterness of sin, have willingly entered these sheltering walls, and are trying to regain their good name, and to make their peace with God."[9] These "voluntary prisoners" were said to live almost leisurely in this *retreat*, according to O'Mahony's 1906 description for *The Irish Monthly: A Magazine of General Literature*:

> We had passed through the green gates and entered the quiet shady lawn which stretched itself in front of the handsome pile of grey-stone buildings, the convent and chapel and the various other edifices of the institution. Here indeed one seemed to have left behind the tired restlessness of the world; the very atmosphere was cooler, balmier. Under the green chestnut-trees which studded the undulating slopes of the lawn were set inviting-looking green seats where one might sit and read or pray.[10]

O'Mahony, visiting during a "retreat from work" where the inmates were celebrating the feast of Mary Magdalene (July 22), did not get to see these "voluntary prisoners" at work, but the reader is assured by the author that "the nuns had spared no pains to make the occasion a pleasant one for 'their children.'"[11] From a rhetorical point of view, referring and thinking of these women as *children*, the sister guardians could justify much of their behavior toward the adult women. They could manage them as one might manage a child by setting rules and regulations, doling out punishments for breaking those rules, as well as directing habits, talk, and dress. At any rate, O'Mahony assures his reader that only the most unruly and impossible of "children" reside in this asylum. For example, the author tells the story of "Mary Agnes,"[12] who has great humor, and is a great "character," as well as a "darling" and a "lovely Lamb," who, although funny, must be kept in check like the misguided *child* she is:

> To look at "Mary Agnes" and to listen to her is to fall into a state of inextinguishable laughter. She has to be kept in check at all times, lest her fun should become too boisterous. One sees her down at the far end of the hall, a demure little figure of patience and self-restraint amongst her sisters; but one glance, or an uplifted finger from the Reverend Mother, brings her to our feet at once; *literally* "to our feet," for she has a childlike trick of falling on her knees beside you, where with more confidence and familiarity she may impart her innocent stories and fun.[13]

The later Magdalenes were also considered *children* in the eyes of this institution. It is amazing to consider that as *children*, they were so easily disregarded by an institution that benefited from their labor. However, as will be revealed regarding the true children and institutional abuse, only certain classes of children and those born to two parents were seen as worthy recipients of real care. Regardless, in 1996 the High Park Magdalene Asylum worked to hide the history of their Magdalenes when they abandoned their "children," the 133 women buried on the convent grounds. As in life, these Magdalene inmates, the so-called "voluntary prisoners" were violated again in death when the Catholic Church destroyed their graves to make way for the real-estate development. Before the graves were destroyed, there was no attempt to contact family members who might still be surviving. In fact, these women were unceremoniously unearthed, their bodies cremated and their ashes shipped to a nearby cemetery where they were reburied in a mass grave without any headstone or remembrance allotted to them. In some ways, this act of burial is not surprising because the Irish Magdalene laundresses were, it seems, rarely buried with recognition. Michael McCarthy in 1903 observed in *Priests and People in Ireland*, "The Sisters of Mercy keep, at Kingstown, one of those nun-managed Magdalene Asylums in which fallen girls are confined, and work, without wages, at the remunerative employment of laundry, until their remains are consigned 'to the nameless graves in the cemetery.'"[14]

Such a practice, however, feels outrageous to modern sensibilities, and so later, after public outcry, a gray headstone was erected in their memory, and although invitations to the unveiling were extended to the church, former nuns, and other officials, not one of the people involved in the Magdalene controversy attended the event: "A double grange on the edge of Glasnevin cemetery, the 133 bodies had been joined by 42 more. Under the heading 'St Mary's High Park, In Loving Memory of, 175 names and dates of death are listed on gray stone, the first in April 1858, and the last in December of 1994. There are no religious trimmings on the grave."[15] Furthermore, Sister Angela Fahy of High Park Convent said, offering her explanation and rationale for the disregard of these women's experiences in the laundry, that the treatment of these women by the church "was a way of that time."[16] However, this excuse held little weight with the survivors of the laundries and family members who were saddened, amazed, and baffled as to why there were no church members at the memorial, or the later ceremony to dedicate an additional monument. These were the ones, the state and the religious institutions, who should have been serving penance for their actions:

> There was not a church collar to be seen at the ceremony to dedicate a park bench to the Magdalen women. Several church representatives had been invited. The Catholic Archbishop of Dublin had been approached to give even a one-line statement. Nothing was forthcoming. The silence surrounding the failure of the Churches (not all institutions were Catholic) and the state to acknowledge their guilt continues, the mainstream media duly obliging. Focus instead is on individual nuns and priests who are given the benefit of trial and appeal by media. The former internees of the institutions are left to be doubted or left to be written off as "victims" or as history.[17]

It should be noted, however, that although the Sisters of Mercy have apologized to the Magdalene survivors — saying they were sorry if their actions caused harm — as author and Irish historian Elizabeth Cullingford points out, there has been no real acceptance of responsibility for those actions:

> Between the conditional and the unconditional apologies, however, Sister Helena O'Donoghue had negotiated, on behalf of the Mercy congregation and seventeen others, a phenomenally advantageous deal with the government (McGarry). In return for contributing 128 million euros to a victim compensation scheme that will cost Irish taxpayers 1.3 billion euros, they secured an indemnity from all future claims (McDonald). Their admission of guilt, therefore, does not entail a full assumption of responsibility; nor has any Irish apology or offer of compensation yet been made to the Magdalenes (Connolly).[18]

Further, there is no doubt that these women would have gone forgotten if the controversy of the 133 women in High Park did not occur; however, as

Maighread Mebdh writes in a poem: "History is pregnant and the truth is pushing out and there's no virtue in silence anymore. The ones who wouldn't bow and the ones who wouldn't swallow prove you can't destroy all spirits with some lies."[19]

Ryan's Report

In late May 2009, the decade-long-awaited *Ryan's Report* was released by the Commission to Inquire into Child Abuse (CICA). Established in 2000[20] by Bertie Ahern, Taoiseach,[21] who had apologized to the victims[22] of childhood abuse on behalf of the Irish state,[23] this report has been hindered and challenged by the enormity of its task — to provide a forum for victims of abuse to tell their stories, to investigate the problems associated with the institutions, and to offer recommendation to avoid further abuse. Additionally, the Commission was stymied by a court case brought by the Christian Brothers, one of the largest providers for the boy's industrial schools in Ireland, which suspended the committee's investigation from September 2003 to March 2004.[24] This report is important on many levels because the institutional asylums, laundries, schools and reformatories were an interconnected and self-perpetuating system of confinement. Further, the report states that 25 percent of those interviewed were children of single mothers. Since being a single mother was often treated as a crime in Ireland, as shown in chapter six, it is fairly safe to conclude that many of the mothers of these children were or became Magdalene laundresses. Further, the report documents several cases of young girls who were placed in the Magdalene laundries, and as such makes this report even more relevant. However, the Commission did not invite adult Magdalenes (those who were placed in the laundries after the age of 18) to address the Committee, and so only those who ended up in the laundries as children or those who were transferred into the laundries as young adults offered testimony. In the end, however, it is clear that the state and religious institutions refused to redress surviving Magdalenes or offer these women any substantive help or apology. Ireland's Magdalenes are still being actively ignored by the state, the religious institutions, and much of society.

While the CICA Committee was working on the report, a collective and bargained redress/compensation fund was negotiated by the state of Ireland with the 18 religious congregations[25] responsible for running many of the institutions in Ireland. A financial liability cap of €127 million was established for those in the juvenile institutions, but as reported by the *Irish Times*, this settlement was seen as being overly favorable to the religious orders.[26] Without a doubt, according to many of the religious orders themselves, the decision to contribute to the juvenile Redress Fund was so that they could avoid more costly litigations later. For example, the Sisters of Mercy, one of the largest religious organizations that ran primary and post-primary schools, as well as several Magdalene laundries, stated that they got involved with the Redress Fund for pragmatic reasons: "Our decision was also informed by a pragmatism in relation to the litigation. The sense that long drawn out litigation proceedings would be what we would be putting out energy into for years and years and years."[27] Likewise, Our Lady of Charity of the Good Shepherd, another formidable provider of asylums and laundries as well as industrial schools, stated that "practical considerations were because of financial restraints. If we went down the road of litigation, it would have cost a huge amount of money and would have gone on for years, as we would see it.... Also, we just didn't want to get ourselves into confrontation with our ex residents and all."[28] In the end, almost all of the congregations decided to contribute to the Redress Fund in order to avoiding having to pay out more money in the long run. But as the *Irish Times* reported on May 23, 2009, the €127 million cap to the fund was a poor estimate of what was needed to help provide care, compensation, and services to the hundreds of people abused by the system, and this redress scheme ignored most of the surviving Magdalenes:

> Even at that time, it seemed a favourable settlement for the religious orders. In 2001, the government's initial assumption was that the cost of the awards would be some €254 million. It proposed that the State and the religious orders would make a 50 per cent contribution towards those costs. By June of that year the estimated cost of compensation had doubled to €508 million. A year later, when agreement was eventually reached, the likely, but unquantified, cost was even higher. It is reported in this newspaper today that €926 million has already been paid out by the State.[29]

Although the orders are not legally bound to contribute more to the fund, after the release of CICA's report, the accused orders have agreed to offer more in compensation (discussed below). As Reuters reported, before the settlement in Ireland, the largest payout was in the United States where the "Roman Catholic archdiocese of Los Angeles agreed in 2007 to pay $660 million to 500 victims of sexual abuse."[30]

The wish to avoid further litigation was also the reason offered by many of the 18 congregations for why they did not offer individual apologies to their victims, but simply stood by a collective apology issued by the Conference of Religious of Ireland (CORI).[31] On January 31, 2002, CORI issued the following apology on behalf of all its religious members to those abused in their institutions:

> We accept that some children in residential institutions managed by our members suffered deprivation, physical and sexual abuse. We regret that,

we apologise for it. We can never take away the pain experienced at the time by these children nor the shadow left over their adult lives. Today the congregations with the State are giving a concrete expression of their genuine desire to foster healing and reconciliation in the lives of former residents.[32]

Although some religious congregations, such as the Sisters of Mercy, offered an individual public apology, most of the religious institutions did not. For example, after the release of the movie *The Magdalene Sisters*, the Sisters of Mercy of the Americas (headquarters in Silver Spring, MD), issued a public apology to former Magdalenes. As reported by Chris Kaltenbach for the LA Times, Stacie Royster, spokesperson for the Sisters, stated that the laundries "represented 'a time in the history of the Catholic Church and religious orders of which we are not proud.... It's not proper to hide from anything.... We're all human; we've all made mistakes. We do reach out and apologize to anyone who may have been abused at the hands of our sisters, or any sisters.'"[33] A similar attempt at an apology was made by the order in Ireland, 1996, but the order felt that the apology was "not successful, because it was perceived as being conditional or incomplete. After the apology, the amount of litigation involving the Congregation increased, and the Sisters felt that this inhibited them in their dealings with former residents."[34] It appears that lessons learned by the Sisters of Mercy in regards to increased litigation was not lost on the other 17 congregations, since many decided not to offer personal apologies to victims. Our Lady of Charity of the Good Shepherd, for example, stated that they agreed with the CORI public apology and that they were willing to listen to ex-residents and their concerns personally: "You know, it has really saddened us a lot and we, like, we would always say, well, look, we are really sorry that these are your memories, that this is how it is, that this was your experience, we are really sorry about that."[35] The Sisters of Our Lady of Charity of Refuge, the order responsible for running and maintaining the Laundry at High Park in Dublin, stated that they backed the CORI apology (reciting it in full to the CICA committee) and further stated that their involvement with the CORI apology and the Redress Fund was to avoid having to pay more money through litigation:

> We were conscious of the five litigation cases that were pending against us at that time and obviously we felt I suppose because there were some that we might hear of others. We felt that it would be easier and quicker and less adversarial than the court process. We would have indemnity following on the litigation which would mean that funds that would be contributed would be directed towards former residents rather than in legal costs and in long trials. We felt that it would give a measure of closure and that we would be enabled to move forward without the long process of legal trials which are hard to prove either way and particularly with so many of the people involved not actually being there.[36]

As the CICA report indicates in its conclusion,[37] and as the above admissions and rationales from these different religious organizations demonstrate, both the state and the separate congregations were very much aware of the amount of physical, mental, and sexual abuse occurring in many of the asylums, schools, and laundries, but did nothing to remedy the problems or address the suffering of the victims. In the conclusion of their report, CICA lays blame in many directions including the State's Department of Education as well as the various religious institutions involved. Regarding the state's failure, CICA states the following: "The Rules and Regulations governing the use of corporal punishment were disregarded with the knowledge of the Department of Education."[38] Similarly, the Committee found that all the participating religious institutions, and not simply a few bad individuals, were responsible for perpetuating abuse under the ideology that "rigid control by means of severe corporal punishment" was needed to control inmates: "The harshness of the regime was inculcated into the culture of the schools by successive generations of Brothers, priests and nuns. It was systemic and not the result of individual breaches by persons who operated outside lawful and acceptable boundaries."[39] Regarding the overall system, a climate of fear existed that discouraged reports of abuse, and those who attempted to run away from the institutions were severely punished. When abuse was reported by family members or the victims, the Department of Education and other prominent parties did not properly investigate.[40] In the end, CICA stated that the institutional system failed those in its care because of the way it was run, including the *lack of inspections* of the institutions and asylums, and, comparing the Irish workings to those more successful efforts in England, the funding problems associated with the vast industrial school system. Quoting from the report at length:

> The defects of the system were exacerbated by the way it was operated by the Congregations that owned and managed the schools. This failure led to the institutional abuse of children where their developmental, emotional and educational needs were not met. The deferential and submissive attitude of the Department of Education towards the Congregations compromised its ability to carry out its statutory duty of inspection and monitoring of the schools. The Reformatory and Industrial Schools Section of the Department was accorded a low status within the Department and generally saw itself as facilitating the Congregations and the Resident Managers. The capital and financial commitment made by the religious Congregations was a major factor in prolonging the system of institutional care of children in the State. From the mid 1920s in England, smaller more family-like settings were established and they were seen as providing a better standard of care for children in need. In Ireland, however, the Industrial School system thrived. The system of funding through capitation grants led to demands by Managers for children to be committed to Industrial Schools for reasons of economic viability of the institutions. The system of inspec-

tion by the Department of Education was fundamentally flawed and incapable of being effective.[41]

Although many other conclusions can be found in these succinct findings, two important and relevant points in relation to this work are central: lack of adequate regulation and inspections of facilities, and lack of adequate funding. Both these facts allowed not only for the existence of abusive conditions but, as was viewed in regards to the laundries from the late 1800s to modernity in Ireland, also the ability to overwork those in the institutions under the guise of financially maintaining a poorly funded system. Yet this reality was often also a cover, allowing various institutions to profit from free labor of its inmates — both young and old.

One point made very clear by CICA's report was that the various institutions were not well inspected. As was demonstrated in chapters six and seven, Ireland, far more than England, objected to the inspection of the religious laundries and other reformatories on the grounds that inspection would interfere with the work of the nuns, that the religious could be trusted explicitly never to commit any wrong, and (later) for reasons of nation building and citizenship, the Catholic religious organizations should be allowed a hand in forming and guiding society's view on poverty and morality. Thus, a hands-off approach was maintained in Ireland regarding the religious reformatory institutions well into the twenty-first century. CICA reports the following regarding the lack of inspection:

- The Inspector was not supported by a regulatory authority with the power to insist on changes being made.
- There were no uniform, objective standards of care applicable to all institutions on which the inspections could be based.
- The Inspector's position was compromised by lack of independence from the Department.
- Inspections were limited to the standard of physical care of the children and did not extend to their emotional needs. The type of inspection carried out made it difficult to ascertain the emotional state of the children.
- The statutory obligation to inspect more than 50 residential schools was too much for one person.
- Inspections were not random or unannounced: School Managers were alerted in advance that an inspection was due. As a result, the Inspector did not get an accurate picture of conditions in the schools.
- The Inspector did not ensure that punishment books were kept and made available for inspection even though they were required by the regulations.
- The Inspector rarely spoke to the children in the institutions.[42]

A Magdalene laundry — site unknown.

As the 2009 report demonstrates, many of the exact same issues regarding the need for inspection of the religious institutions brought up in the Parliamentary debates from 1895 to 1906 are the same today as they were then. Further, as many current reports demonstrate, this issue regarding inspection has still not been resolved.[43] Although the government has promised to have more unannounced inspections to the institutions still in operation,[44] no real change in the law has been made. Thus the lack of proper inspections of religious, educational, and reformatory institutions are still at odds in Ireland. This lack of responsible inspection allowed not only for the existence of abuse, but also for the use of unchecked labor in the name of profit.

Regarding the laundries, profit, and general abuse of inmates, the CICA offers a section of its report dedicated to young girls who were placed in the laundries. As documented in Volume III under chapter eighteen, "Residential Laundries, Novitiates, Hostels and other Out-of-Home Settings," female complainants discussed their time in the residential laundries to the committee, recounting countless hours of unpaid labor, lack of general education, and overall abuse experienced in the laundries. Three of the witnesses reported being submitted to a laundry when at the ages of 10 to 14. One witness testified that she was submitted at 10 years of age, because she was being sexually abused by her step-father:

> I was being abused by my step-father. When I approached my mother, she went to the priest and the nuns and it was decided that I was the one to be sent off.... I was put into the laundry, I was only 10. The people there were horrified, they would say "what are you doing here, sure you're only a child?" The nun said "it's best you don't talk about this, your family will be

disgraced." I was to forget about it ... (*sexual abuse*) ... and it wasn't to be discussed.... I came down with my case, it was tied with twine, and I was put into a laundry van. My mother said "why is she going in a laundry van? She is definitely going to get educated?" They told her I would get an education.[45]

Many of the witnesses stated that they were transferred into a laundry from other institutional settings. Citing a religious orders' wish to gain payment for former care, one young woman, 13 years of age at the time, was told that she was being sent to the laundry to "compensate the Order as her mother had been unable to meet the required payments for her keep in the Industrial School."[46] Other witnesses stated they were moved to the laundries as a result of reporting abuse they received or about abuse they saw others experiencing.[47] All of the women reported the lack of education received,[48] and instead reported being made to work endless hours in the laundries. Regarding the lack of education, one woman reported being hit while telling her mother that she was not receiving an education: "I said I will have to tell her ... (witness's mother) ... about me not getting educated, that's when I got a few little thumps. She ... (religious Sister) ... punched me into the stomach first, and stamped on my toes and said 'Don't tell your mother you are not getting education, your night classes are starting soon.'"[49] When education was provided, it was in relation to hard work, learning the tenants of the Catholic Church, and Gaelic. As discussed in chapter six, the report demonstrates how concepts of Irish citizenship were dependent upon the Catholic faith and a Catholic understanding of morality. For years before Ireland became a free state from England, English law forbid the use of Gaelic. By associating the learning of Irish Gaelic with religious studies, a direct connection between Irish citizenship and identity was linked back to Catholic morality. The inability to learn and to connect these two strains of ideology was deemed the result of the lack of natural intelligence by the facilitators of these religious reformatories: "They called it education, you learned Irish and religion, but none of us could pick it up. There you were, standing up by the wall and you'd get battered again. How could you learn? ... You were 'a dope' and 'a dunce' and ... (they said) ... your mother was not good."[50]

In many cases, education was replaced by "continuous hard physical work in residential laundries, which was generally unpaid." One woman reported long hours, physical abuse, and the lack of medical care:

> Every morning we were up at 5 o'clock in the summer and 6 o'clock in the winter. We slaved all day.... They starved and worked us to death while they lived in luxury. The nuns were all very hard and nasty, they used to shave our hair off ... *distressed* ... we had to suffer in silence. I hope no one has to suffer like us. We had nowhere to run or no one would believe

you.... I often burned myself ... (*while working, ironing*) ... but got no sympathy ... *distressed*.... One time I had a terrible arm, it didn't heal up, I had burned it and the dye of the uniform ran into it, and that was the first time I saw a doctor.[51]

Further, laundry inmates were beaten and battered if they stopped work, broke silence, or was seen in any way as to protest their living and working conditions: "You couldn't laugh or talk in there 'cos you were just battered. A nice nun in the convent talked to us, Sr ... X ... got to hear about it and she just battered us, on the back of the hands, anywhere, and if she got the curtain rail that would go across you. It didn't matter what she had in her hand. She was like a Hitler ... *crying*.... My whole childhood was gone in that place."[52] Further control over the laundry workers were created and maintained by the continuing tradition of changing the inmates names,[53] and humiliating the girls by cutting off their hair and bandaging their breasts flat "so you wouldn't look like a girl, because your body was sin and belonged to the devil."[54] Such physical and emotion abuse helped to keep the Magdalenes into submission and maintain them as unpaid labor, dependent upon their keepers. Indeed, it is a mistake to assume that the institutions and laundries simply worked their inmates only insofar as was needed to financially maintain the individual institutions. As the Executive Summary of the CICA report states, "child labour on farms and in workshops was used to reduce the costs of running the Industrial Schools and in many cases to produce a profit."[55] Profit was a real issue, and unregulated, uninspected farms, workhouses, and laundries became the perfect place for the underside of capitalism to work its magic using unpaid labor up through, in some cases, the twenty-first century.

Who's at Fault in Ireland's Late-Twentieth-Century Laundries?

Although it is important to examine the laws and conditions that allowed for the Irish Magdalene laundries, asylums, and other institutions, it is also important to recognize the perpetuation of such institutions through society and culture. Importantly, CICA's report does a good job at exploring how the Department of Education and the various religious institutions failed hundreds upon thousands of people, but there must also be discussion about a society that fails their poor and those deemed unwanted as well. Accusations have been widely spread throughout Ireland as everyone from religious organizations, to specific nuns and priests, as well as the Irish State, has been blamed for the crimes committed against women and their children living in Ireland's institutions, asylums, and laundries. Further, there is currently a great deal of anger regarding the Christian Brothers' success at making sure that the

CICA report did not "out" the names of the individual priests, nuns, and other lay people responsible for the abuse in this system of institutional containment. However, blame is found in several places. As writer Breda O'Brien writes for the *Irish Times*, "Brothers, priests and nuns were our siblings, uncles, aunts."[56] Thus, blame rests on a society that would allow their daughters and sons to be taken from home, or thrown out of the house, because of *shame*. Once people allow themselves to willingly create outcasts out of their children, they have to assume the responsibility for the backlash. Religion, hopefully, teaches us forgiveness and tolerance, and yet these young girls and boys were shunned by their family first, and second by society: "We all look for someone to blame, but the nuns weren't going out onto the streets taking children in,' says [Maria Luddy]. The girls were sent in by parents and family members and the courts and police. If they hadn't been ... they would have been ostracized."[57] As O'Brien further observes in relation to the CICA report, the religious nuns and Brothers were also part of a repressive Irish society — and everyone failed those who were institutionalized:

> Who were these nuns, Brothers and priests? They were our brothers, sisters, aunts, uncles and cousins, who were shaped by the same repressive society and punitive theology as everyone else, and who were aided and abetted by politicians, An Garda Síochána, the judiciary, the Department of Education, by organisations such as the Irish Society for the Prevention of Cruelty to Children (then NSPCC), and the silent shrugs of many in Irish society. Nor did journalists distinguish themselves, with honourable exceptions such as Michael Viney and Joseph O'Malley. Prominent journalists have admitted self-censorship from fear of being sued and put out of business.[58]

With regard to the laundries specifically, Sister Mary Sarto, a social worker in County Cork and a former mother-and-child home worker, said that "parents would say, 'we don't want you home. You've disgraced the family. Go away.'"[59] But if society is to blame, then, as CICA also reports, so is the state of Ireland that allowed for the intimate marriage of politics and religion without a system of checks and balances, and for having no real support and safety net in place for poor and single mothers in society.

As such, blame can be placed on the state of Ireland for having no social programs available for unwed mothers and their children. Since it was impossible for an unwed mother to work (indeed this is written in the Irish constitution, which only recognizes a woman's place in the home), she could not support herself or her children alone as a single mother. And as many of these unwed mothers were thrown out of their family unit, they had nowhere to turn to and received no real help from the state: "The state clearly did not take its responsibility to these unfortunate children seriously; they were regarded as 'nobody's children'— and treated accordingly."[60] As Smith reports, with the lack of state programs, the laundries themselves were thought of as the best place for these women — that is once their children had been adopted out successfully or else placed in other sites of confinement.[61] Because the Irish Catholic Church was deemed the holders of state morality, and since single mothers and illegitimate children were seen as the epitome of moral degradation, the state seemed to feel at ease with allowing religious organizations to take care of the perceived problem. But as the CICA report demonstrates and as Smith documents in his investigation of the Magdalenes, the major problem comes down to poverty and a lack of practical education. Regarding poverty, not unlike the history that this present work traces, CICA links the history of the institutional schools and reformatories back to the *Poor Relief Laws* of Ireland (1838), the establishment of workhouses, and a general neglect by society to care for its poor.[62] Fundamental to this process was the rise of a capitalist world economic system that divided market centers and labor into core and peripheral sections of society and geography. Within society, labor and class divisions can be better maintained by force, and the interconnection of educational and reformatory institutions, along with the physical, emotional, and sexual abuse, guaranteed a continuation of a severely classed society in Ireland. For women, this meant that they were kept in their deemed place of unpaid labor (in the home or within the various institutions) through legal, moral and societal exceptions, as well as a lack of general education regarding her sexuality and simple reproduction workings.[63] On a legal standing, women were given little to no autonomy. For example, at least in Dublin, up until the 1970s, it was illegal for a single woman to rent a flat; she had to be living with a husband, father or brother. So in a sense, the poor, single mother had nowhere to go except for the mother-and-child homes and Magdalene laundries run by the convents. And talking about the convents, there is blame to lie there as well, because the religious members of the community running these laundries did nothing to stop the abuse they knew was occurring, and inevitably promoted abuse, as many women from the Magdalene laundries and orphanages have testified to. Nuns and Brothers, who formally ran these asylums and laundries, are receiving most of the blame because they were on the frontlines. Trying to defend what was done in the Magdalene laundries, and other similar institutions, the nuns often mention that the women were uneducated and unwanted outcasts of society. One story, refuting this idea, is recounted in Meadbh Gallagher's article, "Reflect Here upon Their Lives," published in the An Phoblacht/ Republican News on Thursday, April 25, 1996:

> "The nuns have been at pains to point out that the Magdalen women were poor illiterate destitutes but I would dispute that totally," Patricia McDonnell says. "My sister-in-law's father had a farm, a butcher's shop and a

dairy herd which supplied all the people within a 10-mile radius with their daily milk." In the early 1940's, the girl, Chrissie, was taken from a Galway village and driven by the local priest to a Magdalen laundry in Dun Laoghaire. Her parents had both died and she was the only daughter in a family of nine. She was 16. For some reason, the parish priest decided that this girl was "in moral danger." He told her brother he'd got her a job in Dublin and the 21-year-old had no reason to doubt the priest's integrity. She simply disappeared into the system. When her brother would inquire how she was, the priest would suggest they ought to leave her alone. When she came out nearly 20 years later, she was really in quite a disgusting condition and weighed about four stone.[64]

Even if the nuns and priests were ignorant about the histories of these girls, blame can be placed on how they treated the women and children in their charge. This is not to say that every nun or priest who worked in these institutions was abusive; however, the evidence is out, and many were. Particular disturbing was the fact that mothers and children were forcibly separated, with the mother kept behind the fortified walls of the Magdalene laundries, while her children were often housed in workhouse orphanages just next door. As Shield recounts, such emotional abuse was par-for-the-course in these institutions:

> A partnership was established between the State providing an annual capitation per child, regulation and inspection, and Catholic Religious Congregations, who provided staff and premises. The system was supported by a network of mother and baby homes and Magdalene Laundries, where unmarried mothers, following the birth and compulsory separation from their child, would work "in penance." The infants were anonymously presented for adoption by Catholic agencies or placed within the schools system. The growth of the system led to 105,000 children during the period 1868–1969 being placed in up to 70 institutions (an average population of 8,000 per year) in a carefully regulated-system involving statutory authorities and voluntary organizations responding to family poverty, juvenile crime, school avoidance, parental death and perceived moral danger, by way of judicial committal and detention [Raftery and O'Sullivan, 1999: 24–6].[65]

The suffering and pain experienced by the mother and child was made worse because they knew they were so close to each other, mother and child, and yet so very far apart. A great deal of time has been spent discussing the Magdalene laundresses who were unwed mothers because the unwed mother who ended up in the laundries far outnumbered the prostitutes. Further, when news spread throughout Ireland about the Magdalene laundries and the victims at Dublin's High Park, most of the stories focused on the plight of the unwed mother in 1940 to 1970 Ireland. Thousands of children were housed in workhouses, orphanages and adopted out of the country, forcibly taken from mothers that wanted them, while the mothers were placed in the Magdalene laundries, forced, often, to do a lifetime of unpaid penance and labor. This particular situation overshadowed the problems of prostitution in Ireland, since the Magdalene Asylums became a place for Irish society to hide away their unwanted women, while profiting off cheap labor.

Unwed Mothers and Their Children

Being an unwed mother holds a heavy stigma in Ireland. A girl that "allowed" herself to become ruined was ruined for the rest of her life in the eyes of Irish family and society:

> This intense disapproval of pregnancy outside marriage was an outcome of many traditional attitudes and prejudices. These included a general social disapproval, found in many countries, which saw these women as shameful and as "damaged goods;" they also included the strong Catholic ethos in Ireland which saw these women as sinners. And there was, perhaps, a trace of the old eugenic attitude — popular throughout the Western world in the early decades of the century — which saw them and their children as inherently inferior.[66]

As Shield also mentions, just like Eve's "seductive curiosity led to the shame of exile," so too did the single mother in Ireland lead to national shame.[67] In Ireland, when an unwed girl got pregnant and was not supported by her family, she had two choices: one, she could place herself into an institution to have her baby, the mother-and-baby homes, or she could be forced into the same institution. Either way, once her family found out that she was pregnant, she was almost always sent away in shame: "The Irish solution to the 'disgrace' of pregnancy outside marriage was to conceal it. Pregnant girls and women were sent to mother-and-baby homes run by religious orders. The neighbours were told they had gone away to work. The babies were adopted or, if they were very unfortunate, went to orphanages."[68] Before the 1970s, most of the women, after giving birth, were then transferred to a Magdalene laundry, serving penance, while their children were fostered out to families as cheap labor, or they were placed in orphanages that were also workhouses. In most cases the women did not want to give up their children, but the state offered no choice, and if the unwed mother could not find someone willing to take her and her child in, the situation was hopeless. During the 1960s, there was an increased interest in adoption, especially from the United States. Now instead of the children being kept in orphanages, they were being adopted out of Ireland, with the mother having no say in the arrangement:

> There is no doubt that adoption was a great advance on what had gone before when single women had their babies in State-run County Homes

and these babies ended up in orphanages or being "fostered" by families who exploited them as a cheap source of labour. Adoption gave the children a chance of a better life. It meant they did not grow up being looked on as inferior because their birth had been "illegitimate" as the law described it.[69]

The people who adopted these children out of Ireland had no idea about what was going on. They were often told that the child was either abandoned at birth or that the birth mother had willingly given the child up. One instance of this happening was with Christopher McCartin, a child adopted out of Ireland to an American couple: "The ultimate irony? He had always assumed he'd been abandoned at birth."[70]

Documenting History—Witness: Sex in a Cold Climate

In March of 1998, Channel 4 in Dublin showed a documentary on the Magdalene laundries by Steve Humphrie: *Witness: Sex in a Cold Climate*.[71] This documentary recognized the lives of women who were sent to the Magdalene laundries in their youth: Phyllis Valentine because she was too pretty, Christina Mulcahy, who was an unwed mother, and Brighid Young, who was brought up in an orphanage attached to a Magdalene laundry. Phyllis Valentine recounts how she was placed into a Magdalene laundry for eight years because she was "'pretty as a picture' and the nuns feared she might 'fall away,' become pregnant and give them yet another mouth to feed. It was a case of prevention rather than cure, and Phyllis was incarcerated in Galway Magdalene Asylum so as not to be a temptation to men."[72] Christina Mulcahy became pregnant, as a result of a wartime romance, and was placed into a Magdalene laundry after her son was forcibly taken away from her: "She recounts how she nearly went out of her mind with grief: 'There was no time to say goodbye' she says tearfully to the camera. It was to be 55 years before she would see her son again."[73] Brighid Young was a child of an unwed mother and was raised in an orphanage attached to a laundry. Her story is especially frightening as she tells the audience how the nuns used the threat of placing young women into the laundries if they did not behave themselves. Many of the young girls, after entering womanhood, were transferred to Magdalene laundries if they could not obtain a job outside, or if they were deemed unruly, or a threat to public morality. After this documentary was aired, hundreds of phone calls came into the help line that Channel 4 had set up. Calls were taken from outraged women — formally of laundries who were still not receiving promised public state assistance, children looking for their birthmothers, and other family members desperately seeking a loved one who was placed into the laundries.

Mr. Allen Hitchen, a counselor specializing in bereavement and sexual problems, said: "There was a great deal of distress. A lot of anger stemmed from the fact that some people had tried, through the Magdalene System, to find out who their mothers or siblings were. They seemed to be hitting a wall of silence. Some of those who had lived through the system said they had tried to tell people that this was going on but no one would believe them."[74]

And still, very few are listening, if lack of action and active redresses for the Magdalenes are any indication of recognition and care. Although redress is being offered and reassessed for those who were children in Ireland's institutional system, Magdalenes continue to be ignored and dismissed. Magdalenism, a form of identity perversion that actively seeks to force a class of women, those who do not agree to the hegemonic power arrangements in society, into to forced submission, is maintained and promoted through both silence and denial. Why does Ireland continue to promote magdalenism? Is it because, as *Ryan's Report* indicates, the state and religious institutions feel that they should not be made to deal with additional cases of litigation? Is it because those responsible believe that the remaining Magdalenes as a generation are dying out and so will soon be nothing more than a bad memory? Is it because those responsible feel that enough redress has been made and there is no more that can be done? Or, possibly, is there a feeling of justification and righteousness in how these women were treated by the system and society? After all, if society maintains that the Magdalene laundries were private charities that admitted "volunteer inmates," then the fault falls on the women committed, not the society that promoted them. As author and Irish historian James Smith observed in a recent article, "Voices of Our Magdalene Women Washed out of History for Too Long": "The Magdalene laundries were excluded from the Residential Institutions Redress legislation. They were deemed private, charitable institutions. Women, the state asserted, voluntarily committed themselves seeking asylum."[75] Yet, Smith rightly points out, the state of Ireland depended, relied on and partially funded the laundries. As such, it is difficult to understand why they remained defined as voluntary and entirely private institutions. Further, insult is added to injury when one considers the 2009 Institutional Child Abuse Bill (ICAB), which was written to reassess and readdress the need for additional redress to the victims of institutional abuse after the release of the CICA report. This bill continues to ignore the Magdalenes in letter and in spirit.

The ICAB recognized that the original definition of "institution" used by the CICA committee was limited and unfair because: "A number of residents of institutions have come forward to make applications to the Redress Board over the years, only to discover that their applications must fail, because the institution in which they were resident is not listed in the schedule."[76] As such this bill extends the definition of institutions: "The proviso is that such a place must, in order to qualify as an 'institution, be in place in respect of which a public body has a regulatory or inspection function."[77] Recalling chapter six and seven, and the active rejection of regulating or inspecting the Magdalene Laundries by Irish state officials, the hypocritical nature of this definition becomes very clear. To qualify for redress, a person had to live in an institution that was subject to regulation and inspection. However, by actively denying, exempting, the Magdalene laundries from regulation and inspection under the *Factory* and *Workshop Acts*, and by suggesting that private religious reform institutions did not need inspection or regulation regarding the working habits of the inmates, the state and religious organizations could maintain an invisible and cheap labor source. They were invisible because they were excluded from state labor laws and so they continue to be excluded under the redress arrangements made for victims of the other public institutions. This is a travesty of justice and respect, because the Magdalenes were very much victims of Ireland's institutional system. Indeed a Magdalene, "Ester," commented after the publication of Smith's article in the *Irish Tribune* on how she was deeply victimized by the system:

> I was a laundry girl from 1959 until 1962. I had a son. Four days before Christmas in 1961 (21 of December), they "discharged" him for adoption to the US. I was wrapping gifts and had no idea he would be gone. I never consented nor was asked. I am now seventy and in poor health. I have been haunted all my life by that last memory of my son struggling to get to me and calling mum as the nuns closed the door.[78]

Yet "Ester" will not be offered redress or additional care for her ailing health because she, like so many Magdalene laundresses, are still being denied and ignored by Ireland and the religious institutions that perpetuated abuse. What should be done to address this travesty concerning women and the Magdalenes? For one, the state, in conjunction with the religious institutions, should maintain a fund that offers pensions for the Magdalenes still living, as well as a fund to assist in the cost for health (physical and mental) care for these women. Both James Smith and Mari Steed, from the group *Justice for the Magdalenes*,[79] and the daughter of a former Magdalene herself, adopted out of Ireland but reunited with her mother years later, calls for not only redress but a purposeful apology to be offered to the Magdalenes from the State of Ireland, as well as an agreement that the state should maintain the Magdalene burial plots: "We assert that the State was an active agent in 'referring' many of these so-called 'voluntary' committals, and as such the State is complicit in and culpable for the abuses therein."[80] Both Smith and Steed are correct; the state is as responsible as the religious institutions and society for the victimization of the Magdalenes. As such, the state should be held accountable for the atrocities visited on the Magdalene laundries and for the perpetuation of magdalenism.

Final Considerations

Ultimately, society must ask itself why it has been so easy to sweep the image of the marginalized woman under the carpet—and behind a wall of silence. Mary Magdalene's image has been dismissed this way, as she became the patron saint for prostitutes and then, farther down the road, for any woman considered dangerous by society. However, unlike Mary Magdalene, true redemption was never possible for the Magdalenes in Ireland, because society had no intention of receiving these women back into the fold. Under the guise of redemption, these women were consistently put down and reminded that they would always be outcasts of society. The perceived sin could never be truly forgiven and repentance never achieved in this life, only sought after by laboring for church and state. Comparison of Mary Magdalene and the Magdalene laundresses presents an interesting picture, since they represent society and a need to strip the identities away from women, dismissing their individual worth and potential. Many saints have dismissed the female gender as being worthless; the many religious orders often dismiss women, while society concurs. And yet is not the image of Mary Magdalene as the repentant prostitute a more realistic role model for women, since she offers us the ability to fall and then to rise again? Unfortunately, just like the early medieval hagiographical text, the *Vita eremitica beatae Mariae Magdalen*'s portrayal of the Magdalene simply as *the Beata Peccatrix* (the blessed sinner), the fallen are told that they must suffer endlessly for past sins. Ireland's Magdalenes would never be allowed to look past their perceived sins, but were asked to emotionally and continually relive the so-called *sin*, eternally repent *the sin*, and to prove herself through service to the church and state. And yet, this Irish case does not stand alone because other peripheral countries such as Australia, Scotland, Canada and other parts of Europe all perpetuated the so-called Magdalene and exploited her labor. Other core market centers such as England and the United States also took advantage of this image, although reform came sooner rather than later, unlike with Ireland. Even today, a form of magdalenism continues to be promoted globally. For example, in Liberia, women and children who are raped are often shunned by their family because of the shame involved. Magdalenism occurs in this instance because the female victim is blamed for this crime and for shaming the family. Here an identity inversion occurs where a perceived sin must be worn forever as a mantel of shame. The current president of Liberia, Ellen Johnson Sirleaf, has worked to change this traditional response by telling of her own personal experiences and working to get a law passed to outlaw rape (passed in 2006).[81] A recent case in Phoenix, Arizona, reported the raping of an eight-year-old Liberian refugee girl by four young boys aged nine to fourteen years of age (also Liberian refugees): "Phoenix police say the boys used an offer of chewing gum to lure the girl to a storage shed at an apartment complex on July 16. There, they allege, the four boys restrained and sexually assaulted her."[82] After the young girl was raped, her family reportedly shunned her for bringing perceived shame onto the family. Although the father now denies this charge, Liberian President Sirleaf was reported as saying that this family was in need of "serious counseling because, clearly, they are doing something that is no longer acceptable in our society here."[83] Regardless, it is apparent from this single story that a modern form of magdalenism is alive and well not only in Liberia, but transported to the United States and many other countries as well. Further, many Middle East countries promote forms of magdalenism through the marriage of state and religious laws designed to control the female population through force and identity inversion, for power, often profit, and control.

In 1843, Ralph Wardlaw wrote his lectures on "magdalenism," where he examined and lamented the state of women in prostitution:

> If the numbers of those females be so great, who, in various ways, more secret or more open, give themselves to this course of life; how much greater must be the number of *the other sex* who are their regular or occasional paramours, their *socii criminis*, partakers in their guilt! The amount of sin, in the eye of Him, of whose law every act of uncleanness is a violation, and in the eye of everyone who has learned to regard that law as "holy, just, and good," is indeed fearful.[84]

Three years before Wardlaw, William Tait had offered his investigation on the problems of prostitution in Edinburgh, locating the "natural causes" of prostitution as a woman's licentious inclination, temper, pride of dress and love, desire of property and indolence.[85] Of the "accidental causes" Tait listed seduction, ill-assorted marriages, lack of pay for female industry, needs of employment, poverty and (lastly) lack of education, ignorance and the bad examples of a Magdalene's parents.[86] Today, magdalenism must be understood in a different, more complete way. Magdalenism must be now understood as the process of identity inversion for the sake of controlling a class of women in the name of moral righteousness and power. Just as Mary Magdalene was wrongly converted into the eternal repentant prostitute, the modern Magdalenes, most of whom were never prostitutes, have been labeled, punished, and sentenced to live out a life of punishment for crimes imagined rather than committed. Society must take this opportunity to restore the true image of the Magdalene and, at the same time, honor and restore the women that bared her name, as well as the stigma of magdalenism, to their rightful place in society.

Chapter Notes

Preface

1. Erner, "Christian Economic Morality: The Medieval Turning Point," 477a.
2. Rollo-Koster, "From Prostitutes to Brides of Christ: The Avignonese Repenties in the Late Middle Ages," 116.
3. Ekelund, Hébert and Tollison, "An Economic Model of the Medieval Church," 113.
4. Wallerstein, *The Modern World-System: Capitalist Agriculture and the Origins of the European World-Economy in the Sixteenth Century*, 67.
5. Haskins, *Mary Magdalen: Myth and Metaphor*, 173.
6. CICA, *Commission to Inquire into Child Abuse*, Volume IV, 6.02.

Introduction

1. The Fabian Society, *Life in a Laundry*, 4.
2. It is the Ultonian Cycle, the second major cycle of Irish myths, where Cuchulain is celebrated. Here is presented the terrible battles over land and cattle between the King of Ulster, Conor Mac Nessa, and the Queen of Connaught, Queen Medb. Called the *Tain Bo Cualigné*, this Ultonian Cycle is the most famous of the Irish tales which is sometimes referred to as the Irish *Iliad*. Cuchulain was the Ulster hero and head of Conor's Red Knights, and was believed to be half-Dana god (fathered by Lugh of the Long Arm) and half human. As a child his name was Setanta. It was only when he was training with the Red Knights, and accidentally killed a guard dog of a wealthy smith, named Cullan from Quelgny, that he got his name Cuchulain. This name was given him because he offered to be a guard dog himself, to protect the man's land until he could train a new dog to take his place. *Cuchulain* means the Hound of Cullan.
3. The Invasion Myths, the oldest Irish myths contain stories about *The Coming of Partholan into Ireland, The Coming of the Nemed into Ireland, The Coming of the Firbolgs into Ireland, The Invasion of the Tuutha De Dannan* (or the people of the god Dana) and finally *The Invasion of the Milesians* (sons of Miled) from Spain, and their conquest of the People of Dana: "With the Milesians we begin to come into something resembling history — they represent, in Irish legend, the Celtic race; and from them the later ruling families of Ireland are supposed to be descended. Apart from the mythological material, the only written evidence from which early Irish history can be reconstructed is the *Leabhar Gabala* or Book of Invasions. This scholarly compilation of oral tradition, annals and genealogies was made in the ninth and twelfth centuries by monks. If the Sons of Miled can be identified with the Gaels, then the People of Dana are evidently gods and are credited with bringing the finer points of civilization to the land. The pre-Danaan settlers or invaders are huge phantom-like figures, which loom vaguely through the mists of tradition, and have little definite characterization" (Rolleston, *Celtic Myths and Legends*, 24).
4. 1530–1603, Grace O'Malley was reportedly a pirate who held great political power in Ireland, not to mention the love of her people. O'Malley is often talked about as a woman dismissing her womanliness in favor of a sword. She became a thorn in the English side, as she plundered English ships for supplies and goods. She was sent to jail several times, but was released. Her final effort for her family and children came when she visited Queen Elizabeth to get her rightful lands and inheritance back from English hands. Rumor has it that not only did

Grace succeed, but was not seen as the savage she was reported to be, but as a refined and educated lady. Grace lived over 70 years.

5. The first woman to serve as Irish president, Robinson worked to transform the largely ceremonial office into a platform from which to campaign for peace, social reforms, and environmental causes.

6. Polman, "Re-discovery of Ireland's 'Forgotten Women' Causes National Scandal," para., 1.

7. Gallagher, "Reflect Here Upon Their Lives," para. 4.

Chapter One

1. Burke, *Attitudes towards History*, 266–67.
2. Burke, *A Rhetoric of Motives*, 22.
3. Pagels, *The Gnostic Gospels*, 55–56.
4. It is now agreed that the Gospel of Mark (A.D. 66–68) was the source for the Gospels of Luke and Matthew.
5. Scholars now conclude that the last eight verses of the Gospel of Mark were added and that the original Gospel actually ended with Jesus' tomb being empty.
6. Haskins, *Mary Magdalen: Myth and Metaphor*, 6.
7. Jn. 16:25, as cited in the *New Revised Standard Version of the Holy Bible*.
8. Jn. 20:1–7.
9. Lk. 24:30.
10. Cahill, *Desire of the Everlasting Hills: The World Before and After Jesus*, 209.
11. St. Augustine, as cited by Ranke-Heinemann in *Eunuchs for the Kingdom of Heaven: Women, Sexuality, and the Catholic Church*, 88.
12. Aquinas, *St. Thomas Aquinas on Politics and Ethics*, 37.
13. Aristotle, as cited by Aquinas in *St. Thomas Aquinas on Politics and Ethics*, 37.
14. Haskins, *Mary Magdalen: Myth and Metaphor*, 40.
15. Ibid., 52.
16. Mt. 16:18–19.
17. Lk. 10:38–42.
18. Ibid., 10:42.
19. Romans, written A.D. 56 or 57. 1 Corinthians, written A.D. 55. 2 Corinthians, written A.D. 56. Galatians, written A.D. 52. Ephesians, written A.D. 63. Philippians, written between A.D. 59 and A.D. 61. Colossians, written A.D. 62. 1 Thessalonians, written A.D. 50. 2 Thessalonians, attributed to Paul, written A.D. 50. 1 Timothy, attributed to Paul, written between A.D. 62 and A.D. 67. 2 Timothy, written between A.D. 62 and A.D. 67. Titus, written A.D. 63. Philemon, written between A.D. 56 and A.D. 62. Hebrews: Traditionally, Paul has been given credit for the book, though there is nothing in the book to suggest that he is the author; and from the standpoint of the style and structure of the book, Paul's authorship is so unlikely as to be excluded from being even reasonably possible; written between A.D. 66 and A.D. 70 (written before the destruction of Jerusalem A.D. 70).

20. Badiou, *Saint Paul: The Foundation of Universalism*, 32.
21. Ibid.
22. 1 Cor. 7:1–4.
23. Rom. 16:3.
24. Phil. 4:2–3.
25. Ranke-Heinemann, *Eunuchs for the Kingdom of Heaven: Women, Sexuality, and the Catholic Church*, 127.
26. Mt. 25:1–7.
27. Lk. 7:36–47.
28. Ibid., 10: 38–42.
29. Mk. 16:9.
30. Pope, "St. Mary Magdalene," para. 1.
31. Cahill, *Desire of the Everlasting Hills: The World Before and After Jesus*, 203.
32. From the Gospel of John, Jesus asks the woman of Samaria for a drink from a well. The woman is surprised about this request because Jesus was a "Jew" and she a Samarian, who, it was said, Jews had no dealings with. Jesus said to this woman: "'Go, call your husband, and come here.' The woman answered and said, 'I have no husband.' Jesus said to her, 'You have well said, "I have no husband"; for you have had five husbands; and the one whom you now have is not your husband; this you have said truly.' The woman said to him, 'Sir, I perceive that You are a prophet'" (Jn. 4:16–19).
33. Haskins, *Mary Magdalen: Myth and Metaphor*, 24.
34. Lk. 8:2.
35. Mt. 8:16 (emphasis added).
36. Lk. 8:2 (emphasis added).
37. Chilton, *Mary Magdalene: A Biography*, 4–5.
38. Butler, "Mary Magdalene Was Female Apostle to the Apostles," para. 15.
39. In 1969 the Second Vatican Council recanted Pope Gregory's pronouncement and removed the stigma of prostitute from Mary Magdalene. Yet the damage had already been done, and people to this day still consider Mary Magdalene a repentant prostitute.
40. Starbird, *The Woman with the Alabaster Jar: Mary Magdalen and the Holy Grail*, 29.
41. Sjöö and Mor, *The Great Cosmic Mother: Rediscovering the Religion of the Earth*, 159.
42. Chilton, *Mary Magdalene: A Biography*, 49.

43. Starbird, *The Woman with the Alabaster Jar: Mary Magdalen and the Holy Grail*, 29. This hostility toward Asherah can be seen in Deuteronomy 16:20: "You must completely destroy all the places where the nations you disposed have served their gods: on high mountains, on hills, under a spreading tree. You must tear down their altars, smash their pillars, cut down their sacred poles, set fire to the carved images of their gods, and wipe their name from the place."
44. Ibid., 30.
45. Ibid., 31.
46. Cahill, *Desire of the Everlasting Hills: The World before and after Jesus*, 203.
47. Picknett, *Mary Magdalene: Christianity's Hidden Goddess*, 66.
48. Chilton, *Mary Magdalene: A Biography*, 19.
49. Haskins, *Mary Magdalen· Myth and Metaphor*, 39.
50. Ibid., 21.
51. Starbird, *The Woman with the Alabaster Jar: Mary Magdalen and the Holy Grail*, 28, It is important to note that the Protestants did not convolute Mary of Bethany with Luke's "sinner."
52. Haskins, *Mary Magdalen: Myth and Metaphor*, 406.
53. St. Jerome's letter was translated by Susan Haskin, the author of *Mary Magdalene: Myth and Metaphor*. This letter was written in 412 and was about Marcella, a wealthy upper-class woman, who "had formed a community with her mother Albinia on the Aventine Hill outside of Rome where Jerome would meet his female disciples" (406). St. Jerome's epithet for Mary Magdalene as "fortified with towers" came from the fact that the Hebrew word Migdol or Magdol meant, "tower."
54. Haskins, *Mary Magdalen: Myth and Metaphor*, 55. Also see Wright, *The Selected Letters of St. Jerome*, 450–51.
55. For example, Mel Gibson's production of "The Passion of the Christ" (2004) depicted the Magdalene as a repentant prostitute as well — perpetuating an unsubstantiated myth.
56. Chilton, *Mary Magdalene: A Biography*, 9.
57. It is interesting to note that in both Matthew's and Luke's accounts of Jesus' lineage, the former prostitute, Rahab (Josh. 2), is part of it. Rahab helped hide the spies in Jericho. This is when the Israelites were under Joshua, and had crossed the Jordan River into Canaan, but their way was blocked by the fortified city of Jericho. Rahab and her family were the only ones from Jericho allowed to live by God. Another former prostitute that is part of Jesus' lineage, or at least playing the whore for the larger good, is Tamar. Tamar, it is written, tricked her father-in-law into sexual relations after her husband died so she could carry on his family line. In the end, God blessed her actions.
58. Lk. 1:26–28; Mt. 1:18–25.
59. Lk. 1:34.
60. Mk. 6:3. It is important to remember that the Catholic Church continues to claim that Mary remained a virgin her whole life and that the so-called brothers and sisters of Jesus, mentioned in Mark, were either distant relatives or brothers and sisters in the "spiritual" sense (all men are my brothers). Yet it would seem very odd to assume that Mary and Joseph never came together in the "biblical" sense, because they were husband and wife.
61. St. Augustine, as cited by Ranke-Heinemann in *Eunuchs for the Kingdom of Heaven: Women, Sexuality, and the Catholic Church*, 127.
62. Ranke-Heinemann, *Eunuchs for the Kingdom of Heaven: Women, Sexuality, and the Catholic Church*, 31.
63. Ibid., 4–5.
64. Ibid., 58.
65. It is ironic that a forgotten and dismissed gospel, which is attributed to Jesus' brother James, would be used not only to prove that the Virgin Mary was and remained a virgin, but to further prove that this brother, James, never existed.
66. James, *Book of James* (Protevangelium). 1924, 19:2.
67. Ibid., 19:2–20:1–4.
68. Chilton, *Mary Magdalene: A Biography*, 20.
69. Ezekiel was a young man taken to Babylon in the first captivity of Jerusalem around 597 B.C. In Babylon he became a type of preacher to the other Hebrew exiles who happened to be allowed to live in a settlement by themselves on the banks of the river Chebar. The entire book of Ezekiel is thought to have been written by himself while in exile in Babylon.
70. Rev. 17:18.
71. Ezek. 16:15.
72. Ibid., 16:26.
73. Ibid., 23: 2–4.
74. Ibid., 23:22.
75. Here is an argument based on a genetic fallacy that suggests that if the origin is bad, so is the offspring. This argument was later taken up and used with the insistence of "bastard" children — those disposable children who somehow are defected because of how they were begat. In Ireland, this genetic fallacy argument would be applied when children were forcibly

taken from single mothers and either adopted out of Ireland or kept in orphanages and workhouses (see chapters 6 through 8 of this work).
76. Hos. 2:1–5.
77. Isa. 1:21.
78. Jer. 5:7.
79. Jl. 3:1–3.
80. Josh. 2:9.
81. Ibid., 6:17.
82. Gen. 38:26.
83. Lev. 21:7.
84. Ibid., 21:14.
85. Ibid., 21:9.
86. Rev. 17:1–2.
87. Ibid., 17:18.
88. Ibid., 18:3.
89. Lev. 15:31.
90. Jn. 4:7–9.
91. Mary Magdalene's Feast Day is on July 22.

Chapter Two

1. Duby, *The Knight, the Lady, and the Priest: The Making of Modern Marriage in Medieval France*, 33.
2. Davis, "Introduction," *The Knight, The Lady, and the Priest: The Making of Modern Marriage in Medieval France*, by Georges Duby, ix.
3. See Davidson and Ekelund, "The Medieval Church and Rents from Marriage and Market Regulations," 215; and Duby, *The Knight, The Lady, and the Priest: The Making of Modern Marriage in Medieval France*, 15.
4. Davis, "Introduction," *The Knight, The Lady, and the Priest: The Making of Modern Marriage in Medieval France*, by Georges Duby, ix.
5. Burke, *Language as Symbolic Action: Essays on Life, Literature, and Method*, 16 (my italics).
6. Davidson and Ekelund, "The Medieval Church and Rents from Marriage and Market Regulations," 215–16.
7. Otis, *Prostitution in Medieval Society: The History of an Urban Institution in Languedoc*, 5.
8. Said, *Culture and Imperialism*, 6–7.
9. Duby, *The Knight, The Lady, and the Priest: The Making of Modern Marriage in Medieval France*, 15.
10. Davidson and Ekelund, "The Medieval Church and Rents from Marriage and Market Regulations," 215–16.
11. Ibid., 216.
12. Ibid., 217.
13. Burke, *Language as Symbolic Action: Essays on Life, Literature, and Method*, 9.
14. Ibid., 11.
15. See Lakoff, "Simple Framing," para. 1; and Sidney Tarrow in *The New Transnational Activism*, 61.
16. Lakoff, "Simple Framing," para. 1.
17. Ibid.
18. Lakoff and Halpin, "Framing Katrina," para. 13.
19. Goffman, *Frame Analysis: An Essay on the Organization of Experience*, 21.
20. Pagels, *The Gnostic Gospels*, 61.
21. Ibid., xvii.
22. Mead, *Pistis Sophia: The Gnostic Tradition of Mary Magdalene, Jesus, and His Disciples*, 47.
23. Jansen, *The Making of the Magdalen: Preaching and Popular Devotion in the Later Middle Ages*, 25.
24. Haskins, *Mary Magdalen: Myth and Metaphor*, 39.
25. Pagels, *The Gnostic Gospels*, 65.
26. Picknett, *Mary Magdalene: Christianity's Hidden Goddess*, 86.
27. Haskins, *Mary Magdalen: Myth and Metaphor*, 40.
28. Lk. 10:38–42.
29. Pagels, *The Gnostic Gospels*, 63.
30. Haskins, *Mary Magdalen: Myth and Metaphor*, 39.
31. Picknett, *Mary Magdalene: Christianity's Hidden Goddess*, 44.
32. Jansen, *The Making of the Magdalen: Preaching and Popular Devotion in the Later Middle Ages*, 25.
33. Bitzer, "The Rhetorical Situation," 218.
34. Ibid., 217.
35. Vatz, "The Myth of the Rhetorical Situation," 226.
36. Ibid., 228.
37. Goodnight, "The Personal, Technical, and Public Spheres of Argument: A Speculative Inquiry into the Art of Public Deliberation," 251.
38. Connell, *Gender and Power: Society, the Person and Sexual Politics*, 134.
39. Ibid., 141.
40. Gramsci, *Selections from the Prison Notebooks*, 12.
41. Ibid.
42. See Buci-Glucksman in "Hegemony and Consent: A Political Strategy," 119; and Gramsci, *Selections from the Prison Notebooks*, 244.
43. Foss, Foss and Trapp, *Contemporary Perspectives on Rhetoric*, 347–51.
44. Karras, "Holy Harlots: Prostitute Saints in Medieval Legend," 4.
45. McDonnell, "'Vita Apostolica': Diversity or Dissent," 17.
46. Ibid.
47. St. Christopher was determined by the

Church Fathers to be more of a legend and less of a real person, so he has been de-sainted, along with St. Patrick, and dropped from the universal calendar of saints.

48. Haskins, *Mary Magdalen: Myth and Metaphor*, 100.

49. As Haskins points out, the importance of relics and their function in medieval society should not be understressed. Not only did relics serve a spiritual function, but they were used to swear on in courts of law, carried in battle for protection, and had numerous other functions as well. Because of the great need for saintly relics, a market in the "discovery" and selling of relics rose internationally: "Their collection evolved into an international business as they were carried north from Italy and Spain, and from the east by entrepreneurs who might be commissioned by "clients," or simply sell to the highest bidders. The trade in relics was to have an extraordinary influence on the economic and social development of the western world, and only increased on the return of the crusaders, especially after the Fourth Crusade, who brought with them relics as numerous as they were spurious" (100).

50. Ibid. Further, Bynum and Gerson (1997) point out, the cult of relics has a long tradition going back to the Romans: "The Roman world maintained strong taboos against moving the dead, dividing their bodies or burying them within city walls. And indeed one of the horrors of martyrdom to the early Christians was the fact that the resulting fragmentation of bodies by execution or burning often made impossible the peaceful and respectful burial owed the dead" (3b).

51. Bynum and Gerson, "Body-Part Reliquaries and Body Parts in the Middle Ages," 3b–4a.

52. Jansen, *The Making of the Magdalen: Preaching and Popular Devotion in the Later Middle Ages*, 36.

53. Ibid.

54. Haskins, *Mary Magdalen: Myth and Metaphor*, 99.

55. Chilton, *Mary Magdalene: A Biography*, 155.

56. Jansen, *The Making of the Magdalen: Preaching and Popular Devotion in the Later Middle Ages*, 18.

57. Chilton, *Mary Magdalene: A Biography*, 155.

58. Jansen, *The Making of the Magdalen: Preaching and Popular Devotion in the Later Middle Ages*, 18–19.

59. Chilton, *Mary Magdalene: A Biography*, 156.

60. Rollo-Koster, "From Prostitutes to Brides of Christ: The Avignonese Repenties in the Late Middle Ages," 127.

61. Vitae were written to expound on what was already known and not known on a particular saint's life. Jansen quotes from *Saints and Their Cults: Studies in Religious Sociology, Folklore and History* (Cambridge: Cambridge University Press, 1983, p. 16): "Lives were written to stimulate devotion and provide examples of piety; ... [and] to further the interest of particular groups or institutions" (37).

62. Misrahi, "A Vita Sanctae Mariae magdalenae (B.H.L. 5456) in an Eleventh-Century Manuscript," 336.

63. Haskins, *Mary Magdalen: Myth and Metaphor*, 117.

64. Jansen, *The Making of the Magdalen: Preaching and Popular Devotion in the Later Middle Ages*, 37.

65. Ibid.

66. See Haskins, *Mary Magdalen: Myth and Metaphor*, 117; and Jansen, *The Making of the Magdalen: Preaching and Popular Devotion in the Later Middle Ages*, 37.

67. It is interesting to note that Queen Sancia of the Kingdom of Naples (1286–1345) established two houses/convents for repentant prostitutes in the mid–14th century, naming one after Mary Magdalene and the other after Mary of Egypt.

68. See Haskins, *Mary Magdalen: Myth and Metaphor*, 117; Jansen, *The Making of the Magdalen: Preaching and Popular Devotion in the Later Middle Ages*, 38; and Misrahi, "A Vita Sanctae Mariae magdalenae (B.H.L. 5456) in an Eleventh-Century Manuscript," 336.

69. The stories surrounding St. Mary of Egypt did not mention her early work in prostitution in connection with monetary or market exchange. But as Karras (1990) points out, this became unpractical in relation to the definition and understanding of the role of prostitution in society and so eventually later versions of Mary's story addressed the financial exchange for sex: "In the earlier Middle Ages, writers who translated or retold the story did not question their sources' statement about Mary's refusal to accept money for sex, but by the fifteenth century the increasing awareness and institutionalization of prostitution made such a detail unrealistic" (9).

70. Haskins, *Mary Magdalen: Myth and Metaphor*, 117.

71. Ibid.

72. Misrahi, "A Vita Sanctae Mariae magdalenae (B.H.L. 5456) in an Eleventh-Century Manuscript," 337.

73. Jansen, *The Making of the Magdalen: Preaching and Popular Devotion in the Later Middle Ages*, 38.
74. Haskins, *Mary Magdalen: Myth and Metaphor*, 115.
75. King Carloman (d. 754) was a son to Pepin the Short and a brother to King Charlemagne. Charlemagne and Carloman both ruled different sections of their father's kingdom, with Carloman ruling the Southern portion. After Carloman died, Charlemagne claimed his brother's portion, sending Carloman's wife and children to the court of Desiderius, an enemy of Charlemagne.
76. Haskins, *Mary Magdalen: Myth and Metaphor*, 115. This story of the Bishop of Autun becomes more believable to many at this time because Vézelay was part of the pilgrimage route (which started in the 11th century). As Christopher Blum states (2005), "By taking the path from Paris to the south, the French knights were not forced to pass Vézelay, which lay on a spur road off the main path across Burgundy's Morvan hills. The French went to Vézelay in 1190, as they had before in 1146 when St. Bernard preached the Crusade there to Louis VII and Eleanor of Aquitaine, because it was a destination for pilgrims in its own right" (143).
77. Jansen, *The Making of the Magdalen: Preaching and Popular Devotion in the Later Middle Ages*, 38.
78. Haskins, *Mary Magdalen: Myth and Metaphor*, 116.
79. Jansen, *The Making of the Magdalen: Preaching and Popular Devotion in the Later Middle Ages*, 38.
80. Rollo-Koster, "From Prostitutes to Brides of Christ: The Avignonese Repenties in the Late Middle Ages," 128.
81. Ibid.
82. Haskins, *Mary Magdalen: Myth and Metaphor*, 118.
83. Jansen, *The Making of the Magdalen: Preaching and Popular Devotion in the Later Middle Ages*, 38–39.
84. Haskins, *Mary Magdalen: Myth and Metaphor*, 118.
85. Jansen, *The Making of the Magdalen: Preaching and Popular Devotion in the Later Middle Ages*, 49–50.
86. Ibid., 53.
87. See Haskins, *Mary Magdalen: Myth and Metaphor*, 118; and Jansen, *The Making of the Magdalen: Preaching and Popular Devotion in the Later Middle Ages*, 54.
88. Misrahi, "A Vita Sanctae Mariae Magdalenae (B.H.L. 5456) in an Eleventh-Century Manuscript," 336.
89. Karras, "Holy Harlots: Prostitute Saints in Medieval Legend," 3.
90. "In England, Mary Magdalen was the supreme patron of lepers. Indeed, the 'Maudlinhouse' was almost synonymous with leper hospital, while the phrase 'mawdlyn lands' often denoted the site of a leper colony" (Jensen 175).
91. Wallerstein, *The Modern World-System: Capitalist Agriculture and the Origins of the European World-Economy in the Sixteenth Century*, 36–37.
92. Ibid., 37.
93. Otis, *Prostitution in Medieval Society: The History of an Urban Institution in Languedoc*, 15.
94. Wallerstein, *The Modern World-System: Capitalist Agriculture and the Origins of the European World-Economy in the Sixteenth Century*, 18–19.
95. Duby, *The Knight, the Lady, and the Priest: The Making of Modern Marriage in Medieval France*, 15.
96. Davidson and Ekelund, "The Medieval Church and Rents from Marriage and Market Regulations," 215.
97. Duby, *The Knight, the Lady, and the Priest: The Making of Modern Marriage in Medieval France*, 12.
98. Davidson and Ekelund, "The Medieval Church and Rents from Marriage and Market Regulations," 223.
99. In the early medieval period, the issue of concubinage was an unclear one, because although it was not a church-sanctioned practice, it was a widely held practice. As such, Brundage (1976) explains how the early canonist jurists viewed the issue as both a "temporary marriage" and as a "clandestine" arrangement: "On the one hand, some of the decretists preferred to treat concubinage as a type of marriage, a temporary marriage, perhaps, as Biship Rufinus (d. 1192) called it, or as an informal, clandestine marriage, as the law professor Huguccio (d. 1210) thought of it. The canonistic doctrine on concubinage, in short, was not wholly clear or consistent" (829).
100. Davidson and Ekelund, "The Medieval Church and Rents from Marriage and Market Regulations," 224.
101. Duby, *The Knight, the Lady, and the Priest: The Making of Modern Marriage in Medieval France*, 23.
102. Ibid., 23–24.
103. Ranke-Heinemann, in *Eunuchs for the Kingdom of Heaven: Women, Sexuality, and the Catholic Church*, 1990, recounts how the Catholic Church was so horrified at the thought of sex enjoyed for other purposes outside of procreation, that "in Emperor Charles V's 'Penal

Rules' of 1532 Article 133 imposed the death penalty for the use of contraceptives — which implied the seeking of sensual pleasure outlawed by the Church" (4).

104. Duby, *The Knight, the Lady, and the Priest: The Making of Modern Marriage in Medieval France*, 27.

105. Ibid., 28.

106. Ibid., 29.

107. Davidson and Ekelund, "The Medieval Church and Rents from Marriage and Market Regulations," 234.

108. Duby, *The Knight, the Lady, and the Priest: The Making of Modern Marriage in Medieval France*, 30.

109. It is important to note that although the church worked to define marriage within the confines of the Catholic Church, this did not mean that marriage was not also recognized as a civil contract as well. In his *Confessions* (1963), St. Augustine demonstrates this fact while reflecting on his mother and father's marriage: "But my mother, speaking lightly but giving serious advice, used to say that the fault was in their tongues. They had all heard, she said, the marriage contract read out to them and from that day they ought to regard it as a legal instrument by which they were made servants; so they should remember their stations and not set themselves up against their masters" (198).

110. Davidson and Ekelund, "The Medieval Church and Rents from Marriage and Market Regulations," 221.

111. Ault, *Europe in the Middle Ages*, 471.

112. Davidson and Ekelund, "The Medieval Church and Rents from Marriage and Market Regulations," 222.

113. Ibid., 232. Davidson and Ekelund also stress the importance of the threat of excommunication because excommunication not only ruled out salvation but also "ostracized an individual from his or her community ... additionally, the threat of excommunication as a penalty for delinquent payment of court fines served to increase Church profit" (236–37).

114. Duby, *The Knight, the Lady, and the Priest: The Making of Modern Marriage in Medieval France*, 31.

115. Ibid., 18–19.

116. See Duby, *The Knight, the Lady, and the Priest: The Making of Modern Marriage in Medieval France*, 19; and Davidson and Ekelund, "The Medieval Church and Rents from Marriage and Market Regulations," 223.

117. Ault, *Europe in the Middle Ages*, 471.

118. Davidson and Ekelund, "The Medieval Church and Rents from Marriage and Market Regulations," 227–28.

119. Ibid., 228–29.

120. Ibid., 233. Also see Charles E. Smith, *Papal Enforcement of Some Medieval Marriage Laws*, (New York: Kennikat Press, 1972), p. 83.

121. Davidson and Ekelund make an important point that by deeming the keeping of a concubine illegal and the offspring of a concubine as illegitimate, the Church was able to increase their own rent-seeking potential: "Had the Church permitted the children of concubines to be classified as legitimate, it would have decreased the Church's rent-seeking prospects by decreasing the incidence of exemptions that the Church could have granted for a fee. Further, by defining these children as illegitimate, any estate bequeathed to such an heir was subject to confiscation by the Church (Goody, 1983, p.77). Concubinage was officially prohibited by the Fifth Lateran Council in 1514 and those found in violation were often fined" (229).

122. Davidson and Ekelund, "The Medieval Church and Rents from Marriage and Market Regulations," 238.

123. For Brundage, the "moralist" is concerned about the ethics of prostitution and the relation of sex or intercourse for the "sake of gain," whereas the jurist looks at the "hire-sale situation" (826).

124. Brundage, "Prostitution in the Medieval Canon Law," 826.

125. Otis, *Prostitution in Medieval Society: The History of an Urban Institution in Languedoc*, 49–50.

126. Ibid., 16. Otis also defines the prostitute as: "*a phenomenon in which a socially identifiable group of women earn their living principally or exclusively from the commerce of their bodies*" (emphasis in original, 2).

127. Rollo-Koster, "From Prostitutes to Brides of Christ: The Avignonese Repenties in the Late Middle Ages," 110.

128. Ibid.

129. Brundage offers several historical accounts where the ideas of promiscuity as well as notoriety are emphasized by the early canonist lawyers. For example, St. Jerome (ca. 342–420) saw a prostitute as a woman who is "available for the lust of many men" (as cited by Brundage, 827). This definition was used by the monk Gratian around 1140 in the *Decretum* law books. Later, in the mid–13th century, a prominent canonist, Cardinal Hostiensis (d. 1271), connected the idea of promiscuity with notoriety when he stressed that "a prostitute was not only sexually promiscuous, she was openly and publically promiscuous" (827).

130. Although the authorities in the early Middle Ages did not attempt to define the pros-

titute specifically, they most likely were inspirited or directed by older Roman law, which did define the prostitute. Otis (1985) cites the Roman jurist Ulpian's definition of a prostitute as "a person engaging in sexual activity with a large number of customers for money or other material remuneration" (2).

131. See Brundage, "Prostitution in the Medieval Canon Law," 827; and Rollo-Koster, "From Prostitutes to Brides of Christ: The Avignonese Repenties in the Late Middle Ages," 110.

132. Rollo-Koster, "From Prostitutes to Brides of Christ: The Avignonese Repenties in the Late Middle Ages," 110.

133. Karras, "Holy Harlots: Prostitute Saints in Medieval Legend," 30.

134. Ibid., 25.

135. Ibid., 29.

136. Rollo-Koster, "From Prostitutes to Brides of Christ: The Avignonese Repenties in the Late Middle Ages," 129.

137. Ibid., 130.

138. Karras, "Holy Harlots: Prostitute Saints in Medieval Legend," 10.

139. Amt, *Women's Lives in Medieval Europe: A Sourcebook*, 39. Originally cited from the 6th-century laws of the Salian Franks. Amt's original source was *The Laws of Salian and Ripuarian Franks*, trans. by Theodore John Rivers (New York: AMS Press, 1986).

140. See Brundage, "Prostitution in the Medieval Canon Law," 830; and Rollo-Koster, "From Prostitutes to Brides of Christ: The Avignonese Repenties in the Late Middle Ages," 110; and Karras, "The Regulation of Brothels in Later Medieval England," 399.

141. Rollo-Koster, "From Prostitutes to Brides of Christ: The Avignonese Repenties in the Late Middle Ages," 110.

142. Otis, *Prostitution in Medieval Society: The History of an Urban Institution in Languedoc*, 9.

Chapter Three

1. Otis, *Prostitution in Medieval Society: The History of an Urban Institution in Languedoc*, 12.

2. Haskins, *Mary Magdalen: Myth and Metaphor*, 169.

3. Rollo-Koster, "From Prostitutes to Brides of Christ: The Avignonese Repenties in the Late Middle Ages," 110.

4. See Karras, "The Regulation of Brothels in Later Medieval England," 399; and Shahar, *The Fourth Estate: A History of Women in the Middle Ages*, 206.

5. Brundage, "Prostitution in the Medieval Canon Law," 830.

6. Rollo-Koster, "From Prostitutes to Brides of Christ: The Avignonese Repenties in the Late Middle Ages," 110.

7. See Brundage, "Prostitution in the Medieval Canon Law," 840; Otis, *Prostitution in Medieval Society: The History of an Urban Institution in Languedoc*, 17; and Shahar, *The Fourth Estate: A History of Women in the Middle Ages*, 208.

8. Otis, *Prostitution in Medieval Society: The History of an Urban Institution in Languedoc*, 77.

9. Ibid., 17.

10. Ibid., as cited by Otis, 18. Otis also offers the important observation that Louis IX and his son took a harsher attitude toward prostitution (19), which was not typical of the general region (21). For example, the ordinance of 1254 allowed for prostitutes to be "expelled from the fields [*de campis*] as well as from the towns," and for their goods to be taken from them (19). The ordinance also carried harsh punishments for anyone who rented a house to a prostitute. Two years later, the laws were softened and then only sent the prostitute away from the "center (*cuer*) of towns, and were to be 'put outside the walls,' thus marking a return to established custom" (20). However, in 1269, Saint Louis returned to the more drastic laws on prostitution, and apparently right before leaving on his second crusade, he ordered that "'notorious and manifest brothels ... to be exterminated, in towns as well as outside them'" (20). It is interesting to note that the focus here changes from punishing individual prostitutes to brothels, which was the normal custom of the times (Brundage, "Prostitution in the Medieval Canon Law," 835).

11. Rollo-Koster, "From Prostitutes to Brides of Christ: The Avignonese Repenties in the Late Middle Ages," 111.

12. See Otis, *Prostitution in Medieval Society: The History of an Urban Institution in Languedoc*, 18; Rollo-Koster, "From Prostitutes to Brides of Christ: The Avignonese Repenties in the Late Middle Ages," 111; and Shahar, *The Fourth Estate: A History of Women in the Middle Ages*, 210. Shahar additionally states that this law can be traced to Avignon in the mid–13th century (210). Further, Otis claims that Jews and prostitutes were seen in a similar light through the eyes of the law: "Like Jews, prostitutes defied the teaching of the Church, yet were tolerated because of the importance of their services in an urban society" (69).

13. Brundage, "Prostitution in the Medieval Canon Law," 834; Otis, *Prostitution in Medieval Society: The History of an Urban Institution in*

Languedoc, 18; and Rollo-Koster, "From Prostitutes to Brides of Christ: The Avignonese Repenties in the Late Middle Ages," 111.
14. Brundage, "Prostitution in the Medieval Canon Law," 834.
15. Cited in Amt, *Women's Lives in Medieval Europe: A Sourcebook*, 197, but originally taken from *Le Livre des Métiers, XIIIe Siècle*, eds. René de Lespinasse and François Bonnardot (Paris, 1879; repr. Geneva: slatkine Reprints, 1980). Tr. E.M.A.
16. Otis, *Prostitution in Medieval Society: The History of an Urban Institution in Languedoc*, 21.
17. Karras, "The Regulation of Brothels in Later Medieval England," 403.
18. Duby, *The Knight, The Lady, and the Priest: The Making of Modern Marriage in Medieval France*, 15.
19. Amt, *Women's Lives in Medieval Europe: A Sourcebook*, 74.
20. Shahar, *The Fourth Estate: A History of Women in the Middle Ages*, 17.
21. Rollo-Koster, "From Prostitutes to Brides of Christ: The Avignonese Repenties in the Late Middle Ages," 112.
22. See Amt, *Women's Lives in Medieval Europe: A Sourcebook*, 210; and Shahar, *The Fourth Estate: A History of Women in the Middle Ages*, 209.
23. As cited in Amt, *Women's Lives in Medieval Europe: A Sourcebook*, 210. Amt's original source was *Memorials of London and London Life in the XIII, XIV, and Vth Centuries*, ed. and trans. by Henry Thomas Riley (London: Longmans, Green, 1868).
24. See Rollo-Koster, "From Prostitutes to Brides of Christ: The Avignonese Repenties in the Late Middle Ages," 112; and Shahar, *The Fourth Estate: A History of Women in the Middle Ages*, 209.
25. Brundage, "Prostitution in the Medieval Canon Law," 835.
26. Shahar, *The Fourth Estate: A History of Women in the Middle Ages*, 209.
27. Brundage, "Prostitution in the Medieval Canon Law," 835.
28. Amt, *Women's Lives in Medieval Europe: A Sourcebook*, 68.
29. Ibid., These laws reflect Sicily of 1231, and Amt's original source was *The Liber Augustalis, or Constitutions of Melfi, Promulgated by the Emperor Fredrick II for the Kingdom of Sicily in 1231*, trans. James M. Powell (Syracuse, NY: Syracuse University Press, 1971).
30. Ibid. (my emphasis).
31. These laws are consistent in that they all assume that only a woman would prostitute herself, never a man.
32. Ibid.
33. Brundage, "Prostitution in the Medieval Canon Law," 837.
34. Ibid.
35. Ibid., 839.
36. Otis, *Prostitution in Medieval Society: The History of an Urban Institution in Languedoc*, 66.
37. Ibid., 67.
38. Ibid., 68.
39. Ibid., 21.
40. Amt, *Women's Lives in Medieval Europe: A Sourcebook*, 57. Amt's original source was *Coutumiers de Normandie, I: Le Très Ancien Coutumier de Normandie*, ed. Ernest-Joseph Tardif (Rouen, 1881). Tr. E.M.A.
41. Cobham, as cited by Shahar, *The Fourth Estate: A History of Women in the Middle Ages*, 209.
42. Brundage, "Prostitution in the Medieval Canon Law," 837.
43. Karras, "Holy Harlots: Prostitute Saints in Medieval Legend," 32.
44. See Rollo-Koster, "From Prostitutes to Brides of Christ: The Avignonese Repenties in the Late Middle Ages," 109; and Shahar, *The Fourth Estate: A History of Women in the Middle Ages*, 209.
45. Otis, *Prostitution in Medieval Society: The History of an Urban Institution in Languedoc*, 32–33.
46. Ibid., 25.
47. Ibid., 26.
48. Ibid., 26–27.
49. Rollo-Koster, "From Prostitutes to Brides of Christ: The Avignonese Repenties in the Late Middle Ages," 109.
50. Otis, *Prostitution in Medieval Society: The History of an Urban Institution in Languedoc*, 29.
51. See Brundage, *Law, Sex, and Christian Society in Medieval Europe*, 548; and Shahar, *The Fourth Estate: A History of Women in the Middle Ages*, 200.
52. Otis, *Prostitution in Medieval Society: The History of an Urban Institution in Languedoc*, 33. It is interesting to note that a side effect of placing the question of prostitution under secular rather than religious rule was that the laws regarding adultery could be relaxed, allowing for more legal prostitution activity to take place: "It was, on the contrary, in towns circumscribed by royal or seigniorial authority that defining an official red-light district became a major concern for the residents, not only in the interest of public order, but also in an effort to limit the king's or lord's prerogative to make adultery arrests. Jurisdiction in cases of morals charges was a powerful means of reinforcing authority over a population; defining an official Hot Street,

within which town residents could not be arrested for adultery, was one way of struggling against that reinforcement of authority" (30).

53. Otis, *Prostitution in Medieval Society: The History of an Urban Institution in Languedoc*, 89.

54. Shahar, *The Fourth Estate: A History of Women in the Middle Ages*, 210.

55. Otis, *Prostitution in Medieval Society: The History of an Urban Institution in Languedoc*, 37.

56. Ibid.

57. See Otis, chapter 3, "Public Houses: Physical Plant, Ownership, and Exploitation" (51–62), for additional information on the running and maintenance of the municipal brothels.

58. Shahar, *The Fourth Estate: A History of Women in the Middle Ages*, 208. As Shahar also notes, taxes were extracted from the brothels that added to the pockets of the seigneur of the town. Many of the seigneurs included churchmen such as "the Bishop of Mainz, who complained in 1422 that the citizens of the town were trying to rob him of his income which had always been due to the seigneur" (208). However, approximately 100 years earlier, taxing prostitutes was considered an ill-conceived idea. As Rollo-Koster points out: "The profitableness of the profession also attracted the authorities. In 1337, after agreeing with the syndics of the town, the marshal of the Roman court (in charge of policing lay curialists) taxed prostitutes and procurers two sols per week. In 1358 Pope Innocent VI, scandalized by the practice, annulled it" (Rollo-Koster 112).

59. Otis, *Prostitution in Medieval Society: The History of an Urban Institution in Languedoc*, 51.

60. Ibid., 88.

61. Rollo-Koster, "From Prostitutes to Brides of Christ: The Avignonese Repenties in the Late Middle Ages," 113.

62. Shahar, *The Fourth Estate: A History of Women in the Middle Ages*, 2.

63. Burke, *The Rhetoric of Religion; Studies in Logology*, 40.

64. Brett, *Humbert of Romans: His Life and Views of Thirteenth-Century Society*, 69.

65. Ibid., 58.

66. Shahar, *The Fourth Estate: A History of Women in the Middle Ages*, 103.

67. Haskins, *Mary Magdalen: Myth and Metaphor*, 149.

68. Humbert, as cited by Haskins, *Mary Magdalen: Myth and Metaphor*, 153.

69. Ibid.

70. Humbert, as cited by Brett, *Humbert of Romans: His Life and Views of Thirteenth-Century Society*, 68.

71. Haskins, *Mary Magdalen: Myth and Metaphor*, 169. It is interesting to note that during the high Middle Ages, women outnumbered men. This lopsided population ratio, along with the new marriage laws by the church, also worked to raise the number of prostitutes. Edward Brett (1984) in his biography on *Humbert of Romans* suggests that one outcome of this population problem was to "place in nunneries and beguinages females from the poor and middle classes as well as those from the nobility" (Brett, 58). This was also the case for prostitutes who had outlived their usefulness in official municipal brothels.

72. Haskins, *Mary Magdalen: Myth and Metaphor*, 167.

73. Humbert, as cited by Brett, *Humbert of Romans: His Life and Views of Thirteenth-Century Society*, 69.

74. Jansen, *The Making of the Magdalen*, 176–77.

75. Haskins, *Mary Magdalen: Myth and Metaphor*, 131.

76. Gold, *The Lady and the Virgin: Image, Attitude, and Experience in Twelfth-Century France*, 94.

77. Shahar, *The Fourth Estate: A History of Women in the Middle Ages*, 210.

78. Shahar, *The Fourth Estate: A History of Women in the Middle Ages*, 252. After Robert of Arbrissel established his abbey at Fontevrault, several men started to complain about Robert to the local bishop because it was felt that Robert was encouraging wives to leave their husbands, "abandon their conjugal duties to pursue a religious life" (Mews and Chiavaroli, 2001, 67). Further it was suggested by Mardob (ca. 1035–1123) that Robert of Arbrissel could not stay chase around so many women (ibid.).

79. Paterson, "Women, Property and the Rise of Courtly Love," 50. There were actually four houses in Robert of Arbrissel's Augustinian Monastic foundation at Fontevrault.

80. Jansen points out in *The Making of the Magdalen*, that Robert of Arbrissel's Magdalene house had several acknowledgments: "Notre Dame for nuns, Saint John the Evangelist for monks, Saint Mary Magdalen for penitents, and Saint Lazarus for lepers. Jacques Dalarun has argued that despite numerous citations in the scholarly literature, there is no medieval evidence supporting the theory that the convent dedicated to the Magdalen segregated the repentant prostitutes from the rest of Arbrissel's followers. This view seems to have originated in the seventeenth century" (178).

81. Gold, *The Lady and the Virgin: Image, Attitude, and Experience in Twelfth-Century France*, 94.

82. Shahar, *The Fourth Estate: A History of Women in the Middle Ages*, 252.
83. Pope Innocent III, as cited by Jansen, *The Making of the Magdalen*, 178.
84. Shahar, *The Fourth Estate: A History of Women in the Middle Ages*, 252.
85. Jansen, *The Making of the Magdalen*, 178.
86. Shahar, *The Fourth Estate: A History of Women in the Middle Ages*, 252.
87. Otis, *Prostitution in Medieval Society: The History of an Urban Institution in Languedoc*, 72.
88. Jansen, *The Making of the Magdalen*, 178.
89. Rollo-Koster, "From Prostitutes to Brides of Christ: The Avignonese Repenties in the Late Middle Age,"116.
90. Brundage, *Law, Sex, and Christian Society in Medieval Europe*, 395.
91. Otis, *Prostitution in Medieval Society: The History of an Urban Institution in Languedoc*, 72.
92. Karras, "Holy Harlots: Prostitute Saints in Medieval Legend," 32.
93. Shahar, *The Fourth Estate: A History of Women in the Middle Ages*, 208.
94. Otis, *Prostitution in Medieval Society: The History of an Urban Institution in Languedoc*, 85.
95. Ibid., 86.
96. Ibid.
97. Ibid., 87.
98. Ibid.
99. Jansen, *The Making of the Magdalen*, 177.
100. Rollo-Koster, "From Prostitutes to Brides of Christ: The Avignonese Repenties in the Late Middle Ages," 116.
101. Ibid.
102. Ibid., 117.
103. Ibid.
104. Otis, *Prostitution in Medieval Society: The History of an Urban Institution in Languedoc*, 73-74.
105. Ibid., 73.
106. Rollo-Koster gives the date as being 1276: "For example, the house in Marseille was founded in 1276 by Bertrand, a pious burgess of the town. He founded a congregation of Augustinians whose mission was specifically to save prostitutes. The congregation was approved by Pope Nicolas III, and the former prostitutes went under the appellation of the *Repenties* of St. Mary Magdalene" (Rollo-Koster, 116).
107. Otis, *Prostitution in Medieval Society: The History of an Urban Institution in Languedoc*, 73.
108. Jansen, *The Making of the Magdalen*, 178-79.
109. Otis, *Prostitution in Medieval Society: The History of an Urban Institution in Languedoc*, 73.
110. Ibid., 74-75.
111. Ibid., 75.
112. Haskins, *Mary Magdalen: Myth and Metaphor*, 172.
113. Otis, *Prostitution in Medieval Society: The History of an Urban Institution in Languedoc*, 73.
114. Jansen, *The Making of the Magdalen*, 179.
115. See Otis, *Prostitution in Medieval Society: The History of an Urban Institution in Languedoc*, 73; and Rollo-Koster, "From Prostitutes to Brides of Christ: The Avignonese Repenties in the Late Middle Ages," 116.
116. Jansen, *The Making of the Magdalen*, 180.
117. Aldobrandesca of Siena's feast's day is April 26.
118. Jansen, *The Making of the Magdalen*, 180.
119. Butler and Walsh, *Butler's Lives of the Saints*, 117.
120. Jansen, *The Making of the Magdalen*, 180.
121. Information originally recorded in the Angevin registers (Jansen 181).
122. Jansen, *The Making of the Magdalen*, 181.
123. Elliott and Warr, *The Church of Santa Maria Donna Regina: Art, Iconography, and Patronage in Fourteenth Century Naples*, 35.
124. Jansen, *The Making of the Magdalen*, 181.
125. Haskins, *Mary Magdalen: Myth and Metaphor*, 172.
126. Jansen, *The Making of the Magdalen*, 181.
127. Otis, *Prostitution in Medieval Society: The History of an Urban Institution in Languedoc*, 74.
128. Rollo-Koster, "From Prostitutes to Brides of Christ: The Avignonese Repenties in the Late Middle Ages,"118. Although mentioned by many medieval researchers, Joëlle Rollo-Koster offers detailed history of this particular Magdalene convent. As such, this section relies heavily on her earlier research.
129. Ibid., 118-19. The Magdalene home in Avignon became a pet project for Pope Gregory XI, as not only did he help get the building constructed, but also the Repenties were offered plenary indulges "*in mortis articulo* and 100 days of indulgences to their benefactors," as well as ex-

empting the community from paying all taxes (Rollo-Koster, 119). Pope Gregory even allowed the repentant sisters to study the Bible. This was an exception granted to the repenties because it was felt that only men could obtain spiritual enlightenment through the study of scripture, not women. Additionally, "Gregory XI went even further in his effort to reform the former prostitutes through education; he permitted the convent to receive nuns from other orders as instructors or to send Repentant sisters to other convents if they wished to further their education" (120).

130. Convent rules as cited by Rollo-Koster, "From Prostitutes to Brides of Christ: The Avignonese Repenties in the Late Middle Ages," 119–20.

131. Rollo-Koster, "From Prostitutes to Brides of Christ: The Avignonese Repenties in the Late Middle Ages,"123.

132. Ibid.

133. See Otis, *Prostitution in Medieval Society: The History of an Urban Institution in Languedoc*, 74; Rollo-Koster, "From Prostitutes to Brides of Christ: The Avignonese Repenties in the Late Middle Ages," 130.

134. As cited by Jansen, *The Making of the Magdalen*, 182. Rollo-Koster stipulates two conclusions from this general rule that is worth reiterating here: "First, women, especially if young and beautiful, were by nature dangerous to themselves and to men. Second, their reform would not only save women but also the masculine community that had enjoyed their charms" (142).

135. Otis, *Prostitution in Medieval Society: The History of an Urban Institution in Languedoc*, 74.

136. Jansen, *The Making of the Magdalen*, 182.

137. Rollo-Koster, "From Prostitutes to Brides of Christ: The Avignonese Repenties in the Late Middle Ages," 121.

138 Jansen, *The Making of the Magdalen*, 182.

139. Ibid., 182–83.

140. Rollo-Koster, "From Prostitutes to Brides of Christ: The Avignonese Repenties in the Late Middle Ages," 121.

141. Jansen, *The Making of the Magdalen*, 182.

142. Rollo-Koster, "From Prostitutes to Brides of Christ: The Avignonese Repenties in the Late Middle Ages," 121.

143. See Jansen, *The Making of the Magdalen*, 183; and Rollo-Koster, "From Prostitutes to Brides of Christ: The Avignonese Repenties in the Late Middle Ages," 121.

144. Rollo-Koster, "From Prostitutes to Brides of Christ: The Avignonese Repenties in the Late Middle Ages," 121.

145. Jansen, *The Making of the Magdalen*, 183.

146. Rollo-Koster, "From Prostitutes to Brides of Christ: The Avignonese Repenties in the Late Middle Ages," 121.

147. Otis, *Prostitution in Medieval Society: The History of an Urban Institution in Languedoc*, 74.

148. Rollo-Koster, "From Prostitutes to Brides of Christ: The Avignonese Repenties in the Late Middle Ages," 122.

149. Ibid., 124.

150. Ibid., 120–21.

151. Ibid., 125.

152. Ibid., 119.

153. Ibid., 132.

154. Otis, *Prostitution in Medieval Society: The History of an Urban Institution in Languedoc*, 73.

155. Ibid., 74–75.

156. Ibid., 74.

157. Ibid., 74–75.

158. Rollo-Koster, "From Prostitutes to Brides of Christ: The Avignonese Repenties in the Late Middle Ages," 117.

159. Otis explains the difficulties for women during this period: "The deterioration of the legal status of women was, to a large extent, due to a conscious movement, a reaction against the 'feminist' literature of the late Middle Ages and the Renaissance. The misogynous attack was first led by Tiraqueau in his *De legibus connubialibus* of 1522–1524, in which he have a clear definition of the legal incapacity of women, prohibiting them from making contracts and acting in justice. The other jurists of the sixteenth century followed suit, and such measures passed even into the reformed customs of the day" (42).

160. Brundage, *Law, Sex, and Christian Society in Medieval Europe*, 521.

161. Rollo-Koster, "From Prostitutes to Brides of Christ: The Avignonese Repenties in the Late Middle Ages," 132. Also see Otis, *Prostitution in Medieval Society: The History of an Urban Institution in Languedoc*, 76.

162. See Otis, *Prostitution in Medieval Society: The History of an Urban Institution in Languedoc*, 44–45.

163. Brundage, *Law, Sex, and Christian Society in Medieval Europe*, 557.

164. Wallerstein, *The Modern World-System: Capitalist Agriculture and the Origins of the European World-Economy in the Sixteenth Century*, 21–22.

165. Ibid., 24.

166. Ibid., 22.

167. Ibid., 27.
168. See Otis, *Prostitution in Medieval Society: The History of an Urban Institution in Languedoc*, 76; Brundage, *Law, Sex, and Christian Society in Medieval Europe*, 251; and Rollo-Koster, "From Prostitutes to Brides of Christ: The Avignonese Repenties in the Late Middle Ages," 132.
169. Otis, *Prostitution in Medieval Society: The History of an Urban Institution in Languedoc*, 57. Besides being rented out, brothels were also sold to the highest bidder. Otis mentions the brothel Montepellier, which the town council agreed to sell in their session of July 25, 1557 (40).
170. Ibid.
171. Ibid., 59.
172. Ibid.
173. Wallerstein, *The Modern World-System: Capitalist Agriculture and the Origins of the European World-Economy in the Sixteenth Century*, 37–38.
174. Ibid., 15.
175. Howell, *Women, Production, and Patriarchy in Late Medieval Cities*, 34.
176. Wallerstein, *The Modern World-System: Capitalist Agriculture and the Origins of the European World-Economy in the Sixteenth Century*, 16.
177. Otis, *Prostitution in Medieval Society: The History of an Urban Institution in Languedoc*, 75.
178. Ibid.
179. Burke, *The Rhetoric of Religion; Studies in Logology*, 4.
180. Wallerstein, *The Modern World-System: Capitalist Agriculture and the Origins of the European World-Economy in the Sixteenth Century*, 86.
181. Howell, *Women, Production, and Patriarchy in Late Medieval Cities*, 33.
182. Bolch, as cited by Wallerstein, *The Modern World-System: Capitalist Agriculture and the Origins of the European World-Economy in the Sixteenth Century*, 87.

Chapter Four

1. Kelly, *A Guide to Early Irish Law*, 68. Kelly also discusses how many sources agreed in a "general ban on female evidence, which one glossator describes as 'biased and dishonest'" (207).
2. It is important to note that in pre-colonized Ireland, there was no such thing as an "illegitimate" child. All children were recognized and their interests protected under the law — a stark contrast to modern Irish law and practice, which will become evident in chapters 6 and 8 of this work.
3. Castells, *The Rise of the Network Society*, 151–52.
4. Chambers, *Granuaile: The Life and Times of Grace O'Malley c. 1530–1603*, 34.
5. Kelly, *A Guide to Early Irish Law*, 232–33.
6. Ibid., 241.
7. MacManus, *The Story of the Irish Race*, 131.
8. MacManus ([1921] 1990) explains that "four generations sprung from one man usually went to each derb-fine — so that in each succeeding generation the groups had to be rearranged" (294).
9. MacManus, *The Story of the Irish Race*, 294.
10. Kelly, *A Guide to Early Irish Law*, xxiii, lists the hierarchal ranking of early Irish society as follows: supreme king (rí ruirech), overking of a few petty kingdoms (rí túath), king of a single petty kingdom (rí túaithe), lord of superior testimony (aire forgill), lord of precedence (aire tuíseo), high lord (aire ard), lord of vassalry (aire déso), prosperous farmer or a strong farmer (bóaire), less prosperous farmer or a small farmer (ócaire), man of middle huts or a semi-independent youth (fer midboth), semi-freeman, tenant at will (fuidir), cottier (bothach), hereditary serf (senchléithe), and the male slave (mug).
11. Kelly, *A Guide to Early Irish Law*, 7.
12. MacManus, *The Story of the Irish Race*, 294.
13. In order to be elected as chief or king, one had to be in perfect physical health and "without physical blemish or deformity" (MacManus, 295). It is interesting to note that this rule is reflected in Irish mythology. Specifically, in the cycle of mythology termed the *Invasion Myths*. Here, a Dana (mythical fairy people of Ireland) named Nuada lost his hand while fighting with another invading group called the Firbogs. Nuada should have become the king and the ruler of the Danaans, but "the mutilation forbade it, for no blemished man might be a king in Ireland" (Rollenston, 107). Instead, the Danaans elected Bres who, apparently, was quite strapping and strong but, as the tale has it, although abundant in brawn — starving in brains. Bres heavily taxed the people and even allowed the Danaans' greatest enemy, the Formorians, to regain power in Ireland. However, his worst and fatal mistake was in not offering hospitality, which has traditionally been one of Ireland's most important, and long-standing, traditions.

In denying hospitality to a Bard (poet) by the name of Corpre, Bres doomed himself when this poet composed what is traditionally considered the first satire in Ireland:
Without food quickly served,
Without a cow's milk, whereon a calf can grow,
Without a dwelling fit for a man under the gloomy night,
Without means to entertain a bardic company,—
Let such be the condition of Bres. (Ibid., 108)

This satire was said to destroy Bres, and finally Nuada was elected in his stead. However, his election depended upon the healing of his blemish — the missing hand. There are two traditions concerning Nuada's recovery of his hand. The first suggests that a silver hand was fashioned for Nuada by his healer, Dianecht — hence the epitaph: "Nuada of the Silver Hand." Later versions of the myths states that a greater healer, the son of Diancecht, actually made the hand grow again from the stump outward.

14. Ellis, *Ireland in the Age of the Tudors: English Expansion and the End of Gaelic Rule*, 41.
15. Kelly, *A Guide to Early Irish Law*, 11–12.
16. Ellis, *Ireland in the Age of the Tudors: English Expansion and the End of Gaelic Rule*, 41.
17. Kelly, *A Guide to Early Irish Law*, xxiii.
18. Based on the population figures of Ireland at this time (which Kelly points out are highly speculative), Kelly, *A Guide to Early Irish Law*, estimates that the "average *túath* could be reckoned to have contained about 3,000 men, women and children," and also contained one scholar (*ecnae*), a churchman, a poet, and a king (4).
19. Ó Corráin, "Prehistoric and Early Christian Ireland," in *The Oxford Illustrated History of Ireland*, ed. R.F. Foster, 25.
20. Ibid., Kelly, *A Guide to Early Irish Law*, 17, places the number at 150 between the 5th and 12th centuries.
21. MacManus, *The Story of the Irish Race*, 293.
22. Ibid.
23. This is not to say that private land ownership was not valued, since nobles and the king did have exclusive private rights to a certain portion of the land.
24. Kelly, *A Guide to Early Irish Law*, 109.
25. Ibid.
26. Ellis, *Ireland in the Age of the Tudors: English Expansion and the End of Gaelic Rule*, 41.
27. A base client is referred to as *Céile gíallnai*, *sóerchéile* equates to a free client, and *céilsine* refers to client-ship (Kelly, *A Guide to Early Irish Law*, 306).
28. MacManus, *The Story of the Irish Race*, 293.
29. Smedley, *Race in North America: Origin and Evolution of a Worldview*, 57.
30. Foster, *The Oxford Illustrated History of Ireland*, 109. While looking at Ireland during the 1500s, Foster states that the most cultivated crop by the Irish tended to be small crops of grain. For the most part, cultivation of green vegetables were unknown: "The systematic production of green vegetables seems to have been unknown in the Irish rural economy, and people supplemented their diet with watercress and other wild herbs, mixed with the ubiquitous butter" (108).
31. Kelly, *A Guide to Early Irish Law*, xxiii.
32. MacManus, *The Story of the Irish Race*, 293.
33. Ibid.
34. Kelly, *A Guide to Early Irish Law*, states that the law-books identify ten different types of *fuidir* (33).
35. Ibid.
36. MacManus, *The Story of the Irish Race*, 294.
37. For a list of surviving wisdom texts, see Kelly, *A Guide to Early Irish Law*, appendix 2, 284–86.
38. For a list of surviving law texts, see Kelly, *A Guide to Early Irish Law*, appendix 1, 264–83.
39. Kelly, *A Guide to Early Irish Law*, 227.
40. Ibid., 232.
41. Ibid.
42. Ibid., 242.
43. MacManus, *The Story of the Irish Race*, 134.
44. Otis, *Prostitution in Medieval Society: The History of an Urban Institution in Languedoc*, 44–45.
45. Brundage, *Law, Sex, and Christian Society in Medieval Europe*, 557.
46. Giraldus Cambrensis, also known as Gerald of Wales (1146–1223) was a medieval clergyman and chronicler who published the *Topography of Ireland* in 1188. A copy of this book translated by Thomas Forester and revised and edited by Thomas Wright (2000) can be found online at http://www.yorku.ca/inpar/topography_ireland.pdf.
47. Kelly, *A Guide to Early Irish Law*, 1.
48. Hegel, *Philosophy of History*, 115.
49. Said, *Culture and Imperialism*, 12.
50. Kelly, *A Guide to Early Irish Law*, 43.
51. Female poets were apparently rare but not unheard of. Kelly, *A Guide to Early Irish Law*, points to the *Annals of Inisfallen* (s.a. 934), and the chronicle of the death of Uallach, daughter of Muinechén. Described as "*banfili Érenn* 'the woman poet of Ireland,'" Uallach was said to be a fully recognized poet (49). However, Kelly

theories that this was a rare occurrence, with most woman "poets" being categorized as a type of sorcerer: "Judgeing by the references in the law-texts, it would seem that most women who composed verse were not legally recognised poets, but satirists who used verse for malicious purposes, in particular sorcery or witchcraft" (ibid).

52. Kelly cites an instance where a poet's satire was thought to have caused death, such as was recorded in 1414 in the *Annals of Connacht* about the death of Lord Lieutenant, John Stanley, which was said to have been caused by *firt filed* or a poet's spell (44).

53. Markale, *Women of the Celts*, 28.

54. Ellis, *Celtic Women: Women in Celtic Society and Literature*, 40.

55. Kelly, *A Guide to Early Irish Law*, 69.

56. Ibid.

57. Duby, *The Knight, The Lady, and the Priest: The Making of Modern Marriage in Medieval France*, 15.

58. Kelly, *A Guide to Early Irish Law*, 231.

59. Liam Breatnach and Aidan Breen, as cited in Kelly, *A Guide to Early Irish Law*, 233–34.

60. Ellis, *Celtic Women: Women in Celtic Society and Literature*, 40.

61. Mahoney, *Whoredom in Kimmage: The World of Irish Women*, 278–79.

62. Cahill, *How the Irish Saved Civilization: The Untold Story Ireland's Heroic Role from the Fall of Rome to the Rise of Medieval Europe*, 76.

63. Squire, *Celtic Myths and Legends*, 158.

64. Ellis, *Celtic Women: Women in Celtic Society and Literature*, 42. Queen Medb is also frequently referred to in the many ancient law books of Ireland.

65. Ibid.

66. MacCana, *Celtic Mythology*, 10.

67. Power, *Sex and Marriage in Ancient Ireland*, 7.

68. The term *Brehon* refers to an official lawgiver in ancient to medieval Ireland. This role was filled by both learned men and women who often traveled from *túath* to *túath* offering their services and, at one time, was considered part of the Druid class of wise men and women. MacManus offers an extensive account of the role of a Brehon:

Instead of filling the position of judge (as usually supposed) the Brehon was rather a legal expert who devoted himself to arbitration — and sometimes to advising — and was paid a fee from his client — a fee that in case of an award was about one-twelfth of the amount awarded. In studying for the profession the Brehon had not only to make himself master of the ancient legal records, and of the very complicated legal rules, the abstruse technical terms, and all the intricate forms in which the law was purposely entangled, but he must also be a genealogist and historian. Through the Brehon was but an arbitrator, so scholarly was he, so skilled in the laws and so wise and weighty in his solemn judgments, that, sitting at Dal, where two witnesses were needed to prove a fact, his words were venerated and his awards sacredly respected — as though they were the awards of a judge consecrated to the judgment seat, and rare was it to find any person hardened enough to evade or reject them. But it should be recorded that there were lawyers, or law arguers — advocates — of a very much lower status, much less learned and much less honoured than the Brehon — men who were paid to argue cases before the Brehon. (130)

69. Power, *Sex and Marriage in Ancient Ireland*, 11.

70. MacManus, *The Story of the Irish Race*, 131.

71. Cahill, *How the Irish Saved Civilization: The Untold Story Ireland's Heroic Role from the Fall of Rome to the Rise of Medieval Europe*, 148.

72. Ibid., 148–49.

73. MacManus offers an extensive list of the different collections of ancient Irish laws, which scholars understand to have existed and the few which we still have access to today. First, there are the Mild Judgments or the *Meill Brethra*, which are thought to have been written in Tara "at the time of Conn, and which has to do with regulations for juvenile sports (and of which only the name remains)" (132). Next, there is what was known as the *Cáin Fuirthime*, which compiled the body of Munster laws (12 books in all) and is also no longer in existence. The third collection, which there is contemporary access to, is called the *Crith Gablach* (theorized as originally being part of the *Cáin Fuirthime*). The fourth collection is the *Book of Acaill*, which is thought to be from the third century and is "attributed to King Cormac MacArt" (ibid.). The fifth and most extensive collection still in existence today is that of the *Senschus Mor*, which are the Irish Brehon civil laws.

74. MacManus, *The Story of the Irish Race*, 129.

75. For a discussion of the documents found in each third of the *Senchas Már*, see Kelly, *A Guide to Early Irish Law*, 243–46.

76. Sjöö and Mor, *The Great Cosmic Mother: Rediscovering the Religion of the Earth*, 259.

77. Most of the laws relating to marriage can be found in the *Cáin Lánamna* or "the law of couples" (Kelly, *A Guide to Early Irish Law*, 70).

78. Though most marriage ceremonies at this time were Catholic ones, the laws governing these marriages were Brehon.

79. Kelly, *A Guide to Early Irish Law*, pinpoints nine different unions: 1) union of joint property, 2) union of a woman on man's property, 3) union of a man on woman's property, 4) union of a man visiting, 5) union when a woman goes away openly with a man, but was not given by her kin, 6) a union where a woman allows herself to be abducted by a man without kin consent, 7) a union where she is secretly visited by a man, but without her kin's consent, 8) those from rape and 9) those shared by "insane persons" (70).

80. Ibid.

81. Ibid. In this arrangement, the woman is called a "'wife of joint authority' (bé cuitchernsa)" (70).

82. Ibid.

83. Power, *Sex and Marriage in Ancient Ireland*, 32.

84. The concubine had several titles, such as *dormuine*, "but a truer title was *ben charrthach*—the loved woman, a term synonymous with *die Geliebte* in German" (Power, 32). Further, this type of union is referred to by Kelly in *A Guide to Early Irish Law*, as a union of a man visiting (*lánamnas fir thathigtheo*) and is a "less formal union in which the man visits the womean at her home with her kin's consent" (70).

85. Power, *Sex and Marriage in Ancient Ireland*, 32–33. The plight of abducted women was also dealt with under the legal system, and neither the woman abducted or her offspring were ignored or "slurred" by the laws.

86. Power, *Sex and Marriage in Ancient Ireland*, 33.

87. Ibid.

88. Ibid. Two different types of rape were recognized by the Brehon Laws; the first being that of a violent possession of a woman sexually, and the second type of rape considered was when a woman was taken by deceit (for example, when she was asleep and could not give her consent). Compared to other parts of Romanized societies, to recognize this type of violation against a woman is not only enlightening, but also refreshing. There were even laws that instructed one on how to deal with a rapist: "The rapist was notified of the charge against him and of the penalty to be exacted. If he did not pay after a number of days, the plaintiff could come and fast at his doorstep, to use a modern expression. If he still remained obdurate, the value of the penalty could be seized in valuables or driven off as cattle" (Power, 20).

89. Ibid.

90. Kelly, *A Guide to Early Irish Law*, 70–71. It is interesting to note that the Church in Ireland at this time tried to oppose the Celtic tradition of polygamy. However, Kelly explains how the *Bretha Crólige* justified the practice by using the Old Testament: "There is dispute in Irish law as to which is more proper, whether many sexual unions or a single one: for the chosen people of God lived in plurality of unions, so that is not easier to condemn it than to praise it" (as cited in Kelly, 71).

91. Ibid.

92. Cahill, *How the Irish Saved Civilization: The Untold Story Ireland's Heroic Role from the Fall of Rome to the Rise of Medieval Europe*, 149.

93. Chambers, *Granuaile: The Life and Times of Grace O'Malley c. 1530–1603*, 80.

94. Power, *Sex and Marriage in Ancient Ireland*, 33–34.

95. As Power states: "The interesting thing about the *coibche* was that it continued to be paid each year for twenty-one years in all, if the marriage lasted that length of time. In the second year the wife kept a third of the amount for herself, while her father and his superior divided the remainder. As years went by, the wife kept a larger part of each year's Coibche. She thus kept adding to her personal property out of her husband's reserves" (34).

96. Power, *Sex and Marriage in Ancient Ireland*, 35.

97. The first group is when separation or divorce is considered "no-fault," and the departing partner could not incur any penalties or have to pay any special compensation, other than the normal division of property: "i) If illness has made the marriage impossible and also if separation is necessary due to some disease. ii) Pilgrimage being made by one of the parties.... iii) Some serious physical blemish or injury, which is not cured or curable, in the opinion of a Brehon, a physician or nobleman. iv) Leaving the territory to seek a friend or avenge an aggression or any such reason. The general notion here is that the absence is likely to be prolonged or perpetual. v) Loss of sanity. vi) If the parties are barren, they may separate without penalty in order to form another union or unions to have children" (Power, 53–54).

98. The second category of separation and divorce, under the Brehon Laws, concerns specifically women and their rights in obtaining a divorce from their husband, as well as receiving compensation for the wrongs that might have been committed against her: "i) A wife whose husband circulates a false story about her among the people. ii) If her husband circulates a satire about his wife which makes her a laugh-

ing-stock among her neighbors and acquaintances, she can leave him without blame to herself.... iii) Any woman who has been struck a blow which blemishes her, is also entitled to separation without blame to herself.... iv) A women who is repudiated for another. v) The woman who is deprived of sexual intercourse by her husband.... vi) If a husband gives his wife a philtre—a charm of some kind—to induce her to sleep with him, this forms grounds for divorce on her side. vii) A woman who is not given what she desires in food and such like things may rightfully divorce her husband without blame" (Power, 54–55).

99. Kelly, *A Guide to Early Irish Law*, 74.
100. Ibid.
101. Power, *Sex and Marriage in Ancient Ireland*, 59.
102. Ellis, *Ireland in the Age of the Tudors: English Expansion and the End of Gaelic Rule*, 41.
103. Power, *Sex and Marriage in Ancient Ireland*, 56.
104. Ellis, *Ireland in the Age of the Tudors: English Expansion and the End of Gaelic Rule*, 41.
105. It is important to distinguish between *kin ownership* and *communal ownership*. As Kelly *A Guide to Early Irish Law*, points out: "The 1865–1901 edition of the Ancient Laws of Ireland almost always translates *fine* as 'tribe' rather than 'kin-group.' This misled Engels and other modern political thinkers into believing that land was held in common by all members of the *túath* in early Ireland. In fact, early Irish society clearly attached great importance to the principle of the private ownership of property, and even extended it to mines and fishing-rights" (105).
106. Kelly, *A Guide to Early Irish Law*, 104.
107. Power, *Sex and Marriage in Ancient Ireland*, 56. The same type of division was also practiced for milk (butter), corn or bacon, wool, the dyeplant (glaisín), and the like.

Chapter Five

1. Polanyi, *The Great Transformation: The Political and Economic Origins of Our Time*, 35–36.
2. See Sayer, *The Violance of Abstraction*, 87; and Marx, "Economic Writings," from *Capital, Volume I*, 234, 236.
3. Marx, "Economic and Philsophic Manuscripts of 1844," in *The Marx-Engels Reader*, 86.
4. On primitive accumulation, Marx states: "The so-called primitive accumulation, therefore, is nothing else than the historical process of divorcing the producer from the means of production. It appears primitive, because it turns the pre-historic stage of capital and of the mode of production corresponding with it" (Marx, "So Called Primitive Accumulation," 871). So, Marx's view of primitive accumulation is rooted firmly in the social, whereas Adam Smith's view, for example, is rooted in the material.
5. Marx," So Called Primitive Accumulation," from *Capital, Volume I*, 876.
6. Ibid.
7. Ibid., 885.
8. Ibid., 875.
9. Ibid., 940.
10. Araghi, "Global Depeasantization, 1945–1990," 338.
11. Simms, "The Norman Invasion and the Gaelic Recovery," in *The Oxford Illustrated History of Ireland*, 60.
12. Wallerstein, *The Modern World-System II: Mercantilism and the Consolidation of the European World-Economy, 1600–1750*, 265. The Williamite War in Ireland is also referred to as the Jacobite War in Ireland—or the War of the Two Kings.
13. Smedley, *Race in North America: Origin and Evolution of a Worldview*, 54.
14. Simms, "The Norman Invasion and the Gaelic Recovery," in *The Oxford Illustrated History of Ireland*, 60. As Wallerstein argues in the *Modern World-System II*, par of the course for modern capitalism was the growth of large estates (85). As discussed in part 1, chapter 2 of this present work, the Catholic Church's laws on marriage and marriage eligibility, which was dependent upon degree of kinship, had the offshoot of limiting family estates, allowing the church to maintain a larger hegemonic role both economically and politically. After the crisis of the 14th century, the increased trend toward long-distance trade, the rise of the state as well as a world economy, large estates started to develop along with Protestantism and capitalism. The main technique of creating these large estates was with the method of enclosing the commons, essentially making what was a public resource a private one (Wallerstein 85–86).
15. Ibid.
16. See Simms, "The Norman Invasion and the Gaelic Recovery," in *The Oxford Illustrated History of Ireland*, 74; and Smedley, *Race in North America: Origin and Evolution of a Worldview*, 54.
17. Polanyi, *The Great Transformation: The Political and Economic Origins of Our Time*, 36.
18. Canny, "Early Modern Ireland, c. 1500–1700," in *The Oxford Illustrated History of Ireland*, 109.

19. Said, *Culture and Imperialism*, 9 (my italics). He further suggests that a great deal of European literature of the 19th century through today assumes a Eurocentric ideology embedded within both text and language. Thus, when briefly examining colonization and Ireland, Said states: "Yet it is greatly true that literary historians who study the great sixteenth-century poet Edmund Spenser, for example, do not connect his bloodthirsty plans for Ireland, where he imagined a British army virtually exterminating the native inhabitants, with his poetic achievement or with the history of British rule over Ireland, which continues today" (8).
20. Smedley, *Race in North America: Origin and Evolution of a Worldview*, 54.
21. Wallerstein, *The Modern World-System II: Mercantilism and the Consolidation of the European World-Economy, 1600–1750*, 123.
22. Smedley, *Race in North America: Origin and Evolution of a Worldview*, 55.
23. Kelly, *A Guide to Early Irish Law*, 99.
24. Ibid., 57.
25. Polanyi, *The Great Transformation: The Political and Economic Origins of Our Time*, 36–37 (my italics).
26. As discussed in chapter 2 of this work, most farmland fell under the category of kinland or *fintiu*. Unlike English law, a family, rather than a single person, owned this land. Private ownership was possible in Ireland, but it was not the normal mode of operation. As Kelly writes: "Most farmland is *fintiu* 'kin-land.' When kin-land is being divided, each heir gets a share which he will work with the help of his wife (or wives), sons, daughters, and perhaps servants or slaves. According to *Críth Gablach*'s picture of society, the average *ócaire* 'small farmer' inherits land worth seven *cumals* [1,492,992 square feet and is worth 24 milch cows], on which he grazes seven cows. The more affluent *bóaire* inherits land worth fourteen *cumals*, on which he grazes twelve cows" (Kelly, *A Guide to Early Irish Law*, 100).
27. As Smedley aptly puts it: "We will recall that, in the late sixteenth century, some Englishmen were beginning to believe that the 'wild Irish,' their prototype savages, were inherently inferior and could never become civilized" (142).
28. Smedley, *Race in North America: Origin and Evolution of a Worldview*, 59.
29. Power, *Sex and Marriage in Ancient Ireland*, 53.
30. Burke, *A Rhetoric of Motives*, 45.
31. Smedley, *Race in North America: Origin and Evolution of a Worldview*, 58.
32. Cambrensis, *Topography of Ireland*, 12. Chapter 4: Of the surface of Ireland, and its inequalities; and of the fertility of the soil.
33. Ibid., 74–75.
34. Ibid., 76. Chapter 20: Of their abominable treachery.
35. Ibid., Chapter 21: How they always carry an axe in their hands instead of a staff.
36. Ibid., 77. Chapter 22: Of a new mode of making a league: a proof of their wickedness.
37. Ibid., Chapter 23: How they love their foster-children and foster-brothers, and hate their own brothers and kindred.
38. Ibid., 70. Chapter 10: Of the character, customs, and habits of this people.
39. Ibid.
40. Written approximately around the same time as the *Topography of Ireland*.
41. Wallace, *The Cambridge History of Medieval English Literature*, 223.
42. Simms, "The Norman Invasion and the Gaelic Recovery," in *The Oxford Illustrated History of Ireland*, 56.
43. Cambrensis, *The Conquest of Ireland*, 12–13. Chapter 1: How Dermitius, Prince of Leinster, took refuge in England, and was restored to his dominions by the king of England.
44. Wallace, *The Cambridge History of Medieval English Literature*, 224.
45. William, *The Pilgrim: A Dialogue on the Life and Actions of King Henry the Eighth*, 66.
46. Araghi, "Global Depeasantization, 1945–1990," 338.
47. Ibid.
48. Smedley, *Race in North America: Origin and Evolution of a Worldview*, 57.
49. Seidman, *Manufacturing Militance: Worker's Movements in Brazil and South Africa, 1970–1985*, 200.
50. *The Annals of the Four Masters* (also referred to as *The Annals of the Kingdom of Ireland* or *Annala Rioghachta Éireann*) chronicle of medieval Irish History and recounts historic events from the great deluge or flood (said to have occurred 2,242 years after creation) to 1616. Translation of the Annals can be found online at http://www.ucc.ie/celt/published/T100005A/.
51. Sidney, as cited in Chambers, *Granuaile: The Life and Times of Grace O'Malley c. 1530–1603*, 84.
52. Ibid.
53. Chambers, *Granuaile: The Life and Times of Grace O'Malley c. 1530–1603*, 93.
54. Buci-Glucksman, "Hegemony and Consent: A Political Strategy," 117–18.
55. Ibid., 119. Also see Gramsci, *Selections from the Prison Notebooks of Antonio Gramsci*, 244.
56. Weber, "The Types of Legitimate Domination," 122.

57. Smedley, *Race in North America: Origin and Evolution of a Worldview*, 57 (my italics).
58. Lennon, *Sixteenth-Century Ireland: The Incomplete Conquest*, 56.
59. Ibid.
60. Ellis, *Ireland in the Age of the Tudors 1447–1603: English Expansion and the End of Gaelic Rule* 11.
61. *The Annals of the Four Masters*, M1537.19.
62. Chambers, *Granuaile: The Life and Times of Grace O'Malley c. 1530–1603*, 56.
63. Smedley, *Race in North America: Origin and Evolution of a Worldview*, 57.
64. Ibid.
65. Ellis, *Ireland in the Age of the Tudors 1447–1603: English Expansion and the End of Gaelic Rule*, 15.
66. Chambers, *Granuaile: The Life and Times of Grace O'Malley c. 1530–1603*, 63.
67. Ellis, *Ireland in the Age of the Tudors 1447–1603: English Expansion and the End of Gaelic Rule*, 15.
68. Glenn, *Unequal Freedoms*, 1.
69. Marshall, *Citizenship and Social Class and Other Essays*, 248–49.
70. Ibid, 249.
71. Ibid.
72. Ibid.
73. Connell, *Gender and Power: Society, the Person and Sexual Politics*, 26.
74. Ibid.
75. Engels, "The Patriarchal Family," 65.
76. Ibid.
77. Ibid., 65–66.
78. Ibid., 66.
79. Ibid.
80. Kandiyoti, "Bargaining with Patriarchy," 275.
81. Ibid., 278.
82. Stone, *The Family, Sex, and Marriage in England 1500–1800*, 93.
83. Ibid.
84. Canny, "Early Modern Ireland, c. 1500–1700," in *The Oxford Illustrated History of Ireland*, 113.
85. Marx," So Called Primitive Accumulation," from *Capital, Volume I*, 881–82.
86. Chambers, *Granuaile: The Life and Times of Grace O'Malley c. 1530–1603*, 113.
87. It is interesting to note that Irish law did not permit legal divorce until 1995.
88. Stone, *The Family, Sex, and Marriage in England 1500–1800*, 136.
89. Ibid., 36.
90. Ibid., 35.
91. Ibid.

Chapter Six

1. The Fabian Society, *Life in a Laundry*, 4.
2. Similar case studies to those in Ireland can be found with England's other peripheral states at the time: Australia, Scotland, and Canada. This chapter focused on Ireland as the notable case study of peripheral laundries.
3. Finnegan, *Do Penance or Perish: Magdalen Asylums in Ireland*.
4. Smith, *Ireland's Magdalen Laundries and the Nation's Architecture of Containment*.
5. Mullan, dir., *The Magdalene Sisters*.
6. Humphries, dir, *Sex in a Cold Climate*.
7. Wallerstein, *The Modern World-System II: Mercantilism and the Consolidation of the European World-Economy, 1600–1750*, 123.
8. Held, "The Development of the Modern State," in *Modernity: An Introduction to Modern Societies*, 81.
9. Wallerstein, *The Modern World-System: Capitalist Agriculture and the Origins of the European World-Economy in the Sixteenth Century*, 15.
10. Held, "The Development of the Modern State," in *Modernity: An Introduction to Modern Societies*, 82.
11. Polanyi, *The Great Transformation: The Political and Economic Origins of Our Time*, 146.
12. Bloy's article, "The 1601 Elizabethan Poor Law," can be found at http://www.victorianweb.org/history/poorlaw/elizpl.html.
13. Ibid., para. 6.
14. Ibid., para. 7–8.
15. Levinson, *Encyclopedia of Homelessness*, 654a-b. Further, a full transcription of the Act can be found at http://www.workhouses.org.uk/index.html?poorlaws/1601intro.shtml.
16. Bloy, "The 1601 Elizabethan Poor Law," para. 13.
17. Ibid., para. 14.
18. Browning and Douglas, *English Historical Documents, 1660–1714*, 464.
19. Bloy, "The 1662 Settlement Act," para. 1. Bloy's full article can be viewed at http://www.victorianweb.org/history/poorlaw/settle.html.
20. Bloy, "The 'Workhouse Test Act' (1723)," para. 3. Bloy's full article can be viewed at http://www.victorianweb.org/history/poorlaw/testact.html.
21. Bloy, "Gilbert's Act (1782)," para. 1–4. Bloy's full article can be viewed at http://www.victorianweb.org/history/poorlaw/gilbert.html
22. Polanyi, *The Great Transformation: The Political and Economic Origins of Our Time*, 100.
23. Ibid., 82. Polanyi quotes the recommendation: "When the gallon loaf of bread of a definite quality 'shall cost 1 shilling, then every

poor and industrious person shall have for his support 3 shillings weekly, either procured by his own or his family's labour, or an allowance from the poor rates, and for the support of his wife and everyone other of his family 1 shilling 6 pence; when the gallon loaf shall cost 1/6, then 4 shillings weekly, plus 1/10; on every pence which the bread price raises above 1 shilling he shall have 3 pence for himself and 1 pence for the others.'"

24. Ibid.

25. Levinson, *Encyclopedia of Homelessness*, 677b–678a.

26. It should be noted that Australia did not have official poor laws as Ireland, England, Scotland and Wales adopted. However, many of the same conditions existed in Australia, making it an ideal place for the workhouse as well. Further, the Sisters of Mercy, an order that originated in Ireland and ran many of the Irish Magdalene Houses, located orders in Australia, bringing with them certain traditions, ideas and in essence was able to reproduce social, economic, and political norms associated with a Magdalene laundry.

27. It is estimated that between 1838 and 1843, 112 workhouses were erected in Ireland with 18 more still being built. These institutions were not enough when the Irish famine of 1845–1851 hit — causing forced immigration to Canada and Australia.

28. Writing about Lady Arabella Denny, Crookshrank and Cole in *History of Methodism in Ireland* wrote: "While in the city Wesley seized the opportunity of waiting on Lady Arabella Denny at her beautiful residence, now known as Lisaniskea, Blackrock. The philanthropic character of this noble lady is well known. In 1765 she was presented with the freedom of the city of Dublin as a mark of esteem 'for her ladyship, for her many great charities and constant care of the poor foundling children in the city workhouse.' She also founded the Magdalene Asylum in Lesson Street, which was opened in 1766, and was the first institution of the kind in Ireland. Her ladyship died in 1792, aged eighty-five years" (372).

29. This date appears to be in question. Raughter, "A Discreet Benevolence: Female Philanthropy and the Catholic Resurgence in Eighteenth-Century Ireland," lists the date at 1767. The 1864 Parliamentary Gazetteer of Ireland (125a), Crookshrank and Cole (372), Wright (119), and O'Toole, "The Sisters of No Mercy," all place the establishment of the Lesson-Street Magdalene Asylum at 1766. However, *Thom's Almanac* puts the date at 1765, noting the following about the Asylum in 1850: "Magdalen Asylum, Leeson-Street, Founded by Lady Arabella Denny; opened June 11, 1765. *Patroness*, Her Royal Highness the Duchess of Gloucester.—*Vice-Patroness*, Mrs. J. Digges La Touche. *Governesses for Life*, Countess of Castlestuart, Marehioness of Thomond, Mrs. James, Mrs. Woodward, and Hon. Mrs. Henry Hamilton.—*Governesses*, Countess of Farnham, Countess of Longford, Lady Elizabeth Brownlow, Lady Ema Vesey, Mrs. William Disney, Mrs. Boyd, Mrs. Wise, Hon. Mrs. Newcombe, Baroness De Robeck, Lady Gort, Hon. Mrs. Pakenham, Mrs. Singer, Mrs. Bessonet, and Mrs. C. Browen.— President, His Grace the Archbishop of Dublin.—*Guardians*, Earl of Roden, Rev. Sir Richard Wolseley, bart., Lord Decies, Baron De Robeck, Rev. Doctor Wall, F.T.C.D., B.C. Lloyd, Hon. And Rev. Dean Bernard, Rev. George Blacker, Dr. Collins, William Digges La Touche, esq., William Brooke, esq., J.H. Otway, esq., Rev. Thomas Digges La Touche, James Bessonette, esq., Q.C., Theophilus Digges La Touche, and William Watson, esq.—*Guardians for Life*, Rev. Mr. Jessop, Lord Bishop of Killaloe and Kilfenora, and Henry Hamilton, esq.— *Honorary*, Rev. Dr. Nash, Rev. R.J. Hobson, and Rev. H. Woodward.—*Annual Subscribers*, John Schoales, esq., and Surgeon Maurice Colles.— *Treasurers*, Messrs. David C. La Touche & Co. *Chaplain*, Rev. J.H, Singer, D.D., S.F.T.C.D.— *Assistant Chaplain*, Rev. J. Lowe.—*Physician*, Dr. Fras. Barker.—*Surgeon*, Maurice Colles. Esq.— *Superintendent Matron*, Mrs. Sarah Arundell.— Secretary and Providore, Mr. John Dale. Washing, mangling, glazing, and needle-work, executed at the shortest notice" (658).

30. Luddy, *Women in Ireland, 1800–1918: A Documenentary History*, 10.

31. Wright, *An Historical Guide to the City of Dublin, Illustrated by Engravings and a Plan of the City*, 119

32. Finnegan, *Do Penance or Perish: Magdalen Asylums in Ireland*, 8.

33. Parliamentary Gazetteer of Ireland, 1846, 125a.

34. Taylor's publication reads more like a lengthy propaganda pamphlet for religious institutions than a critical and factual account of the Irish religious houses. Regardless, it is a valuable resource.

35. Taylor, *Irish Homes and Irish Hearts*, 107–8.

36. Ibid., 108.

37. The following historical documents mention the Donnybrook Magdalen Asylum: Keogh, *The Irish Catholic Directory, Almanac and Registry with Complete Ordo in English*, listing "Superioress, Mrs. Barden. Chaplan, Rev. James M'Veigh," p. 157. Thom's *Irish Almanac* offers

the most extensive listing: "General Magdalen Asylum, Donnybrook. This Institution was founded in 1798, for female penitents of every religious persuasion, under the care of the Sisters of Charity, and provides in every respect for fifty penitents. It is in the premises lately occupied by the Castle School, and hence has many obvious advantages for washing and making up family and fine linen. All kinds of plain needlework also executed. A confidential person will be sent to receive directions for any work to be done at the Establishment; and letters by post addressed 'To the Superintendent, St. Mary Magdalen's Asylum, Donnybrook,' will be attended to. Benefactions received by the Most Rev. Archbishop Murray; J.C. Bacon, esq., by the Tresurer, A. O'Brien, esq., 5, Mountjoy-square, east; and by the Governesses, Mrs. Codd, Mrs. Boylan, Mrs. Devereaux, Mrs. O'Brien. The Committee of Governesses meet at the Asylum every Thursday" (657). Finally, there is Taylor's 1867 description in *Irish Homes and Irish Hearts* (29–30), as well as a brief discussion by Gilbert (1893), *Woman's Mission*, 238.

38. Taylor, *Irish Homes and Irish Hearts*, 27–28.

39. Ibid., 28.

40. Batchelor, "'Industry in Distress': Reconfiguring Femininity and Labor in the Magdalen House," 3.

41. Ibid., 16.

42. Ibid. Finnegan does discuss that the York Penitentiary and a Glasgow Magdalene Institution did make an effort to teach basic reading and writing skills that were later extended (19th century) to include classes in geography, music and math. Yet this was the exception in Ireland. Indeed, most of the laundries ended up being run by the Good Shepherd Nuns as well as the Sisters of Mercy. Both orders focused only on "religious instruction," "pious readings" and prayers: "These alternated with the silences, and all were extended to the work" (149–50).

43. Ibid., 3–5.

44. Taylor, *Irish Homes and Irish Hearts*, 28–29.

45. Finnegan, *Do Penance or Perish: Magdalen Asylums in Ireland*, 33.

46. See Luddy, *Women and Philanthropy in Nineteenth-Century Ireland*, 22; and Finnegan, *Do Penance or Perish: Magdalen Asylums in Ireland*, 13.

47. See Luddy, *Women and Philanthropy in Nineteenth-Century Ireland*, 22. The following historical documents lists the Sister of Mercy's Magdalen Asylum: Keogh, *The Irish Catholic Directory, Almanac and Registry with Complete Ordo in English*, 208a. N.a., *The Religious Houses of the United Kingdom: Containing a Short History of Every Order and House Compiled from Official Sources*, 193. N.a., *The Irish Catholic Directory and Almanac*, 266, 267.

48. Taylor, *Irish Homes and Irish Hearts*, 192.

49. Finnegan, *Do Penance or Perish: Magdalen Asylums in Ireland*, 50.

50. See Taylor, *Irish Homes and Irish Hearts*, 139; and Finnegan, *Do Penance or Perish: Magdalen Asylums in Ireland*, 51. Additional historical accounts of this Asylum can be found in the following sources: Keogh, *The Irish Catholic Directory, Almanac and Registry with Complete Ordo in English*, 185, 186. N.a., *The Religious Houses of the United Kingdom: Containing a Short History of Every Order and House Compiled from Official Sources*, 159. N.a., *The Irish Catholic Directory and Almanac*, 233. Regarding this later source, the following information was listed for the Asylum in 1907, where apparently 100 Magdalene inmates resided: "Convent of the Good Shepherd, Limerick — *Superioress*, Mrs. Haugh; Chaplain, Rev. S. Connolly. 78 Sisters (including the Novices) in Community, who have care of a *Magdalen Asylum*, where over 100 poor penitents are protected and trained to industry. They have also under their care a Female Reformatory, which numbers over 40 children, an Industrial School numbering 130, and an 'Angels' Home,' for the girls discharged from their Industrial School, when out of employment. The inmates of the different institutions embroider vestments in gold and silver, chenille and silk; they also make exquisite Limerick Lace, Rochets, Albs, Altar Falls, etc., to order" (233).

51. Finnegan, *Do Penance or Perish: Magdalen Asylums in Ireland*, 51.

52. Ibid., 33.

53. Monsignor Kinseley of Kilkenny, as cited by Luddy, *Women and Philanthropy in Nineteenth-Century Ireland*, 97.

54. Ibid., 101.

55. Finnegan, *Do Penance or Perish: Magdalen Asylums in Ireland*, 9.

56. Woodward, *Essays and Sermons*, 462.

57. Luddy, *Women in Ireland, 1800–1918: A Documenentary History*, 255.

58. The Sisters of Mercy ran the Cork Magdalene Asylum, which was founded on July 29, 1872. Historical documents that mention this asylum include the 1887 *Religious Houses of the United Kingdom* (159), Taylor's *Irish Homes and Irish Hearts* (152–53), and finally Manner's 1881 *Notes of an Irish Tour* (98).

59. Finnegan, *Do Penance or Perish: Magdalen Asylums in Ireland*, 36.

60. Taylor, *Irish Homes and Irish Hearts*, 153.

61. Manner, *Notes of an Irish Tour*, 98. Fur-

ther, Manner's observation that the sister was offered command over all the Magdalene Asylums is substantiated by Finnegan: "Sister Mary of our Lady of the Sacred Heart Coppinger, on the other hand, also from an unusually distinguished background, was to spend her life in the Penitents' Section. During her Novitiate the young women was named First Mistress of Penitents at Cork — a unique position in view of the Foundation's association with the Contagious Diseases Acts; and a post which she held for over half a century" (60).

62. Luddy, *Women and Philanthropy in Nineteenth-Century Ireland*, 107.

63. Finnegan, *Do Penance or Perish: Magdalen Asylums in Ireland*, 42.

64. 1897–1898 Brisbane, Australia Sisters of Mercy Magdalene Laundry Advertisement, included in *the Handbook of Information for the Colonies and India*, x.

65. The Fabian Society, *Life in The Laundry: Fabian Tract No. 112*, 10.

66. Ibid., 9

67. Ibid.

68. Ibid. Because religious institutions were not legally required to report earnings, many did not. But it is interesting that out of the few records found, most institutions consistently reported an overall yearly loss of around £200 or so. For example, Hayter in 1875, *Notes on the Colony of Victoria: Historical, Geographical, Meteorological, and Statistical*, states that Melbourne's refuge for fallen women (the Magdalen Asylum at Abbotsford) received £1,495 from the government, nothing from private contributions, £5,472 "from other sources," with a total expenditure of £7,120, making a loss of £153 (entry 584, p. 219). Vagabon, in the then-famous *The Vagabon Papers: Sketches of Melbourne Life, in Light and Shade*, also reporting on the same house in 1876, stated that "the receipts from all sources, including the Parliamentary grant of £950, and £2,045 realized by the penitents' labour, were £4,807. The expenditure was £5,400, or not, £25 *per capita*. Over £860 was expended in building, repairs, fittings, and furniture. New buildings are, in fact, sadly needed for the health and comfort of the inmates" (197). Not only is a slight loss shown for the Magdalene asylums reported on in Australia, but in Ireland as well. Because of the consistency of slight financial losses when asylums did report their financial laundry reviews, and also because of the overall complaints the Magdalene laundries received regarding unfair and unregulated completion, it is important that we examine these numbers with great suspicion. The Magdalene laundries had much to lose by showing profit margins. Further, because inspectors or officials of any kind were not required to check validity of these numbers, but simply took what reporting was received at face value, we should again be cautious at reading much into the consistent show of profit loss.

69. In this section and elsewhere, McCarthy actually expresses concern regarding how workhouses were becoming religious institutions: "On the facts stated, which apply to almost every similar board in Catholic Ireland, I believe that at no remote period, unless Irish public opinion takes a healthier trend, the Poor Law Union Workhouses will become religious institutions, managed at a profit, like the national and industrial schools and reformatories... while the orders of nuns will fill the female posts, getting the actual work done free by pauper labour; as they get it done at present whenever they can" (454–55).

70. McCarthy, *Priests and People in Ireland*, 455.

71. Ibid., 456 (emphasis in original).

72. Annual Report of Chief Inspectors of Factories, 1900, 387, as cited by The Fabian Society, *Life in The Laundry: Fabian Tract No. 112*, 10.

73. Smith, *Ireland's Magdalen Laundries and the Nation's Architecture of Containment*, 47.

74. The Fabian Society, *Life in a Laundry*, 10.

75. This law was changed to 13 with the amendment made in 1875.

76. Mead, Bodkin and Britain, *The Criminal Law Amendment Act, 1885, with Introduction, Notes, and Index*, 44.

77. Ibid., 42.

78. Ibid., 31. Of course, most sexual crimes including rape and incest are not done in the company of witnesses, and thus this portion of the law served to condemn the victimized rather than protect them.

79. Bunreacht na hÉireann (Constitution of Ireland), Article 40:6.1.

80. Ibid., Articles 41.2.1–2.

81. The Code of Cannon Law, 1369.

82. Mahoney, *Whoredom in Kimmage: The World of Irish Women*, 178.

83. Power, *Sex and Marriage in Ancient Ireland*, 11.

84. Taillon, *When History was Made: The Women of 1916*, 1.

85. Ibid., xvii.

86. James Smith, *Ireland's Magdalen Laundries and the Nation's Architecture of Containment*, focus on the process of Catholic national identity building following Ireland's successful bid for independence in the beginning of the

20th century. Although it can be argued that from a legal standpoint this relationship between the Catholic Church and the Irish state became solidified, the actual project of national identity building within the confines of Catholic morality can be traced to the 1600s and Ireland's final struggle against colonization. Although the Catholic faith has long existed in Ireland, identification with the Roman Catholic Church and their particular set of morals did not occur early on, but developed as a reaction against Protestant England and the growth of the capitalist world system, as is discussed in chapter 5 of this work.

87. Smith, *Ireland's Magdalen Laundries and the Nation's Architecture of Containment*, 3.

88. Finnegan, *Do Penance or Perish: Magdalen Asylums in Ireland*, 18.

89. Smith, *Ireland's Magdalen Laundries and the Nation's Architecture of Containment*, 3

90. Ibid., 46.

91. Ibid., 49.

92. Ibid., 46. By defining the laundries as voluntary and charitable intuitions, the state and church can better disavow their personal responsibility. In a sense, the entering female becomes the scapegoat because it was her decision, as it is argued, to enter the asylum. No one forced her. But the illusion of choice is not the same as freedom of choice. Further, because the laundries continued to be unregulated and uninspected, no one really knew, outside of the inmates and those who ran the institutions, what occurred behind these cloistered walls.

93. Ibid., 52.

94. CICA, *CICA Investigation Committee Report Vol. 1*, 38: 2.14.

95. CICA's Investigation Committee Report also traces the institutions back to the poor law of 1598 and the later workhouses for the poor (35: 2.01–2.02.).

96. Smith, *Ireland's Magdalen Laundries and the Nation's Architecture of Containment*, 45.

97. Ibid., 11.

98. Moral danger was a concept that was widely defined and preemptively applied. Some of the Magdalene's accounts include being placed in the institutions as a result of being too attractive, or because of rape. Other accounts include the death of the mother and the daughter being left to care for a house full of men. In each above situation, the girl in question was deemed in moral danger and sent to a laundry. See Polman, "Re-discovery of Ireland's 'Forgotten Women' Causes National Scandal," 1993.

99. CICA, *CICA Investigation Committee Report Vol. 1*, 38: 2.14–2.15.

100. Smith, *Ireland's Magdalen Laundries and the Nation's Architecture of Containment*, 53.

101. Ibid., xv.

102. Linda Mahood, in *The Magdalenes*, recounts, for example, the long history associated with the Glasgow Magdalene Asylum in Scotland. In 1841 an act of Parliament combined a girl's juvenile reformatory with the Magdalene asylum, and created the House of Refuge for Females. As a result, the Magdalene asylum in Glasgow no longer existed as a separate institution for over 20 years. By 1850, however, there were concerns that by incarcerating juvenile offenders, the institution resembled more of a "penal character" (106). In the protester's view, and those who wished to reestablish the Magdalene asylum, the Magdalene was not a criminal: "[It] was offensive and irritating to the women, as it gave their department a penal aspect, quite opposed to its real character, for, notwithstanding the stigma of the name common to both, the two branches differed entirely" (ibid.). However the tendency toward moral reformatory continued and a Glasgow Magdalene home for wayward girls called Lochburn (a relative of the earlier House of Refuge for Females and Magdalene asylum) applied much of the ideology used on the early Magdalene homes. Mahood recounts a September 17, 1958 mass escape where 26 girls (between ages 15 and19) had scaled down a ladder and dropped from a wall. All the girls claimed mistreatment, that they were held as prisoners and had been beaten: "Two days later there was another 'breakout' and William Hannan M.P. assured the public that the Institution would be looked into by the Secretary of State for Scotland" (165).

103. McElwee, "Tragedy of Magdalene A Lesson for Present," para. 25.

104. Polman, "Re-discovery of Ireland's 'Forgotten Women' Causes National Scandal," para. 17.

105. As cited by Finnegan, *Do Penance or Perish: Magdalen Asylums in Ireland*, 20.

106. Polman, "Re-discovery of Ireland's 'Forgotten Women' Causes National Scandal," para. 17.

Chapter Seven

1. As cited in Dodd, *An Account of the Rise, Progress, and Present State of the Magdalen Hospital, for the Reception of Penitent Prostitutes*, 22.

2. Gray, *A History of English Philanthropy from the Dissolution of the Monasteries to the Taking of the First Census*, 164.

3. Stone, *The Family, Sex, and Marriage in England 1500–1800*, 340.

4. Ibid.

5. Ibid., 336.

6. Hickman, *Courtesans: Money, Sex and Fame in the Nineteenth Century*, 86.

7. Stone, *The Family, Sex, and Marriage in England 1500–1800*, 334.

8. Haskins, *Mary Magdalen: Myth and Metaphor*, 233.

9. Stone, *The Family, Sex, and Marriage in England 1500–1800*, reports that the three most advertised subjects in the 18th-century periodicals were "cures for venereal disease, cosmetics and books — in that order" (379).

10. Painting your mistress as the Magdalene actually was practiced by many aristocrats. As Haskins points out, there are many examples of this: "In the late fifteenth and early sixteenth centuries, artists such as the Fleming Jan Gossaert had depicted noble women in this guise, as in the portrait believed to be of Isabel of Austria (1501–1526), sister of the Holy Roman emperor, Charles V, and that of Louise de Brabant. Pier di Cosimo painted an unknown sitter as Mary Magdalene (c. 1580, Rome, Galleria Nazionale di Palazzo Barberini), as did Domenico Puligo (1525, Florence, Palazzo Pitti) and II Poppi (c. 1580, Florence, private collection), the latter two coldly erotic Mannerist images rather than saintly portraits" (292).

11. Haskins, *Mary Magdalen: Myth and Metaphor*, 291.

12. Ibid., 294.

13. Ibid., 294–95.

14. Batchelor, "'Industry in Distress': Reconfiguring Femininity and Labor in the Magdalen House," 4–5.

15. Stone, *The Family, Sex, and Marriage in England 1500–1800*, 392.

16. Batchelor, "'Industry in Distress': Reconfiguring Femininity and Labor in the Magdalen House," 5.

17. Stone, *The Family, Sex, and Marriage in England 1500–1800*, 392.

18. Boucherett et al., *The Condition of Working Women and the Factory Acts*, 2. The following abbreviations apply: s. refers to shillings and d. refers to sixpence; 20 shillings to a pound, and 12 pence to a shilling (240 to a pound).

19. Ibid., 3.

20. Ibid., 10.

21. Earnings for living off of 14s. a week can be found in Boucherett et al., *The Condition of Working Women and the Factory Acts*, 5–6.

22. A double-bedded kitchen is equivalent to an all-in-one living space or studio.

23. Earnings for living off of 7s. 6d. a week can be found in Boucherett et al., *The Condition of Working Women and the Factory Acts*, 7.

24. Batchelor, "'Industry in Distress': Reconfiguring Femininity and Labor in the Magdalen House," 16.

25. Nathaniel Lardner (1684–1768), the famous English theologian and writer, firmly objected to the term "Magdalen house for penitent prostitutes" because he realized that Mary Magdalene was not a prostitute and therefore should not be associated with such a venture: "It appears to me a great abuse of the name of a truly honourable, and I think truly excellent woman. If Mary's shame had been manifest, and upon record, she could not have been worse stigmatized: whereas the disadvantageous opinion concerning the former part of her life is founded only in an uncertain, and conjectural deduction" (Lardner and Kippis, 246).

26. Stone, *The Family, Sex, and Marriage in England 1500–1800*, 392.

27. It is suggested that Dr. Johnson was the first to publish an appeal for the prostitute: "It cannot be doubted but that numbers follow this dreadful course of life, with shame, horror, and regret; but, where can they hope for refuge? The world is to their friend, nor the world's law" (Johnson, as cited by Turberville in *Johnson's England*, 330).

28. William Dodd, *An Account of the Rise, Progress, and Present State of the Magdalen Hospital*, 2–4.

29. Hanway, *An Historic Account of the British Trade Over the Caspian Sea*, 308.

30. Hanway, as cited by Moxham in *Tea*, 33–34.

31. Sangster and Bennett, *Umbrellas and Their History*, 27.

32. Inwood and Porter, *A History of London*, 289.

33. Haskin, *Mary Magdalen: Myth and Metaphor*, 304.

34. Ibid.

35. Hanway, as cited in Haskin, *Mary Magdalen: Myth and Metaphor*, 305.

36. Ibid., emphasis in original.

37. Traditionally a magistrate's courts were held within their private residence.

38. Gray, *A History of English Philanthropy from the Dissolution of the Monasteries to the Taking of the First Census*, 164. Dodd, *An Account of the Rise, Progress, and Present State of the Magdalen Hospital*, also lists the following as founders of the Magdalen-Home: Robert Nettleton, George Wombwell, John Dorrien, John Thorton, Thomas Preston, and Charles Dingley (5).

39. Timbs' account seems to be taken directly from Dodd's account in *An Account of the Rise, Progress, and Present State of the Magdalen Hospital*, which states that the home was opened in August, 1758, to eight "unhappy objects" (5).

40. Timbs, *Curiosities of London*, 54. The author also mentions one of the original benefactors, Omychund: "Among the names of the earliest benefactors occurs that of Omychund, the black merchant of Calcutta. He bequeathed between this and the Founding Hospital 37,500 current rupees, to be equally divided. Unfortunately, however, 'a portion only of this magnificent legacy could be extracted from the grasp of Hurzorimal, his executor, notwithstanding the zealous interference of the Governor-general (Warren Hastings) and other eminent functionaries" (Brownlow, as cited in Timbs, 540).

41. Gray, *A History of English Philanthropy from the Dissolution of the Monasteries to the Taking of the First Census*, 165. This reasoning of the "more innocent" is not unlike the rationale of the first fallen in Ireland (see chapter 6 of this work).

42. Timbs, *Curiosities of London*, 540.

43. Feltham, *The Picture of London for 1803*, 160.

44. Chart reproduced from Dodd, *An Account of the Rise, Progress, and Present State of the Magdalen Hospital*, 6.

45. Women were encouraged to stay for approximately three years, and only those who did not have venereal diseases could be admitted; the rest went to hospitals.

46. Haskin, *Mary Magdalen: Myth and Metaphor*, 307.

47. Batchelor, "'Industry in Distress': Reconfiguring Femininity and Labor in the Magdalen House," 14–15.

48. Jane Shore (d. 1527?), mistress of Edward IV and of Thomas Grey, 1st M. of Dorset; forced to do penance by Richard III, according to historical tradition. She was familiar to the 18th century as the heroine of a tragedy by Nicholas Rowe.

49. Walpole, *The Letters of Horace Walpole*, 38–39.

50. Mogg, *Moggs Picture of London and Visitor's Guide to Its Sights*, 1848, 158–59.

51. Feltham, *The Picture of London for 1803*, 160.

52. Timbs, *Curiosities of London: exhibiting the most rare and remarkable objects of interest in the metropolis, with nearly sixty years' personal recollections*, 540.

53. Haskin, *Mary Magdalen: Myth and Metaphor*, 312.

54. Ibid., 317.

55. Batchelor, "'Industry in Distress': Reconfiguring Femininity and Labor in the Magdalen House," 3–5.

56. Smith, *Ireland's Magdalen Laundries and the Nation's Architecture of Containment*, 3.

57. Smith, *Ireland's Magdalen Laundries and the Nation's Architecture of Containment*, xv.

58. Viault, *English History*, 259.

59. It is important to note that until the *Registration Act of 1837*, which required everyone to register births, marriages and deaths under English law, it was impossible to know how old anyone was and so impossible to really enforce many of these restrictions. See Thompson (Barrister-at-Law), *The Law Journal Reports for the Year 1896*, 79.

60. Ibid.

61. Ibid., 259.

62. Jeans, *Factory Act Legislation*, 1892, 14.

63. Ibid., 78.

64. Ibid., 79. Jeans writes that the distinction between workshops and factories continued to be vague even after the 1878 legislation: "The terms 'factory,' 'workshop,' and 'domestic workshop,' in the Act of 1878, are now hardly more than survivals of the past, which serve to mark the historical progress of legislation. To-day there exists no really fundamental distinction between a 'factory' and a 'workshop,' or an ordinary and a 'domestic' workshop" (ibid.).

65. Malcolmson, *English Laundresses: A Social History, 1850–1930*, 82.

66. Smith, *Ireland's Magdalen Laundries and the Nation's Architecture of Containment*, xv.

67. View the full amendment proposal in *The Parliamentary Debates*, 1901, ei–eii.

68. *The Parliamentary Debates*, 1901, ei.

69. "(b) A woman, young person, or child must not be employed continuously for more than five hours without an interval of at least half an hour for a meal" (ibid., eii).

70. Provisions included the following for all laundries that used steam, water or any mechanical power: "(a) A fan or other means of a proper construction must be provided, maintained, and used for regulating the temperature in every ironing room, and for carrying away the steam in every washhouse in the laundry; and (b) All stoves for heating irons must be sufficiently separated from any ironing-room, and gas irons emitting any noxious fumes must not be used ; and (c) The floors must be kept in good condition and drained in such manner as will allow the water to flow off freely" (ibid.).

71. Ibid.

72. "The provisions of this Act prohibiting the employment of women within four weeks after childbirth, and of children under the age of twelve years, shall apply to the laundry in like manner as to a factory or workshop" (ibid.).

73. Ibid. Boucherett, Blackburn and Boucherett in *The Condition of Working Women and the Factory Acts*, published 1896, argued that a female laundress would not be able to support herself if the laws forbidding night work and

limiting hours were instituted (11). Boucherett further suggests that if women's ability to work longer hours and at night thereby lowering their wages, that "other" means of support (suggesting prostitution) would be sought and necessary (ibid.).

74. *The Parliamentary Debates*, 1901, eiii.
75. Ibid., 651.
76. Ibid., 656–57.
77. Ibid., 658. Although historically alternative forms of inspection would be employed regarding the Magdalene Laundries (especially in Ireland), there is little information regarding how such inspections should be conducted. It appears that the main difference resides in pre-arranged inspections — that is, inspections where always pre-announced in the religious and reformatory institutions, and surprise inspections never occurred.
78. Ibid.
79. Ibid., 660.
80. Ibid., 661
81. Ibid., 662.
82. Ibid.
83. Ibid., 664.
84. Ibid., 663. Mr. Tennant reads a letter sent to the Archbishop by Miss Ella Pease regarding the Morpeth Home of Industry: "I have heard from three members of the 'Morpeth Home of Industry' Committee, and they are all strongly in favour of homes and institutions such as this being put under the Factory Acts. The other member who is in Norway at the present moment agrees with us, I know. So I can say all the managers of the home are unanimous on the subject. We have all felt how difficult it is to prevent matrons from overpressing girls, even when their committees do all they can to prevent it, and when, as with us, there is plenty of money. I know, however, one or two institutions where there is not much money, and where the committees are at fault as well as the matrons, and a terrible lot of overwork goes on, and until there are women inspectors nothing will stop this continuing" (ibid., 663).
85. Ibid., 674.
86. Ibid., 673.
87. Ibid., 675.
88. Ibid., 665.
89. Ibid., 665–66.
90. Ibid., 666.
91. Ibid.
92. Ibid., 666–67.
93. Ibid., 676.
94. Ibid., 676–77.
95. Ibid., 677.
96. Ibid., 678.
97. The argument tends to hold little weight, since the Irish M.P.s consistently bring up the fact that ladies tour the laundries on a regular basis and that the nuns welcome such visitations. Therefore the question one is left with is not whether a woman in general is a problem, but a woman with state authority is at issue. It can also be argued, considering Ireland's later stance toward women working outside the home, that an independent female wage-earner with authority was seen as a threat to the institution and to the nation.
98. Ibid., 679.
99. Group et al., *A Historical Dictionary of British Women*, 12b.
100. Anderson, *Women in the Factory*, 182.
101. Malcolmson, *English Laundresses: A Social History, 1850–1930*, 84.
102. Anderson, *Women in the Factory*, 182–83.
103. Malcolmson, *English Laundresses: A Social History, 1850–1930*, 85–86.
104. Ibid., 87.
105. *The Parliamentary Debates (Authorised Edition); Fourth Series*, 1906, 13.
106. Ibid., 16–17.
107. Malcolmson, *English Laundresses: A Social History, 1850–1930*, 88.
108. Some of publications include Bishop Wilson's *Knowledge and Practice of Christianity — an Essay towards the Instruction for the Indians*. There was also an anonymously authored piece called *Exhortation to Chastity*. All of these works were required reading for the inmates at the Magdalen-House. Edward Jerningham wrote a piece called *The Magdalens: An Elegy* as well as *The Nunnery* and *The Nun*, all which took their inspiration from the inmates at the Magdalen-House.
109. Kelly, *Memoirs of a Magdalen: or, the History of Louisa Mildmay*, 102–3. Other notable Magdalene (fictionalized) autobiographies include: *The Histories of Some Penitents in the Magdalen-house, as Supposed to be Related by Themselves* (1760), and *The Magdalen, or Dying Penitent, Exemplified in the Death of F.S.* (1759).
110. *No Name* was originally serialized in "All the Year Round" publication, and finally published book form on December 31st of the same year.
111. Serialized in *All the Year Round* and published in three volumes in July of the same year.
112. Haskin, *Mary Magdalen: Myth and Metaphor*, 329.

Chapter Eight

1. CICA, *Investigation Into Child Abuse, Volume III*, 18.45.

2. Ibid., 18.52.
3. Finnegan, as cited by Culliton, "Last Days of a Laundry," para. 11.
4. Scanlan, *Culture and Customs of Ireland*, 71.
5. The entire report and history can be read online at http://www.childabusecommission.ie.
6. Smith, *Ireland's Magdalen Laundries and the Nation's Architecture of Containment*, 2, 19.
7. Ibid., 55.
8. Polman, "Re-discovery of Ireland's 'Forgotten Women' Causes National Scandal," para. 4.
9. Taylor, *Irish Houses and Irish Hearts*, 89. Emphasis added.
10. O'Mahony, "In a Magdalen Asylum," in *The Irish Monthly: A Magazine of General Literature*, 374.
11. Ibid.
12. It is important to note that the names of the women who entered the Magdalene asylums were changed in order to divorce them from their former life. In effect, it did nothing more than to hide the Magdalenes' identity from a larger system — making these women nameless and invisible.
13. O'Mahony, "In a Magdalen Asylum," in *The Irish Monthly: A Magazine of General Literature*, 375–76.
14. McCarthy, *Priests and People in Ireland*, 419.
15. Gallagher, "Reflect Here Upon Their Lives," para. 4.
16. Ibid.
17. Ibid., para. 30.
18. Cullingford, "'Our Nuns Are Not a Nation': Politicizing the Convent in Irish Literature and Film," 15.
19. Mebdh, as cited in Gallagher, "Reflect Here Upon Their Lives," para. 9.
20. CICA, *Investigation Into Child Abuse, Executive Summary*, 1.
21. The Taoiseach is the Irish Prime Minister.
22. CICA, *Investigation Into Child Abuse, Volume I*: "On behalf of the State and of all citizens of the State, the Government wishes to make a sincere and long overdue apology to the victims of childhood abuse for our collective failure to intervene, to detect their pain, to come to their rescue" (1.1).
23. *The Irish Times*, "Reopening the Abuse Deal," para. 1.
24. CICA *Investigation Committee Report, Volume I*; the Christian Brothers sought to stop the investigation from specifically naming accused abusers: "This case sought judicial determination, inter alia, of the constitutionality of the investigation Committee's approach to making findings of abuse against elderly or deceased Brothers or those who could not properly answer the allegations" (1.24).
25. The 18 congregations are: The Rosminian Institute of Charity, the Dominican Order, the Sisters of Mercy, Our Lady of Charity of the Good Shepherd, the Presentation Brothers, The Religious Sisters of Charity, The Christian Brothers, The Daughters of Charity of St Vincent de Paul, The Sisters of Our Lady of Charity of Refuge, The Brothers of Charity, The Daughters of the Heart of Mary, The De La Salle Brothers, The Sisters of St Clare, The Presentation Sisters, The Sisters of St Louis, The Hospitaller Order of St John of God, The Sisters of Nazareth, The Oblates of Mary Immaculate (CICA, *Investigation Into Child Abuse, Volume 1*, 1.81).
26. *The Irish Times*, "Reopening the Abuse Deal," para. 2–3.
27. CICA, *Investigation Into Child Abuse, Volume I*, 1.97.
28. Ibid., 1.101.
29. *The Irish Times*, "Reopening the Abuse Deal," para. 3.
30. Crimmins, "Pope 'Visibly Upset' over Irish Abuse Report," para. 9.
31. CORI's website can be found at http://www.cori.ie.
32. CICA, *Investigation Into Child Abuse, Volume I*, 1.80.
33. Kaltenbach, "Nuns Apologize for Order's Role in Irish Laundries," para. 3–6.
34. CICA, *Investigation Into Child Abuse, Volume I*, 1.95.
35. Ibid., 1.99–1.100.
36. Ibid., 1.122.
37. The conclusions can be read online at http://www.childabusecommission.com/rpt/04-06.php.
38. CICA, *Investigation Into Child Abuse, Volume IV*, 6.09.
39. Ibid., 6.10.
40. Ibid., 6.11–6.13.
41. Ibid., 6.02–6.06.
42. Ibid., 6.06.
43. Edwards, "Dead Rats Found in Croydon School's Drinking Water Tank," para. 3.
44. Seaver, "Widespread Abuse of Irish Children in Catholic Church-run Institutions," para. 4.
45. CICA, *Investigation Into Child Abuse, Volume III*, 18.10.
46. Ibid., 18.13.
47. Ibid.
48. Ibid., 18.14.
49. Ibid., 18.66.

50. Ibid., 18.45.
51. Ibid., 18.25.
52. Ibid.
53. Ibid., 18.58.
54. Ibid., 18.57.
55. CICA, *Investigation Into Child Abuse, Executive Summary*, 38.
56. O'Brien, "Brothers, Priests and Nuns Were Our Siblings, Uncles, Aunts."
57. Smith, "A Full Heart and Empty Arms," para. 23.
58. O'Brien, "Brothers, Priests and Nuns Were Our Siblings, Uncles, Aunts," para. 5.
59. Smith, "A Full Heart and Empty Arms," para. 33.
60. *The Irish Times*, "Magdalen Scandal," para. 2.
61. Smith, *Ireland's Magdalen Laundries and the Nation's Architecture of Containment*, 47.
62. CICA, *Investigation Into Child Abuse, Volume I*, 2.02.
63. Smith, *Ireland's Magdalen Laundries and the Nation's Architecture of Containment*, 15.
64. Gallagher, "Reflect Here Upon Their Lives," para. 6–8.
65. Shield, "Special Section: 'Forty Seven, Today You are Nine': Systematic Abuse in Irish Childcare Institutions," 27.
66. O'Morain, "State Involvement in Mistreatment of Children Exposed," para. 3–4.
67. Shield, "Special Section: 'Forty Seven, Today You are Nine': Systematic Abuse in Irish Childcare Institutions," 28.
68. O'Morain, "State Involvement in Mistreatment of Children Exposed," para. 5.
69. Ibid., para. 8.
70. Smith, "A Full Heart and Empty Arms," para. 10.
71. Humphries, a powerful, socially minded documentary filmmaker, has also directed such documentaries as: *A Secret World of Sex* (1988) and *Forbidden Britain* (1994).
72. Goldstone. "Too Pretty To Be Allowed Out," para. 8.
73. Ibid., para. 9.
74. Donnelly, "Helpline Callers Express Anger and Distress," para. 3.
75. Smith, "Voices of Our Magdalene Women Washed out of History for Too Long," para. 7.
76. ICAB, p. 2.
77. Ibid.
78. Ester, Comment #1 (July 26, 2009 at 2:06 A.M.), in Smith's "Voices of Our Magdalene Women Washed out of History for Too Long."
79. *Justice for the Magdalenes* can be found online at http://www.magdalenelaundries.com.
80. Steed and Smith, as cited by McGarry in "Call for Apology to Survivors of Laundries," para. 3
81. N.a., "'Shame' Felt by Young Assault Victim's Family Decried," para. 12.
82. Ibid., para. 5.
83. President Sirleaf, as cited in "'Shame' Felt by Young Assault Victim's Family Decried," para. 8.
84. Wardlaw, *Lectures on Magdalenism; its Nature, Extent, Effects, Guilt, Causes, and Remedy*, 51.
85. Tait, *Magdalenism; An Inquiry into the Extent, Causes, and Consequences, of Prostitution in Edinburgh*, chapter 3, part 1, on "Natural Causes": 83–92.
86. Ibid., part 2 on "Accidental Causes": 94–145.

Bibliography

Agnew, Patty. "Tracing a Sometimes Unholy History." *The Irish Times*, September 20, 1997.

Altmann, Barbara K., ed. *The Court Reconvenes: Courtly Literature across the Disciplines*. University of British Columbia, July 25–31, 1998. Selected Papers from the Ninth Triennial Congress of the International Courtly Literature Society, 9. Woodbridge, Suffolk: Brewer, 2003.

Amt, Emilie, ed. *Women's Lives in Medieval Europe: A Sourcebook*. New York: Routledge, 1993.

Anderson, Adelaide Mary. *Women in the Factory*. London: E.P. Dutton, 1922.

The Annals of the Four Masters. 2002. http://www.ucc.ie/celt/online/T100005E/text004.html (accessed October 13, 2008).

Aquinas, St. Thomas. *St. Thomas Aquinas on Politics and Ethics*. Translated by Paul Sigmund. New York: W.W. Norton, 1988.

Araghi, Farshad A. "Global Depeasantization, 1945–1990." *The Sociological Quarterly* 36, no. 2 (1995): 337–68.

Augustine, St. *The Confessions of St. Augustine*. Translated by Rex Warner. New York: Mentor, 1963.

Ault, Warren O. *Europe in the Middle Ages*. Revised Edition. Boston: D.C. Heath, 1946.

Badiou, Alain. *Saint Paul: The Foundation of Universalism*. Translated by Ray Brassier. Stanford: Stanford University Press, 2003.

Batchelor, Jennie. "'Industry in Distress': Reconfiguring Femininity and Labor in the Magdalen House." *Eighteenth-Century Life* 28, no. 1 (2004): 1–20.

Bitzer, Lloyd. "The Rhetorical Situation." *Contemporary Rhetorical Theory*, edited by John Louis Lucaites, Celeste Michelle Condit and Sally Caudill, 217–25. New York: Guilford Press, 1999.

Bloy, Marjie. "Gilbert's Act (1782)." The Victorian Web: Literature, History, & Culture in the Age of Victoria. May 6, 2006. http://www.victorianweb.org/history/poorlaw/gilbert.html (accessed April 23, 2009).

———. "The 1601 Elizabethan Poor Law." The Victorian Web: Literature, History, & Culture in the Age of Victoria. May 6, 2007, http://www.victorianweb.org/history/poorlaw/elizpl.html (accessed April 23, 2009).

———. "The 1662 Settlement Act." The Victorian Web: Literature, History, & Culture in the Age of Victoria. May 06, 2007. http://www.victorianweb.org/history/poorlaw/settle.html (accessed April 23, 2009).

———. "The 'Workhouse Test Act' (1723)." The Victorian Web: Literature, History, & Culture in the Age of Victoria. May 06, 2007. http://www.victorianweb.org/history/poorlaw/testact.html (accessed April 23, 2009).

Blum, Christopher O. "Vézelay: The Mountain of the Lord." *Logos* 8, no. 3 (2005): 141–64.

Boucherett, Emilia J., Helen Blackburn, and Blackburn Boucherett. *The Condition of Working Women and the Factory Acts*. London: Elliot Stock, 1896.

Brazil, Maureen. "Time to Raise the Profile of Women's Role in Scripture." *The Irish Times*, August 27, 1996.

Brett, Edward Tracy. *Humbert of Romans: His Life and Views of Thirteenth-Century Society*. Toronto, Ontario: Pontifical Institute of Mediaeval Studies, 1984.

British India & Queensland Agency Company. *Handbook of Information for the Colonies and India*. Brisbane: Watson, Ferguson, 1897.

Browning, Andrew, and David Charles Douglas. *English Historical Documents, 1660–1714*. New York: Routledge, 1996.

Brundage, James A. *Law, Sex, and Christian Society in Medieval Europe*. Chicago: University of Chicago Press, 1987.

———. "Prostitution in the Medieval Canon Law." *Signs* 1, no. 4 (1976): 825–45.

"Bunreacht na hÉireann (Constitution of Ireland)." Dublin, Ireland. July 1, 1937. http://www.taoiseach.gov.ie/attached_files/html%20files/Constitution%20of%20Ireland%20(Eng)Nov2004.htm. (accessed April 23, 2009).

Burke, Kenneth. *Attitudes towards History*. Second Edition. Los Alton: Hermes, 1959.

———. *Essays toward a Symbolic of Motives, 1950–1955*. Selected, arranged, and edited by William H. Rueckert. West Lafayette, IN: Parlor Press, 2007.

———. *A Grammar of Motives*. Berkeley: University of California Press, 1969.

———. *Language as Symbolic Action: Essays on Life, Literature, and Method*. Berkeley: University of California Press, 1966.

———. *A Rhetoric of Motives*. California Edition. Berkeley: University of California Press, 1969.

———. *The Rhetoric of Religion; Studies in Logology*. Berkeley: University of California Press, 1970.

Butler, Alban, and Michael J. Walsh. *Butler's Lives of the Saints*. San Francisco: Harper San Francisco, 1991.

Butler, Diana. "Mary Magdalene was Female Apostle to the Apostles." *The Seattle Post-Intelligencer*, March 28, 1997, Late Edition: All.

Bynum, Caroline Walker, and Paula Gerson. "Body-Part Reliquaries and Body Parts in the Middle Ages." *Gesta* 36, no. 1 (1997): 3–7.

Cahill, Thomas. *Desire of the Everlasting Hills: The World Before and After Jesus*. New York: Doubleday, 1999.

———. *The Gift of the Jews: How a Tribe of Desert Nomads Changed the Way Everyone Thinks and Feels*. New York: Doubleday, 1998.

———. *How the Irish Saved Civilization: The Untold Story Ireland's Heroic Role from the Fall of Rome to the Rise of Medieval Europe*. New York: Anchor, 1995.

Cambrensis, Giraldus. *The Conquest of Ireland*. Edited by Thomas Wright. Translated by Thomas Forester. Cambridge, Ontario: In Parentheses, 2001.

———. *Topography of Ireland*. Edited by Thomas Wright. Vol. Medieval Latin Series. Cambridge, Ontario: In Parentheses, 2000.

Canny, Nicholas. "Early Modern Ireland, c. 1500–1700." In *The Oxford Illustrated History of Ireland*, edited by R.F. Foster, 104–60. Oxford: Oxford University Press, 1998.

Castells, Manuel. *The Rise of the Network Society*. Malden: Blackwell, 1996.

Catholic Church. "The Code of Cannon Law." Edited by The Canon Law Society Of Great Britain and Ireland. The Canon Law Society Trust, 1983. http://www.deacons.net/Canon_Law/book_6.htm. (accessed April 23, 2009).

Chambers, Anne. *Granuaile: The Life and Times of Grace O'Malley c. 1530–1603*. Dublin: Wolfhound Press, [1979] 1998.

Chilton, Bruce. *Mary Magdalene: A Biography*. New York: Doubleday, 2005.

CICA (Commission to Inquire into Child Abuse). "CICA Investigation Committee Report, Executive Summary." *Commission to Inquire into Child Abuse*. May 20, 2009. http://www.childabusecommission.com/rpt/pdfs/CICA-Executive%20Summary.pdf (accessed May 25, 2009).

———. "CICA Investigation Committee Report, Volume I." *Commission to Inquire into Child Abuse*. May 20, 2009. http://www.childabusecommission.com/rpt/pdfs/CICA-VOL1-01.PDF (accessed May 25, 2009).

———. "CICA Investigation Committee Report, Volume II." *Commission to Inquire into Child Abuse*. May 20, 2009. http://www.childabusecommission.com/rpt/pdfs/CICA-VOL2-01.PDF (accessed May 25, 2009).

———. "CICA Investigation Committee Report, Volume III." *Commission to Inquire into Child Abuse*. May 20, 2009. http://www.childabusecommission.com/rpt/pdfs/CICA-VOL3-01.pdf (accessed May 25, 2009).

———. "CICA Investigation Committee Report, Volume IV." *Commission to Inquire into Child Abuse*. May 20, 2009. http://www.childabusecommission.com/rpt/pdfs/CICA-VOL4-01.PDF (accessed May 25, 2009).

———. "CICA Investigation Committee Report, Volume V." *Commission to Inquire into Child Abuse*. May 20, 2009. http://www.childabusecommission.com/rpt/pdfs/CICA-VOL5-00.pdf (accessed May 25, 2009).

Collins, Wilkie. *No Name: A Novel*. New York: Harper & Brothers, 1893.

Connell, R.W. *Gender and Power: Society, the Person and Sexual Politics*. Stanford: Stanford University Press, 1987.

Crimmins, Carmel. "Pope 'Visibly Upset' over Irish Abuse Report." Reuters.com. Edited by Mark Trevelyan. June 8, 2009. http://www.reuters.com/article/worldNews/idUSTRE55755A20090608 (accessed June 11, 2009).

Crookshank, C.H., and Richard Lee Cole. *History of Methodism in Ireland*. Belfast: R.S. Allen, Sons & Allen — University House, 1885.

Cullingford, Elizabeth Butler. "'Our Nuns Are Not a Nation': Politicizing the Convent in Irish Literature and Film." *Éire-Ireland* 41, nos. 1–2 (Spring/Summer 2006): 9–39.

Culliton, Gary. "Last Days of a Laundry." *The Irish Times*, September 25, 1996.

Davidson, Audrey B., and Robert B. Ekelund, Jr. "The Medieval Church and Rents from Marriage and Market Regulations." *Journal of Economic Behavior & Organization* 32 (1997): 215–45.

Davis, Natalie Zemon. "Introduction." In *The Knight, The Lady, and The Priest: The Making of Modern Marriage in Medieval France*, by Georges Duby, translated by Barbara Bray, vii–xiii. London: Penguin, 1983.

Defoe, Daniel. *The Fortunes & Misfortunes of the Famous Moll Flanders, & C.* New York: E.P. Dutton, 1930.

Dodd, William, C. Chapman, and Charlotte Smith. *An Account of the Rise, Progress, and Present State of the Magdalen Hospital, for the Reception of Penitent Prostitutes: Together with Dr. Dodd's Sermons. To Which Are Added, the Advice to the Magdalens, with the Psalms, Hymns, Prayers, Rules.* Fifth Edition. London: W. Faden for the Charity, 1776.

Donnelly, Rachel. "Helpline Callers Express Anger and Distress." *The Irish Times*, March 20, 1998.

Duby, Georges. *The Knight, the Lady, and the Priest: The Making of Modern Marriage in Medieval France.* Translated by Barbara Bray. London: Penguin, 1983.

Edwards, Anna. "Dead Rats Found in Croydon School's Drinking Water Tank." Thisiscroydontoday.co.uk. June 12, 2009. http://www.thisiscroydontoday.co.uk/latestnews/Exclusive-Dead-rats-Croydon-school-s-drinking-water-tank/article-1070534-detail/article.html (accessed May 12, 2009).

Ekelund, Robert B., Jr., Robert F. Hébert, and Robert D. Tollison. "An Economic Model of the Medieval Church; Usury as a Form of Rent Seeking." *Journal of Law, Economics, & Organization* 5, no. 2 (1989): 307–31.

Elliott, Janis, and Cordelia Warr. *The Church of Santa Maria Donna Regina: Art, Iconography, and Patronage in Fourteenth Century Naples.* Aldershot, England: Ashgate, 2004.

Ellis, Peter Berresford. *Celtic Women: Women in Celtic Society and Literature.* Grand Rapids: William B. Eerdmans, 1995.

Ellis, Steven G. *Ireland in the Age of the Tudors 1447–1603: English Expansion and the End of Gaelic Rule.* New York: Addison Wesley Longman, [1995] 1998.

Engels, Friedrich. "The Patriarchal Family." In *The Multicultural Classic Reading*, edited by Charles Lemert, 65–67. Boulder: Westview Press, [1884] 2004.

Erner, Guillaume. "Christian Economic Morality: The Medieval Turning Point." *International Social Science Journal* 57, no. 185 (2005): 469–79.

Feltham, John. *The Picture of London, for 1803: Being a Correct Guide to All the Curiosities, Amusements, Exhibitions, Public Establishments, and Remarkable Objects, in and Near London; with a Collection of Appropriate Tables.* London: Lewis, 1802.

Finnegan, Frances. *Do Penance or Perish: Magdalen Asylums in Ireland.* New York: Oxford University Press, 2001.

Fitzpatrick, David. "Ireland Since 1870." In *The Oxford Illustrated History of Ireland*, edited by R.F. Foster, 213–75. Oxford: Oxford University Press, 1998.

Foss, Sonja K., Karen A. Foss, and Robert Trapp. *Contemporary Perspectives on Rhetoric.* Third Edition. Long Grove: Waveland Press, 2002.

Foster, R.F. "Ascendancy and Union." In *The Oxford Illustrated History of Ireland*, edited by R.F. Foster, 161–212. Oxford: Oxford University Press, 1998.

Francis, M.E. "Penitence." Edited by the Rev. Matthew, S.J. Russell. *The Irish Monthly: A Magazine of General Literature* 34 (1906): 373.

Gallagher, Meadbh. "Reflect Here Upon Their Lives." *An Phoblacht/Republican News*, April 25, 1996.

Gilbert, Mrs. John T. (Rosa Mulholland). "Philanthropic Work in Ireland." *Woman's Mission: A Series of Congress Papers on the Philanthropic Work of Women*, edited by Baroness Angela Georgina Burdett-Coutts, 228–47. New York: Scribner's, 1893.

Glenn, Evelyn Nakano. *Unequal Freedoms.* Cambridge: Harvard University Press, 2002.

Goffman, Erving. *Frame Analysis: An Essay on the Organization of Experience.* Cambridge: Harvard University Press, 1974.

Gold, Penny Schine. *The Lady and the Virgin: Image, Attitude, and Experience in Twelfth-Century France.* Chicago: University of Chicago Press, 1987.

Goldstone, Katrina. "Too Pretty To Be Allowed Out." *The Irish Times*, March 14, 1998.

Goodnight, G. Thomas. "The Personal, Technical, and Public Spheres of Argument: A Speculative Inquiry into the Art of Public Deliberation." *Contemporary Rhetorical Theory*, edited by John Louis Lucaites, Celeste Michelle Condit and Sally Caudill, 251–64. New York: Guilford Press, 1999.

Gramsci, Antonio. *Selections from the Prison Notebooks.* Edited by Quintin Hoare and Geoffrey Nowell Smith. Translated by Quintin Hoare and Geoffrey Nowell Smith. New York: International, [1971] 2005.

Gray, B. Kirkman. *A History of English Philanthropy from the Dissolution of the Monasteries* to the *Taking of the First Census.* London: P.S. King & Son, 1905.

Hanway, Jonas. *An Historical Account of the British Trade over the Caspian Sea: With a Journal of Travels from London through Russia into Persia; and Back through Russia, Germany and Holland.* London: Mr. Dodsley, 1753.

Haskins, Susan. *Mary Magdalen: Myth and Metaphor.* New York: Riverhead Books, 1993.

Hauser, Gerald A. *Vernacular Voices: The Rhetoric of Publics and Public Spheres.* South Carolina: University of South Carolina, 1999.

Hayter, Henry Heylyn. *Notes on the Colony of Victoria: Historical, Geographical, Meteorological, and Statistical.* Melbourne: G. Skinner, Acting Govt. Printer, 1875.

Hegel, Georg Wilhelm Friedrich. *Philosophy of History.* Translated by John Sibree. New York: American Home Library, [1813] 1902.

Held, David. "The Development of the Modern State." In *Modernity: An Introduction to Modern Societies,* edited by Stuart Hall, David Held, Don Hubert and Kenneth Thompson, 55–89. Malden: Blackwell.

Hickman, Katie. *Courtesans: Money, Sex and Fame in the Nineteenth Century.* New York: Perennial, 2004.

A Historical Dictionary of British Women. Second Revised Edition. New York: Europa, 2003.

Howell, Martha C. *Women, Production, and Patriarchy in Late Medieval Cities.* Chicago: University of Chicago Press, 1986.

Humphries, Steve, dir. *Sex in a Cold Climate.* 1998.

Inwood, Stephen, and Roy Porter. *A History of London.* New York: Carroll & Graf, 1998.

The Irish Catholic Directory and Almanac. Dublin: J. Duffy, 1907.

The Irish Times. "Magdalen Scandal." Editorial. March 20, 1998.

James, M. R. (translation and notes). *Book of James (Protevangelium).* Oxford: Clarendon Press, 1924. http://www.gnosis.org/library/gosjames.htm (accessed October 11, 2008).

Jansen, Katherine Ludwig. *The Making of the Magdalen: Preaching and Popular Devotion in the Later Middle Ages.* Princeton: Princeton University Press, 2000.

Jeans, Victorine. *Factory Act Legislation: Its Industrial and Commercial Effects, Actual and Prospective, Being the Cobden Prize Essay for 1891.* London: T. F. Unwin, 1892.

Johnson, Heather. "Subsistence and Control: The Persistency of the Peasantry in the Developing World." *Undercurrent* 1, no. 1 (2004): 55–65.

Kaltenbach, Chris. "Nuns Apologize for Order's Role in Irish Laundries." LAtimes.com. August 4, 2003. http://articles.latimes.com/2003/aug/04/entertainment/et-nuns4 (accessed June 12, 2009).

Kandiyoti, Deniz. "Bargaining with Patriarchy." *Gender & Society* 2, no. 3 (1988): 274–90.

Karras, Ruth Mazo. "Holy Harlots: Prostitute Saints in Medieval Legend." *Journal of the History of Sexuality* 1, no. 1 (1990): 3–32.

———. "The Regulation of Brothels in Later Medieval England." *Signs* 14, no. 2 (1989): 399–433.

Kelly, Fergus. *A Guide to Early Irish Law.* Dublin: Dublin Institute for Advanced Studies, 1988.

Kelly, Hugh. *Memoirs of a Magdalen: or, the History of Louisa Mildmay.* London: W. Griffin, 1767.

Keogh, Rev. Canon, P.P. *The Irish Catholic Directory, Almanac and Registry with Complete Ordo in English.* Dublin: J. Mullany, 1876.

Kiberd, Declan. "Irish Literature and Irish History." In *The Oxford Illustrated History of Ireland,* edited by R.F. Foster, 275–338. Oxford, UK: Oxford University Press, 1998.

Lakoff, George. *Don't Think of an Elephant! Know Your Values and Frame the Debate.* White River Junction: Chelsea Green Publishing, 2004.

———. "Simple Framing." Rockridge Institute. February 14, 2006. http://www.iterasi.net/openviewer.aspx?sqrlitid=azzswl0zceuhdkgf69vepw (accessed August 2, 2009).

———, and John Halpin. "Framing Katrina." *The American Prospect.* October 7, 2005. http://www.prospect.org/web/page.ww?section=rootandname=ViewWebandarticleId=10391 (accessed December 18, 2008).

Lardner, Nathaniel, and Andrew Kippis. *The Works of Nathaniel Lardner.* London: W. Ball, 1838.

Lennon, Colm. *Sixteenth-Century Ireland: The Incomplete Conquest.* New York: St. Martin's Press, 1995.

Lentin, Ronit. "Pregnant Silence: (en)gendering Ireland's Asylum Space." *Pattern of Prejudice* 37, no. 3 (2003): 310–22.

Levinson, David. *Encyclopedia of Homelessness.* Thousand Oaks: Sage, 2004.

Luddy, Maria. *Women in Ireland, 1800–1918: A Documentary History.* Warwick: Cork University Press, 1995.

———. *Women and Philanthropy in Nineteenth-Century Ireland.* New York: Cambridge University Press, 1995.

Luquet, Wade. "The Contribution of the Sisters

of Mercy to the Development of Social Welfare." *Affilia* 20, no. 2 (2005): 153–68.

MacCana, Proinsias. *Celtic Mythology*. New York: Bedrick, 1985.

MacManus, Seumas. *The Story of the Irish Race*. Old Greenwich: Devin-Adair, [1921] 1990.

Maher, Eamon. "John McGahern and His Irish Readers." *New Hibernia Review* 9, no. 2 (Samhradh/Summer 2005): 125–36.

Mahoney, Rosemary. *Whoredom in Kimmage: The World of Irish Women*. New York: Anchor Doubleday, 1993.

Mahood, Linda. *The Magdalenes: Prostitution in the Nineteenth Century*. London; New York: Routledge, 1990.

Malcolmson, Patricia E. *English Laundresses: A Social History, 1850–1930*. Urbana: University of Illinois Press, 1986.

Manners, John James R. *Notes of an Irish Tour*. London: William Blackwood and Sons, 1881.

Markale, Jean. *Women of the Celts*. Rochester: Inner Traditions, 1986.

Marshall, T.H. *Citizenship and Social Class and Other Essays*. Cambridge: Cambridge University Press, 1950.

Marx, Karl. "Economic and *Philosophic* Manuscripts of 1844." In *The Marx-Engels Reader*, edited by Robert C. Tucker, 66–125. New York: W.W. Norton, 1978.

———. "Economic Writings." In *Capital*, Volume I, by Karl Marx, 214–43. New York: Vintage Books, [1876] 1977.

———. "So Called Primitive Accumulation." In *Capital*, Volume 1, by Karl Marx, 871–913. New York: Vintage Books, [1876] 1977.

McCarthy, Michael John Fitzgerald. *Priests and People in Ireland*. Dublin: Hodges, Figgis, 1903.

McDonnell, Ernest W. "'Vita Apostolica': Diversity or Dissent." *Church History* (Cambridge University Press) 24, no. 1 (March 1955): 15–31.

McElwee, Niall. "Tragedy of Magdalene A Lesson for Present." *The Irish Times*, March 20, 1998.

McGarry, Patsy. "Call for Apology to Survivors of Laundries." *The Irish Times*, July 6, 2009. http://www.irishtimes.com/newspaper/ireland/2009/0706/1224250105643.html (accessed July 27, 2009).

———, and Padraig O'Morain. "Service for Victims and Abuse Gets Buried." *The Irish Times*, March 21, 1998.

Mead, Frederick, Archibald Henry Bodkin, and Great Britain. *The Criminal Law Amendment Act, 1885, with Introduction, Notes, and Index*. London: Shaw & Sons, Fetter Land and Crane Court, E.C., 1885.

Mead, G. R. S., trans. *Pistis Sophia: The Gnostic Tradition of Mary Magdalene, Jesus, and His Disciples*. Mineola: Dover, 2005.

Mews, Constant J., and Neville Chiavaroli. *The Lost Love Letters of Heloise and Abelard: Perceptions of Dialogue in Twelfth-Century France*. The New Middle Ages. New York: Palgrave, 2001.

Misrahi, Jean. "A Vita Sanctae Mariae magdalenae (B.H.L. 5456) in an Eleventh-Century Manuscript." *Speculum* 18, no. 3 (1943): 335–39

Mogg, Edward. *Moggs Picture of London and Visitor's Guide to Its Sights*. London: E. Mogg, 1848.

Moxham, Roy. *Tea: Addiction, Exploitation, and Empire*. New York: Carroll & Graf, 2004.

Mullan, Peter, dir. *The Magdalene Sisters*. 2002.

New American Standard Bible. La Habra: Foundation Press Publications, 1973.

New Revised Standard Version of the Holy Bible. Grand Rapids: Zondervan Publishing House, 1989.

O'Brien, Breda. "Brothers, Priests and Nuns Were Our Siblings, Uncles, Aunts." *The Irish Times*. May 23, 2009. http://www.irishtimes.com/newspaper/opinion/2009/0523/1224247209586.html (accessed June 6, 2009).

———. "Magdalen: Whose Forgotten Victims?" *The Sunday Business Post*, May 4, 1998.

Ó Corráin, Donnchadh. "Prehistoric and Early Christian Ireland." In *The Oxford Illustrated History of Ireland*, edited by R.F. Foster, 1–52. Oxford: Oxford University Press, 1998.

O'Mahony, Nora Tynan. "In a Magdalen Asylum." Edited by the Rev. Matthew, S.J. Russell. *The Irish Monthly: A Magazine of General Literature* 34 (1906): 374–77.

O'Morain, Padraig. "State Involvement in Mistreatment of Children Exposed." *The Irish Times*, May 1, 1991.

Otis, Leah Lydia. *Prostitution in Medieval Society: The History of an Urban Institution in Languedoc*. Chicago: University of Chicago Press, 1985.

O'Toole, Fintan. "The Sisters of No Mercy." *The Observer*. February 16, 2003. http://www.guardian.co.uk/film/2003/feb/16/features.review1/print (accessed May 13, 2009).

Pagels, Elaine. *The Gnostic Gospels*. Vintage Books Edition. New York: Vintage Books, 1989.

The Parliamentary Debates (Authorized Edition); Fourth Series. First Session of the Twenty-Eighth Parliament of the United Kingdom of Great Britain and Ireland. Vol. CLXII. London: Wyman and Sons, 1906.

The Parliamentary Debates (Authorized Edition);

Fourth Series. Second Session of the Twenty-Seventh Parliament of the United Kingdom of Great Britain and Ireland. Vol. XI. London: Wyman and Sons, 1901.

The Parliamentary Gazetteer of Ireland. Vol. II. Dublin: A. Fullarton, 1846.

Paterson, Linda. "Women, Property and the Rise of Courtly Love." In *The Court Reconvenes: Courtly Literature Across the Disciplines: Selected Papers from the Ninth Triennial Congress of the International Courtly Literature Society, University of British Columbia, 25–31 July, 1998,* by Barbara K. Altmann, Carleton W. Carroll. International Courtly Literature Society. Congress, 41–56. DS Brewer, 2003.

Picknett, Lynn. *Mary Magdalene: Christianity's Hidden Goddess.* New York: Carroll & Graf, 2003.

Polanyi, Karl. *The Great Transformation: The Political and Economic Origins of Our Time.* Boston: Beacon Press, [1944] 2001.

Polman, Dick. "Re-discovery of Ireland's 'Forgotten Women' Causes National Scandal." *Knight-Ridder/Tribune News Service,* October 24, 1993.

Pope, Hugh. "St. Mary Magdalene." *New Advent.* Robert Appleton Company. 1910. http://www.newadvent.org/cathen/09761a.htm (accessed October 10, 2008).

Power, Patrick C. *Sex and Marriage in Ancient Ireland.* Dublin: Mercier Press, 1997.

Ranke-Heinemann, Uta. *Eunuchs for the Kingdom of Heaven: Women, Sexuality, and the Catholic Church.* Translated by Peter Heinegg. New York: Doubleday, 1990.

Raughter, Rosemary. "A Discreet Benevolence: Female Philanthropy and the Catholic Resurgence in Eighteenth-Century Ireland." *Women's History Review* 6, no. 1 (1997): 465–87.

The Religious Houses of the United Kingdom: Containing a Short History of Every Order and House Compiled from Official Sources. London: Burns & Oates, 1887.

"Reopening the Abuse Deal." Irishtimes.com. May 23, 2009. http://www.irishtimes.com/newspaper/opinion/2009/0523/1224247212995.html (accessed June 6, 2009).

Rollenston, T.W. *Celtic Myths and Legends.* Second Edition. New York: Dover, [1921] 1990.

Rollo-Koster, Joëllo. "From Prostitutes to Brides of Christ: The *Avignonese* Repenties in the Late Middle Ages." *Journal of Medieval and Early Modern Studies* 32, no. 1 (2002): 109–44.

Rousseau, Jean-Jacques. *Émile.* Translated by Barbara Foxley. London: Orion Publishing Group, 1997.

Said, Edward W. *Culture and Imperialism.* New York: Vintage Books, 1994.

Sangster, William, and Charles Henry Bennett. *Umbrellas and Their History.* London: Effingham Wilson, Royal Exchange, 1855.

Sayer, Derek. *The Violence of Abstraction.* New York: Blackwell, 1987.

Scanlan, Margaret. *Culture and Customs of Ireland.* Westport: Greenwood Publishing Group, 2006.

Seaver, Michael. "Widespread Abuse of Irish Children in Catholic Church-run Institutions." *Global News Blog/The Christian Science Monitor.* May 21, 2009. http://features.csmonitor.com/globalnews/2009/05/21/report-widespread-abuse-of-irish-children-in-catholic-church-run-institutions/ (accessed June 12, 2009).

Seidman, Gay. *Manufacturing Militance: Workers' Movements in Brazil and South Africa, 1970–1985.* Berkeley: University of California Press, 1994.

Shahar, Shulamith. *The Fourth Estate: A History of Women in the Middle Ages.* Second Edition. New York: Routledge, 2003.

"'Shame' Felt by Young Assault Victim's Family Decried." CNN. July 24, 2009. http://www.cnn.com/2009/CRIME/07/24/liberia.arizona.juvenile.assault/index.html (accessed July 27, 2009).

Shield, Paul. "Special Section: 'Forty Seven, Today You are Nine': Systematic Abuse in Irish Childcare Institutions." *The Group-Analytic Society* (London) 39, no. 1 (2006): 25–35.

Simms, Katharine. "The Norman Invasion and the Gaelic Recovery." In *The Oxford Illustrated History of Ireland,* edited by R.F. Foster, 53–103. Oxford: Oxford University Press, 1998.

Sjöö, Monica, and Barbara Mor. *The Great Cosmic Mother: Rediscovering the Religion of the Earth.* Second Edition. San Francisco: HarperCollins, 1991.

Smedley, Audrey. *Race in North America: Origin and Evolution of a Worldview.* Boulder: Westview Press, 1999.

Smith, James M. *Ireland's Magdalen Laundries and the Nation's Architecture of Containment.* Notre Dame: University of Notre Dame Press, 2007.

Smith, James. "Voices of Our Magdalene Women Washed out of History for Too Long." *Tribune News.* July 12, 2009. http://www.tribune.ie/news/home-news/article/2009/jul/12/voices-of-our-magdalene-women-washed-out-of-histor/ (accessed July 27, 2009).

Smith, Leef. "A Full Heart and Empty Arms." *Washington Post,* February 20, 2001.

Society, The Fabian. *Life in the Laundry: Fabian Tract No. 112*. London: Fabian Society, 1902.

Squire, Charles. "The Irish Iliad." In *Celtic Myths and Legends*, by Charles Squire, 158–83. New York: Gramercy Books, 1994.

Starbird, Margaret. *The Woman with the Alabaster Jar: Mary Magdalen and the Holy Grail*. New Mexico: Bear, 1993.

Stone, Laurence. *The Family, Sex, and Marriage in England 1500–1800*. New York: Harper & Row, 1979.

Taillon, Ruth. *When History Was Made: The Women of 1916*. Dublin: Colour Books, 1996.

Tait, William. *Magdalenism; An Inquiry into the Extent, Causes, and Consequences, of Prostitution in Edinburgh*. Edinburgh: Rickard, 1840.

Taylor, Fanny. *Irish Homes and Irish Hearts*. London: Longmans, Green, 1867.

Thom, Alexander. *Thom's Irish Almanac and Official Direction, with the Post Office Dublin City and County Directory, for the year 1850*. Dublin: Alexander Thom, Printer and Publisher, 1850.

Thompson (Barrister-at-Law), James Eyre. *The Law Journal Reports for the Year 1896; Cases Decided by the Judicial Committee and the Lords of Her Majesty's Privy Council, and in The House of Lords (Scotch and Irish Appeals)*. Edited by John Mews, W.E. Gordon and A.J. Spencer. Privy Council, Vol. LXV. London: Stevens and Sons, 1896.

Timbs, John. *Curiosities of London: Exhibiting the Most Rare and Remarkable Objects of Interest in the Metropolis, with Nearly Sixty Years' Personal Recollections*. London: Longmans, Green, Reader, and Dyer, 1868.

Turberville, A.S. *Johnson's England—An Account of the Life & Manners of His Age*. Vol. I. Oxford: Clarendon Press, 1933.

Vatz, Richard E. "The Myth of the Rhetorical Situation." In *Contemporary Rhetorical Theory*, edited by John Louis Lucaites, Celeste Michelle Condit and Sally Caudill, 226–31. New York: Guilford Press, 1999.

Viault, Birdsall S. *English History*. McGraw-Hill's College Core Books. New York: McGraw-Hill, 1992.

Wallace, David. *The Cambridge History of Medieval English Literature*. Cambridge: Cambridge University Press, 2002.

Wallerstein, Immanuel. *The Modern World-System I: Capitalist Agriculture and the Origins of the European World-Economy in the Sixteenth Century*. San Diego: Academic Press, 1974.

———. *The Modern World-System II: Mercantilism and the Consolidation of the European World-Economy, 1600–1750*. New York: Academic Press, 1980.

Wardlaw, Ralph. *Lectures on Magdalenism; its Nature, Extent, Effects, Guilt, Causes, and Remedy*. Glasgow: Maclehose, 1843.

Walpole, Horace. *The Letters of Horace Walpole, Earl of Oxford: Including Numerous Letters Now First Published From the Original Manuscripts*. Edited by J. Wright. Vol. III. Philadelphia: Lea and Blanchard, 1842.

Wardlaw, R. *Lectures on Magdalenism: Its Nature, Extent, Effects, Guilt, Causes, and Remedy*. New York: Redfield, 1843.

Weber, Max. "The Types of Legitimate Domination." In *The Multicultural and Classic Reading*, translated by Charles Lemert, 112–15. Boulder: Westview Press, [1918] 2004.

William, Thomas. *The Pilgrim: A Dialogue on the Life and Actions of King Henry the Eighth*. Edited by J.A. Froude. London: Parker, Son, and Bourn, West Strand, 1861.

Wollstonecraft, Mary. *Mary, or the Wrongs of Woman*. New York: Oxford University Press, 1976.

Woodward, Rev. Henry. *Essays and Sermons*. Fourth Edition. London: Duncan & Malcolm, Paternoster Row, 1844.

———. "Sermon X." In *Sermons*, by Rev. Henry Woodward, 112–28. Dublin: Oxford University Press, 1866.

Wright, F.A., trans. *The Selected Letters of St. Jerome*. New York: Putnam's, 1933.

Wright, George Newenham. *An Historical Guide to the City of Dublin, Illustrated by Engravings and a Plan of the City*. London: Burns & Oats, 1825.

Index

abandonments 133–134, 145, 158, 163, 174, 194
abductions 57, 94
An Account of the Rise, Progress, and Present State of the Magdalen Charity 174
Ad mulieres malas corpora 73
Adalgar (Bishop of Autun) 53
Adoption Act 166
adultery 68
Agnes of Montepulciano 78
Ahern, Bertie (Taoiseach) 201
áige fine (Irish: the head of the tribe) 110
Ailill (Husband to Queen Medb) 104–105, 109
Aix-en-Provence, France 54, 67
Albi, France 70–71, 76
Aléaume (medieval monk) 53
Amelia 176
Amorous Repository 169
Amt, Emilie 63, 67, 69
An Gorta Mór (The Great Irish Famine 845–1852) 158
Anderson, Adelaide 190–191
The Annals of The Four Masters 123, 126
Annual Report of Chief Inspectors of Factories 135, 160
Apostola Apostolorum (Apostles' Apostle) 20, 52; see also *Beata Peccatrix* (Apostle to the Apostles)
Araghi, Farshad 115, 122
Arles, France 65
Armadale 195
Asquith, Herbert Henry 186
Ault, Warren O. 59
Australia 3, 10, 113, 158–159, 166, 216
Avignon, France 66, 77, 80–86
Avignonese Repenties 80–86

Badiou, Alain 21
Balilon (Badilus) Medieval monk 53
Ballyetaighs (Irish: division of land) 97
Basil 195
Batchelor, Jennie 171, 182
Beata Peccatrix (Apostle to the Apostles) 48, 52, 55, 216; see also *Apostola Apostolorum* (Apostles' Apostle)
Bentham, Jeremy 197
Bernard of Clairvaux 50
Bitzer, Lloyd F. 46
Blind Beak 176
borough town 115
Bothach (Irish: class distinction) 98
Boucherett, Emilia 172–173
Bow Street Runners 176
Brehon Laws 3, 10, 12, 94–101, 105–107, 110–112, 118, 125–132, 163
Brinckerman, Rev. Arthur 161
British Parliament 6, 13
brothel(s) 65, 68, 71, 75–76, 81, 87
Brundage, James A. 61, 67–68, 75, 85, 100
Bulwer-Lytton, Robert (Earl, Member of English Parliament) 191
Burgundy, France 53
Burke, Bridget 148
Burke, Kenneth 4, 17, 40–41, 43, 47, 119

Cahill, Thomas 19, 25, 104, 106
Calvinistic sensibility 85–86, 100
Cambrensis, Giraldus 100, 119–122
The Cambridge History of Medieval English Literature 121
Campion, Edmund 118
Canada 3, 10, 113, 166, 216
Canny, Nicholas Patrick 116
Capital 114
capitalism 88–89, 114–115, 137, 140, 182
capitalist world system 2, 9, 64, 86–89, 165–166
Carcassone, France 77
Cardinal George of Armagnac 84
Carrigan Committee Report 161, 164, 166
Castells, Manuel 95
The Castle of Otranto 179
Catholic Canon Laws 13, 99–100, 103, 161–162, 164
Catholic Church 8–13, 19–21, 27, 29, 31, 41–

42, 45–46, 57, 59–60, 63, 72, 75, 85, 94, 100, 106, 113, 131–134, 136, 152, 157–158, 164, 182, 188–192, 203
Céiles (Irish: tenants living on land) 98
celibacy 31
Celtic Mythology 105
Celtic Myths and Legends 109
Cétmuinter (Irish: a man's chief wife) 108
Chambers, Anne 96, 108
Chilton, Bruce 25–28, 34, 50
Christian Brothers 201, 208–209
Chronicle of Colmar 77
Church of Saint-Maximin 50
Church of the Saint Sauveur at Aix 54
citizenship 9, 93, 95, 99–100, 113, 128–129, 133–134, 164–166, 182, 187, 190, 205, 207
clandestine marriages 57–58
Cobham, Thomas 69
coerced labor 89; *see also* slavery
Coibche 110
Collins, Wilkie 2, 13, 194
colonization 2, 3, 9, 12, 93–94, 113, 115, 122, 134, 136–137
Colossians 21
Commission to Inquire into Child Abuse (CICA) 3, 165, 196, 201–210, 214
concubines 57, 60, 108
The Condition of Working Women and the Factory Acts 172
condoms 169–170
Conference of Religious of Ireland (CORI) 202–203, 211
conhospitae (Irish: female priests) 107
Connell, Raewyn W. 47–48, 129
Conquest of Ireland 121
Consolidation Act 183
Contagious Diseases Act 5, 153, 156, 161, 163, 181
Convent at Mercy's Laundry at Wexford 160
core market centers 2, 9, 89, 93, 115, 136, 149, 168, 192
Corinthians (1) 21–22
Corinthians (2) 21
Cork's Good Shepherd Convent at Sunday's Well 5, 138–139, 142–143, 146–147, 150–151, 154–155, 156
Courtesans 169
Covent Garden Magazine 169
Criminal Law Amendment Act 161–162, 164, 192
Cullingford, Elizabeth 200
Culture and Imperialism 4, 42
Cumal (Irish: 1,492,992 square feet of land) 117
Cunningham, Peter 180
Curiosities of London 176
custom of gavelkind 96

d'Alife, Niccolò 79
Davidson, Audrey B. 41–42, 57, 59
Davis, Elynor D. 41

Davis, Mark 5, 138–139, 142–143, 146–147, 150–151, 154–155, 157
De genesi ad Litteram 20
De modo prompte cudendi sermons 72
Defoe, Daniel 13, 182, 194
deliberative rhetoric 46
derb-fine (Irish: tribal family groups) 96
Deuteronomy 35
Devon Female Penitentiary 153
Dilke, Sir Charles 186
Dillon, John (Irish Member of Parliament; East Mayo, Ireland) 187–190
Dingley, Robert 171, 173–174, 178, 180
Disappearance Theory 115
Divide and Conquer Policy 12, 128
divorce 110–111, 118, 132–133, 163; *see also imscarad*
Do Penance or Perish: Magdalen Asylums in Ireland 4, 136, 156
Dodd, William 5, 13, 173, 177, 180
Donnybrook Green Magdalene Asylum (Ireland) 149
Dublin's Foundling Hospital 145
Duby, Georges 40, 57–58, 66, 102

Earl of Kildar 126
Easter Rising 163, 164
Ed Eruditione Praedicatorum 72
Ekelund, Robert Burton, Jr. 41–42, 57, 59
Elizabethan Poor Laws (Poor Law Act of 1601) 140–141, 144; see also *Old Poor Law*
Ellis, Peter Berresford 103
Ellis, Steven G. 96, 97–98, 102, 111, 126–128
Engels, Friedrich 129–133
England 2, 9–10, 12–13, 89, 93–94, 117, 119, 130–134, 137, 140, 149, 158, 166, 168–195, 197, 205, 216
English Laundresses: A Social History, 1850–1930 184
English Philanthropy 169
The Enlightenment 42
Ephesians 21
Exeter Female Penitentiary 153
Exhortation to Chastity 178
Ezekiel 35

Fabian Society 159
Factory Acts (laws) 9, 13, 95, 137, 140, 159, 163, 172, 181–190, 196, 215
fallen woman 17, 39, 66, 74, 75, 78, 81, 88, 135–136, 145, 156–157, 168–169 177, 179, 182, 197, 199, 216
Feast of Imbolc 108
Féine (Irish: general body of a tribal group) 98–99
Feltham, John 177, 180
Feudalism 56, 87, 89, 96, 114–115, 137
Fielding, Henry 171, 176, 182
Fielding, Sir John 13, 173, 176, 180
Fifth Lateran Council 60

Index

Fili (Irish: poet or bard) 101
Fille-dieu 77
Finnegan, Frances 4, 136, 152–153, 156, 167, 196
Fontevrault Abby 74
Foster, R.F. 97
Foucault, Michel 48
Fourth Lateran Council (1215) 58,
Frame Analysis: An Essay on the Organization of Experience 4
Framing 43, 55
Francesco Sansovino 81
French Wars (1793–1815) 144
Fuidir (Irish: semi-freemen or a tenant "at will") 97, 99
Fulk of Neuilly 75, 77
Furtum Sacrum (holy theft) 53

Galatians 21
Gallagher, Meadbh 210
Gaul(s) 51, 54
gender (creation of) 46–47
Genesis 36, 58
Germany 77–78, 191
Gilbert's Act 141, 144
Gladstone, Herbert 192
Glasgow Magdalene Asylum 153
global depeasantization 115, 118, 122
Gloucester Magdalene Asylum 153
Gnostic Gospels 44–45, 51, 53
Goffman, Erving 4, 43
The Golden Legend 55
Goodnight, Thomas 4, 46
An Gorta Mór (The Great Irish Famine 845–1852) 158
Gospel of James (apocryphal) 33
Gospel of John 18–19, 26, 28, 38
Gospel of Luke 18–19, 23–31, 37–38
Gospel of Mark 18–19, 26–27, 30–31, 37
Gospel of Mary (Gnostic) 44
Gospel of Matthew 18–19, 29–31, 37
Gospel of Thomas 21, 44
Gramsci, Antonio 47–48, 125
Gray, Benjamin Kirkman 169
Gray, Thomas 178
The Great Social Evil 181
The Great Transformation 114, 140
Guasbert du Val (Biship of Narbonne) 80
A Guide to Early Irish Law 102, 107

Hand-book of London: Past and Present 180
Hanway, Jonas 5, 13, 171, 173–175, 178, 180
The Hanway Act 175
harlot 34–37, 66, 73; *see also* prostitute; whore
Harris's List of Convent Garden Ladies 169
Haskins, Susan 4, 21, 28, 44, 49, 51, 177, 180
Hauser, Gerald 4
Hays, Mary 195
Hebrews 21, 35

Hegel, Georg Wilhelm Friedrich 101, 114
hegemony 46–48, 55–56, 59, 66–67, 95, 125, 127–128, 140, 153, 178
Held, David 4, 137
Henry I 121
Henry II 121
Henry VII 125
Henry VIII 12, 125–127, 131
Henry of Le Mans 74
Hickey, Michael G. 17
Hickman, Katie 169
High Park Magdalene Laundry 1, 8, 13, 198–200, 211
An Historical Account of the British Trade Over the Caspian Sea 175
A History of London 175
The History of Tom Jones 176
Hobhouse's Act 183
Hope, Mr. James (English Member of Parliament-Sheffield, England) 187
Hosea 35
How the Irish Saved Civilization 104
Howell, Martha C. 89
Hull Home of Hope 153
Humbert de Romans 72–73
Humphrie, Steve 213
Hundred Year War 56, 70, 86

identification 17, 43, 119
illegitimacy 14
imscarad (Irish: divorce) 110; *see also* divorce
Institutional child Abuse Bill (ICAB) 214
Instruction for the Conduct of Women, and Virtue in the Humble Life 178
Ireland 2, 7–13, 62, 81, 93–112, 113–134, 135–167, 168, 181–182, 186–191, 196–218
Ireland in the Age of the Tudors 96
Ireland's Magdalen Laundries and the Nation's Architecture of Containment 4, 136, 164
Irish Catholic Church 14, 93, 100–101, 107, 199, 207, 210
Irish Constitution 13, 161–165
Irish Homes and Irish Hearts 148, 156
The Irish Monthly: A Magazine of General Literature 198
Irish Poor Laws 144
The Irish Times 103, 201–202, 209
Irish Tribune 215
Isaiah 35
Italy's early Magdalene convents 79

Jansen, Katherine Ludwig 44–45, 50, 51, 53, 77, 79
Jericho 36
Jesus Christ 20–29, 31–32, 34, 37–38, 44–45, 49, 51–53, 72–73, 170, 181, 188
Joel (Book of) 36
John the Baptist 30
Joseph 32
Josephus, Flavius 51

Joshua 35–36
Judges 35
Julie, or the New Heloise: letters of two lovers who loved in a small town at the foot of the alps 195
Justice for the Magdalene 5–6, 195, 215

Kaltenbach, Chris 203
Kandiyoti, Deniz 130
Karras, Ruth Mazo 48, 62
Kelly, Fergus 96, 98–103, 106–111
Kelly, Hugh 193
Kéroualle, Louise de (Duchess of Portsmouth) 171
King Charles VII 71
Kneller, Godfrey 171
The Knight, The Lady, and The Priest 40
Knowledge and Practice of Christianity —*An Essay towards the Instruction for the Indians* 178

La Sainte-Baume 55
Lacauue, France 70
Lady Arbella Denny 12, 145, 152
Lakoff, George 4, 43
Lambert, Mr 160
lánamnas (Irish: Marriage/union) 106–111
lánamnas comthinchuir (Irish: union of joint property) 107
lánamnas fir for bantinchur (Irish: Union where a man is supported on a woman's property) 107, 109
lánamnas mná for fertinchur (Irish: union where a woman is supported on a man's property) 107
land enclosure 2, 9, 94–95, 116
Lazarus 24, 27–28, 53
Leamy, Edmund (Irish Member of Parliament; Kildare North, Ireland) 188–190
Lectures on Magdalenism 7
Lesson-Street Magdalene Asylum 145, 148
Leviticus 35, 37
The Liber Augustalis Laws 68
Liberia, West Africa 216–217
Life in a Laundry 159
Liverpool Female Penitentiary 153
Liverpool Magdalen Institution 184
Luddy, Maria 4, 153, 209
Lynch, Mss. 152

MacCana, Proinsias 105
MacManus, Seuman 96–97, 99
MacMurrough, Dermont 121
MacOliverus Bourke 124
The MacWilliam (Irish: title of Mayo petty kingship) 123–124
The Magdalen House (England) 145, 168–169, 173, 174–181
The Magdalen Rule Book 175
Magdalene cults 11, 50

Magdalene laundresses 1, 71, 201, 216; *see also* Magdalenes; repenties
Magdalene Refuges 152
The Magdalene Sisters 136, 203
Magdalenes 2, 14, 18, 80, 94, 167–170, 175, 178–180, 192–196, 199–203, 208, 214, 215, 216; *see also* Magdalene laundresses; repenties
magdalenism 4, 7, 9–12, 14, 25, 41, 55, 62, 66–67, 71, 93–95, 112, 133, 136, 167, 169, 214, 216, 217–218
Mahoney, Rosemary 103
The Making of the Magdalen: Preaching and Popular Devotion in the Later Middle Ages 4
Malcolmson, Patricia 190
The Man of Fashion's Companion 169
Manchester Asylum for Female Penitents 153
Manderville, Bernard de 173
Manners, John James R. (7th Duke of Rutland) 139, 151, 156
Manufacturing Militance 123
March Laws 12, 105, 126, 164
marriage 1, 11, 37, 41, 56–60, 65, 74, 106–111, 135, 137
Marseilles, France 51–54, 61, 66–77
Marshall, T.H. 129
Martha of Bethany 21, 24–28, 44, 53
Marx, Karl 88–89, 94, 114, 116, 122, 131
Mary Magdalen: Myth and Metaphor 4
Mary Magdalene 1, 8–10, 13, 17–21, 23–29, 34, 38–39, 41–47, 49–55, 62, 73–74, 78, 80, 84–85, 118–119, 156–157, 167, 170, 175–176, 198, 216–218
Mary of Bethany 11, 24, 53
Mary of Nazareth 30, 31–32, 34; *see also* Mother Mary; Virgin Mary
McCarthy, Michael John Fitzgerald 138, 160, 199
McCartin, Christopher 213
McDonnell, Ernest 47
McElwee, Niall 167
Mebdh, Maighread 201
Memoirs of a Magdalen: or, the History of Louisa Mildmay 193
Menou Mathiew 77
meretrix publica (to publically earn a living/medieval term for prostitutes) 61–62, 66
Misrahi, Jean 52
M'Kenna, Reginald (Member of Parliament-Monmouthshire Northern, Wales) 187
The Modern World-System 4, 137
Mogg, Edward 180
Moll Flanders 194
monopoly (on medieval economics) 41–42, 59
monopoly (on salvation) 41–42, 57
Montague, George 179
Montpellier, France 69–70, 77, 84
The Moonstone 194
More, Hannah 179, 195

mother-and-baby homes 164–165, 209–210, 212
Mother Mary 11, 23, 29–30, 33, 156; *see also* Mary of Nazareth; Virgin Mary
Mulcahy, Christina 213

Nakano-Glenn, Evelyn 128
Narbonne, France 70, 77
Nationalism (nation building) 93, 95, 137, 149, 160, 182, 187, 190
Nemed (Irish: meaning privileged but also the name of a race that myth states invaded Ireland) 97, 101
The New Magdalen 194
New Picture of London and Visitor's Guide to its Sights 180
New Poor Laws 144–145
Nîmes, France 70, 75
No Name 194

O'Brien, Breda 209
Ó Corráin, Donnchadh 97
Offences Against the Person Act (1861) 161–163
O'Flaherty, Murrough-na-dTuadh 127–128
Old Poor Laws 141, 144; see also *Elizabethan Poor Law*
O'Mahony, N.T. 198–199
O'Malley, Grace (Gráinne Uí Mháille) 7, 96, 108, 124
Order of the Good Shepherd Magdalen House in Sheffield, England 186
Order of the Good Shepherd Magdalene Mission in Limerick 152
Order of the Good Shepherd Nuns 88, 136, 149, 152, 167, 186, 202, 203
Otis, Leah Lydia 41, 56, 61, 64, 69, 70–71, 75–77, 84–85, 87–88, 100
The Oxford Illustrated History of Ireland 97

Pace, Edward Aloysius 155
Pagels, Elaine 44, 45
Panopticon Penitentiary 197
Parliament Debates of Great Britain (1895–1907) 183–192
peripheral market centers 2, 9, 12, 89, 93, 115, 117, 135–137, 149, 160, 168, 197, 216
permanence theory 115
Peter of Roissac 75
Peter the Chanter 75
Pheobe of Cenchrea 22
Philemon 21
Philippians 21–22
The Philosophy of History 101
Phoenix, Arizona 217
Picknett, Lynn 27, 44–45
Picture of London, for 1803: Being a Correct guide to All the Curiosities, Amusements, Exhibitions, Public Establishments, and Remarkable Objects, in and Near London 180
The Pilgrim 122

pilgrimages 49
Pistis Sophia (Faith Wisdom) 44
Place's Law 171–172
Polanyi, Karl 114, 116–117, 140–141, 144
Polygamy 108, 118
Poor Laws 137, 140–141, 163, 165
Poor Relief Laws of Ireland 210
Pope Adrian IV 121
Pope Innocent III 74–75
Pope Gregory IX 1, 8, 11, 25–26, 60, 78,
Pope Gregory XI 80, 83
Pope Nicolas II 77
Pope Nicolas IV 78
Pope Siricius 32
Pope Urban II 74
Power, Patrick C. 107, 109, 163
Priests and People in Ireland 199
Primitive Accumulation 114, 116, 134
The Prison Notebooks 47
prostitute(s) 1, 8–9, 23, 24–27, 29, 34, 36, 55, 60, 62, 64–73, 75, 78–88, 94 134–136, 145, 153, 158, 163, 167, 181–182, 194, 211, 217; *see also* harlot; whore
prostitution 3, 8, 10–12, 60, 62, 64, 67–73, 85, 88–89, 135, 149, 156, 166, 169, 171–172, 181–182
Protestant(ism) 85–86, 95, 100, 130–133, 145, 166
Proverbs 35

Queen Elizabeth I 7, 12, 124–125, 127–128, 131
Queen Medb 7, 102, 104–105, 107, 109
Queen Sancia 79–80

Race in North America 98, 116
Rahab 36
The Rambler 174
The Ranger's Magazine 169
Ranke-Heinemann, Uta 32
rape 108, 158, 163, 216
red light districts 65, 69–70
Reddan, Miss 152
Redmond, John (Irish Member of Parliament; Waterford, Ireland) 186
Redress Fund 201–203, 214–215
Reid, Sister Meta 167
Renshaw, Charles (English Member of Parliament; Renfrewshire Western, England) 187
Repentant Sisters of Saint Catherine 84
Repentant Sisters of Saint Mary Magdalene of the Miracles of Avignon 80–86
repenties 1, 8, 80–86, 89, 145, 163, 212; *see also* Magdalene laundresses; Magdalenes
Revelations (Book of) 37
Reynolds, Joshua 13, 173
Rhetoric of Motives 17
rhetorical situation 46
rí ruirech (Irish: supreme king) 97
rí túath (Irish: Petty Kingdoms) 97
Richie, Baron Charles Thomson 185, 186

The Rise of the Network Society 95
Robert of Arbrissel 74–75, 78
Robert the Wise 79
Rollo-Koster, Joëlle 51, 53, 61, 67, 76, 77, 80–81, 83–85
Romans 21–23
Rousseau, Jean-Jacques 195
Roussillon, Count Girart de 53
Royster, Stacie 203
Rudolph of Worms 78
Ryan's Report 3, 14, 95, 197, 201–208, 214

Said, Edward 4, 42, 101
Saint Agnes 52
Saint Aldobrandesca of Siena 78
Saint Ambrose 32
Saint Anthony 71
Saint-Antoine des Champs 75
Saint Augustine 20, 31–32, 65–66
Saint Bernard 28
Saint Bridget 102
Saint Jerome 28, 58
Saint Jovinian 32
Saint Louis 77
Saint Mary of Egypt 52
Saint Maurice of Hildesheim 78
Saint Maximinus 53–54
Saint Patrick 96, 100–101, 106
Saint Paul 11, 21–23
Saint Paul: The Foundation of Universalism 21
Saint Thomas Aquinas 20
La Sainte-Baume 55
Sainte-Marie-Madeleine at Vézelay (France) 11, 50–51, 53
saintly relics (Cult of Relics) 49–51
Santa Maria Egiziaca 79
Santa Maria Magdalena 78–79
Sarto, Sister Mary 209
Scotland 3, 113, 166, 216
Seasreachs (Irish: about 120 acres of land) 97
The Second Collection of Psalms and Hymns Used at the Magdalen Chapel 193
secular marriage 57; *see also* marriage
Seidman, Gay W. 123
Senchus Mor (Statute Law of Patrick) 99, 106
sencléithe (Irish: hereditary serf) 98
Settlement Laws 141
Sex and Marriage in Ancient Ireland 107
Sex in a Cold Climate 16
Shahar, Shulamith 67, 71
Sheffield Independent 187, 189
Shield, Paul 211–212
Sicily, Italy 68
Sidney, Sir Henry 124
Simms, Katharine 115, 121
Simon Peter 19, 21, 27, 31, 44–46
single mothers 158, 163–164, 212–213
Sirleaf, Ellen Johnson 217
Sisters of Charity 148, 156, 198, 202
Sisters of Mercy 88, 136, 152, 158, 199–201

Sisters of Mercy Galway City Magdalene Asylum 152
Sisters of Mercy of the Americas 203
Sisters of Our Lady Charity of Refuge 203
slavery 88–89, 94, 130, 163; *see also* coerced labor
Smedley, Audrey 98, 116–119
Smith, James 4, 136, 164–166, 197, 209, 214–215
Society of the Suppression of Vice 173
Some Considerations upon Streetwalkers 194
Sorores Poenitentes Beatae Mariae Magdalenae 77
Sorores Repentite Hospitalis S. Marie Magdalene de Spina 78
Speenhamland System 144
Spence, Joseph 179
Squire, Charles 109
Starbird, Margaret 27
Steed, Mari 215
Stone, Lawrence 130, 169
The Story of the Irish Race 96
Summa Theologia 20
sumptuary laws 66
surrender and regrant policy 126

Táin Bó Cuailnge 104, 109
Tait, William 217
Talbot (Oxford University) 186
Taylor, Fanny 138, 143, 147, 149–150, 156–157, 198
Tennant, Harold J. (English Member of Parliament) 186, 189
Thessalonians (1) 21
Thessalonians (2) 21
Thomas, William 122
Timms, John 176
Timothy (1) 21–22, 44
Timothy (2) 21
Tinchor (Irish: dowry) 107, 110
Tinnscra (Irish: bride price) 110
Tinól (Irish: a type of wedding present) 110
Titus 21
Tocqueville, Alexis de 153
Topography of Ireland 100, 119–122
Toulon, France 67
Toulouse, France 65, 71, 77, 87–88
Townsend Street (Dublin) Magdalene Asylum 148
train déidenach (part three of the *Senchas Már*) 106
train medónach (part two of the *Senchas Már*) 106
train toísech (part one of the *Senchas Már*) 106
Treaty of Limerick 115
Túaths (Irish: Territorial kingdom space) 97, 99

Unequal Freedoms 128
United States 3, 10, 149, 166, 216

Valentine, Phyllis 213
Vatz, Richard 46
Vernacular Voices: The Rhetoric of Publics and Public Spheres 4
Virgin Mary 17–19, 29, 31, 33–34, 38–39, 43, 73–75, 118–119, 157; *see also* Mary of Nazareth; Mother Mary
virgin(ity) 11, 18, 29, 31–34, 37, 39, 68, 74, 78, 135–136, 157
Vita apostolica 47, 51, 53–54
Vita apostolico-eremitica 51, 54
Vita eremitica 51–54; see also *Vita eremitica beatae Mariae Magdalen*
Vita eremitica beatae Mariae Magdalen 51–53, 216; see also *Vita eremitica*
Voragine, Jacobus de 55

Wakefield, Priscilla 195
Wallace, David 121
Wallerstein, Immanuel 2, 4, 56, 64, 86–87, 89, 117, 137
Walpole, Horace 2, 178, 180
Walpole, Robert 178
Wardlaw, Ralph 7, 217
Waterford Institute of Technology (Ireland) 167
Weber, Max 125

Welch, Saunders 171
whore 18, 29, 34–36, 38, 72, 157; *see also* harlot; prostitute
Whoredom in Kimmage: The World of Irish Women 103
"Wild Irish" (Irish population characterized as) 116–122
William of Auvergne 77
Williamite War (1689–1691) 115
Wilson, Bishop 178
Witness: Sex in a Cold Climate 213
Wollstonecraft, Mary 195
Women and Philanthropy in Ninteenth-Century Ireland 4
Women in Ireland, 1800–1918: A Documenentary History 4
Women in the Factory 190
Women, Production, and Patriarchy in Late Medieval Cities 89
Woodward, Rev. Henry 153
Workhouse Laws 12
Workhouse Test Act 141, 144
Workshop Acts 13, 95, 183, 215
Wright, George Newenham 145

York Refuge 153
Young, Brighid 213

www.ingramcontent.com/pod-product-compliance
Lightning Source LLC
Chambersburg PA
CBHW030616230426
43661CB00053B/2006